I AM
RUTH
LICHTENSTEIN, ARNSTEIN, PADDOCK, BLOHM, BOYLAN,
DUNKINSON
and this is My Story

Ruthie
by Ruth Eda Dunkinson

Print ISBN: 978-1-09838-260-5

eBook ISBN: 978-1-09838-261-2

LIVED

I have lived in the city

I have lived in apartments

I have lived in efficiencies

I have lived in camps

In New York

New Hampshire, Maine

And Colorado

I have camped in tents

I have lived on a boat

I have crossed the sea

I have lived in a B & B

I live in the mountains

And live in a house

In the woods.

I have lived

For Josie, Joslyn, Jacob and
Mother Januarius
Who taught me to read and write.

TABLE OF CONTENTS

Lived v

Family Tree 1

Introduction 7

PART ONE **9**

Chapter 1: The Old Country 11

Chapter 2: Hans and Gina 21

Chapter 3: Two Women and a Baby 28

Chapter 4: The Real World 38

Chapter 5: Nicky Arnstein and Me 46

Chapter 6: My Summer Camp Experience 54

Chapter 7: 1944 to 1957 61

Chapter 8: Visitations With My Father... 76

PART TWO **89**

Chapter 9: A Day at the Beach.. 91

Chapter 10: Leaving Home 100

Chapter 11: Dismal Swamp... 104

Chapter 12: Finishing the Journey 108

Chapter 13: Across the Gulf Stream 113

Chapter 14: Cuba... 123

Chapter 15: Returning Home 133

Chapter 16: Ocean Reef Club 136

Chapter 17: Deceived 146

Chapter 18: My Wilder Side 150

Chapter 19: Pregnant and Alone 154

PART THREE **165**

Chapter 20: Roger and Jerry 167

Chapter 21: Jane 179

Chapter 22: A Fresh Start 181

Chapter 23: The Lowe Museum Art Show 184

Chapter 24: The Meeting 188

Chapter 25: The Arrival 192

Chapter 26: Our Vacation Trip... 194

Chapter 27: The Wedding 211

Chapter 28: Married with Children and Animals... 215

Chapter 29: The Art Show Circuit.. 218

Chapter 30: Jim Boylan's Children 223

Annette 223

James, Jr. 224

Stella... 225

Suzette 226

Jerry and Timothy.. 240

Chapter 35: We Rode Motorcycles 248

Chapter 36: Raccoon Gun Shop.. 253

PART FOUR..**263**

Chapter 37: Marshall House Bed & Breakfast 265

Chapter 38: Disastrous Letter 285

Chapter 39: Miracle... 287

Chapter 40: Jim Boylan.. 298

Chapter 41: Life with Tony.. 299

Chapter 42: Grandkids.. 311

Epilogue 314

A Closing Thought... 315

FAMILY TREE

GREAT GRANDPARENTS

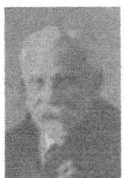

Joseph Rothchild *1842-1924*
Ruth's Great Grandfather. Married to Clara Isengarten. Father of August, Eda, Helena and Bruno Rothchild.

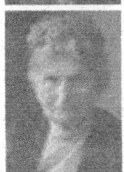

Clara Isengarten *1845-1935*
Ruth's Great Grandmother. Married to Joseph Rothchild. Mother of August, Eda, Helena and Bruno Rothchild.

GRANDPARENTS, GREAT AUNTS AND GREAT UNCLES

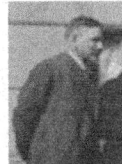

August Rothchild *1870-1961*
Ruth's Great Uncle. Married to Paula Epstein. Paula and August had no children.

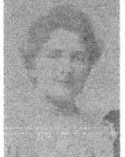

Eda Rothchild *1874-1912*
Ruth's Grandmother. First wife of Berthold Rosenthal. Mother of Regina and Ella Rosenthal.

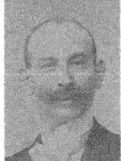

Berthold Rosenthal *1866-1934*
Ruth's Grandfather. Married to Eda Rothchild until her death. Remarried to Helena Rothchild.

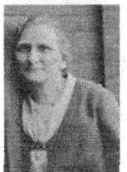

Helena Rothchild *1876-1962*
Ruth's Great Aunt. Second wife of Berthold Rosenthal. Helena had no children.

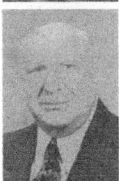

Bruno Rothchild *1890-1964*
Ruth's Great Uncle. Married to Flora Stein. Father of Robert and Walter Rothchild.

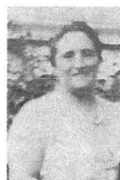

Flora Stein *1884-1971*

Ruth's Great Aunt. Married to Bruno Rothchild. Mother of Robert and Walter Rothchild.

PARENTS, AUNTS AND UNCLES

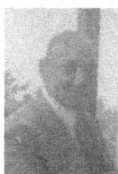

Herman Lissner

Ruth's Uncle. Married to Ella Rosenthal.

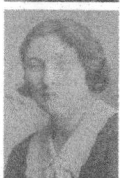

Ella Rosenthal *1901-1943*

Ruth's Aunt. Daughter of Eda Rothchild and Berthold Rosenthal. Married to Herman Lissner. Ella had no children.

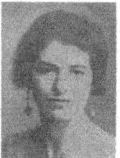

Regina Rosenthal *1906-1991*

Ruth's Mother. Daughter of Eda Rothchild and Berthold Rosenthal. Married to Hans (Hank) Lichtenstein. Remarried to Emanuel (Nicky) Arnstein.

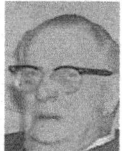

Hans Lichtenstein *1902-1977*

Ruth's Father. Married to Regina Rosenthal. Remarried to Margot Schoenhwez.

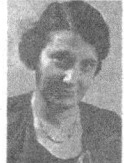

Margot Schoenhwez *1908-2005*

Second wife of Hans Lichtenstein. Margot had no children.

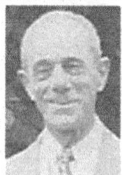

Emanuel (Nicky) Arnstein *1882-1968*

Raised Ruth. Married to Mildred Little. Remarried to Regina Rosenthal.

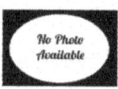

Mildred Little *1887-1930*

First wife of Emanuel Arnstein. Mother of Ruth Arnstein (not to be confused with the author) and Eugene Arnstein.

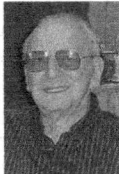

Robert Rothchild *1919-2004*

Ruth's first cousin once removed. Son of Bruno and Flora Rothchild. Father of Kenny Rothchild (1946). Grandfather of Matthew (1972) and Adam Rothchild (1976).

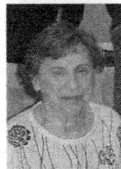

Florence Silverman *1922-2005*

Married to Robert Rothchild. Mother of Kenny Rothchild. Grandmother of Matthew and Adam Rothchild.

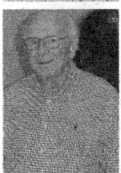

Walter Rothchild *1923-2007*

Ruth's first cousin once removed. Son of Bruno and Flora Rothchild. Married to Vivian Arbuckle. Father of Richard Rothchild (1956). Grandfather of Lindsey (1986) and Max Rothchild (1990).

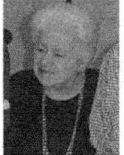

Vivian Arbuckle *1928-2012*

Married to Walter Rothchild. Mother of Richard Rothchild (1956). Grandmother of Lindsey (1986) and Max Rothchild (1990).

RUTH AND HUSBANDS

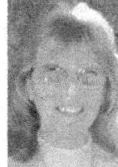

Ruth Lichtenstein Arnstein Paddock Blohm Boylan Dunkinson *1937*

The author of this memoir. Daughter of Hans Lichtenstein and Regina Rosenthal. Raised by Regina and Nicky Arnstein. Married to James Paddock. Remarried to Roger Blohm. Remarried to James Boylan. Remarried to Anthony Dunkinson. Mother of Jerry Blohm.

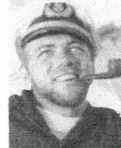

James Paddock *1933-1983*

Ruth's first husband. Father of Jerry Blohm, who would later take his step-father's surname.

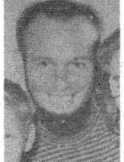

Roger Blohm *1941-2009*

Ruth's second husband. Adopted and raised Jerry Blohm. Roger had no other children.

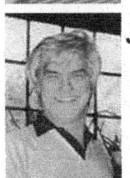

James Boylan *1933-2010*

Ruth's third husband. First married to Irene Willes. Remarried to Ruth. Father of James Jr, Stella, Annette, Timothy and Suzette Boylan.

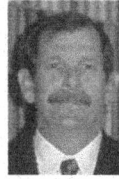

Anthony Dunkinson *1959*
Ruth's current husband. First married to Carol Jack (1959). Father of Samantha (1979) and Travis Dunkinson (1982).

CHILDREN, IN-LAWS, AND GRANDCHILDREN

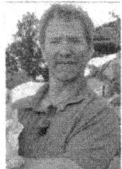

Jerry Blohm *1962-*
Son of Ruth Lichtenstein and James Paddock. Raised by Ruth and Roger Blohm. Married to Meredes Siu. Father of Josephine Blohm (2003), Joslyn Blohm (2010), and Jacob Blohm (2012).

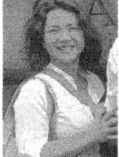

Mercedes Siu
Ruth's Daughter In Law. Married to Jerry Blohm. Mother of Josephine Blohm (2003), Joslyn Blohm (2010), and Jacob Blohm (2012).

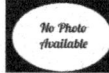

James Boylan Jr *1957-2019*
Ruth's stepson. Son of James Boylan.

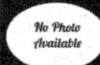

Stella Boylan *1959*
Ruth's stepdaughter. Daughter of James Boylan.

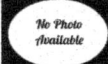

Annette Boyaln *1960*
Ruth's stepdaughter. Daughter of James Boylan.

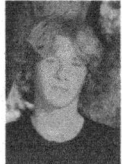

Timothy Boylan *1962*
Ruth's stepson. Son of James Boylan.

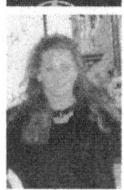

Suzette Boylan *1967-1998*
Ruth's stepdaughter. Daughter of James Boylan. Mother of Jennifer Perez (1990).

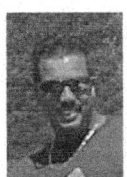

Wilfred Perez *1964-2007*
Father of Jennifer Perez (1990)

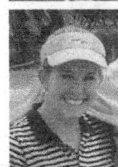

Samantha Dunkinson *1979*
Ruth's stepdaughter. Daughter of Anthony Dunkinson and Carol Jack. Married to Mike Hulsman (1979). Mother of Sean and Katie Hulsman.

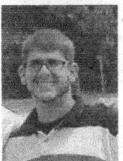

Travis Dunkinson *1982*
Ruth's stepson. Son of Anthony Dunkinson and Carol Jack.

GRANDCHILDREN AND STEP GRANDCHILDREN

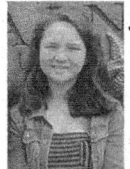

Josephine Blohm *2003*

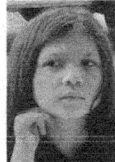

Joslyn Blohm *2010*

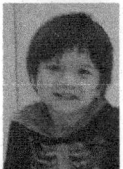

Jacob Blohm *2012*

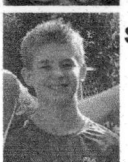

Sean Hulsman *2005*

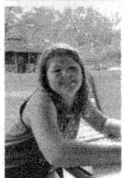

Katie Hulsman *2008*

Lichtenstein Family

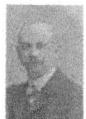

Heinrich Lichtenstein
1873-1955

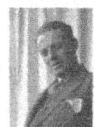

Hans J Lichtenstein
1902-1977

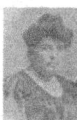

Mathilda Frank
1861-1947

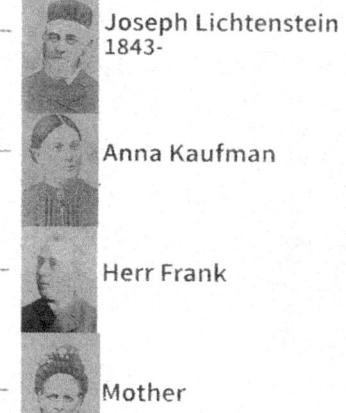

Joseph Lichtenstein
1843-

Anna Kaufman

Herr Frank

Mother

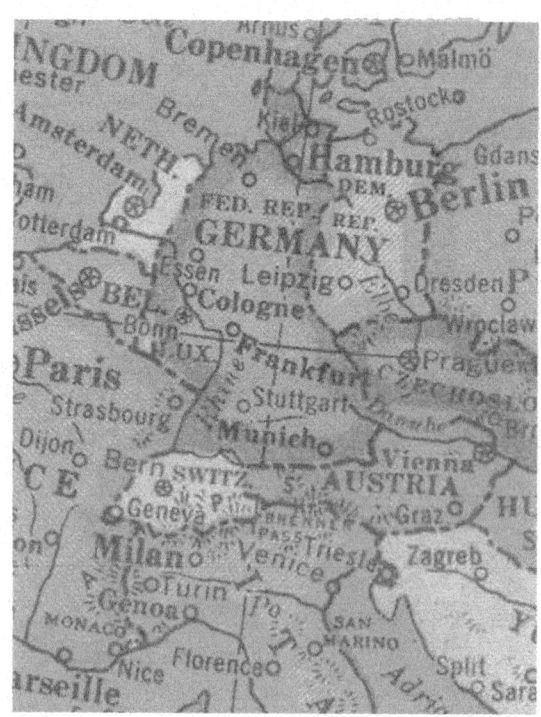

INTRODUCTION

My Jewish ancestors had lived for generations in Germany. There they birthed and raised their children and had successful businesses. They survived World War I and lived in temporary peace. Then, in 1933, Adolph Hitler entered the political arena, and his radical ideology threatened the mere existence of their lives. To escape tyranny and the impending war, it became necessary for the family to depart their homeland.

My mother, Regina Agnes Rosenthal, aka Gina, came from Kiel, located on the Baltic Sea in the northern capital of Schleswig-Holstein. She sought refuge in the land across the sea on the SS Europa, arriving in New York harbor on May 31, 1934.

On February 7, 1936, my step-grandmother Helena Rothschild Rosenthal was born in Thuringia in Erfurt in the black forest. She was my aunt. She was able to have all their belongings sent to America. She had delayed her passage until the death of her ninety-year-old mother, Clara, in 1935. She departed Germany on the SS Washington, docking in the Manhattan harbor.

On December 10, 1936, my father, Hans Lichtenstein, aka Hank, came from Frankfurt in Hessen state by the Oder River in west-central Germany. He came across the ocean on a ship named Washington, tying-up in the New York harbor. To escape Nazi Germany, my father's parents Heinrich and Matilda Lichtenstein, aka Opa and Oma, arrived on the SS New York on November 11, 1938, docking in the New York harbor. Our family was now complete.

Their exodus cast my fate to be born, thankfully in the United States of America.

PART ONE

CHAPTER 1:

THE OLD COUNTRY

My great grandparents, Joseph and Clara Rothschild had four children – August, Helena, Eda, and Bruno. In the beginning, they lived in Thuringia in the Black Forest. Upon moving to Kiel, they lived in an ornate four-story apartment-type home with chambermaids to care for the chores.

Eda married Berthold Rosenthal. He was bald, mustached, wore glasses, and smoked cigars. They had two girls, Ella in 1901 and Regina in 1906. Eda was a strict but loving and attentive mother. She instructed her children in the adage,

"Children should be seen and not heard."

Eda taught her girls embroidery and dressed them in clothes befitting children of a well-to-do family. Each day she took them outside to walk and exercise, and in winter, they ice-skated.

Eda, Ella, and Gina ascended to the upper floors for the grandparents' customary visit at four o'clock every afternoon for candies, pastries, and coffee for the adults, and cocoa for the youngsters.

Despite the age difference, Ella and Gina were very close. Ella was always watching out for her younger sister. Ella was quiet, reflective, and devoted to her studies of medicine. Gina was a precious child with brown eyes and hair cascading down her back. A German Shepherd she encountered, when a young child, left her with a deep-rooted fear of dogs. She, however, did cherish her cat Hippolet. While attending school, she was educated in English, a great asset on her several trips to America with her Uncle Bruno.

Tragedy struck in 1912 when Eda passed away from ruptured appendicitis, leaving Berthold alone to raise his young children. Aunt Helena was a spinster, devoting her time to working in an orphanage. She agreed to marry Berthold and help raise her nieces.

Berthold owned an extensive home-furnishing store in Kiel, supplying draperies and oriental carpets from Persia. Should you spy Berthold striding down the street, he personified a prosperous businessman, dressed very stylishly in an overcoat and hat. Berthold spent twenty-five years of his life in this store, making a very comfortable living for his family. To commemorate his years of success, he received a silver engraved plaque from nine businessmen and one woman congratulating him for his dedication.

As Gina matured Berthold trained her in the store. At sixteen, Gina was a dynamo of energy at a quarter-of-an-inch less than five feet; she was energetic, aggressive, fun-loving, impatient, always walking fast and taking tiny steps. Gina became a clerk learning about the business and working closely with her father. She often remarked later in life,

"My father would have loved the computer."

Gina related an incident about her father's life, she said,

"My parents employed chambermaids in the household. On one occasion, my father became involved with one of the women. When he dallied, his conscience prevailed, and he bought Helena delicate porcelain figurines to make up for his indiscretion." Poor man, he must have frequently dallied as I have a well-stocked china cabinet.

The second event she related,

"When things were changing in Germany, and a call came for the citizens to destroy their firearms, Father took the pistol he kept in the store, walked down to the waterfront, and tossed it in the Baltic Sea."

It was too early to know what the fate of the Jews in Germany would be. Berthold passed away in 1924 at the age of sixty-six.

In 1929, Gina was twenty-three and dating regularly. She enjoyed dancing and going out to nightclubs, where American Jazz was fashionable. True love had not entered her life until one day a friend introduced her to Hans. He was a well-dressed, attractive, redheaded man, five-feet-nine-inches tall, clean-shaven, ruddy skin, and light blue eyes slightly cross-eyed, a trait he bestowed upon his only daughter. He had a cocky attitude to go along with his quick temper and good humor. He was a traveling salesman for Golo shoes arriving in Kiel in the northern part of Germany. A uniformed chauffeur drove him around in a Modern Model T Ford truck.

Work truck, as it was, it still impressed Gina. It was love at first sight. The gay side of Germany was the scene of their whirlwind affair.

The signs of war aborted their courtship and did not permit them the time to become better acquainted. And so plans were made to reunite in the new country.

Hans Liechtenstein was the only child of Heinrich and Matilda. Hans' father had come from a family of five siblings. In 1872, with permission from the Polish Government, Heinrich's father, Joseph, and mother, Anna, and their children emigrated from Wischograd, Poland to Frankfurt, Germany and they became citizens of the Royal Prussian Government.

Hans and his parents were merchants in Frankfurt before the Nazis shut down the Jewish businesses. The time had come to leave Germany. Neither he nor his parents had ever traveled to the United States. In their attempt to emigrate, officials delayed them, demanding sufficient proof of funds or employment in the new country. Hans required financial help, which came from Gina's Uncle Bruno. Bruno, a businessman dealing in electrical supplies, traveled back and forth from Germany to America. He married an American woman Flora Stein, who gave birth to my cousins Walter and Robert, affectionately called Bobby.

Today, January 5, 2021, I have before me a letter written on August 10, 1991. It comes from Edith Mendel, the daughter of Dr. Mendel. I had heard my mother mention the Mendels, but I had not heard of the following:

"I wonder if you ever knew that my father signed the affidavit for your dad to come to this country. The refugee had to be related to the sponsor. He also had to guarantee his support for his first five years in this country. This is something that not one of the Rothschilds' dearest and closest friends (her reference would be Bruno, who did not care for my father) was willing to do. But my father could not bear to think of a man's life being weighed in the scale against a little white lie to Uncle Sam, so his new 'cousin' entered the U.S.A."

Edith continued to write that her father signed for eighteen people until whatever department in charge took a closer look. They examined his income tax report and decided that he could not possibly support that many people! (Doctors did fairly well in those days but rarely hit big money.) So, the powers in charge decided that he had to deposit five thousand dollars in the bank in the names of any further "cousins" he would bring over. I might proudly add that he never lost a single penny on any one of them.

My uncle Bruno was not the sponsor of my father. I was shocked to read this letter. I believe my mother wanted to keep the information from me as I thought highly of my uncle, which may have changed my feelings.

My grandparents were unable to arrange passage and arrived later.

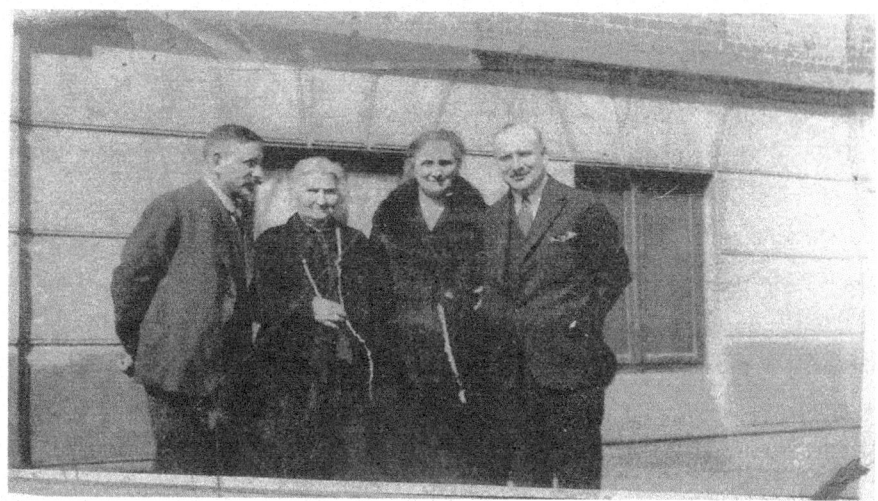

August Clara Helena & Bruno Rothchild 1913-1914

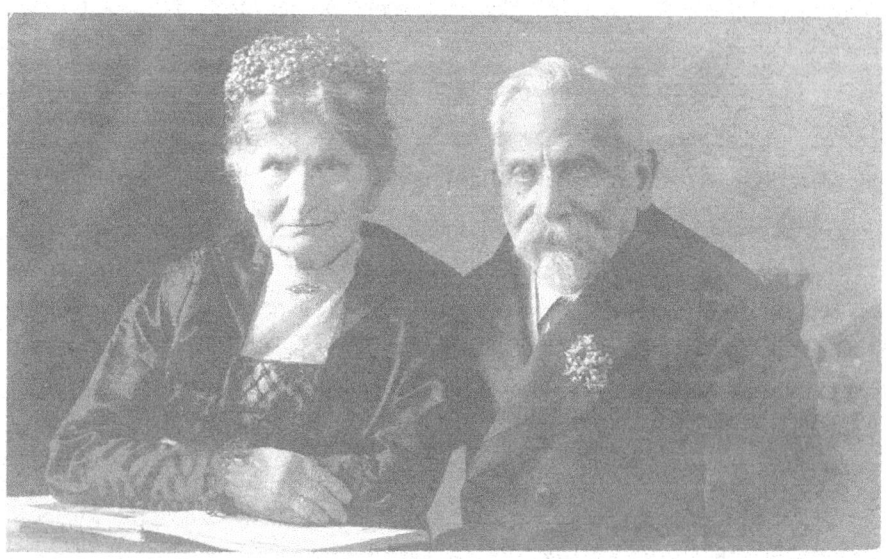

15 December 1919, Clara & Jospeh Rothchild

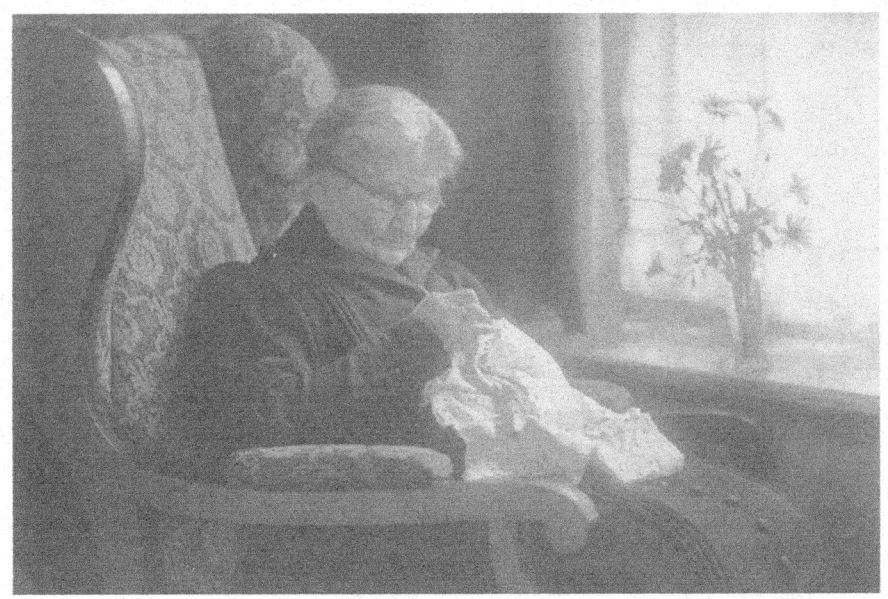

Clara Rothchild Germany

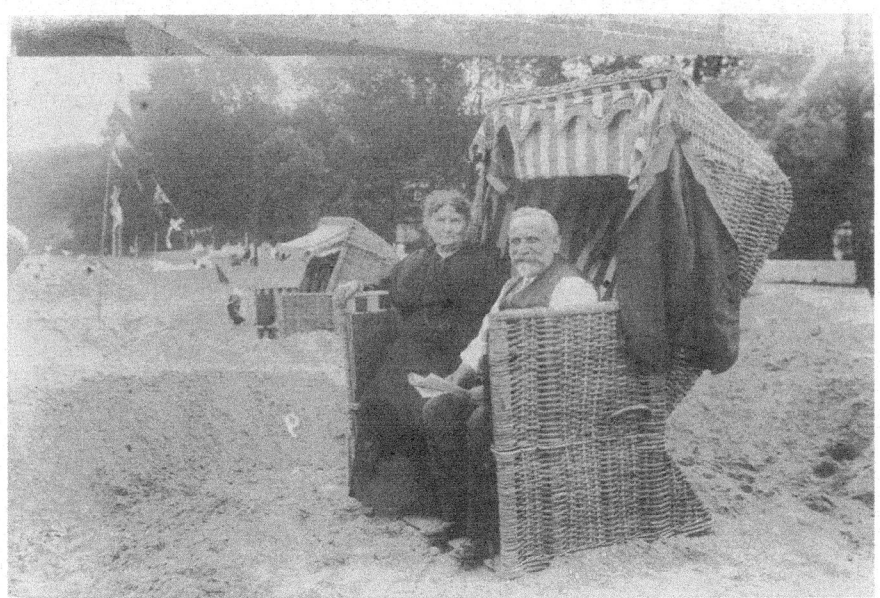

At the Beach, Clara & Joseph Rothchild

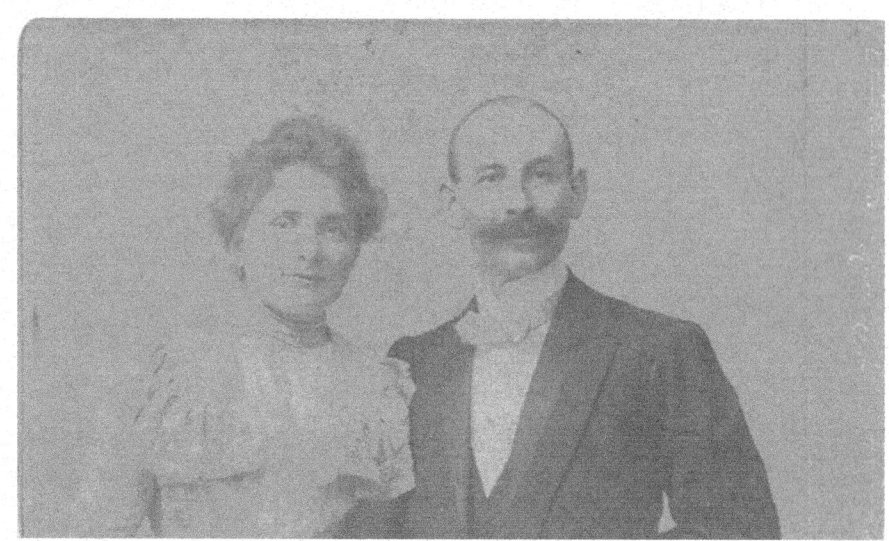

Eda Rothchild & Berthold Rosenthal 1899 Wedding Picture

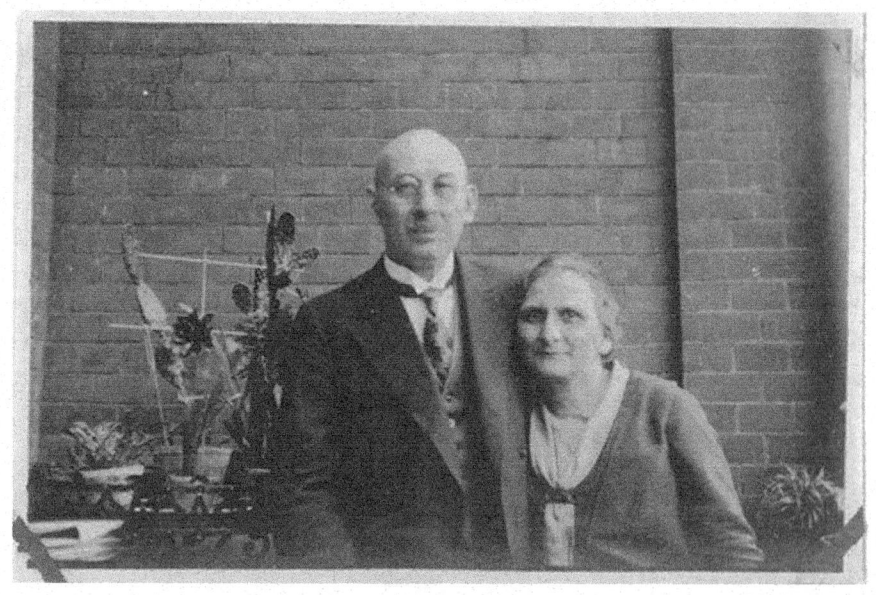

Berthold Rosenthal & Helena Rothchild 1928

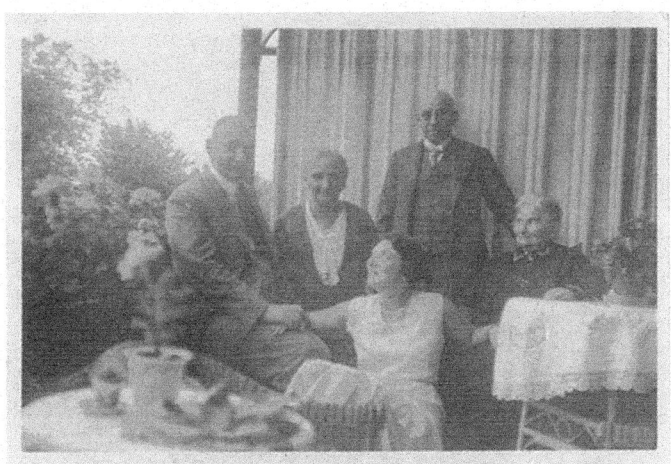

Ella – died during the war 1943 Herman, Helena, Berthold, Clara, Ella seated ca. 1932

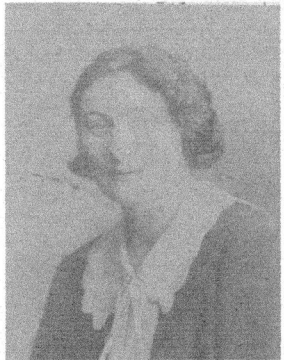

Ella

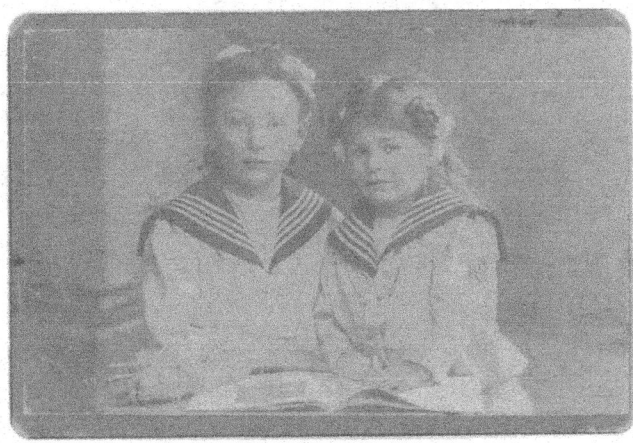

Ella 8 yrs old & Gina 3 yrs old

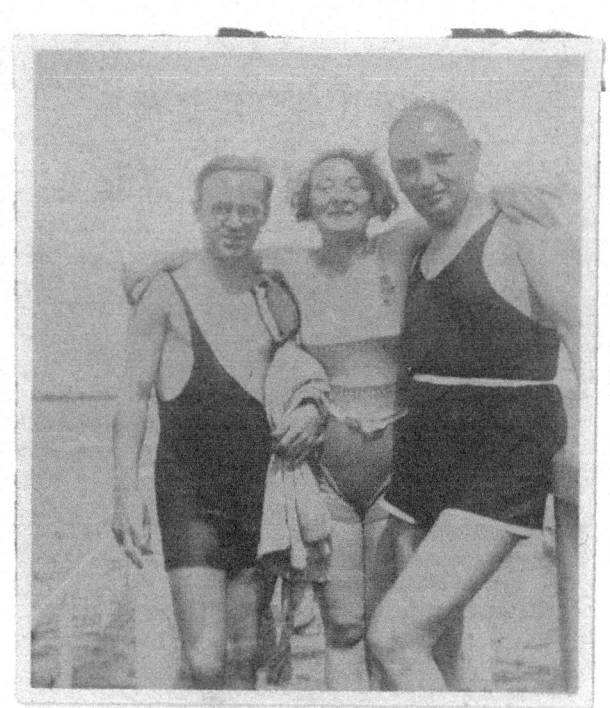

Ella & Herman Lissner Circa 1935

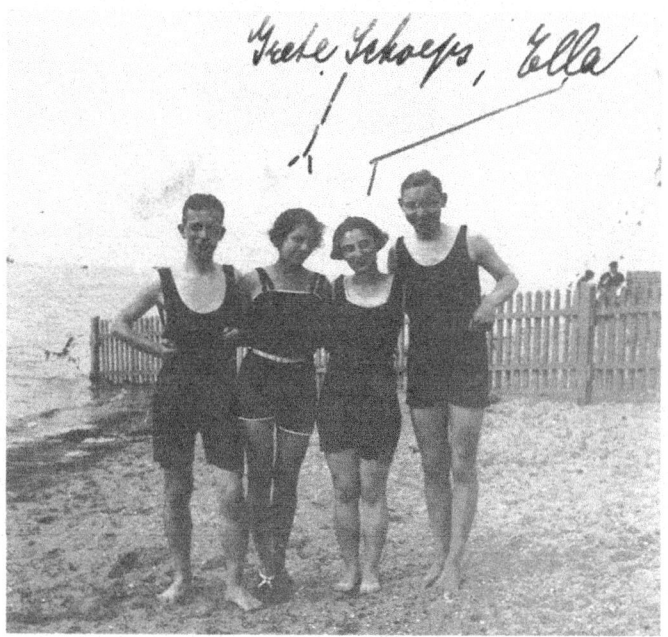

Grete Schoeps, Ella

1923

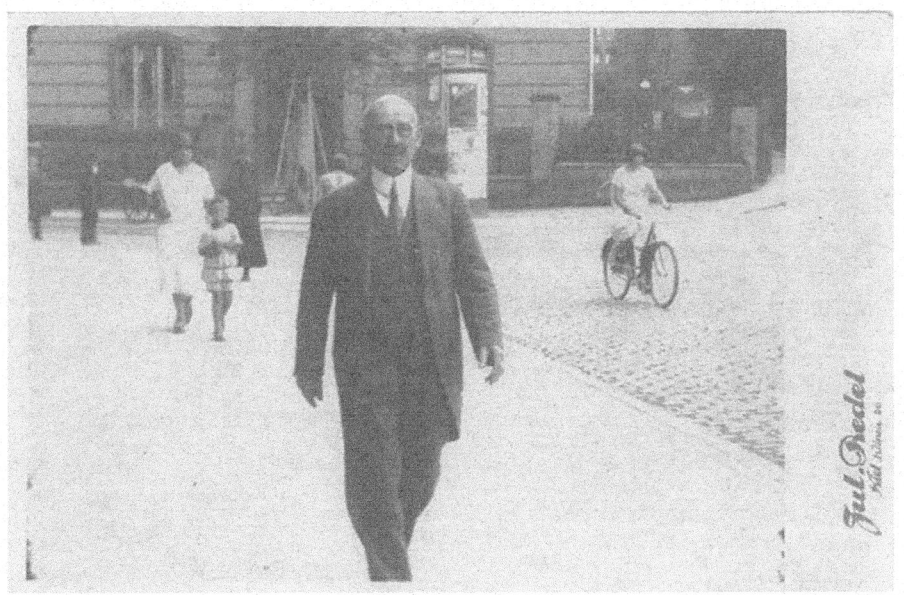

Berthold Rosenthal

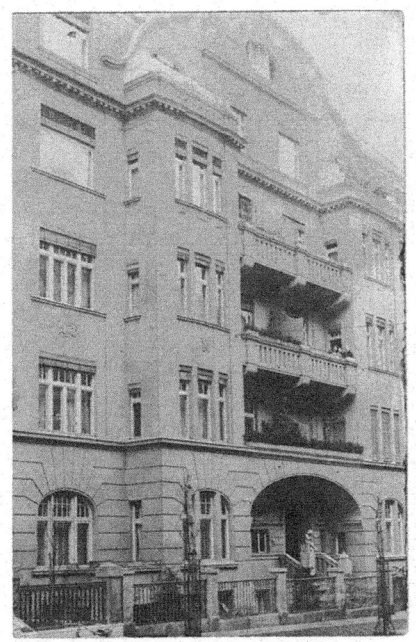 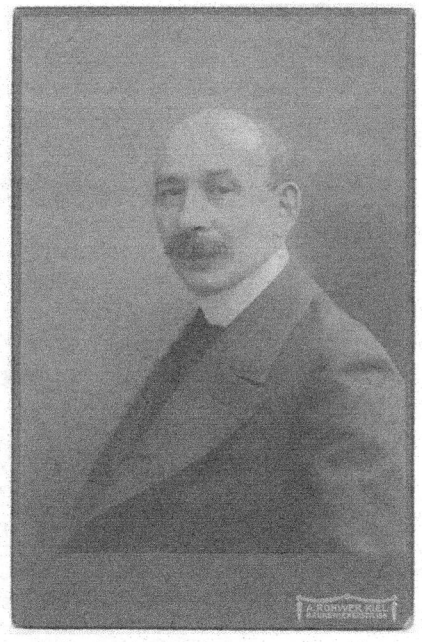

Rothchild, Rosenthal Kiel, Germany

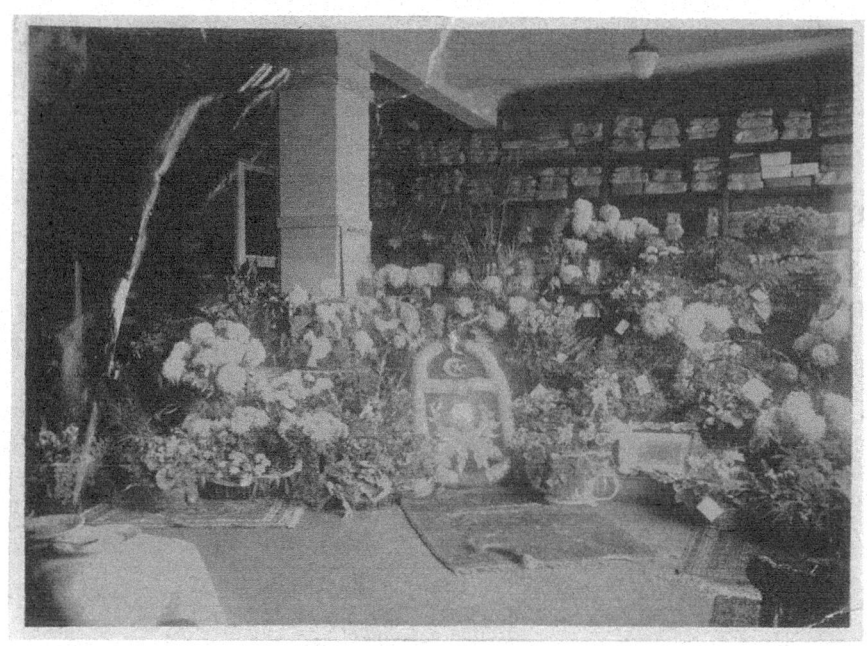

November 1919 Rosenthal 25 year anniversary Berthold's store

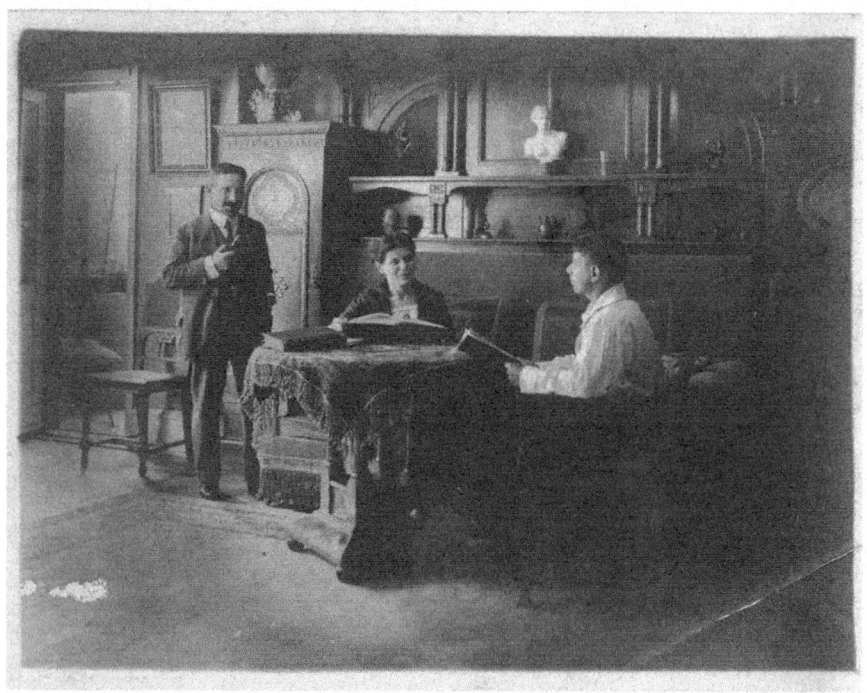

Berthold standing with pipe, customer & employee at store

CHAPTER 2:

<hr>

HANS AND GINA

By a Justice of the Peace, Hans and Gina were married in a civil ceremony in Newark, New Jersey, on New Year's Eve, 1936. Her words of warning to me:

"Never marry on a holiday, in the event things do not work out well."

Along with Helena, they set up housekeeping. A year later, Heinrich and Matilda arrived from Germany and moved in with the family. There were five adults, and only two were capable of finding jobs. Gina was able to find employment at the Haines Department store in the curtain and drape department. She gained her experience while working with her father.

Hans worked in manual jobs at the docks. Loading and unloading the cargo vessels at the Port of Newark, the busiest container shipping port on Newark Bay.

By March, Gina realized she was pregnant. She went to her mother, Helena,

"Was it honestly time to have a baby? We are just settling in, and things are rough now. Oh, Mutter, I will not be able to continue working, and you will have to take care of the baby. I'm thirty, really; how many more years do I have to have a child?"

"Ginschin, this is wonderful. It is a good start in the new country. The child shall be an American. Yes, I will take care of the child. Everything will work out." Her answer gave Gina a much more positive outlook.

All my life, while my mother was still alive, I heard the story of how I was almost born on Thanksgiving Day. It had been a day with Uncle Bruno; I called him Brupa Aunt

Flora and cousins Walter, aka Wawa and Bobby. Aunt Flora, a short round woman, had prepared a proper American Thanksgiving feast.

Suddenly, while eating turkey, stuffing, potatoes, and vegetables Gina developed labor pains. Close to panic, Cousin Bobby sprang into action and took Mother and Grandmother to the hospital, only to return hours later with a still pregnant Gina. My father was neither present on that day, nor for my birth four days later; he was on a sit-down strike. If he had walked away, he would have had to cross the picket line and pay a fine to the union bosses and inevitably lose his job.

On November 30, 1937, Ruth Eda Lichtenstein was born in the Presbyterian Hospital in Newark, New Jersey. My mother, Regina Agnes Rosenthal Lichtenstein, chose Ruth's name as it was diminutive and not too many modifications could be added or subtracted other than Ruthie. Gina wanted a counterbalance for the long last handle.

Hans did not get home from the sit-down strike for two days. Upon seeing his new daughter, he announced,

"The child has a chicken neck."

Dad would play with me, throw me in the air, and listen to me squeal. One memorable day he tossed me too high, and my little head struck the ceiling lamp. There was no damage to me, but the commotion it wrought as Grandma Helena came to my rescue was detrimental.

It did not take long for things to deteriorate. Helena was a domineering woman who wanted to run things, and Hans was a German man who felt that was his position. Helena would tell him,

"Hans, you have to learn more English, then you can get ahead in life."

She spoke German and French and, with a distinct German accent, she spoke English well. Smattering his English with German words and a heavy southern accent made him difficult to understand. Stubborn as he was, even considering learning better English was unthinkable. His retort to her was,

"No, I don't need to learn more English. I have a job, and they understand me fine. You stay out of my business."

He did not like his mother-in-law at all. I do not think she or the rest of the family cared for him. When I got older, he used to tell me,

"She was a bitch."

Grandmother Tilley wanted to entertain me. I was barely a year old. She gave me a box of something, and when I shook it, it made a noise. I was fascinated with the new toy. When Helena spotted what I had in my hand, she became agitated with Tilley,

"How can you give something like this to a child? Can't you read English? It is a package of aspirins."

She grabbed the package from my little hand, and I started screaming. Helena tried to quieten me to no avail until Mother picked me up.

The conflict and drama in the house caused my mother to scream. She was a spiteful woman, and with intention, she meant to annoy her in-laws. Gina was well aware that orthodox Jews do not eat bacon. To show her dislike of kosher customs and the old country religious laws, she spitefully cooked bacon, burning it and smelling up the house. Tilley came out of her room saying,

"*Oh, was ist das?*"

Her face showed disgust; she wrinkled her nose, dabbed her mouth to dispel the odor, shook her head, and looked at Gina.

"*Was machst Du Ginchen?*"

Hans came into the kitchen after hearing the tone of his mother's voice, and I followed him.

Upon entering, he asked,

"*Gina was ist das?*" Seeing a potential argument, he said, "Ruthie, leave the kitchen,"

"Don't talk to her in such a harsh tone, Hans; she's just a baby," Gina screamed at him.

"What is going on here?" Helena inquired, sticking her head into the kitchen. Looking at Gina, she demanded, "What is that smell?"

"Mutter, its bacon, don't you know?" Gina responded.

"Gina, this was not necessary. *Ach*, it smells terrible."

Hans looked at Helena and said in a nasty tone, "Raus mit Dir. I'll handle this." Disgruntled, Helena left the kitchen and went to her room.

In the kitchen, Hans and Gina were still arguing. "Gina, why did you do this?"

"Because I'm tired of all the fuss about the food. Every time I open the icebox door, your mother sticks her head out of the bedroom door and asks me what I'm doing. I live here too; I can go into the icebox."

"But why would you cook bacon when you knew it would make trouble?"

"Make trouble; everything is trouble; I cannot move an inch around here; someone is always watching me. Your dad is the only kind person here. He always asks me how I am. He hardly ever comes out of his room because he is afraid to say anything wrong. Tilley is always saying, 'Shh, shh.'"

Hans was frustrated; he could not make sense out of the whole thing. He thought Gina was unreasonable. His face turned red; he was losing control. He pushed Gina, and she fell to the kitchen floor.

Looking down at Gina, Hans venomously shouted,

"That is what you deserve, Gina. No more nonsense like this again." Being in the hallway, I heard it more than I saw it. And I quickly ran to Mommy's side.

"Mommy, Mommy, Daddy put you on the floor."

Getting up, she hugged me. "Ruthie, I'm OK. Daddy did not mean it."

One day on a visit to Aunt Flora and Uncle Bruno, I immediately told them, "Daddy threw Mommy on the *kitcen* floor." I could not say the word correctly.

Life in the apartment had become unbearably stressful. Privacy was at a premium. The old folks never left the house, and the new couple could not escape, even for an evening of pleasure. To Gina's distress, the marriage was not working. Had there been a time when this family could have gotten to know one another, it might have worked in their favor, but everyone was a stranger. The short courtship had not allowed for any conversation between the parents of each partner. Thrown together, due to circumstances, was proving to be a considerable hardship.

My father and my maternal grandmother were never going to get along. The bickering between the two was constant. There was no way out of this chaos except dissolution.

Divorce was not prevalent in 1939. Recorded state files show that under times of duress, such as war, it became more common. Divorce usually took three years of separation before the decree would become final.

Gina's grandparents were married for fifty years. Hans' parents were married at least forty-five years.

In the end, Gina decided that she could not raise a child, work a job, and take care of the home alone with the constant stress level. They arranged to dissolve an unhappy marriage.

Over the years, there were no repentant words. The bitterness remained to the end.

Dad, Oma, and Opa sat in the living room, watching the progress of our move. I went to Dad's side and whispered, "I will miss you, Daddy," tears in my eyes. He gently patted me on the head, and in a choking voice, he muttered,

"Be a good girl Lizbet."

It was his pet name for me. I gave him a big smile through my tears. I walked over to my grandparents and smiled shyly; in a quiet voice, I said,

"Goodbye."

Oma took my hand and kissed it while Opa leaned forward and put his arm around me, and kissed my cheek. It was sad we had to leave. Of course, at three, I was unsure why we had to depart, but Dad always stayed in my life.

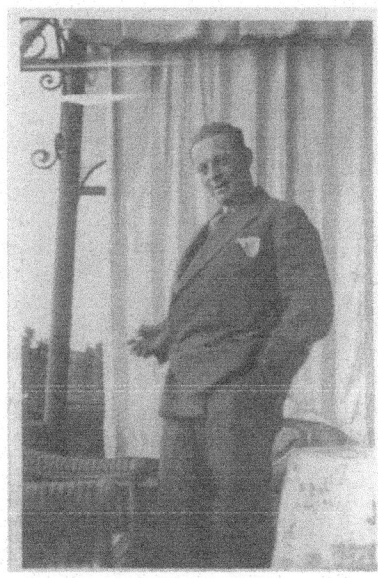

Hans Lichtenstein. Lichtenstein,
Germany 1934

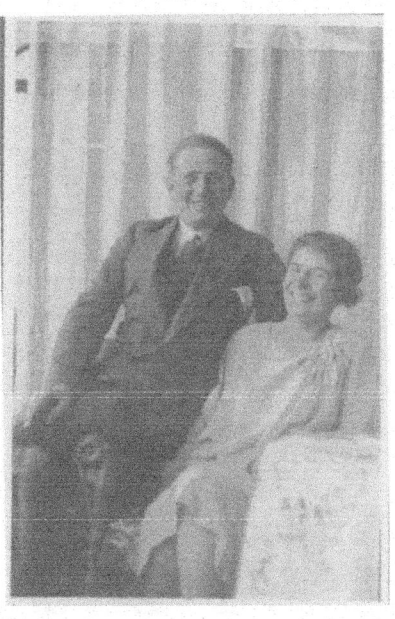

Gina Rosenthal & Hans Lichtenstein
Germany 1934

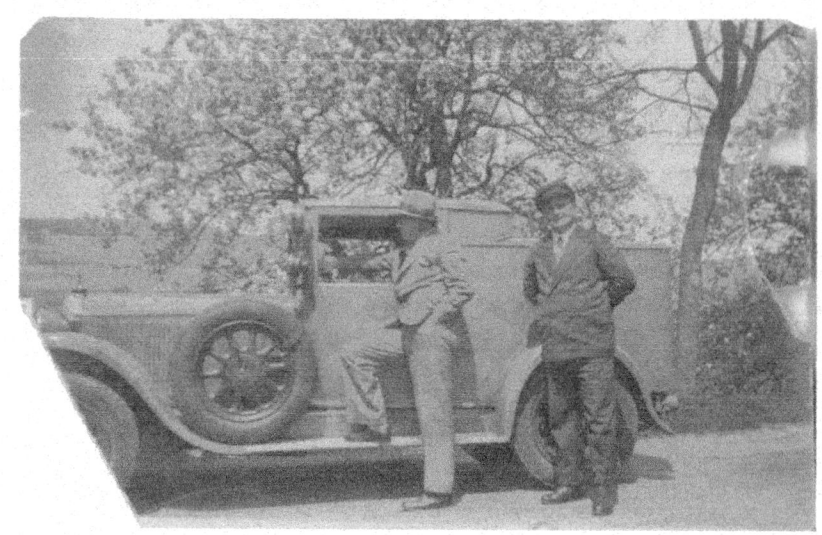

Hans Lichtenstein with Ford pickup & chauffer 1931-1932

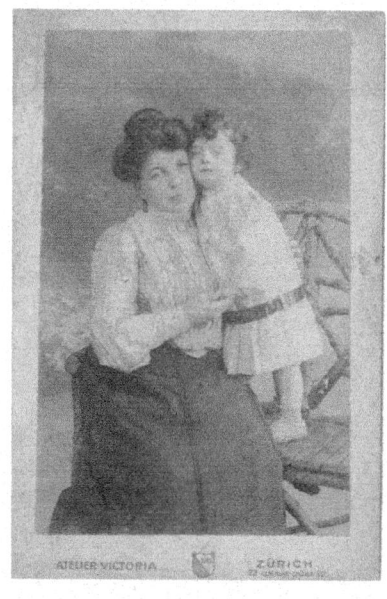

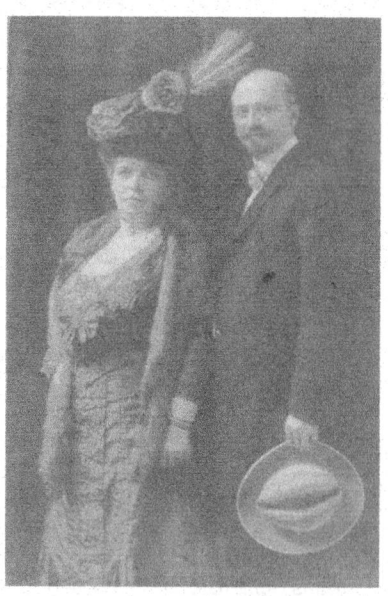

Matilda & Hans Lichtenstein,

Germany 1905

Heinrich & Matilda"

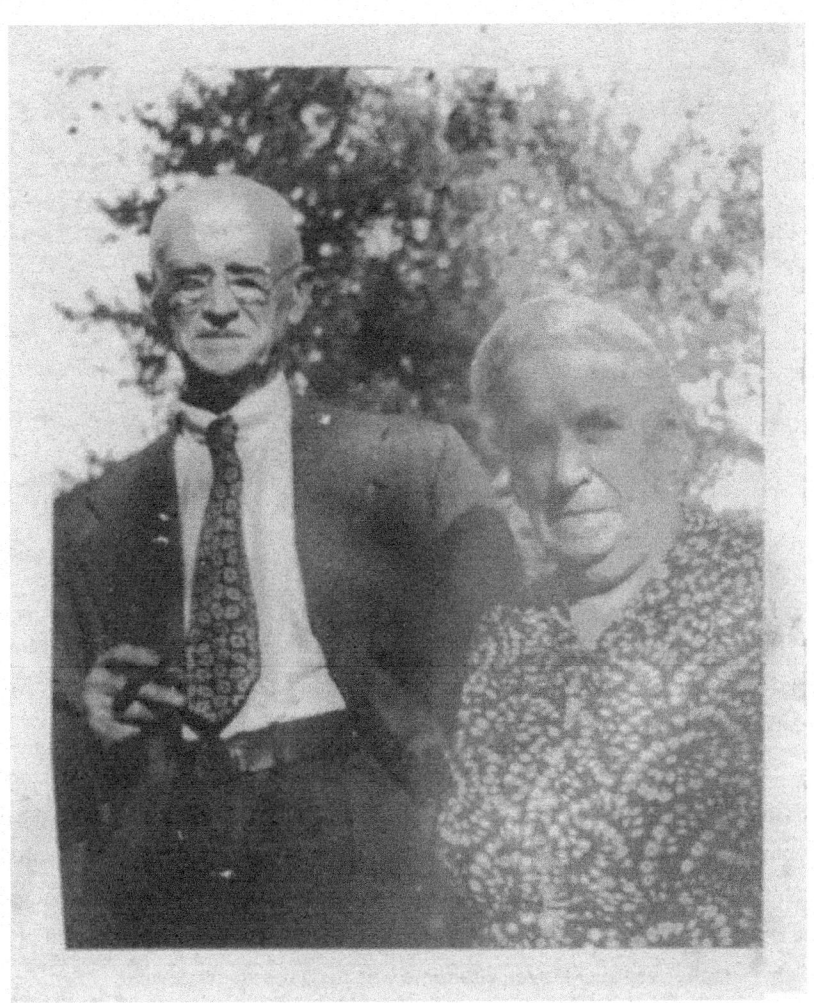

Heinrich & Matilda Lichtenstein 1945-1946

CHAPTER 3:

TWO WOMEN AND A BABY

From three to six, Mom, Grandma and I, moved from one rental house to another around Essex, and Union County, New Jersey. We had no vehicle, so we had to travel in the cab of the moving van.

Once settled into our new house, Mom unpacked the Victorian family heirloom from Germany, where it hung outside the family home in Kiel, Germany. It is a thin, black wrought iron, four-sided filigree, custom electric light, made in Italy. On each side is a slightly curved, circular yellow, red, blue, and green glass orb, which casts a colorful sub-dued incandescent glow. I remember distinctly my mother climbing on a chair to fasten the light in each subsequent foyer. Grandma watched; she would caution,

"Gina, be careful; you know a chair is not a ladder."

"Yes, Mother, I know, I can do this."

Grandma cared for me as Mom worked. Uncle Bruno had a factory making Christmas angels, and he gave Mom a job. It was machine sewing, making clothes for the angels.

I remember various details from the time I was very young. Peter, a neighbor, and I would ride our tricycles up and down the block. His mother invited me to lunch at their home, and he treated me to the unpleasant ordeal of throwing his egg up all over his plate. I thought it was disgusting. I tried not to look at him.

At our following location, my grandma enrolled me in a daycare center. There I encountered my first Negro. He was a slim man and appeared very tall. He was a gentle soul dealing with small children, helping us up on step stools to wash our hands; and placing our bags in cubbyholes, too tall for our tiny frames.

Our next move was to Elizabeth, New Jersey. I was probably four-and-a-half. It was an apartment complex opposite a park where Nene, short for Helena, took me for walks in my stroller. There were many leaves in the grass where the squirrels scampered. I clapped and made happy sounds; I liked to watch the little squirrels.

Grandma had a doctor's appointment and asked the neighbor to watch me for a few hours.

Whatever I did to upset that lady must have been awful. She told me,

"I'm going to put you in a frying pan and hold you out the window."

"No, please don't put me out the window," I begged.

I was so glad to see my grandma when she came to pick me up. I told her, "I had a frightening experience. That is not a nice lady."

This is my Christmas memory of my Cousin Walter, who was home on leave serving in the Army in World War II. Our presents were under our lighted Christmas tree with Mom's angel on top. The door flung wide, and dressed in his red suit Santa appeared. What a thrill –Santa was in our house. I sat on his lap and tugged on his white beard. It only took a few minutes for me to realize it was my Cousin Wawa. I had a fondness for him as he often played with me before growing up and leaving for the service. I was a bit timid as a toddler, and he gifted me a large brown Teddy Bear with glass eyes. My family thought my affection for the sizable bear would make me more assertive. The bear did the trick. They should have given me a smaller bear.

On February 13, 1986, my mother turned eighty-years-old, and I was forty-nine. She began to relate a story to me that I had heard all my life. Certain parts I had not remembered or been told.

"When you were a three-year old child, in 1941, your grandmother rented a large house on 10th Street and Madison Avenue in Newark, New Jersey."

I had no memory that Grandma rented the house, although I had heard the address over the years, which is the case of many of the things Mom was saying. However, I let her ramble on and tried not to interrupt.

"When we first moved in, there was a 'Morning Kindergarten' on the first floor, and a married couple occupied the third floor. The living room, dining room, sunroom, and

29

kitchen were on the first floor. Our sleeping arrangements were on the second floor, but we were able to use the kitchen. After we lived there for a while, the kindergarten moved out, and so did the couple. The house was much too big for just the three of us." I knew none of those particulars as they had nothing to do with me.

Mom continued, "Grandma decided we should take in a boarder for the third floor to supplement the family income. I had just recently separated from your father and was working all the time in a specialty shop selling drapery and curtains."

I knew my mom was selling home goods as that is what her father sold in Germany. So, this was not a revelation.

"OK, Ruth, I know you know much of this story, but it does my heart good to reminisce a little now."

"Grandma had many friends. One was Clara Husserl, the wife of our family doctor that delivered you. One day while Clara was visiting, she brought up the subject of this young man that was her student. We listened to Clara tell us about him. Clara said, 'He is in bed at this time and is getting very little care where he is living. The young man met a bandleader while performing in another town and offered him a job in his hometown of Newark. The bandleader also rented him a room in his house with his family, but the rent was high. He got sick and was unable to work for a few nights, and the bandleader didn't pay him for his absence from work, but he still wanted the rent. The bandleader had introduced Liberace to me as I'm a well-known piano teacher.'"

"Hold on, Mom, before Clara told you, did you know she was a well-known teacher?"

"No, I did not know that. I was always working when Clara came to visit. That was the first time I had seen her in a year. I remember this story more because my mother told me. Ruthie, let me go on; that is where it gets more interesting. So, as I was saying, this is what Clara said to Grandma; 'My student, Walter, was already an accomplished pianist, having played with the Chicago Symphony for a short time, and he had also made a record of his classical music. He brought the record to me so that I would have an idea of his talents. On the reverse side of the record was a jazz piece he had put together. I listened to the classical side, and then the jazz side. He protested when I turned the record over to the jazz side as he felt he was a serious musician and wanted to follow that line of play. He desired to become a concert pianist. He proclaimed that the jazz record was for fun. Upon hearing the jazz, I was most impressed and suggested I assist him in cultivating this side of his music. Although his heart was with Mozart, Beethoven, Brahms, and Bach, he realized the merit of my suggestion and spent hours working with me.'"

Once again, I interjected my thought.

"Clara had not told you his name; then, it would not have meant anything to you."

"Yes, that is true. But next, Clara did tell his name and asked, 'Helena, will you rent to this young man, named Walter Liberace, your vacant studio apartment?'"

"Your Grandmother told her, 'Yes, I can.' I am sure your Grandma was pleased that she did not have to hunt up a tenant. It's always better to have someone recommended."

Mom gathered her thoughts and continued, "I was home on the cold January night when our new boarder arrived wearing a camel's hair coat and carrying his only suitcase. He was about eighteen, with a full head of black curly hair. Grandma was impressed with his kind manner. She showed him the rooms, which he told us were much larger than those he was currently renting, and with great pleasure, he agreed to move in. He had the entire upstairs of the house, two rooms with a bath. We were having lentil soup for dinner that night, and we invited him to join us."

I asked my mom, "Didn't you ask him any questions during dinner?"

"Yes, I inquired how long he had been playing the piano, and his response was, 'I have been playing since I was a small child. My family is a family of music lovers, and they say I was a child prodigy.'"

"'And where do you come from?' Your Grandma interrupted."

"He said, 'I was born in Milwaukee, Wisconsin.'"

"Then, Grandma asked, 'What is your real name?'"

"Many people ask me that, as in show business, I only go by my last name. My parents named me Wladziu Valentino Liberace. My mother loved Rudolph Valentino, and that is why she gave me that middle name."

Mom wanted to know what we should call him. Was it Mr. Liberace or Walter? So, she asked, "Can I call you Walter?"

'Yes, Ma'am, please do.'

Mom continued with her story, and she said, "In the months that followed, after asking if he could make some changes, he decorated his part of the house. The room had a large bed with a solid headboard and baseboard, which he painted black and trimmed with gold. He then made drapes from a material, which your Grandma had given him. He also bought a black table to match the bed."

I knew this. I listened attentively, hoping to catch something new.

Mom rambled on,

"I recall that terrible luck followed him. No sooner had he moved in he lost his job. He needed to make a living and pay his bills, so he immediately began looking for another job.

Employment was scarce, and when his agent was able to find him work, it often took him out of town. Times were rough; remember Ruthie, the war was going on, and he had to accept what he could get. He had one-night engagements in New York and Baltimore. He played in Toronto, Canada, and came home with a towel from the Mt. Royal Hotel.

When he had money, he would spend it freely. He bought me a red leather rose for my spring coat. He purchased Grandma a lovely wooden tray.

Grandma was a prudent person; she suggested he save money. We had a porcelain renaissance man that stood high up on a bookcase, and he would put his money under there."

Mom said Grandma told him,

"The figurine is an antique inkwell from Germany. Unfortunately, during our move to this country, the insides were broken, leaving a hollow space."

That is a description of the piece where Liberace put his money. The item is white porcelain, at one time, decorated with gold. The man sits relaxing on a leaf-decorated pedestal. He wears a plumed hat, knee-length fluffed britches, and his sword tied to his left side. His right arm is in a sling across the front of his chest. His bent left elbow is upon his left knee, and his left hand is holding his head. His below-shoulder-length hair hangs over the back of his stylish coat with fluffed sleeves that match his britches. He is a picture of utter despair.

Mom had more of the story to tell.

"There were times that Walter could not find work at all. During these days, he would do things around the house. Walter cooked, cut the grass, and made little dolls out of clothespins for you. Walter became more than a boarder; he was more like a family member, and eventually, we stopped collecting rent.

Liberace liked to call you Haschen; In German it means little rabbit. One day, he told you that he was going to paint your picture. Liberace curled your hair in Shirley Temple curls, sat you down, and took your picture. He knew you could not sit still, so he painted your portrait from the photo. He matted the drawing with his silk handkerchief, framed it, and signed it on the back."

We seldom took the picture off the wall, but Mom removed it to show it to me. It says: 'To Gina – In remembrance of the many happy hours I spent with your charming little daughter Ruth Eda Lichtenstein. Most sincerely, Walter Liberace, August 20, 1941.'

Mom continued. "Remember I was working in the kitchen. Walter came in and handed me the portrait. It was lovely; there is still a wonderful likeness." And she smiled at me and touched my cheek. "I will never get rid of it; you are still my little girl."

She had more to say about Walter. "Above all, I remember how considerate he was. I had to go to New York one day and had a heavy suitcase to carry. Walter was not busy that day, so he offered to tote it and came to New York with me. I and Grandma would go to the movies together and when we were both out of the house, Walter would care for you. One day you had gone into the pantry, and you were unable to get out. Grandma could not get the door open, but Walter came to her assistance and opened the door." Now, I did remember that. I was crying, afraid that I was locked in and unable to get out.

Mom kept talking, "After a few months, he was able to purchase a small upright piano, which he placed in the sunroom at the front of the house. Friends and family would come over to listen to him play, and he enjoyed the audience. He practiced long and hard for a contest at the Julliard School of Music. He didn't win." Ah! A revelation, I knew nothing about the concert.

"Oh, I remember, at another time, Liberace had never seen the ocean. His first sight of the sea was a family outing when we all went to the beach during the only summer he stayed with us."

My mom's memory was remarkable as she continued, "Then, one day, Walter's agent called with a job that was to take him out of town for a long engagement. And so, he left us. Years later, I saw him perform at the Roxy in New York."

It was my turn to tell Mom that I remembered that, in 1953, when I was sixteen, he gave a concert at Carnegie Hall. Afterward, we went backstage, and as soon as he saw me he called out Haschen. To our amazement, he had not forgotten. I was embarrassed and wanted to hide. I blushed, feeling shy.

My mother also mentioned, "Your Cousin Bobby once wrote Liberace saying, 'One day, you will appear at the Hollywood Bowl.' His prediction became a reality."

"Our Walter became known the world over as Liberace. Even with fame and fortune shadowing his every move, he remained attentive to us. He especially would welcome the rest of the family and me at his performances. All I had to do was give my name at the front door, and shortly after that, someone would come, find us and usher us backstage, or to his dressing room, to visit for a spell. He never forgot my mother Helena's kind treatment of him."

Today I like to say Liberace was my babysitter. It is hard to believe that this young man became so famous, and I knew him when I was a baby, and he was a teenager.

The way Mom talked about Grandma serves as a reminder that she shared so many moments in our lives. It is difficult to think that she left us fourteen years ago. Her picture in my mind is as clear as yesterday. I can still hear her advising me not to waste time. She said once, "We should be born old and get younger each year. Then, we can make better use of the knowledge we have acquired."

I told Mom I thoroughly enjoyed our afternoon together.

"I am amazed you remembered all these details." I hugged her and declared, "I love you, Mom."

Our final move in New Jersey was to Orton Parkway in East Orange. It was a neighborhood of single-family homes. Little did we know how life-changing this move would be!

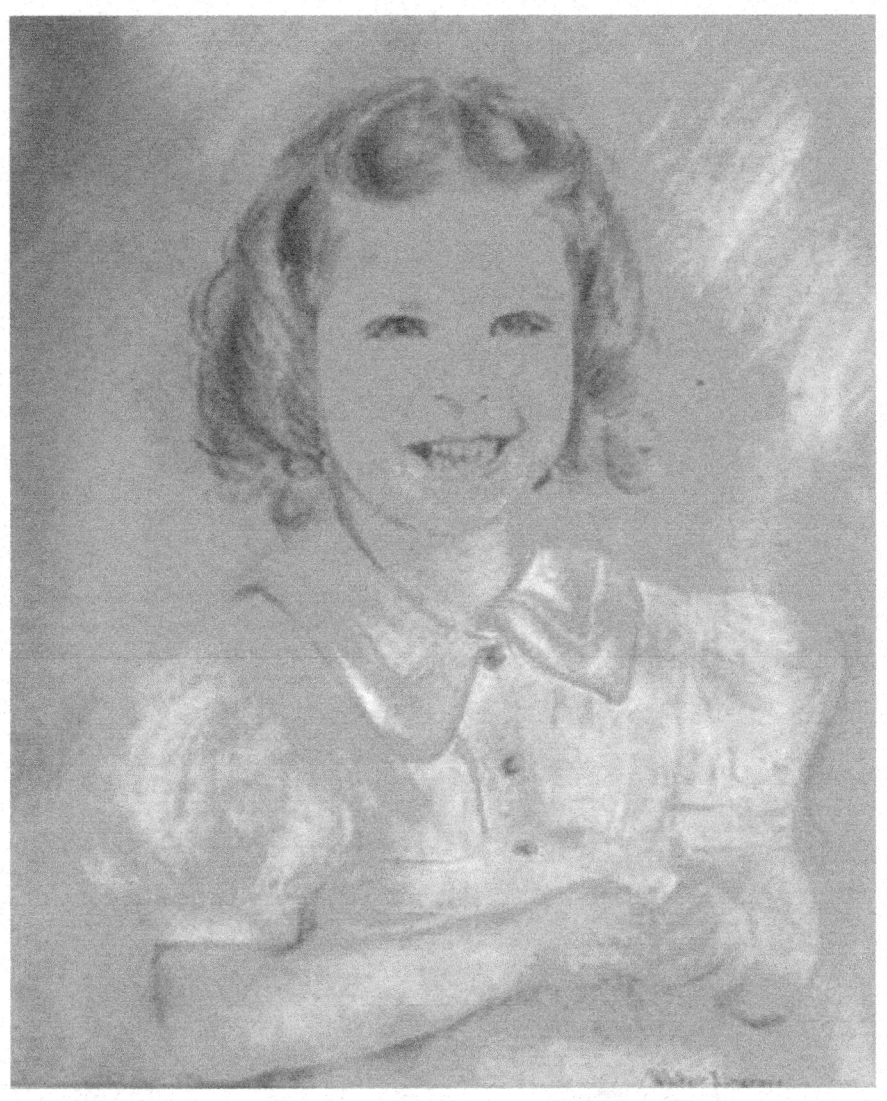

Picture by Liberace when Ruth was 3 yrs old. He curled my hair for the picture

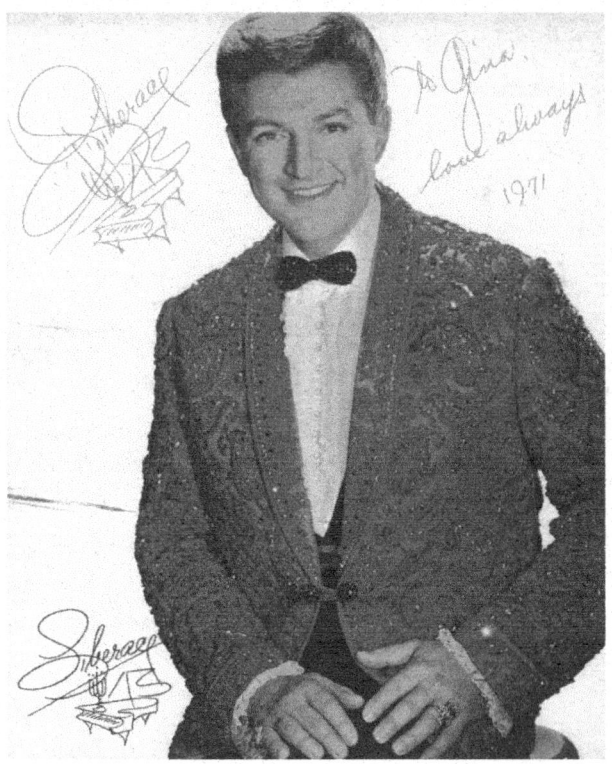

Liberace

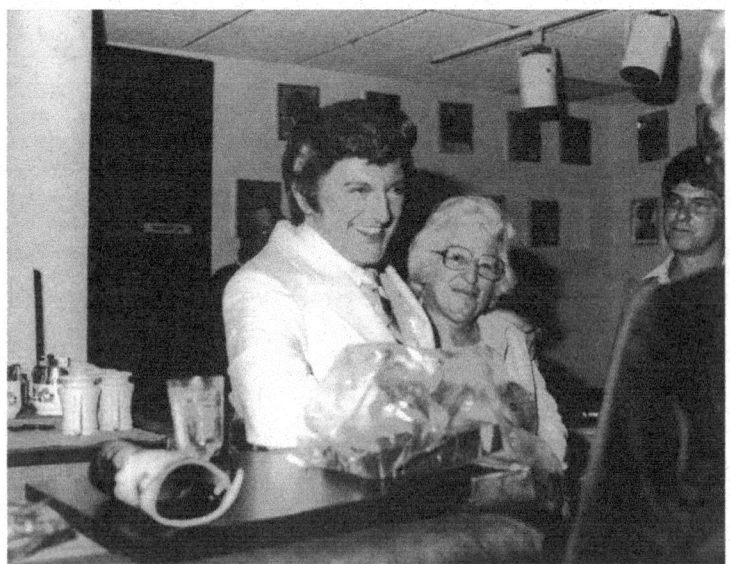

Liberace and mom

ADMINISTRATOR:
Barbara J. Shaw

September 28, 1993

Ms. Ruth Boylan
Marshall House
   Bed and Breakfast Inn
PO Box 865
Marshall, NC 28753

Dear Ruth,

Thank you so much for both writing and talking with us by
phone. The memories that you shared with us were so real
and we especially loved the copy of the drawing.

I have spoken with our publicist, Jamies James, in an
effort to corroborate your recollections. Although he was
not working for Liberace in those days, he did recall Liberace's
memories of those difficult times and remembered his living
with a family in that area.

We looked through our archival material for dates and places
which might correspond. Indeed, you told us that your Mother's
home was at Madison Ave. and 10th Street, facing 10th and
we show Liberace living at 7915 10th in Newark in 1941.
The drawing is dated 1941.

As far as we can determine, your memories are accurate and
the drawing was done by Liberace. It is a delightful drawing
and one to be proud to own.

Please stay in touch with us and visit the Museum if you
get a chance.

Sincerely,

Barbara Shaw

Barbara J. Shaw
Administrator

BJS/fg

CHAPTER 4:

THE REAL WORLD

On December 7, 1941, the bombing of Pearl Harbor brought America into World War II against Germany, Italy, and Japan.

It was now six years since my family had left Germany. During those years, we hopped, skipped, and jumped from one rental house to another. Retired Judge Felsenheld was the owner of our new rental home in East Orange, New Jersey. He was a cranky, cantankerous fart who smoked smelly Havana cigars. To this day, I have a loathing for cigars. He lived on the first floor, and we on the second. He liked my grandma because she cooked his breakfast, but he did not care about me. I had been forbidden anywhere near the dining room while he was eating. He called me a chatterbox and complained that I never sat still.

My mother applied, along with many other women, for a job at General Electric. "Rosie the Riveter" was the name J. Howard Miller gave to the women. Early each morning, Gina marched onto the assembly line, where she made parts for bombs and torpedoes for submarines.

On the bulletin board one morning, an announcement read, one of Regina Lichtenstein's torpedoes sank a German ship. Excitedly, that evening she told Grandma, who was delighted with the news.

I had just turned four; I was a small, sickly child and stayed home with Grandma. One day, a man knocked on the door. Cautiously, Grandma answered, and after he announced that he was our neighbor, Emanuel Arnstein, living just four doors down, Grandma invited him in.

He explained, "I have followed the government recommendations to plant a 'Victory Garden.' It should inspire people 'to sow the seeds of victory.'"

"Vegetables at the market are expensive; they charge double their cost. The child needs good nutrition to grow."

"Here," and he put his hand out with a bunch of beets, carrots, and greens. "I just pulled these from my garden this morning; I am sure she will like them."

After he left, my grandma cornered me in the kitchen, telling me, "Ruth, he is a nice man, you must be polite to him; he brings us food. I do not know much about him, but he seems to be a good person."

On the following visit, Mr. Arnstein asked Grandma to call him Nicky. He said,

"Mr. Arnstein is too formal. I received this nickname many years ago; I'll tell you all about it another time."

It became a practice for Nicky to visit our home and talk to Grandma, but he also stopped over to chat with me and inquired, "Would you like to walk Rags, my Scottish Terrier, around the block with me?"

"Oh, yes, I have never had a dog; my mom likes cats." Then, I told him, "Mom thinks about me all the time. One day she brought a cat home for me. She had picked it up at the Animal Shelter. It was a black and white cat, and it meowed and meowed all night. It jumped up in the high window in the stairwell and would not come down and would not stop meowing. The Judge insisted it leave. What a shame, she had to take it back to the shelter."

Grandma spoke to me often, telling me, "Ruthie, healthy children should spend time outside. Go out and play; the fresh air will do you good. In Germany, we went outside to play every day; you stay inside too much." So, out I went.

Our neighbors were a friendly bunch assembling two doors down from our house in front of Doc Keller's home. Nicky was there, so I wandered over, and Doc Keller asked me to sit on his lap. He moved around some trying to adjust me on his knees, and then, Nicky said, "No, Ruth, don't sit there; I would like you to go home." I did what he said and found out later that Doc Keller liked to fondle little girls. It hurt my feelings; I knew I didn't do anything wrong. When Nicky told me he was not a nice man, I felt exonerated.

My ensuing incident should have told me to go out was dangerous. Grandma hired a painter at the request of the Judge. I was playing in the backyard, and the painter was in the shed. "Come here, you little girl. I want to show you something." He did not want to show me the color of the paint. He had unzipped his pants and had pulled out his penis, which he wanted me to lick. I was embarrassed; I knew there was something wrong and ran to Grandma, who quickly ran out of the house saying words I had never heard before.

There was another nasty moment while playing with the kids on the street; one child yelled, "Kike." The boy was hateful and threw rocks at me. I was too young to understand his religious prejudice.

The word *kike* came into existence during 1900–05 when German Jews were immigrating to America. Instead of using an X on their papers, they wrote Kike making the designation that they were Jewish. The immigration officers used the word like shorthand to divide population groups. Assigning documents to the new arrivals, they found many names began or ended with ki or ky. It quickly became slang and a derogatory term for any Jewish person.

I had no idea there were so many evil people in the world. I had a lot to learn.

Being sick so often, I was spoiled and still slept in a crib when I was five or six. I had painful earaches and German measles. My tonsils regularly had inflammation that I lived with until I was nineteen, and then I suffered an adult tonsillectomy. Nene would play a game of hairdresser with me. I would slide down to the open slots of the crib, and she would comb and curl my hair. She was an awesome grandma, the epitome of what a grandmother should be. Of course, I loved my mom, but she always had to work in a short time; that would change.

My next adventure was first grade. I can't remember much about it as I had been out frequently and missed much work and time. I remember one afternoon after school; I was walking home when I spotted a pigeon at the curb near a car wheel. The bird was flat, and I bent down to pet the poor dead bird. To this day, I cannot handle anything dead. I had a strong love for animals and birds. It hurts my heart that the bird was deceased.

We knew the war was in progress in the real world as the air raid sirens screeched at odd hours in the night. Eugene, Nicky's son, was the air raid warden, walking the streets at night, ensuring all the neighbors kept their windows covered so that the enemy could not see any light. Gene had a limp, so he served his country at home.

I also participated in the war effort. Every time we opened a can of food, it had to be open at both ends, and Mom let me step on it to flatten it. The metal collected went toward the war effort. I was proud that I could help.

An early morning knock made me jump. I thought it was Nicky, so I ran to the door, and there stood a stranger in dark glasses and a black coat. In a commanding voice, he said, "Little girl, is there an adult at home?"

"Yes, sir, there is."

"Please get them for me; it is important."

I ran off quickly to call Nene. As I listened, I could hear the word FBI. Nene made a call to Nicky and asked him to come over and watch me. Then, the FBI took her away. I was afraid, and Nicky told me it would turn out OK.

"Why did that man take Nene?" I asked.

"I'm sure it is a mistake," Nicky told me.

It was hours before she came home. The FBI accused her of being a spy. Mom was working at a high-security plant. How was it possible for Grandma to be a spy? We had moved so much in such a short time; they assumed we were trying to cover our tracks. Naturally, it was not so. Grandma had to call Uncle Bruno, and he straightened the entire matter out to their satisfaction.

Nicky had been a patient man and waited for Mom to get her divorce. At that time, in New Jersey, it took a long time. The New Jersey law only allowed divorce on the grounds of adultery, how she proved that I, of course, have no idea.

It did not take long, once the divorce was final, for Nicky to propose to Mom. I knew we would never live with my real Daddy again.

Nicky wrote five letters to my mom before their marriage on April 4, 1944. In a red leather-locked attaché, she had hidden and saved these letters. Before this time, I had not opened nor searched through it. They express all his deep feelings for her. The one I have chosen is more explicit in the outpouring of his emotions. He wrote it on November 18, 1943.

E. ARNSTEIN
81 SOUTH MUNN AVENUE
EAST ORANGE, NEW JERSEY

in your case it is quite a different matter.
I have found in you what I seek most, not only
a true friend but also a beacon light, showing
me the way into a new world of happiness. I
cannot begin to express my sentiments in sufficient
appreciation for your beautiful thoughts and kind
acts. Yes, indeed, I have learned to worship you
more than anything else and if all my prayers
are answered your life will be filled with God's
blessings and the finer things which make it
worth living.

Just think! If we had permitted outside
opinions to govern us how different the results
might have been. Thank God we had the courage
of our own convictions to by-pass the curiosity
seekers and meddlers.
together into a union of happiness. I personally
have travelled far and wide and met all sorts
and conditions of people upon whom I can
only look as an element of the masses, but

As time elapses the eventful day is growing
nearer and just a little more patience is all
that is necessary and before we realize it the
happy day will dawn.

E. ARNSTEIN
61 SOUTH MUHN AVENUE
EAST ORANGE, NEW JERSEY

Let us be of good cheer which will surely
champion our cause to a successful finish,
I sincerely hope that all of the above words will
convey to you in no uncertain manner my inner-
most feelings

Yours forever,
Nicky

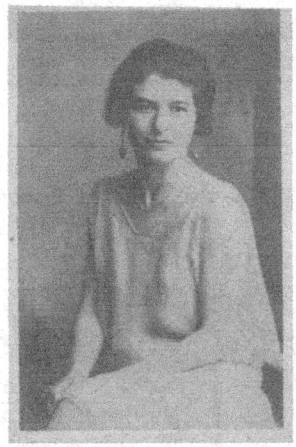

Regina Rosenthal worked for General Electric

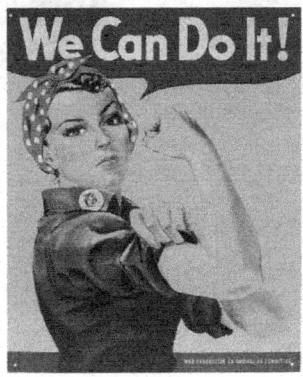

Rosie the Riveter

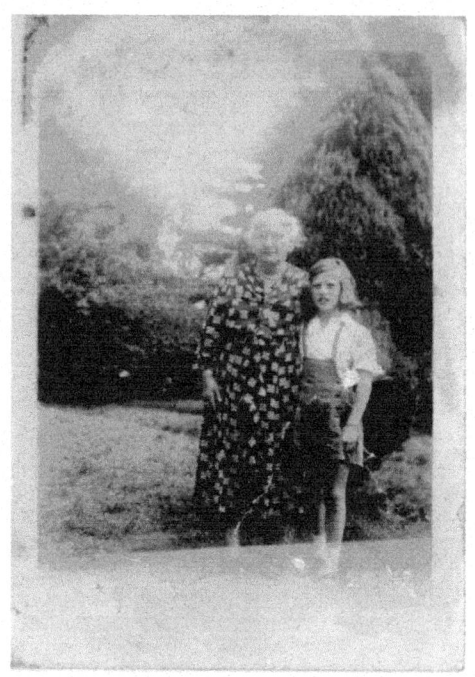

1944 Ruth Lichtenstein, 6yrs old & Grandma Helena

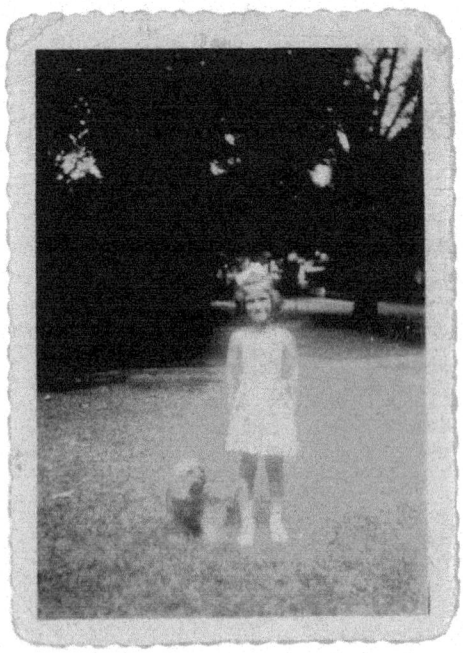

Ruth Lichtenstein & Nicky's dog Rags 1943 East Orange, NJ

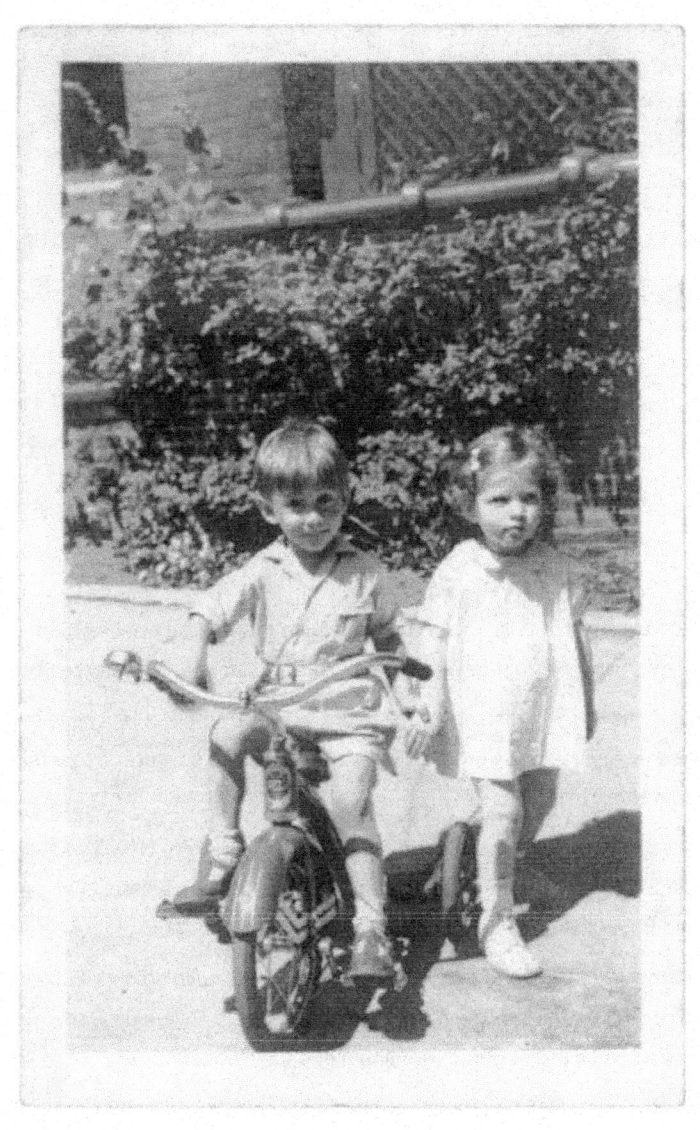

Ruth Lichtenstein 2 ½ yrs olf, Wally Cacasmere, 3 yrs old Newark , NJ 1939

CHAPTER 5:

NICKY ARNSTEIN AND ME

Once the divorce was final, Nicky and Gina married on April 4, 1944, in a simple private ceremony by the Justice of the Peace in East Orange, New Jersey.

Nicky was now my resident father figure. He and Mom wanted me to call him Dad, and I obliged. In my heart, my birth father was my dad, and so, I prefer to refer to my new stepfather as Nicky in my story.

After they were married, we moved from New Jersey to New York, except Rags, Nicky's little Scottie dog. Nicky said, "It is not right to have an animal in an apartment." I wish we had taken the dog.

We now lived on the eighth floor of an apartment building constructed in 1911. It was in Upper Manhattan on Riverside Drive across from Riverside Park, completed in 1902. It was a scenic thoroughfare running along the Hudson River.

676 Riverside Drive's apartment building entrance had a gold-colored revolving door opening onto an expansive lobby with marble floors. A mural on the wall depicted a bygone era with horse-drawn carriages. It reflected an ambiance of former times that were soon to fade away completely. There was a doorman in uniform, and he was also the elevator man.

From every window of our apartment, there was a view of the Hudson River and the George Washington Bridge. Across the broad expanse of water, we could see the Palisades of New Jersey and the famous Palisades Amusement Park.

In wartime the Hudson was a metallic gray mass with churning white caps rolling off her rough, jagged waves. Freezing temperatures brought floating ice to the busy waterway and slowed down the behemoth ships as they plodded through the dangerous channel.

The train yard next to the river often kept me amused, counting different types of cars. First, the mighty locomotive, then covered hoppers carrying grain, sand, clay, boxcars loaded with freight, flat wagons with oversized lumber loads, and the versatile gondolas filled with building supplies. The Westside elevated highway ran along the Hudson over the train tracks.

The apartment was a two-bedroom, two-bath unit along with quarters for a maid. I got the maid's room just after the kitchen and before the dining room, but that was great. It had a window, a bathroom, a bathtub, and a sink in the room.

Nicky taught me how to catch a ball in a long hallway that ran from the living room to the dining room. He attempted to improve my hand-to-eye coordination.

"Look, I caught it."

"Just keep your eye on the ball, and you'll catch it every time."

My parent's area was in the middle of the hall. Talking about my parents, now that they were married, maybe I could get a brother or sister. Of course, that would never happen; they slept in separate beds.

As an only child, I was always around grown-ups. I would listen to them talk; they did not know I overheard some old biddy say, "Poor child, she is not pretty; she is so skinny and wears those glasses and has buck teeth."

That was something a child should not hear. It made me feel self-conscious. I can remember Nene saying on numerous occasions, "Your hair is your crowning glory." Perhaps, the rest of me was lacking.

With the blended family, all the furniture including Grandms's belongings came to the new apartment.

In our living room, Grandma's large bookcase spanned an entire wall. It was dark walnut, with beveled glass, and on the shelves were German books. A delicate glass cabinet displayed porcelain figurines of dancing ladies; vases with lovely flowers; a big gray elephant; a brown dog; many other treasures. There was a green couch stuffed with horsehair, a companion chair in red, and an antique white lamp with figures portraying a masquerade ball. We had red and blue Persian rugs brought from Grandfather Berthold's store.

Nicky brought a red couch and a large dining room table into the marriage, which could seat six people comfortably, and twelve people when opened. It was as shiny as a mirror, and I could see my face in it. Mom and Grandma would dust all this furniture, and I had to bend down, or crawl under it, to clean the bottoms.

To add to what we had, as a wedding gift, Nicky and Mom went to an antique store in the city and brought home a marble table and a complete set of white gold-rimmed Theodore Haviland china, which she seldom used.

My mom did not have to get up at 6:00 a.m. anymore to chase a bus down the street to get to work on time. Grandma was always home. Nicky was an old-fashioned man; he said, "In my day, women did not work outside the home."

Plus, he was a jealous man and kept Gina always in sight. It was usually a duo when it came to shopping. He was even envious of Liberace.

On a quiet Sunday morning, while Mom, Grandma, and I casually sat in our living room, Nicky decided to tell us his story. "I have been a widower for twelve years. My wife, Mildred died of cancer, leaving me with two children; Eugene was ten, and Ruth was fourteen. Ruth is now twenty-eight and married to Lou Leeds. She has a daughter, the cutest child, Susie, and one on the way. Eugene, I like to call him Gene, is just twenty-two and unmarried. Poor fellow, he was born with a clubfoot, but he manages. With a house-keeper, I raised the children.

You already know that I am Jewish, I do not follow the faith, but my family did. My name Emanuel means, 'God is with us.' They were disappointed with my marriage to Mildred as she was a gentile. I forfeited my inheritance for love. Instead, my children received the money, and I only got blue-chip stocks and now live off the dividends."

He stopped for a moment, took a sip of coffee, and smiled at my mom. Nicky was a quiet man; he spoke softly and slowly so that we would all grasp his words. He glanced around the room, and then kept talking, "I was living with Ruth and Gene and my widowed Sister Rose. She had been married to Ben, who blew her inheritance. There is another sister Etta, married to an attorney living in Baltimore. I do not have a close relationship with them. Etta's husband managed the papers for my family, cutting me out of the will."

He then went on to tell us, "I am retired as I suffered a severe heart attack years before and was advised not to do any strenuous activities."

He paused again, looked down for a moment, lit his pipe, and hesitated as though he was now going to divulge some great mystery.

"As you know, my given name is Emanuel Arnstein, but I acquired the nickname Nicky in the 1920s. An actress Fanny Brice was married to Nicky Ornstein, a professional gambler and con artist in Chicago. I also came from Chicago, and that connection and strange coincidence brought about my nickname. Some people call me Manny, which is what my sister Rose likes to call me." And then he said, "Ruthie, let me tell you, your mother's name Regina means Queen, so I am married to a queen." We all laughed at his statement, and Mom blushed.

He appeared proud of himself with his captured audience. Helena asked to leave the room for a moment, and he waited until she came back.

"When I was a younger man, I drove over a million miles selling cans of paint for the family-owned business. I moved heavy boxes of paint cans and got a hernia. That is something I never took care of, and subsequently, I wear a hernia belt.

I was one of the first to possess a Model T Ford. I was a little wild in my day. I busted broncos in the streets of the Loop and jumped onto moving freight trains during a blizzard." He would brag about these feats on more than one occasion.

He was five foot seven, a thin man, and about one hundred and forty pounds. He was balding, had a large nose, a kind manner, and always smoked his Kay woody pipe. His fingers were dirty from regularly lighting it and pressing the tobacco into it.

We had lunch after his 'tell-all' session. Then, Grandma went into her room, where she spent most of her time sewing or relaxing. I found a chair to read in, and Mom kept busy knitting a sweater for me.

Nicky busied himself with the stock market. One of my favorite pranks, aside from tying his shoelaces together under the dining room table, was to flick the newspaper when he was reading the small print of the stocks. I came to find out that the move to New York was the primary reason to make phone calls to his stockbroker, at no charge. New Jersey calls were long-distance. He did tolerate my devilish behavior, but he was not an affectionate man. Did not hug and kiss, and when company came to visit, his greetings were a bit standoffish and just a handshake.

When friends arrived, they played cards; Canasta was the game of the day. Occasionally, Nicky would have a glass of port wine.

If Nicky were not reading the paper, he would be watching our sixteen-inch black and white TV, the first family in the neighborhood to have one. My favorite programs were *Howdy Doody* and *Uncle Milty* (Milton Berle). He watched golf, boxing, football, basketball, and baseball. We watched ball games together, but he never took me to the Yankee Stadium, maybe because I was a girl. I regret to this day that he did not.

The other thing he would do was the crossword puzzle in the *New York Times*. He was a cruciverbalist. He had the most extraordinary command of the English language, ejecting forth a magnitude of profound, august phraseology. He would never spell a word for me; he always said, "Look it up."

Nicky's breakfast invariably consisted of two, three-minute eggs, cracked open in a bowl, two pieces of toast, and coffee. After eating, he immediately began to walk around the apartment, raising his legs in a march-like percussion to encourage the urge to eliminate. The evening routine was to have dinner at six o'clock sharp. Everyone came to the table, and mother washed while Nicky dried the dishes. That was the only household task he did.

Each day, Nicky would go out in the evening to get the five-cent newspaper. He would dress, just for this occasion, in a hat, scarf, and coat. When he came home, he wrote in his little book the expenditure of five cents. I learned the meaning of the word curmudgeon, which I felt defined him until I learned otherwise. He would say, "Penny wise and pound foolish." I came to a better realization of my stepfather. The little book with the five-cent notation was undoubtedly penny-wise, but pound-foolish was more characteristic of Nicky. He paid for my private Catholic school, the orthodontist, my eyes, a camp, college, and eventually a car.

When I talked to my stepdad, I had to look him in the eye. I knew I had to do that, but he always reminded me, "Ruth, why do you look away when I am talking to you? We have discussed this matter before; it is polite to look at a person when they talk to you."

"Yes, I know that. I am looking at you."

I was feeling a bit annoyed. I did not like correction, and it was not my fault I was cross-eyed.

Immediately taking the matter to my mother, they decided that I would have an operation before starting school in Manhattan. Mom would have done it before, but neither she nor my dad had the money for it.

I was put to sleep with ether and had a lovely dream of Japanese Geisha ladies dressed in their traditional ceremonial dress. My folks brought me home with bandages over my eyes, guiding me down the street like a blind child. The first thing I saw was a coloring book with an apple on the top of William Tells' head. The operation was a success for forty years, and then the muscles in my eyes became weak. They turned walleyed, in medical terms, Strabismus. I tried to correct it in 2007, but it was unsuccessful.

Nicky took me to the Orthodontist for braces. It was a ride in the trolley car to the Bronx. The office was in a poor, pitiful neighborhood. The doctor's sister lived across the street. Nicky commented on more than one occasion, "I hope you never have to live in such a neighborhood once you begin working." He showed compassion for others, wanting me to realize people had to make concessions. I didn't like to go to the dentist; he had a severe problem; apparently, no one was aware of it. He always closed the office door just before he gave laughing gas to his young patients. While we were under the influence, he would open up our blouses and have a feel. My friend had a similar experience. We were just too embarrassed to tell our parents. Some years later, Dr. Halphan moved out to Long Island; his wife was always in the room when he attended to me. Do you think she knew?

Twenty years later, I decided to go through braces again. The dental industry had made advancements from the metal bands to clear synthetic sapphire brackets. These orthodontic appliances cemented to the front of the teeth gave them a more aesthetic appearance. This time the dentist extracted my eye teeth, making room for my teeth to move. Today, I have unwanted spaces between my teeth, and my front teeth still protrude. Truthfully, I feel it is because I did not wear my retainers long enough. They are far from perfect, but they are mine. I will not mention the joy of two wisdom teeth extractions in New York and one in Florida.

Shortly before I began school on September 9, 1944, when I was almost seven years old, The Great American hurricane slammed into New York. Its winds and rains were lashing at our windows late at night, pouring water in relentlessly. Mom and Grandma raced back and forth, replacing towels at the front windows. We could not see a thing outside, but it sounded like the end of the world. In the calm of the morning, we saw the destruction it had wrought. A massive oak tree had blown across the promenade area of Riverside Park running along Riverside Drive. Many of the neighborhood kids were soon jumping up, on, and over the giant tree. I wanted to be in on the fun also, only to be back upstairs, and Grandma pressing a cold knife to the large welt on my forehead.

Playtime was about to end as school loomed large on the horizon.

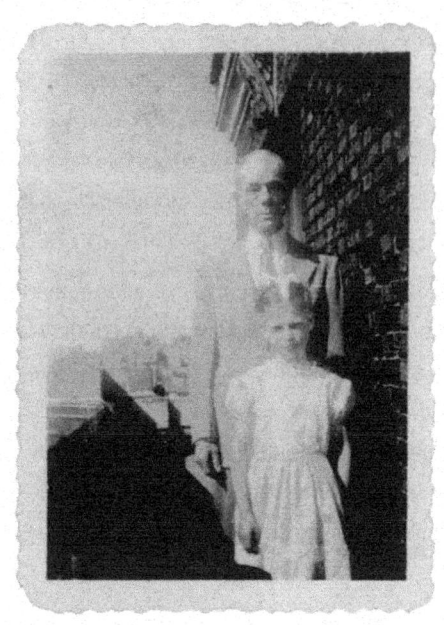

Daddy 1946 Nicky Arnstein, Ruth Arnstein 8 yrs old 676 Riverside Drive NYC

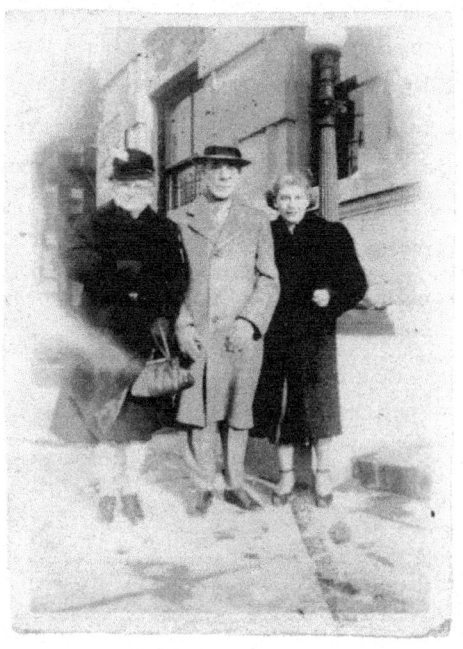

In front of Riverside Drive, NYC Helena, Nicky & Gina

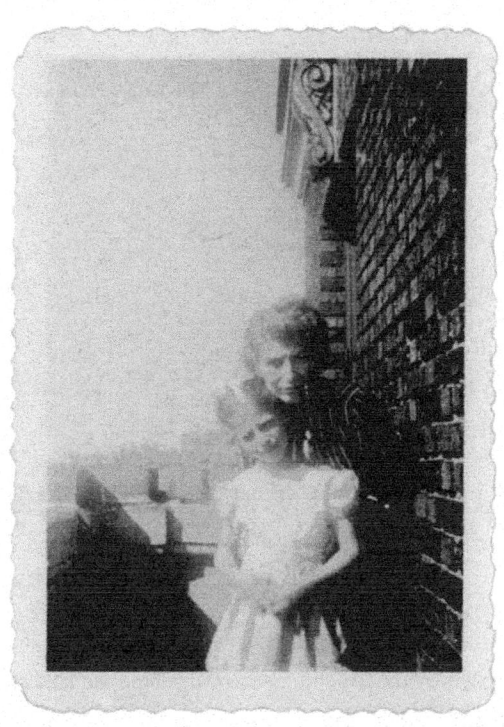

1946 Mother and Ruth Arnstein, 8 yrs old 676 Riverside Drive NYC

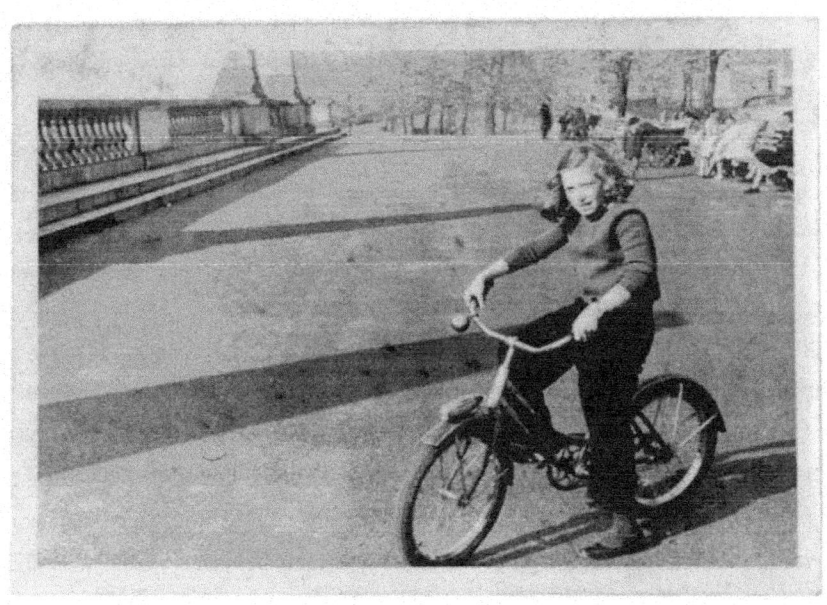

Ruth Arnstein, Riverside Drive, Ruth learning to ride bike, 13 yrs old

CHAPTER 6:

MY SUMMER CAMP EXPERIENCE

The city that had everything was a sweltering, depressing, humid asphalt rock in the summertime. Nicky sent me to summer camp this time, and did so for the next eleven years. I loved camp and never missed my family.

For the first three years, from 1945 to 1947, I attended Camp Grotowhitt in upstate New York. I caught chicken pox along with six other girls. Quarantined from the other campers, we looked a site with Calamine lotion on our faces and elsewhere. It was the savior to quieten the itching.

Once I was well, Eugene, Nicky's son, came to visit. He brought his adopted son, Douglas, along, and we spent the afternoon swimming in the lake. I wish I had gotten to know Gene better, but we were seventeen years apart. He was a quiet man, went to M.I.T., and worked at Electric Boat in Mystic, Connecticut. Gene married Grace when he was thirty-one; she was older and never divulged her age. They were unable to have children and adopted Douglas when he was three and Nanette as a newborn. At the age of fifty-one, Eugene's premature death from lymph node cancer left Grace alone with the two children. Douglas was a handful to manage, and at twelve, he drowned while walking on a frozen lake. Grace was a gentle, stoic soul who bore her dual grief admirably.

For the next six years, from 1948 to 1953, I went camping at Camp Winnataska on the shores of Little Squam Lake in Holderness, New Hampshire, in the White Mountains.

During those years, the most common name was Ruth; there were seven of us. Renamed 'Little One' by the campers reduced the confusion.

Little Squam ran into Big Squam and subsequently into the vast Lake Winnipesaukee. Spruce, maple, fir, and birch trees formed the background of the camp. Rustic cabins peppered the hillside dropping down toward the lake. A counselor and a counselor in training managed each residence. Five or six girls populated the bungalows with one bathroom for all.

Our German director Dr. Herford was a strict disciplinarian, and he had particular rules we had to obey. We had to sweep our floor, maintain the bathroom, and make our beds with hospital corners. Mrs. Haskell, the assistant in charge of the girls, performed weekly inspections.

The first requirement in the morning; we appear for reveille with the bugle's blowing and the Pledge of Allegiance. Each evening all campers stood on the grounds for the ceremonial flag lowering, and then the sound of taps. Two girls folded the banner military-style and placed it in Dr. Harford's hand.

Dr. Harford demanded us to keep our wooded grounds neat.

God forbid if a camper dropped a paper wrapper, we heard the words of the director, "Would you drop the paper in your living room?"

The camp was not all rules and regulations. I participated in many sports. Once a week, Dr. Hertford took a small riding group to Meredith's stables. One day during the ride, my horse decided to lie down. I was able to eject myself with no consequences.

The instructor told me, "Immediately, get back on the horse so you don't become afraid of the animal."

I played shortstop during baseball; basketball was my least favorite, too much running back and forth. Volleyball was a game for tall people. I thought I was too short to get the ball over the net, but I had a friend Naomi who had been coming to camp as long as I had. She was taller by two inches than I, with short brown hair and light brown eyes. She would assist the balls coming my way. We were a great team – Naomi and Ruth, it was fate that we were best friends. We also played archery; it was challenging, and we bet our arrows against each other as to who would make the most bull's eyes. I seldom won as she was a better sportswoman. Naomi had a better grasp of the bow, winning hands-down most times. Among all the activities offered, I favored water sports. At canoe time, one of my cabin mates and I carried our canoe and paddles to the water's edge. The stronger person would regularly be in the stern to guide the boat and the weakest one in the bow. I was always in the front as I invariably was the weaker paddler. Under a watchful eye, we tipped the canoe over and swam under it to the air pocket. I also liked to stand on the canoe's stern and advance it forward by bouncing up and down on the gunnels. It made me feel powerful to be able to move it all by myself.

Little Squam was precisely half a mile across to the town side. With a combination of crawl and breaststrokes, I swam with other girls to the opposite shore and back. That exercise was a one-time event. I did not wish to do that again. It seemed simple at first, but by the end, I was breathless and had rubber arms.

Practicing on the diving board, I felt accomplished completing a dive. One rule was to wear rubber unattractive bathing caps, which were the style of the day. These were happy times until one hot summer day I was swimming, and suddenly my face became swollen, my lips became large, and my eyes small. The camp director drove me to the doctor. It was determined a bee bit me, or the gasoline from a passing boat had affected me. I had to lie down on a skinny cot while the doctor gave me a shot, which did the trick. I was back in the water swimming the next day, and it never occurred again.

Among the upper class in Germany, the art of fencing and dueling was prevalent. We learned that the scar above Dr. H's lip came from his younger days. He wanted his challenges to serve as a lesson for his students to understand the art of fencing, outfitting us in steel mesh face masks and white protective clothing, socks, and gloves. Our foils had blunt ends with a protective cushion. We learned the basics of advance and retreat, to position our arms, hold the foil, and lunge.

Each year, we performed a play. That year it was by Louis Carroll. I recited the poem Jabberwocky.

Twas brillig, and the slithy toves
Did gyre and gimble in the wabe:
All mimsy were the borogroves,
And he mome raths outgabe.

Beware the Jabberwock, my son!
The jaws that bite, the claws that catch!
Beware the Jubjub bird, and shun
The frumious Bandersnatch!

Another year we performed Gilbert & Sullivan's H.M.S. Pinafore.

Campers worked tirelessly setting up the stage for each act. They stitched and created costumes for the actors.

The recreation hall where we had arts and crafts was at the bottom of a hill. Supposedly making the descent easier, small steps were dug in the ground. When the hall was empty, Naomi and I would play chopsticks on the piano. On the way there, she fell down the steps, arms and legs flying everywhere, and I laughed so hard I almost lost her friendship.

Many late afternoons, I would leave the cabin and walk to the lake. I sat on a rock as the sunset made the calm waters glow. When alone, it was a time to reflect and imagine I was an Indian princess. The rocky shoreline offered river rocks for skipping across the stream, and when Naomi accompanied me, we competed. Sunset heralded dinnertime in the tabled dining hall.

Mrs. Briggs, coming from South Carolina, had been our Negro cook for years. She was capacious in her kitchen apron. I was a skinny kid, and she took a liking to me. She wanted to fatten me up and came to the table whispering, "Come to the back door after mealtime." There she doled out chocolate pudding, apple pie, and other leftover desserts. It was customary on Saturday evenings to have large bonfires burning until midnight.

Each one of us held a stick with a marshmallow on top to roast to the flames. After ghost stories, our voices rose in song familiar to us all.

One of the worst situations that could happen was the death of a camper. In 1952, several counselors in training took out a canoe and paddled across the lake to Holderness.

On the return trip, a motorboat sideswiped their canoe, throwing all the occupants into the water. Winfred Douglas drowned. From then on, management secured all the canoes, and no more after-hours use was allowed. Dr. H. told of the foolishness of the act and the dire result. I downed my head as he dedicated a prayer to Winfred. Her parents came to camp, and we saw the devastating affect her death caused. Winfred was seventeen and an only child. For days, we mourned the sad loss of one of our own.

Camp ended on a high note. It was a year of unforgotten friendships, accomplished goals, summer fun, and sadness. We were learning what life had to offer. As we said our farewells and with a few parting tears, we promised to meet next year for a renewed blissful summer.

Naomi and I stayed in touch, and one winter day, she and her parents came from Baltimore to New York and invited me to dinner at Long Champs Restaurant. I was unused to such a fancy place. My favorite was shrimp cocktail, but when I dipped my shrimp into the red horseradish sauce and put it in my mouth, I was on fire. That was the hottest food I had ever eaten.

In 1969, a card arrived in the mail informing me that Dr. Herford had passed away on August 24th. A buried memory surfaced of him carrying a cane across the grounds of his beloved camp.

In 1954, I attended Sanborn Camp in Florissant, Colorado, near Pike's Peak. Getting there was an experience in itself. My folks took me to New York's Penn Station to meet other campers and board the Colorado Springs train. We had to change trains in Chicago. While in Chicago, a few girls and I walked out of the station to look around. Nicky was born in Chicago. He always talked about breaking broncos in the Loop in 1900 when he was twenty-three years old. The Loop is the downtown hub of the financial center. The Union Train Station, of course, was not located in the Loop. We saw the elevated train system known as the 'L' that runs one-hundred and two miles above Chicago streets. It started its operation in 1892.

Back on the train, we had some fun playing strip poker. A Negro conductor knocked and stuck his head in the door. I had forfeited my blouse, not knowing my way around the game, and covered up quickly with a towel. He questioned, "What are you young people doing? Don't you get yourselves in any trouble now?" The boys playing innocent spoke up, "We are not doing anything."

The change of trains placed Pullman cars on the rails for sleeping and dining as we were traveling overnight. The Pullmans were ushered into the marketplace in 1893 during a time when train travel was more popular. In our compartment, we had bunk beds and bath facilities.

We arrived in Colorado Springs the next day and bused to our location at Florissant, which has an elevation of eight thousand two hundred feet. This mountain atmosphere was much higher than we were accustomed to. The camp required that we rest for three days before starting any activity, or we may pass out. I was now a cowgirl wearing boots, western shirts, and Wrangler jeans.

It was a coed camp with the boys at a different location. Dances took place twice during the camp season. The trending song for that summer was "Blue Moon".

The boys came to our camp, otherwise there was no mingling with the girls. I danced with one short boy from Chicago, who told me, "My Dad was on Iwo Jima in 1945 during World War II when the soldiers raised the flag after the battle." He was not a talkative fellow. I tried to draw him out, but the music and other conversations drowned us out. It was not going to be a lingering relationship.

We had excursions out of the camp to a roller rink in Colorado Springs. We visited an old mining camp Cripple Creek. In 1890, loaded ore deposits were found and mined there, creating the last Colorado gold rush.

My favorite experience was riding our horses to a campsite away from the camp and spending one night camping out under the vast Colorado skies with millions of stars watching us. Looking up, I felt so small and insignificant against the sprawling sky. I wondered if we were the only people in this vast universe. In the morning, we rounded up the horses, saddled, bridled them, and rode back to the camp.

Almost every day, during the afternoon, hail fell, covering the ground and it rapidly melted away under the summer sun.

Maine was my last year of camping at Camp Sunnydale in 1955. I was now an experienced horse person, so they thought. I became the assistant horseback riding instructor and a counselor in training (CIT). I rode bareback in the coral, stood upon the horse, and fell a few times. I had to manage the tack and put halters and saddles on for class. After class, I had to walk the horses around the corral to cool them down, and then brush them. The only boy in the camp was the official horseback riding instructor. I had plenty of attention.

Just like my other camps, there were swimming activities, sports, and crafts.

Each year, Nicky and Gina would come up to the camp on visiting day. They would rent a cabin close to a lake so that Nicky could go fishing.

When I was in Colorado, they did not visit.

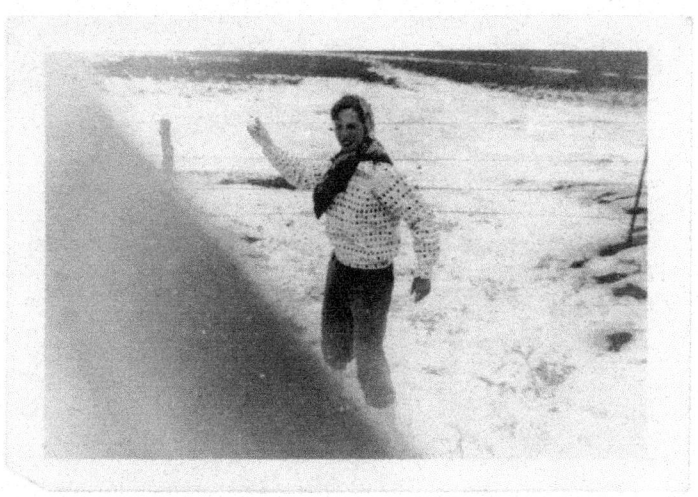

1954 Colorado, Ruth Arnstein – 17 yrs old

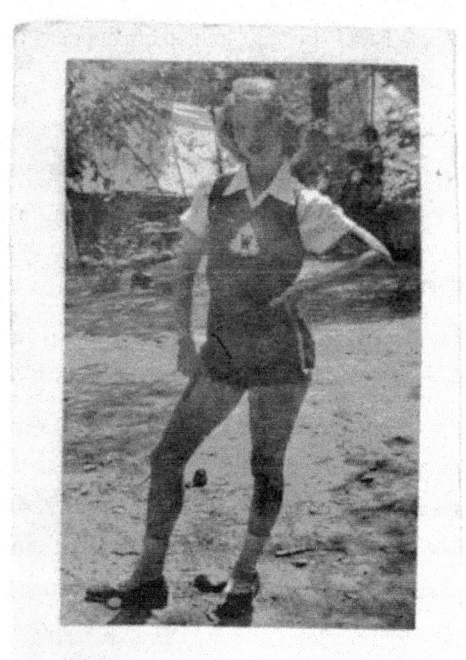

1953 Camp Winataska, Ruth Arnstein – 16 yrs old

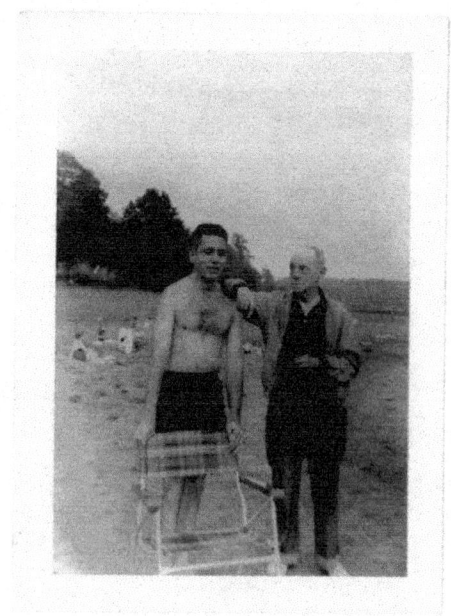

Eugene Arnstein, Nicky Arnstein 1944

CHAPTER 7:

1944 TO 1957

It was due time to begin a new school. The Public School that I should have attended was just off-Broadway, on the fringes of Harlem. Nicky did not think it appropriate for a little Jewish girl to go to school with all black children.

Before beginning a new school, Nicky did not want people to know that my mother was a divorcee. The way to hide this family embarrassment was to change the child's name to match the parents. Just switch it, no legal papers, my birth certificate read Lichtenstein. My father, Hans, wanted me to keep the name Lichtenstein; he would not permit Nicky to adopt me. That made no difference to Nicky; all my school papers would read Arnstein from that time forward.

Five blocks down Riverside Drive was the Saint Walburga's Academy. A Catholic school taught by nuns attired in black robes belonging to the Holy Child Jesus Society. I took a test to determine which grade I should enter. It should have been the second grade, but as I had been sick a good part of my first grade in East Orange, the nuns decided I lacked elementary education, so I had to repeat the first grade.

Henceforth, I was one year older than all my other classmates when I went to Saint Walburga's from 1944 to 1950.

The school was a splendid example of Gothic Revival architecture built in 1911.

A sizable white marble statue of Michelangelo's Pieta was in an alcove on the marble stairs between floors. A small chapel on the first floor always contained abundant snapdragons and gladiolus. Sister Januarius showed us by applying a small amount of pressure to the snapdragon bloom; it would open like a mouth. The flowers emitted the scent of spring and a feeling of serenity.

A wooden fence around the backyard protected us during recess and picture taking. Our first and second graders watched the upper-level girls exhibiting their talents playing basketball and admired their skill.

The school was girls only with thirteen girls in our class. We had to wear uniforms, a jumper of maroon, and white long sleeve blouses. We covered a wide range of nationalities. Caroline, Constance, and Angela were Italian, Ann was Chinese, Dorothy and I were Jewish, Geraldine and Elizabeth were Irish, Acacia and Velma were Puerto Rican, Simone was French, and there were Dottie and Hope. Elizabeth, Dorothy, and I were the best of friends and known as the Three Musketeers.

In the second, third, and sixth grades, I had the same teacher, Sister Januarius. She called me a chatterbox and put her hand in front of my mouth. I would kiss her hand and make her laugh.

During one history class, I looked out the window and exclaimed, "There goes Henry Hudson." That set the whole room laughing and Sister Januarius too.

Keeping my pencil sharp was an obsession. Located near the windows overlooking the river was a manual turn sharpener. It became a routine to visit this site and sharpen away. Sister Jan still remembers my fixation to hone my writing instrument to the sharpest point possible.

On Good Friday, I remember one year, Sister took the three of us across the George Washington Bridge. We began on 140th Street to one-hundred-eighty-first street and across the bridge. We girls were on roller skates, Sister Jan walked, and we agreed not to talk from noon until three o'clock, the hours that Jesus hung on the cross. Every year since this outing, I have thought of this devoted nun. In 1999, when my time was not so pressing, I visited a Catholic retreat in the mountains of Hot Springs, North Carolina. They looked up the Catholic diocese that I contacted and could get in touch with my Sister Januarius. Now known as Rosemary McCarthy, presently she is a fantastic ninety-seven-year-old woman.

Every year in June, all the grades had graduation ceremonies, and this particular day we were to go shopping for my graduation shoes. On this spring day, I was roller-skating in front of our apartment building. One of the neighborhood kids, Leon, decided he wanted to jump over my head while on skates. He missed and hit me square in the chest. I hit my head on the sidewalk.

When Mother called me, I told her, "I don't want to go to Tom McCann today."

"We have to go today."

"No, I don't feel well."

"What can be the matter with you? You were fine this morning. You just want to stay and play."

So, I went with my parents on the subway to the shoe store. I was already feeling nauseous on the train.

When we arrived at the store, I told Mom, "Mom, I feel nauseous." Then, I threw up on Nicky's shoe. He hailed a cab to take us home.

We did not have a car; if we did, it would have been convenient to take me to the Doctor.

A few years later, I had my last graduation at St. Walburga's; I was thirteen and sorry to move on. We were leaving the neighborhood.

Today, the Fortune Society owns the academy. It houses homeless individuals from prison transitioning back into society.

While I was going to Catholic School, my father, Hans, was more concerned about my Jewish religious education. Mother's family was Reform Jews, meaning that the Jewish law was a general guideline rather than restrictions and obligations. My father's parents were Orthodox Jews keeping a Kosher home, therefore, strictly obeying the edicts. My father insisted I attend Jewish Sunday School and learn about the religion of my birth.

The Temple was the Congregation of Rodeph Shalom, located on 83rd Street in Manhattan. Nicky took me on the subway every week. Hans lived in New Jersey, so I guess that is why Nicky had to take me. During class, I learned the bread's blessing and the prayer for Hanukkah, which I have never used at a service. In my one attempt at being Jewish, my dresser went up in flames when I lit the Menorah to celebrate Hanukkah. I had left some paper lying around, and it caught fire. Christmas and Hanukkah come in relatively the same time, and so while I lit the candles, a Christmas tree resided in our living room.

The temple building was also a Community Center where Mother did some sewing as a volunteer. While she volunteered, I attended Girl Scout meetings.

At home, she had a sewing machine and sewed many of my dresses. I was fond of the dresses she made for me. I have happy memories of standing on a stool while she measured the hem.

"I can't do this if you keep moving around, Ruth." Mom scolded, "You must stand still and stop jittering, or I will hit you with one of these pins." Of all the ensembles she made for me, my favorite was an ice-skating skirt with a blue corduroy on top, and a red felt inside. I wore it once when Mom and Nicky brought me to an indoor rink in Brooklyn. But, I wore it more frequently with my dad, who took me skating often.

While in Catholic School, I attended religion class daily. I believe for services, I wore a head covering, and the priest spoke in Latin. At the Synagogue, I had a few hours each Sunday of religious training. During services, the Rabbi opened the Arc, and a Torah scroll carried around the pews of the Synagogue. The Rabbi spoke in Hebrew, and the men wore yarmulkes, and devoted women wore head coverings. I had made one friend Harriett. At Catholic school, I had many friends. I got more training in Catholicism than in Judaism and felt more at ease at the Catholic school. I have no idea how long I attended the Temple.

One winter day, I was sleigh riding in Riverside Park. A small dark boy stood at the bottom of the hill with arms outstretched. I tried to avoid him, which I did, but my sled had rusty runners and did not obey my command. I ran into the cast iron fence with my head, splitting it open. My blood ran in the snow, and it soiled my pea coat. Elizabeth and I walked three blocks to the drug store to see if the pharmacist could help me out.

"Little girl, go home." At home, I tried to wash the blood away in my sink while Elizabeth tried to distract Mom. She did not like the sight of blood, especially if it was coming from her daughter. As soon as she saw me, she cried out, "Oh my God, what have you done this time, Ruth?" As quickly as they could slide into their coats, we were off to the doctor in a cab.

Once again, it would have been handy to have a car to take me to the doctor to have my head stitched up. The accident put me in bed for a week.

It was my birthday week, and I received a watch with a second hand that I showed to everyone. I had never seen a timepiece with a second hand, and it delighted me.

When I was sick for any length of time, I stayed in my grandmother's room. It was like a throwback to the old country; an old dresser with a marble top, an oval mirrored armoire, chair, and an oval table where my great-grandmother used to make lovely doilies and tablecloths. I learned as all children in Europe knew how to embroider, crochet, and knit.

Nene enjoyed classical music and wanted me to learn to appreciate it. When a younger woman, she found the music enchanting. One of her favorites was the NBC

Symphony Orchestra with Arturo Toscanini conducting the music of Beethoven. I sat with her for hours and listened, not only when I was sick, but at other times, too.

To enhance my music appreciation, in our dining room was an upright piano where I took my lessons. Oh! I remember those lessons well. I would automatically learn the pieces, but the problem was that I would memorize the mistakes too. Why did my folks think that any type of music lesson was appropriate for me? I was tone-deaf.

My parents, especially my granny, felt that, "Music should be an integral part of the life and mind of a young person."

Nicky felt, "Music was a key to middle-class ways, brought socialization, culture, and breeding."

That is why I had music lessons.

During one of the lessons, I had this terrible stomach ache, but had to read a new music sheet. I had to practice anyway, since there was a concert coming the following week. It was the first day I became a woman; I was thirteen. My mom had timed a private conversation about the life of a woman the week before this mishap. She came into my bathroom when I was in the tub. I scurried under the water; what was she doing here?

"I need to have an important conversation with you."

"Now, while I am in the tub?"

"Yes, no one is around, and I want to talk to you about something serious."

Oops, what have I done?

And so, while she sat on the closed toilet seat, she explained about my first 'period.' I think it embarrassed her to talk about it. Instead of explaining it in her own words, she read from a book. I was shocked.

"What do you mean? I will bleed, wow."

"Ruthie, it means that you have reached womanhood."

Then, she explained about intercourse. "Do you mean people do that, ugh?" Bewildered, I pulled the plug and let the water drain.

My mom picked the exact time to tell me about the birds and the bees. After our conversation, I was one day a child, the next day, a woman. I didn't feel like a woman, and I was not too fond of this transformation.

Easter morning, I was spending time with Grandma. We sat in the living room at 676 Riverside Drive. I asked her, "Do you remember when you made a German pancake?

It had split apart when you flipped it." I loved German pancakes; they were so large and fluffy, and she made them in an iron skillet.

"Yes, I remember, you were so delighted that I was able to make it whole again." We both laughed. Then, the mood became serious. "Ruthie, I must tell you something; I think you are old enough to understand."

"What are you going to tell me?"

She told me that she was not my real grandmother, "Mother's mother Eda died when she was four years old. Eda had bad pain in her side, and by the time she got to the doctor, her appendix exploded." "Back when your mother was small," Grandma explained, "There was no such thing as penicillin; Eda died of the poison that went through her body. Gina's father did not know how he was going to raise Gina and her sister Ella. I was not married, and I was very close to my sister Eda, your mother, and Ella. Your grandfather, Berthold, who was Eda's husband, asked me to marry him and take care of the children. I raised both your mother and Ella. That is how I became your grandmother."

I didn't know what to say, lost for words; I was surprised and saddened.

"Grandma, I love you. It does not matter to me if you are not my real grandmother; you are my real grandmother." She was very happy, and with tears in her eyes, she hugged me.

Not long after Grandma and I had our conversation, one of our family's most tragic events occurred on a day when the mailman came to the door with a special delivery letter from Germany. My mother and grandmother ran into Mom's bedroom, and soon I heard sobs. Mom told me very little except that Ella and her husband Herman were dead. Years later, I found out that the Nazis wanted to take them to the camps. Ella was a renowned eye doctor, and she was afraid she would have to operate on her people. They had attempted to come to America, but Herman was a polio victim, and the United States would not accept people with that illness. They committed suicide just before a letter arrived from the Cuban council saying they could come to Cuba.

April 12, 1945, Newspaper headlines read, "President Roosevelt is Dead leaving vice president Truman in charge."

Harry S. Truman became the 33rd President of the United States. He told reporters. "I felt like the moon, the stars, and all the planets had fallen on me." I was eight years old when this happened, and I remember the passing of FDR.

It was Victory in Europe, or VE Day, May 8, 1945. In June of the same year, New York honored General Dwight D. Eisenhower with the largest ticker-tape parade the city had ever seen. It came down West 86th Street, where Aunt Flora and Uncle Bruno lived. They had an apartment on the fifth floor, and I was able to see General Ike waving to the crowds of cheering people on the streets. People were hanging out of apartment house windows, applauding in appreciation. Aunt Flora carried quite a bit of weight, she was looking out the window, and suddenly she slipped, no, not out the window, but in the living room and broke her arm.

"On Oct. 27, 1945, New York City was the site of the most spectacular homefront display of American military might the nation had ever seen. Navy Day was in effect a monumental victory lap, coming seven weeks after the signing of the Japanese surrender in Tokyo Bay aboard the USS Missouri. Now the 'Big Mo' and other stars and supporting players from the Pacific Fleet had come home. Along a six-mile stretch of the Hudson River, 47 warships gathered—battleships, aircraft carriers, cruisers, destroyers, submarines, and submarine chasers." (Copied from the *Wall Street Journal*, October 26, 2015)

I stood on our rectangular-shaped balcony, jutting clumsily from three of our windows. It was an awkward configuration. The only way into the structure was to climb through the window. The one in our living room was perfect for waving at the decked-out vessels on VE Day, sailing down the Hudson River. My hair in pigtails, pinned on top of my head, watching in complete amazement. I wore a pink gingham dress with a bow in the back.

The building is now a condominium, and the balconies are gone.

Our neighborhood was changing, and it was time to leave the city. Mother had a cousin Gretel in Forest Hills, and she wanted to be closer to her. I could never figure out why, as we seldom saw them. Once we moved to Forest Hills, we got a car. Nicky picked out a light blue Pontiac, four-door sedan. He was to be the only driver as Mother had never driven. In time, she learned.

My new school was Steven A. Halsey Junior High School. The public school was coed, and I was unaccustomed to boys in the class. I would blush if called. They were teaching things that I had already learned in my other school. My Catholic education had covered a wide range of subjects. It was somewhat dull; there was less homework, less discipline. When a nun left the room, no one said a word. Here the kids talked while the teacher was speaking. That first year I received a letter from Sister Jan. She told me the class missed me and hoped I was doing well in my new surroundings.

I made friends with some of the girls, and we formed a club called Jugs, Just Us Gals. We would go to the movies together, bowling and ice-skating at the rink in Flushing Meadows. It was in a building left standing from the 1939 World's Fair. It was a very long walk around the grounds. A chain-link fence surrounded the area, and to cut short the hike, we climbed the obstruction except for Joyce, whose pants got hung up on the barbs of the fence, and after we finished laughing, we got her down.

While walking around the grounds, we found the buried time capsule. Placed in the park on September 23, 1938, and not opened until 6939. Wow! What would life on earth be like by then? Would we even be living on this planet? Perhaps, we would be living somewhere above this sphere. It sparked an engaging conversation.

My Junior High graduation was in June 1953. Instead of having it at school, it was in Kew Gardens, Queens, in the movie theater. I wore a white dress, and all the accessories were white except for a pink corsage on my left shoulder. Rochelle and I posed for pictures after the event.

The commencement song was "I Believe," with lyrics, "I believe for every drop of rain that falls, a flower grows ... " Englebert Humperdinks was the singer.

After graduation, as a special gift, Mom planned two Saturday's each month, just for the two of us. Grandma and Dad had always been around and we seldom had mother and daughter time together. The New York City Center presented theater performances, and she enjoyed the live theater, and it made an impression on me at the age of thirteen.

I remember all the performances, and a special actor: Jose Ferrer, who played *Cyrano de Bergerac*. We also saw: *Shrike*, *Richard III*, the operas *Aida*, *Carmen*, *La Boehme*, *Die Fledermaus*, and *Madam Butterfly*.

Forest Hills High School was my next stop. I loved English, and typing, shorthand not so much. My math teacher recommended a general math class; therefore, I did not have to take geometry. I walked to school with friends; ate tuna fish sandwiches in the lunchroom, and large pretzels after school from a street vendor, which I shared with my friends. Since 1820, these pretzels have sold on the streets of Philadelphia and New York. They had a softer inside like bread and a shiny exterior like a bagle, but more delicate and covered with salt.

I took French classes, and Grandma helped me with them. She could speak German, French, and English. I always had to pronounce the French words correctly. She was a demanding teacher, but she did it for me.

During the lessons, Mom ironed on an ironing machine known as a mangle. It was thirty-six inches across and had a roller fourteen inches in diameter. The flat, curved hot metal iron pressed down on the cloth that lay across the round roller. She pressed the sheets and fancy tablecloths that her grandmother Clara had made.

In 1955, I was seventeen. Mom came into my room with the sad news that a city bus had tragically killed Opa when he stepped off the curb. "That is terrible," I cried. "I loved him; he was my only Grandpa." I thought about him, and the times we spent together. He was the first of my family to die. I was unable to attend the funeral. I would never see him again.

While in high school, at the behest of a friend who suggested we attend a Civil Air Patrol meeting, I met Ray Colucci. He wore a uniform and a hat, making him all the more attractive. Friday night was meeting night, and I never missed a session. After Ray and I went out, it turned out to be my first sexual encounter. On a school afternoon, I stopped at his home; I wanted to show him the pearls I got from Aunt Gretel for my 17th birthday. Unexpectedly, his mother came home from work early. Like little mice, we scurried from her bedroom.

We went to school dances, movies, restaurants, and hotel rooms. To keep our rendezvous secret, we made out in the stairwell of my apartment building. To protect me from the cold concrete, Ray laid his coat on the ground when we made out. He gave me his CAP wings; we were going steady. I thought the relationship was going somewhere. After two-and-a-half years of dating, one evening, standing in the stairwell, Ray told me,

"I met a girl at work, and I'm going to marry her; she is pregnant."

I was shocked, "I thought you were faithful to me." What a fool I was.

"How long have you been dating her?"

"I met Pat at work at Revlon. She is in the same department as me."

"You did not answer me. How long have you been dating her?"

"Ah, I got the job about ah, ah six or seven months ago. For four months, I've seen Pat for four months."

"And you got her pregnant? Pretty stupid. What happened to you using rubbers?"

"I did. I did not know this would happen. I felt sorry for Pat as she has a little boy. Someone else got her pregnant and left her. The boy is a little slow."

"You felt sorry for her, you simpleton; she wanted a father for her kid, and she knew a soft touch when she saw one. She knew just what she was doing. Now you are going to be a father to someone else's kid and have a baby?"

"It looks that way. We have already set a date."

"Well, isn't that nice? Were you going to wait until you were married to tell me?"

"No, I wanted to tell you. I still love you, but I have to do this."

"You are an imbecile. Have a happy marriage, you idiot."

By then, I was crying. How could Ray do this to me after all these years? I wasn't using dirty words back then, but what a bastard.

"Is she Catholic?"

"Yes."

"Your mother would have never let you marry me. God forbid I'm Jewish, so, instead, you marry a nice Catholic girl with one child, and now she is pregnant again. You think she can get away with wearing a white dress, maybe a purple one."

I was getting hotter by the minute. I wanted to inflict pain. I didn't want to look at him - the lout, cheater, liar. I wanted him to be gone. Teary-eyed, I walked away.

Ray was not the boyfriend I thought he was. If my thoughts of marriage had materialized, I think he would have been a cheating husband. It was best for me that it did not work out. I was eighteen when it was all over. I got on with my life.

On an April afternoon, we were a group of three teenage couples heading to Greenwich Village for a night out. It was a daring act to take the subway to the sophisticated part of town. A strip joint was our destination. We were trying to act grown-up in an atmosphere of artists and educated hippie individuals. We found a bar advertising semi-clad women in provocative poses. As the dancers began their performance, we guessed, among ourselves, if they were male or female. The fair sex won out at first, and then doubt crept into our decisions. Oh, wow, the girls were boys. The drag queens put on a spectacular show. Now we knew more about the other side of life.

For part of one summer, I worked for Cousin Vivian, Walter's wife. She worked under her maiden name Arbuckle in the fashion industry. She had established quite a name for herself, and she wanted to teach me about the trade. When she opened a small children's boutique in Teaneck, New Jersey, I went to work for her. It was something new for me. I unpacked and hung up stylish clothes for kids, helped customers, and swept the floors inside and out. I liked working with people and benefitted from what Vivian passed on to me. The job was to arouse my interest in retail and fashion, and it achieved that goal.

In the early part of 1956, while I was in high school, I got a job at Bloomingdales on Lexington Avenue. I worked in the linen department on Thursday evenings and every other Saturday. Nothing spectacular ever happened until the day Marilyn Monroe came to our floor. She was impossible to recognize, all bundled up with a high collar fur coat. As word filtered around the floor, I glanced about and possibly saw her.

My last day of work was a warm June day. I dressed in a blue checked scoop neck cotton dress, which I inherited from my mother's cousin's wealthy daughter-in-law. With that, I wore blue Ansonia three-inch heels. It was a Thursday, I took the subway into Manhattan, and when I got off work, they were striking. The only way home was across the 59th Street Bridge. A two-level cantilever bridge 3724 feet, almost three-quarters of a mile long. The walkway was grated metal with openings every three-quarter of an inch. My stylish heels kept getting caught in the grating. The bridge connects the borough of Queens to Manhattan. It is a scary feeling to have cars overhead and cars within reach.

There were hundreds of stranded workers bedraggled, hot, and thirsty finally arriving in Long Island City. The bar was packed, not that I would have gone in, but on the curb, a man with a red Cadillac stopped asking, "Who needs a ride?" I was quick to respond and sat in the front seat. My feet were killing me.

In 1956, I graduated high school, and for graduation, my gift was a trip with the family to Washington, DC. I had been reading about President Lincoln, so visiting Ford Theater was top on my list. We also visited the home of Dr. Samuel Mudd. I felt like I was reliving history. We took pictures at the Lincoln and Jefferson memorials and visited The National Gallery of Art. The display of the Sacrament of the Last Supper by Salvador Dali was inspirational.

Nicky, on a whim, decided to visit his sister Etta in Baltimore. Never mind that he had not seen or talked to her in years. He knocked on her door, and the three of us stood expectantly waiting for her to answer. She refused to open the door announcing, "Go away; I do not want to see you."

Rose was Nicky's younger sister. Rose was now my Aunt Rose, thin to the bone, and had been left destitute by Ben, her dead husband. Rose floated between Nicky's home, her niece Ruth, and her son Benjamin and wife Valerie. She stayed for two or three months, and then moved on. Aunt Rose slept on a convertible couch in the living room. Wearing her light peach-colored negligee of silk chiffon and matching robe, she seldom dressed before eleven.

Her thinning gray hair curled in a sausage roll around the edge of her head. She smoked steadily, carrying her ashtray with her wherever she went. Should she acciden-tally drop her long ash on the carpeted floor, she rubbed her foot over it, grinding it into the carpet.

After graduation, at the urging of Cousin Vivian, I attended Tobe-Coburn School for Fashion Careers. Part of the curriculum consisted of learning how to sell retail. We had to find a job, which I located at B. Altman Department Store for the Christmas of

1957. The jewelry counter was my assignment. That year the most sought-after piece of Jewelry was Aurora Borealis. Swarovski, collaborating with Christian Dior, was the inventor experimenting with metal on crystal, achieving fabulous rainbow colors. It was a well-known phenomenon in colors and the gem's versatility picking up color from the fabric. The women swarmed to the counter for earrings, pendants, and necklaces. I enjoyed this phase of my education but left the school a few months later. The girls were cliquish, and I did not feel accepted. They came from Florida and Washington, DC, from well-to-do families, and I could not financially compete. Conversations of foreign travel and fur coats, I was not in their league.

I was finally the right age to drive, and I wanted a car. One day, I called a girlfriend, and we walked a few blocks to a used car dealership. For ten dollars, I bought a Buick. I drove it home and told my folks. Nicky felt this was an inappropriate car for me. He spoke to me with an unaccustomed severe emphasis, "What have you done? You know I disapprove of credit. I pay cash, and that car is too big for you." Days later, I returned my foolhardy purchase. He bought me a 1954 white Chevy convertible. He paid for the car, and I paid him ten dollars a month. At first, Nicky tried to teach me how to drive and said, "You will never stay between the lines." He then thought it a better idea to send me to driving school, so I would learn the proper way to handle a car. I failed the first driving test because I was unable to parallel park. For the second test, I blundered because the officer said, "Make a right turn." I did, but the light was red. I finally got my license on the third try.

First cars are always at the mercy of inexperienced drivers. It was a rainy day in the Bronx, on a wet cobblestone street; I made a turn and skidded into a concrete wall protecting railroad tracks below, rearranging my right fender.

Nicky was in the hospital for something minor. While he was gone, I drove his Pontiac. There was a post on the right side of our parking spot in the apartment house's basement garage. On re-parking it, I hit the post and damaged the right-side door. I located a repair shop, and for ten dollars, they fixed it. I borrowed the ten dollars from Mom, but did not tell her why I needed the money. When I told her, she said, "Nicky would have never seen it; he never gets in the car on that side."

A few years later, on a winter morning, after I had put many, many miles on my car and left a boyfriend or two behind, white smoke billowed from the hood of my beloved car. My car knowledge was negligible, and antifreeze, not a word in my vocabulary, had never touched my radiator. That was the beginning of my destructive vehicular life and my love and hate affair with Detroit. The Chevy was history.

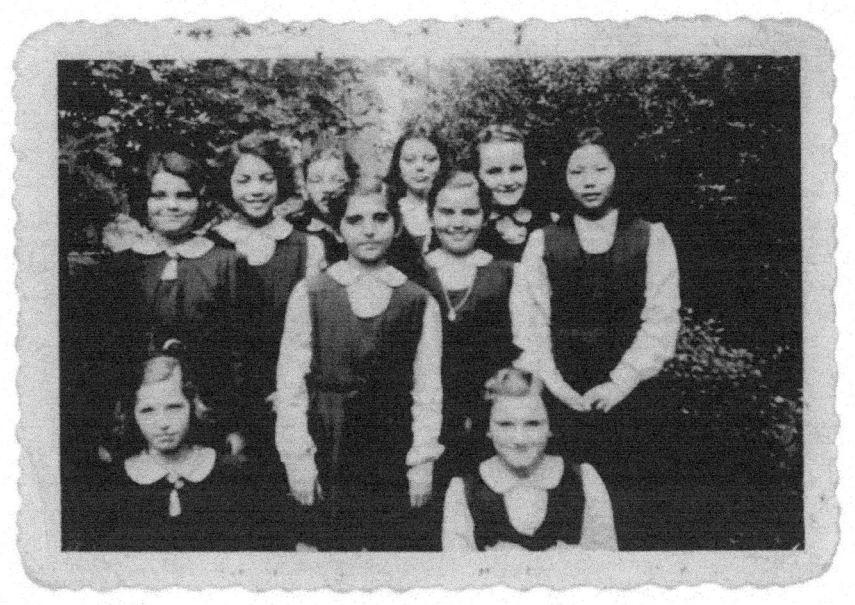

1949 Classmates with Ruth Arnstein: Elizabeth, Dorothy, Conny, Carolyn, Angela, Gerry, Ann, Acasia, Hope

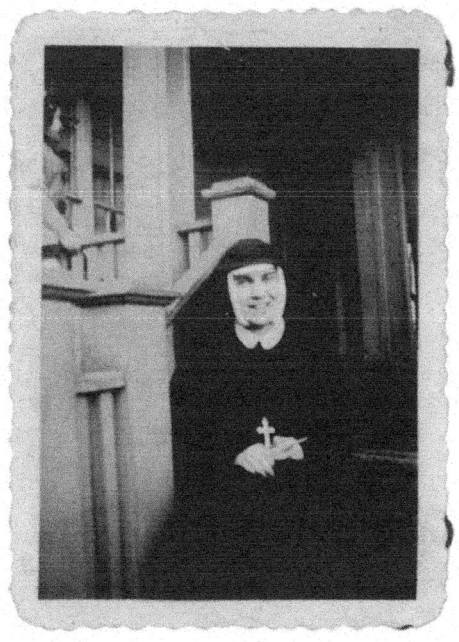

Mother Januarius 1949 Grades 2, 3, and 6. Favorite teacher, St. Walburgers Academy Order of the Holy Child

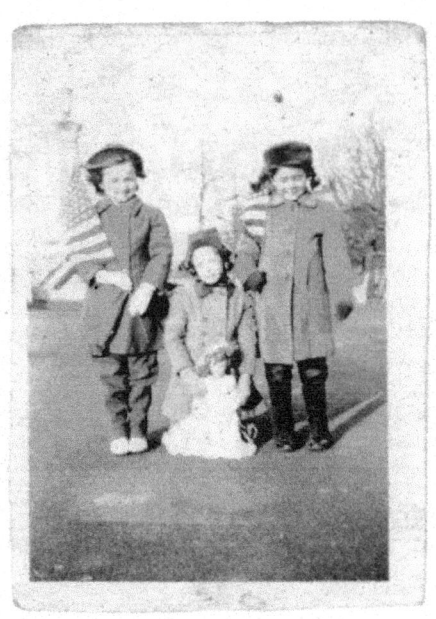

Elizabeth, Ruth & Dorothy Best friends 1946 Ruth Arnstein 9 yrs old

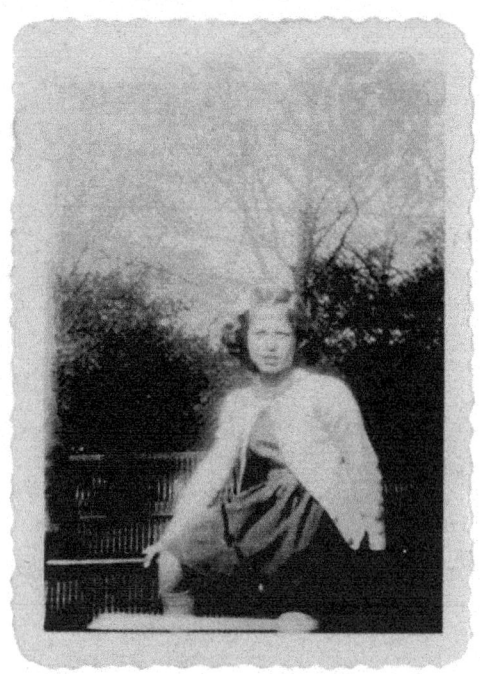

Ruth Arnstein 1947 – 10 yrs old

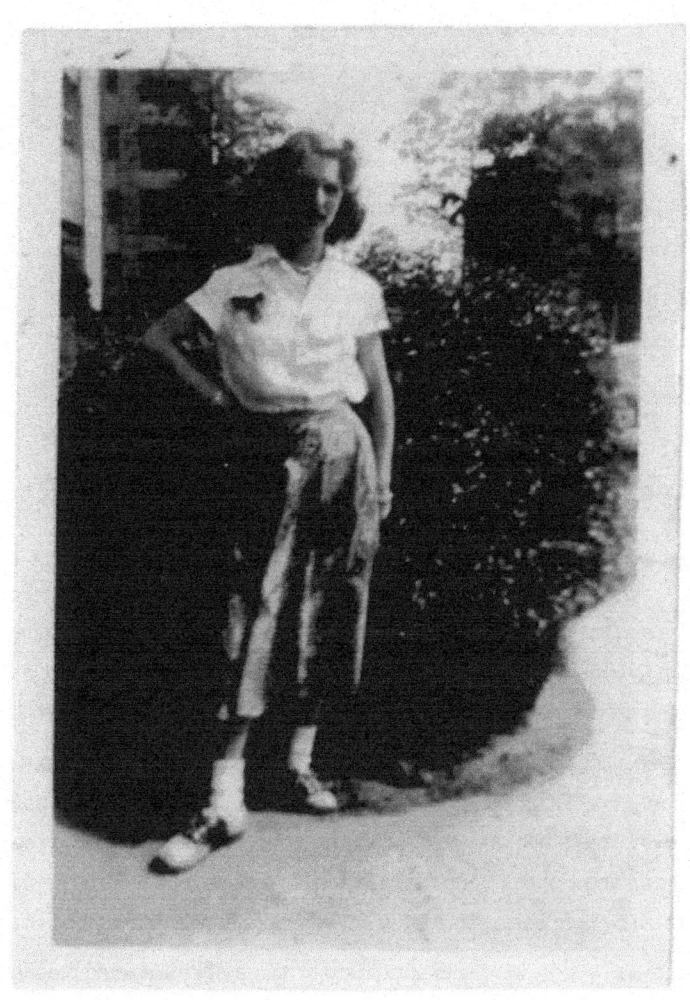

Ruth Arnstein 1953 – 16 yrs old

CHAPTER 8:

VISITATIONS WITH MY FATHER

Mom and the courts had given my dad visitation every two weeks. When we were living in East Orange, I only saw my dad a few times. Sometimes, he did not make it, and when the support checks did not arrive on time, Mom did not let me see him.

When picking me up at our house in East Orange, he stood in the doorway, waiting for me to come out. Then, he would help me into his old Plymouth coup parked in our empty driveway. I remember my father driving us to his garage; he went in to see someone leaving me standing at the entrance. I could see cars inside, but he told me, "Just wait, do not come in; I'll be right back." This is the cover picture on the front of the book.

There was a story Mom told about Dad in his garage, "He attempted to fix something on a car, and when completed, he had parts remaining. I always wondered how the car ran." Mom said. We would laugh about this little family story.

Now Mommy never spoke of him or told me anything about his family. I wondered how she felt about him.

Dad and I drove to his Irvington apartment where he lived with Opa and a little dog, which he brought along occasionally. I am sure it was hard for him to figure out what to do with a toddler with whom he spent such little time. He would tell me, "My sweet Ruthie, one day is not enough with you. I would love to spend more time, but I have to work." When he held me to his chin, it was rough but I did not mind. I loved my daddy. These visits were short, although as I grew they became longer.

Upon returning, Mom only asked what we did. I did not tell her; I thought she would disapprove. When I was about six, he took me to Asbury Park in New Jersey. There were gaming wheels like a carnival, and Dad liked to put money down and see what sort of prize he could win for me. I was just tall enough to look over the gaming counter where he was tossing a ring toward a slew of bottles. I usually went home with a stuffed animal, but we always had fun. For pennies back then, he bought me sticky, gooey pink cotton candy and chocolate ice cream that ran down the side of the cone and dripped on my dress. Of course, I loved to go to different places, but most importantly, I valued the time I spent with my dad. I loved him and was so happy to go out with him.

Once our family moved to New York, for our visits I met Dad on the street of our apartment building. Nicky did not want him in our apartment anywhere near my mother. Not that she wanted to see him; the love was gone. Nicky made all the arrangements by phone. He hated it when I spent time with my dad. If I were to speak of my father in our home, I had to refer to him as 'X;' in my mind, I did not think this was appropriate. Nicky did not even know him, and to be jealous of a man my mother thought nothing about now. He was showing a lot of disrespect to my dad.

My father waited for me in front of the building, wearing his felt fedora hat cocked a bit toward the back of his head and smoking his Lucky Strike. He still drove the older model Plymouth, invariably in a dark color. I used to look out my bedroom window, see these cars, and wonder what they would look like if they had zebra stripes or tiger markings. To me, they looked like gangster automobiles. They had manual gearshift levers referred to as four-on-the-floor. The average price of a new car was eight hundred seventy dollars, and gas cost eleven cents a gallon. Dad would sit me on his lap in front of the steering wheel, and we made believe I was driving.

He would make funny comments as I tried to hold the wheel on which he kept a firm grasp. I was not able to touch the pedal because I was too short. Instead of the beach, we often went to Palisades Amusement Park across the river in New Jersey. It covered thirty acres of a summer family-oriented outdoor playground. It began operation in 1898 and remained open through 1971. The attraction was rides, fun houses, games of chance, and a carnival atmosphere, all of which brought people flooding to the park. Moms and dads with their kids, baby carriages, and teenager'ghys hand-in-hand paraded through the midway past the stalls. Young girls in skirts and blouses, and boys in pompadour haircuts, combs protruding from back pockets, and one T-shirt sleeve rolled neatly holding their cigarette packs. Carney operators called from their booths when we walked by, "Come on, Dad; win a prize for your little girl."

On our visits to the park, we rode bumper cars that Dad enjoyed racing; we would go around chasing each other to bump our small vehicles together and laugh every time we contacted. Dad lifted me onto the merry-go-round, and on each turnaround, he watched for me. We played on pinball machines, and he shot at moving ducks. I think gambling on the wheels of chance was his favorite. Dad gave me the nickels or dimes, and I plunked them on the numbers. We won a lion with a full mane and a tall giraffe.

Mother insisted I give them away when I went camping.

One time, Dad won a small teddy bear. He was carrying it around, and when he went into the bathroom, he kept it in his hand, forgetting to give it to me. When upon returning, Dad was hitting it on the head; his cigarette had ignited the bear. He stood in front of me, beating it, and we laughed and laughed. He took it home as a reminder of our day together.

It was Sunday, August 14, 1944; my father brought Grandpa along, which was an extra treat as Opa seldom accompanied Dad. Driving back to New Jersey over the ever-familiar George Washington Bridge, we headed for Palisades Park. As we walked around the midway, I pointed to Opa the giant Ferris wheel, which loomed high above the park. He saw the roller coaster Skyrocket, and he remarked, "Do you ride on that machine, Ruthie?"

"No, Opa, I am afraid it goes so fast and makes all that noise."

It operated from 1926 until 1944. We followed Dad down the midway. As Opa and I walked, he put his hand on my shoulder, giving me an affectionate squeeze. We watched as my father played a few games of chance before we settled in for our lunch.

Dad chose a spot close to the Skyrocket. It was an enormous ride gliding along on its rails. Most buckets had three people across protected by support in front that kept them from falling out and provided a secure handle to grasp. The riders were holding tightly to these rails and grimacing with mouths agape, screeching as it sped down, and then swung up, wobbling on the tracks, swaying as it rose and fell. Up and down it went. It was somewhat scary. We agreed we would not attempt to try it.

Suddenly, Dad said, "I see smoke coming from the rails."

Just then, a fire broke out. Flames began creeping forward on the wooden structure. Screams of joy turned into shrieks of terror.

"Kommen Sie Vater, Ruthie, take my hand. We must go to the car."

People were frantic, hastily exiting from the coaster buckets, scrambling to their automobiles. When we reached our car, I was delighted to find a charming little doll in the back seat.

"How did this doll get in the car, Dad?"

"I don't know. Someone must have put it in the wrong vehicle." I was seven years old, and I believed him.

When I got home, Mother was beside herself; she just knew I was at the park. She protectively hovered over me, hugging me and took my hand, and led me to the living room window where we could see the flames. Reports in the newspaper the following day claimed the fire demolished 85 percent of the park. Wow, we were there on what turned out to be a historic day.

Palisades was the cream of parks, but we changed direction and went to Coney Island when it burned. It is a residential neighborhood in Brooklyn with a boardwalk park, a crowded beach with umbrellas and blankets, and many little kids running in the sand and into the water. There were families on the sand, but the teenagers made lots of noise, played loud music, and pushed into people on the boardwalk. Dad said, "They act like hoodlums." I could not defend them; I thought they were loud and brash.

"Next time we come, we bring our suits."

"I would like that."

The boardwalk had a very different feeling from Palisades Park. It was the beach and scanty clothing that changed the feel.

However, this time we stayed on the boardwalk, played some arcade games, looked at the many rides and decided to see the Ripley's Believe-it-or-not museum. We saw the excellent Cyclone ride; we were not getting on that one either. We found the famous Nathan hotdog stand, and that was our lunch for the day.

A stop at a restaurant was part of our day. I liked that, and Dad had no problem spending some money. So different from Nicky, who watched every penny spent.

In upper Manhattan off-Broadway, we found a Jewish delicatessen. Dad ordered matzo ball soup and generously salted it. As we left I saw the money on the table and took it, handing it back to my father.

"No, Ruthie, that's the tip." I went back and laid it on the table. Nicky and Mom never took me out to eat, so how would I have known?

On another weekend, we went to Chinatown in lower Manhattan, where crowded narrow streets housed the largest Chinese population in our Western Hampshire. The restaurant was a small place with a red entrance door and colorful oriental decorations. The Americanized Chinese food was tasty, and we tried to eat it with chopsticks, laughing at each other. My mom bought canned Chinese food, and I doubt she and Nicky would have gone out to eat Chinese. Had it not been for my dad, I wouldn't have had these experiences.

I loved to go into New York City with its hustle and bustle. Crowds gathered in every corner, and I could hear voices from around the world. Trucks and cars were lumbering through jammed city streets, shouting obscenities. The vibe of New York City is an exhilarating joy mixed with apprehension and euphoria. Even as a child, I could feel it. The city was alive. At night, it was as a shining bright star emblazoned with illumination.

Dad took me to Rockefeller Center, a twenty-two-acre conglomerate encompassing a variety of entertainment venues in midtown Manhattan.

Radio City Music Hall was the first place on our schedule that day. We came to see the Rockettes Spectacular Christmas show and the movie. The entire building and lobby are splendid. They made me feel like I was entering a palace, and that was the intention of John D. Rockefeller when he had it built at the height of the Depression in 1932. He wanted it to be a place where regular people could attend at affordable prices. The Rockettes are a seasonal precision dance team of twenty-six girls performing high kicks similar to the cancan dancers of the Moulin Rouge of Paris. All the girls kicked their legs high in unison. Dad liked the pretty girls, and I was fascinated with the dance routine. That was the first and only time I went there, so the event stayed with me.

On another Sunday, we went to the lower outdoor rink at the Rockefeller Center.

A gold-colored monumental iconic eighteen-foot-tall sculpture of Titan's Prometheus floats above the skaters, watching over the lower plaza rink. Prometheus is a Greek legend who brought fire to humankind. It is the most photographed piece of art in the Rockefeller Center. Behind the statue carved in red granite, slate these words written by Aeschylus from the sixth century, "Prometheus, teacher in every art, brought the fire that hath proved to mortals a means to mighty ends."

While I skated, Dad relaxed at a swank coffee shop surrounding the outside of the rink.

He bought petit fours to accompany his coffee, and as I glided around I stopped at his table and ate one. They were incredible pastries, my favorites.

One time, as we were going down the steps, we nearly bumped into Judy Garland and Liza Minnelli, who were on their way up. Oh! I wish we could have stopped and talked to them. They were in a hurry.

Directly across the street is Saint Patrick's Cathedral. I visited it several times, but Dad had no desire to stop there.

We visited the Wollman Skating Rink in Central Park. I was no stranger to the Wollman Rink; I would go with friends on Saturdays. Dad only saw me on Sundays. He enjoyed watching me skate and told me, "This reminds me of a frozen pond in Germany. In those long-ago days, I wore skates too."

The Central Park Zoo was also on his agenda. It is a small zoo of six-and-a-half acres located on Fifth Avenue and begins at 64th Street. The idea started about 1859, although to bring it to fruition took until 1934. The zoo is small, although the park itself is eight hundred and forty three acres. Frederic Olmsted had designed the park's walking paths and foliage to make a lovely getaway for city dwellers. Across the street from Central Park, there is a multitude of high-end residential apartment buildings. Dad and I enjoyed the smaller zoo. We could take in all it had to offer.

The next time I saw my father, we went to the Bronx Zoo. It is two hundred sixty five acres, and it was opened in 1899. It is the most significant metropolitan zoo in the United States. We were there for the first showing of the duck-billed platypus. The platypus originated in Australia and was one of the earliest mammals to exist twelve million years ago before the dinosaurs' extinction.

They are bottom feeders, storing food in their cheeks. They live twenty years in captivity and only twelve in the wild. Although Dad was an animal lover, neither he nor I wanted to keep one as a pet in the bathtub.

He thought of all these attractions to broaden my view and show me glimpses of people and places with whom I would not have become familiar. He liked to drive, and some of the attractions were quite far.

We drove out to the Catskill Game Farm, three-and-a-half-hours from New York City in the Catskill Mountains, where tame deer ran free. I was able to touch them, an experience I would never accomplish with a wild one. A mean goose that bit my pants chased me. I caressed baby lambs; their coats contained lanolin secreted from the sebaceous gland keeping them dry. I could feel their oil on my hands.

We took a trip to the Howe Caverns in Schoharie County in upstate New York. Mohawk Indians once occupied the land, which they called 'floating driftwood.'

In 1842, Lester Howe discovered his cows were wandering to a cluster of bushes where the air coming forth from the ground was a constant fifty-two degrees. Upon investigation, he found caves and an underground river. It was not until 1929 that they opened to the public. An elevator took us to the level where we entered a boat that traveled on the river for eighty minutes. Howe Caverns are the second most visited tourist attractions in New York to surpass only Niagara Falls. Cave wonders were another adventure I would never have considered had my dad not introduced me to them. Within the sphere of his reachable surroundings, he wished to discover what his new home had to offer. Therefore, I think he enjoyed the things we did as much as I did. I feel it made me into a more discerning person. He opened up new worlds to me, and I am forever grateful.

On one of our Sundays, we took a cruise up the Hudson River for the entire day. The Hudson River Valley is still a pristine scenic landscape, perhaps looking the same as it did in 1524 when Giovanni de Verrazzano navigated it. The Verrazzano-Narrows Bridge between New York and Staten Island carries his name. We made a stop onshore and looked through a tower- viewer, which is a mounted telescope. He dropped a coin in the machine, and we saw down the river.

In the fall, we took a ferry to Liberty Island and the Statue of Liberty, a French gift on October 28, 1886. This colossal sculpture designed by Frederic Auguste Bartholdi and constructed by Gustave Eiffel, who made the skeleton for it. He also built the Eiffel Tower in Paris. It shipped in pieces to the New York Harbor. Its copper coating gives it its natural weathered green look. She is the Roman goddess Libertas (Liberty), holding erect the torch of freedom. In her left hand is a tablet with the dates of the Declaration of Independence. At her feet is a broken chain standing for the bonds of oppression and tyranny. Erected on an island in the New York Harbor just a ferry ride away, she saw Dad when he came from Germany. This trip meant a lot to him as he had suffered at the hands of the Nazi government. We climbed the spiral staircase to the torch. At that time, people were still able to access the arm. Not too many years later, the city closed it off to the public; it was unstable.

My dad had hardly any family to visit except a distant cousin in a New York apartment. I think his name was Uncle Leo. The place was dark with older furnishings. There was nothing for me to do while they talked. I can't remember going back a second time. Neither can I recall visiting another family in upper Manhattan again. I think his name was Kurt; they had two children younger than I was. Dad was so proud to introduce me as his daughter. I did not know these people, and it embarrassed me to be the center of attention.

As time went on, he brought a lady friend named Margot along for the Sunday visit. She was different from the other women he dated; she showed an interest in me. I liked her and was glad when they married.

Margot has a story of her own, but I will only tell a small portion here. She was living in Cleveland with her husband after she came from Shanghai, China. After he died, her cousin Edith requested that she come to live with them in New Jersey. Edith's husband Max subscribed to the *Aufbau* Newspaper founded in 1934. It aided in connecting German-speaking Jews. Max saw a request from a man looking for a woman. He suggested Margot answer it. She was shocked and said, "Max, I would never do such a thing."

So, Max answered it for her. He got an answer-back, gave it to her, and she followed through and met my father. Hans and Margot were well suited to each other. They laughed, played cards, and enjoyed their life together. Margot was an excellent cook, which made Dad happy.

After his garage days, Dad worked for the Kinney Parking Company. There was a shed on the property with a propane stove to keep the men comfortable in winter. On Friday nights, after paychecks came, they would have a friendly game of poker. One winter night, the heater blew up, and my father suffered third-degree burns on the left side of his face and hands.

After Grandpa died and Dad retired, they moved to Phoenicia in the Catskill Mountains. It is a rural hamlet boasting three-hundred-and-nine people in 2010, probably less when they lived there. Phoenicia is a recreational mecca for New Yorkers escaping from town. Sixteen miles from my dad's front door was the town of Woodstock, where on August 17, 1969, the infamous music festival took place.

He and Margot remodeled a one-hundred-year old farmhouse. It resembled a duplex with separate entrances for each floor. The plan was for Edith to come and live with them after Max died. She would then have her private apartment on the second floor. At four o'clock every afternoon, they got together for coffee time and pastry.

Margot opened a knitting shop in a part of the house. She could not have lived off the income generated by her little store, but she enjoyed being a shopkeeper. Dad reverted to his original occupation of a salesman. He was a traveling shoe salesman in Germany before the big war, so selling Fuller Brush to mountain residents and hotels was perfect. Hank liked to talk to people and drive through the mountains. Occasionally, he took Margot with him so she could socialize with the ladies.

Margot told a little story about Opa, whom she called Heinrich. His daily walks took him to the Garden State Parkway, which was under construction at the time. When he came home, he would tell her, "Margot, they do not know what they are doing." It became a family joke.

The joke continued in Marshall when they were rebuilding the bridge over the French Broad River. Margot looked out the window of the Marshall House and said, "Ruthie, they don't know what they are doing."

That is not the end of the story. My relationship with Margot deepened with time, but that comes later.

I have mentioned places my father took me to in and around the city. His goal was to keep me occupied and do things I would enjoy and remember. Perhaps, I didn't see him as often as I would have liked to, but we had loads of fun and many different adventures for the time we had together. Later in life, he was there for me when I needed him the most.

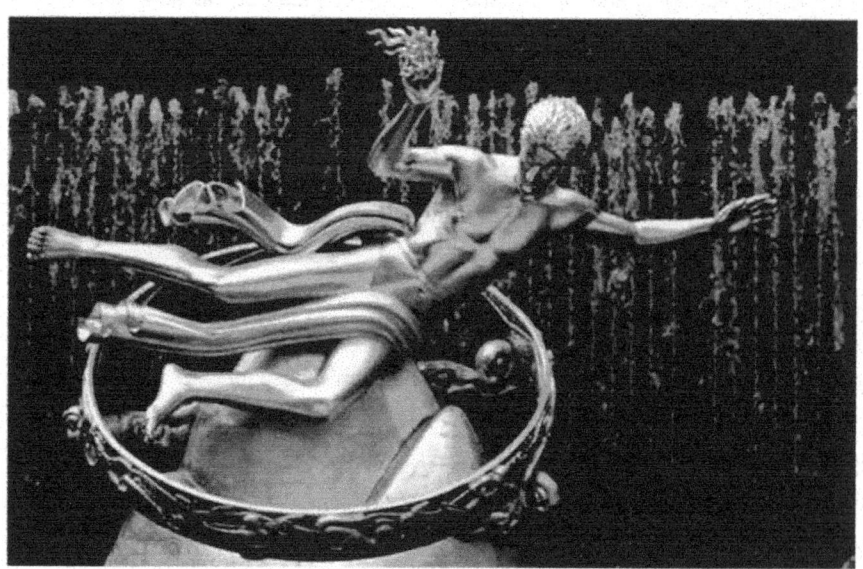

Prometheus, gilded cast bronze by Paul Manship, 1934; at Rockefeller Center, New York.

© Marcin Wasilewski/Fotolia

"Prometheus, in Greek religion, one of the Titans, the supreme trickster, and a god of fire. His intellectual side was emphasized by the apparent meaning of his name, Forethinker. In common belief, he developed into a master craftsman, and in this connection, he was associated with fire and the creation of mortals."

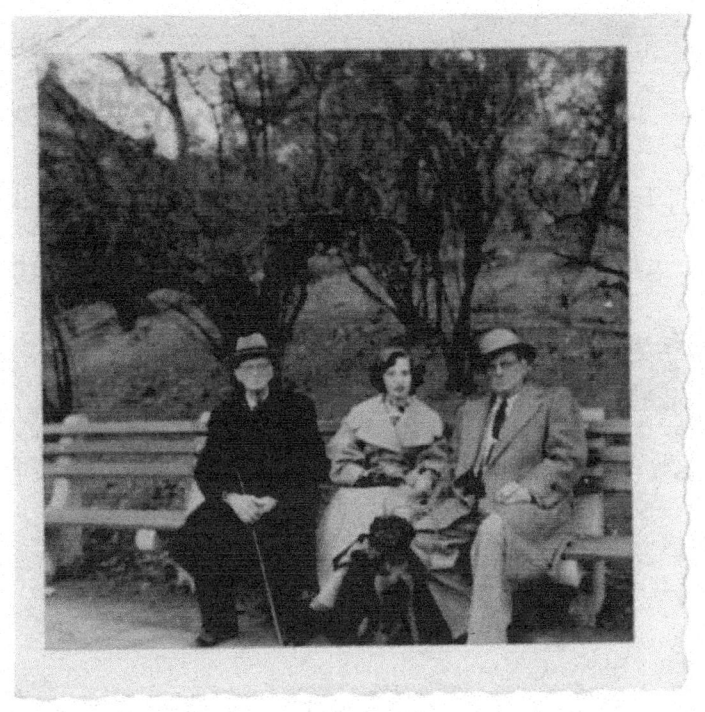

Ruth Arnstein in special blue coat, Father & Grandfather ca. 1955

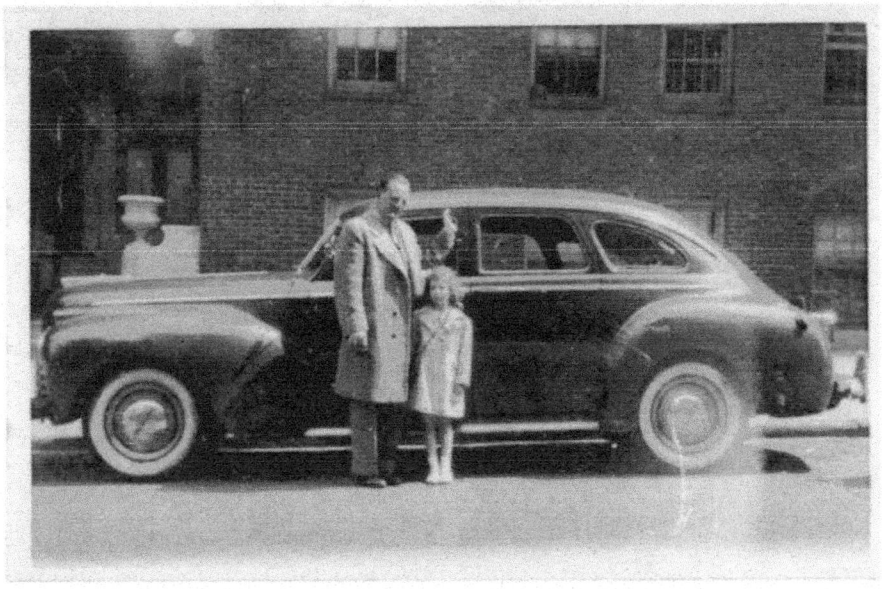

Hans and Ruth Lichtenstein, 5 yrs old, Plymouth 1942

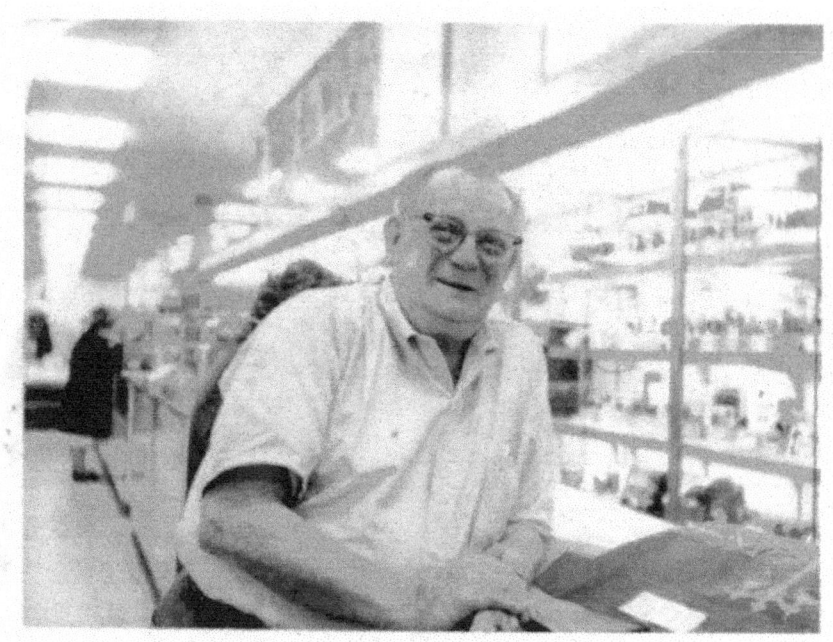

My dad Hans Lichtenstein

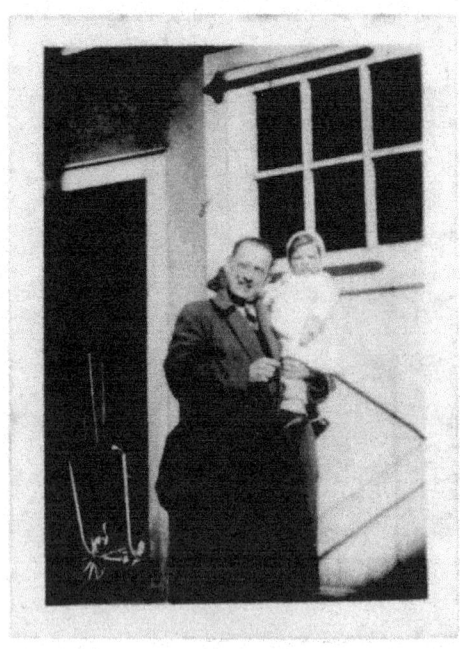

My dad Hans 1937, Me under 1 yr old

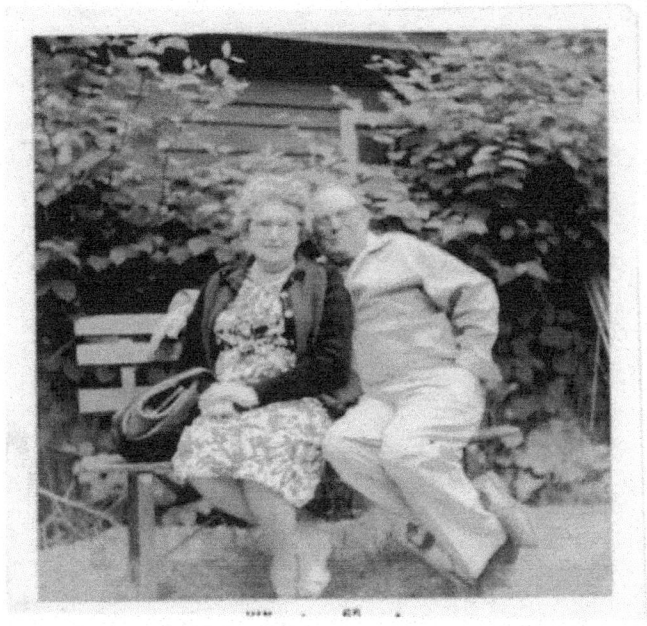

Margot (2nd wife/stepmother" & Hans (she called him Hank)

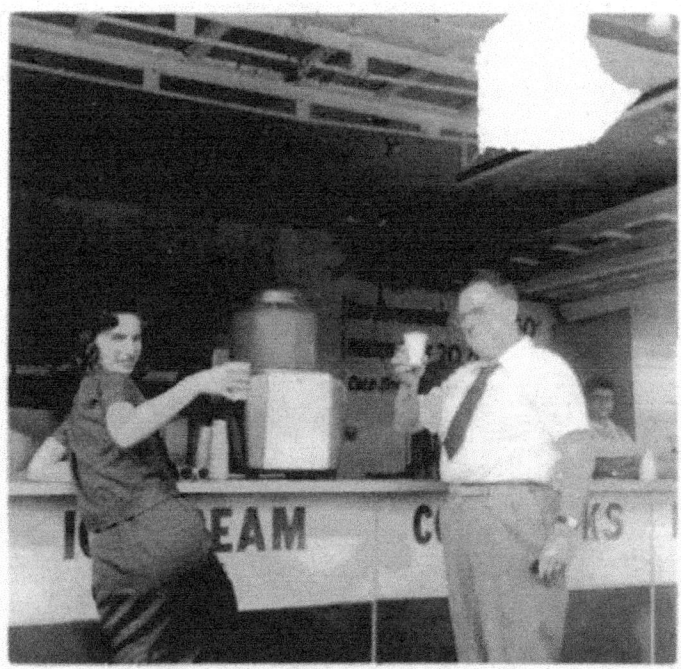

Asbury Amusement Park, Hans and Ruth Arnstein 15/16 yrs old

PART TWO

CHAPTER 9:

A DAY AT THE BEACH

Fifty years passed before I learned more about the handsome man that picked me up on Jones Beach in New York on July 4, 1958.

It would be hard to say I did not notice him immediately. He sat on a beach towel next to the enormous black radio with an extended antenna.

Jones Beach had always been my favorite getaway; thus, on this first summer holiday of the year, I headed for the shores of the Atlantic

Over the years, this ocean and I would become well acquainted.

There were crowds on the beach of pale white-skinned and black bathers. Little children romped in the sand, building forts and sandcastles. Colorful umbrellas and lounge chairs dotted the landscape. I looked about for a place to spread my towel. Amid blankets and towels everywhere, I placed my beach towel close, but not too close to this attractive man, but close enough so he would notice me. I had brought my portable radio and tuned to the sounds of Satchmo Armstrong, who was celebrating the birth of our Nation. He was the iconic Fourth of July Yankee Doodle Dandy.

I swabbed sunscreen on, rested peacefully on my towel for a few moments while I let the sun warm me. Then awkwardly, I proceeded to the water. My clumsy walking on the hot pearly deep sand made me feel self-conscious. I stepped forward gingerly, one small step at a time, in an effort not to burn the souls of my feet on the uneven surface of the sand.

It was still early in the year; the water's gradual warming had not occurred yet, leaving it feeling icy against my hot body. I slowly inched my way as the waves broke around my feet. I could feel the sand between my toes receding as the water flowed out to sea. I cautiously advanced into the rough surf and sand-laden waves. Too turbulent, my ninety-eight-pound body was no match for the harsher waves. Swimming was not possible, so I just took a quick dunk. Cooled and invigorated, I slowly returned to my towel.

Refreshed, feeling a bit bold, I stretched out on my towel more in the direction of the fellows just a few feet away. Every muscle was etched perfectly by his bronze tan. When he turned, I saw he had blond hair, clean-shaven with ocean blue eyes. Handsome and exuding sex. He was with a friend whom I heard him call Dick. Dick was a short, chubby blond curly-haired jovial fellow. Dick kept his eyes on me, nudging his friend to make an advance.

I was twenty years old, five-feet-two-inches tall, with long wavy flowing dirty blond hair, and blue-green eyes with glasses. My black bathing suit with a V-shaped bodice inlaid with white accentuated my curvy figure.

I stretched out on my towel, and very soon, a dark shadow covered the sun.

Squinting, I glanced up at chubby Dick.

"Excuse me, miss, would you like to join us over there?" He pointed to his friend.

"I think I could arrange that," I responded with my typical New York sarcasm.

Slowly collecting my belongings, I sauntered their way.

Cupid introduced his friend, "Glad you came over. That is my friend Jim, and my name is Dick." Dick made the introductions. I formally introduced myself,

"Glad to meet you, Dick, as I nodded to Jim. My name is Ruth," and so the conversation began. My first question was about the large black box.

"This is a ship to shore radio that we use on boats; here on the beach, I can pick up the conversation of the fishing boats," Jim said.

Dick chimed in, ready to brag about his friend.

"Jim just came back from Cay Sol. There is an oil rig out in the ocean, and the oil company employed Jim to take their executives out fishing on the company yacht." Dick explained.

I was supposed to be impressed. Where was Cay Sol? I had never heard of the place. I was fascinated, trying to hide my naiveté.

"So what are you doing in New York?"

"Jim is a charter boat captain; he wants to buy a boat that he can use as a charter fishing boat," Dick explained.

Informative information – was I the ploy to find the boat, a means to an end. Rich Jewish girl, oh he did not know I was Jewish, or a city girl with a Daddy with deep pockets. In my jaundiced mind today in my older age, I speculate if this could have been the case, he gets the boat; I get the guy. I get to leave the bright lights of the city for a Podunk town in Florida. Maybe not a bad deal!

We talked for a long time, and we're hitting it off.

"Well, I guess it's time to go; it's getting late," I said, and Jim and Dick both stood up, and I saw that Jim was five-foot-eight inches tall about one-hundred-thirty-pounds; Dick was a bit shorter and quite a bit heavier. "Sorry, I dress like a beach bum; I hate to wear shoes. I have lived on a boat most of my life in the Florida Keys." Jim exclaimed.

"Lucky man."

I drove my white 1954 convertible Chevy, and he sat behind the wheel of his 1950 green convertible Caddy. Keeping up side-by-side, convertible tops down as we sped to the "Catch 'um" bar and grill in Freeport, where we had agreed to meet. Later on, he showed me the charter boats at the Freeport docks; all went well, too well. I called my mother and advised her I would not be home. That was very unusual. The nights being out were something I never did, so Mom knew something was up.

Two weeks later, we had rented an apartment in Freeport. Dick was with us, and we planned a sham wedding. Dick made up a phony marriage license, and we presented ourselves to my parents as husband and wife. My folks would have been awful upset if they thought I was not married. We told them we ran off to Atlantic City. To this day, I have never been to Atlantic City. I changed my name and all my identification to Ruth Paddock. Months later, an ex-boyfriend Ray Collucci, whom I dated through high school, told my folks we were not officially married. He will show up in my story later.

As a wedding present, my stepfather Nicky Arnstein put up the collateral for a boat we purchased in Freeport, Long Island. She was a twenty-six-foot Norseman, with a white wooden hull, twin-screw engines, and a large cockpit for fishing. Jim placed a fighting chair in the middle of the deck, he had a seat on the port side to steer the boat, and I sat on the starboard side. She had a cabin with two bunks, a small galley, head, and a mahogany transom where we had a professional painter scribe in gold leaf the chosen name of "Bambino" plus the port name "Freeport, NY." She came equipped with a floating compass placed in the center of the front console, and outriggers on either side were making her look like a real fishing boat.

We got a slip at the Freeport docks among many other fishing boats.

Before the weekend, the head boat owner, which accommodated more customers, came over and asked Jim to take out his Japanese visitors' large party. The head boat left the dock at eight in the morning and returned about six-thirty. All the wives and I were on the pier and saw the excitement on the head boat as she neared. People crowded around to view the catch. A Mako shark hung from the stern of the charter boat. Mako shark is one of the most dangerous marine predators for humans. It is fearless and can suddenly attack any prey that looks interesting to the Mako shark. It weighed at least nine hundred pounds. The shark had multiple rows of teeth. Jim extracted some as a souvenir for the anglers. The newspaper showed up and took pictures of the shark and all the smiling Japanese fishermen. Jim sliced the shark into Mako steaks and sold them to local restaurants. It was good eating.

We had a few bookings to fish for mackerel. I was his crew, helping to hook lines and talk with the customers. I was a city girl; I did not know anything about fishing. I had never fished in my life. I learned to tie leader wire and handle the line when we hooked a fish, but I could not bring the fish into the boat; the Captain had to do that.

My friend Betty invited us to her birthday party. Of course, everyone wanted to see my new guy. We had been out fishing that afternoon for mackerel. We had to churn the water to catch mackerel. Chumming consisted of fish parts placed in a bucket and handfuls thrown in the water to attract the fish. I wore a glove to do this; I would not put my hands in that disgusting mess. Most of the mackerel we caught was six inches to ten inches long. These were tinker mackerel, a smaller mackerel variety. I had a gift in mind that I thought would be a big hit at the party. One sweet little fish about four inches long, nicely curled, fit perfectly in a box with a red ribbon. As a joke, I presented this to Betty. Everyone laughed, but she did not want to keep the little fish. We were not the charming couple; we exited soon after gifting.

One day an old friend of Jim's called from Ocean City, Maryland. He wanted him to take out a charter of six people on one of his large Mathews fishing boats. It was an excellent opportunity for us.

We drove to Maryland in my Chevy with the top down. We found a rooming house with a shared bath across the way from our room. It did not take long for us to get into trouble. We were taking a bath together when the landlady came screaming down the hall at us.

"What do you think you are doing? That is not allowed." She wanted to kick us out, but Jim sweet-talked her into letting us stay.

The next day we had the charter, and I had to be the crew. I still did not know what it entailed to prepare for a larger fishing party. There was ice to load onto the boat, all the rods and reels required checking; food that the mandatory beer, placed on ice, necessitated. The vessel had to be spotless, scoured with a brush, and hosed down. That became my job.

We were ready when six large beer-drinking men boarded the boat. My job was to see that the lines don't get tangled, untangle when needed, and get whatever customers wanted. Matthew boats have a barrel bottom. If the sea is the least bit rough, the boat rolls; for a novice like me, this was a terrible boat; it made me sick. I wanted to go somewhere and throw up. Someone suggested I lie down in the cabin and eat pickled pig's feet. The thought made me feel sicker; no pickled pigs feet for me. I followed his other suggestion but found the inside cabin confining, unbearably hot, and muggy with no air circulation. It made me feel more nauseated, and I thought it was the worst thing to do. I would rather be on the deck, getting sick in front of everyone, and be embarrassed to death. I went to the flying bridge for air, accidentally knocking a can of beer down to the deck. By the time I yelled, "Watch out below," the can had hit the deck, exploded spewing beer on every-one. I felt so self-conscience, although the fresh air was making me feel better. Everyone survived the beer blast, the men were catching fish, but I knew I was no mate.

My poor performance during the charter caused a terrible argument. I was so upset I just wanted to go back home. To keep me there, Jim sneakily removed the rotor from my car. Was this going to be a controlling relationship? It was my first taste of what was to come.

The following day we left, and on the way home, in a raging rainstorm, the canvas top of my convertible ripped. We had to stow the top and travel home in the rain.

The business had been slow. It was October, and the bluefish was usually running at this time. This year proved to be different; the fish did not show up. Business for us was not happening.

We were planning our trip to Florida, and before we left New York, I wanted to get a dog. That would be my first dog. We purchased Rex a solid Brindle Boxer with a white chest from Bide-A-Wee Kennel on Long Island. Owners who had to leave the country placed him there. The previous owners had trained him well. Jim would throw balls, and Rex would jump in the water and bring them back. This game could go on indefinitely. Next, Jim threw a fifteen-inch two-by-four board into the water from the dock. Rex jumped off the dock into the water and brought back the piece of wood. He was terrific, bringing them back to land and asking for more. My favorite picture of Rex is when he brought us that board.

Cold weather was slowly creeping down the coast. We decided to travel south; the Florida Keys were our destination.

Jim's friend Dick stayed in Freeport, and I never saw him again.

With our new dog Rex and all our belongings loaded in a steamer trunk, including my pink reading chair packed in the fishing boat's stern, we left Freeport, New York, heading to the Florida Keys.

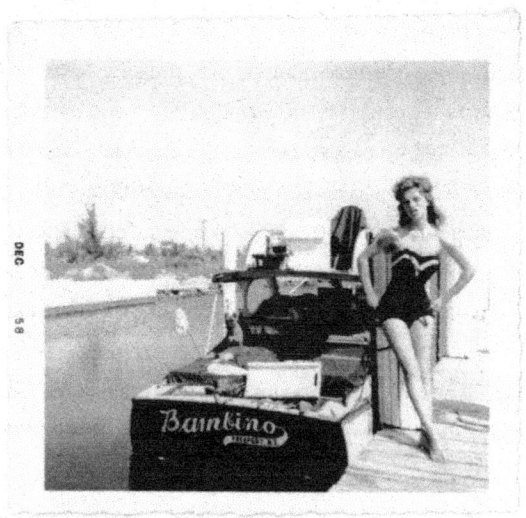

Ruth Paddock 1958, Vaca Key, FL

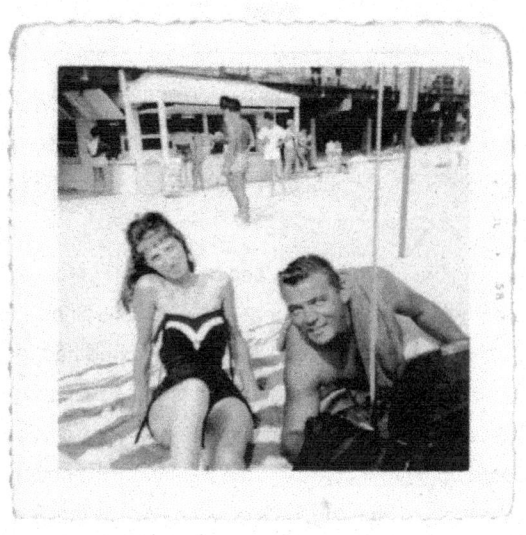

July 4, 1958 Jones Beach, NY Ruth Arnstein & James Paddock

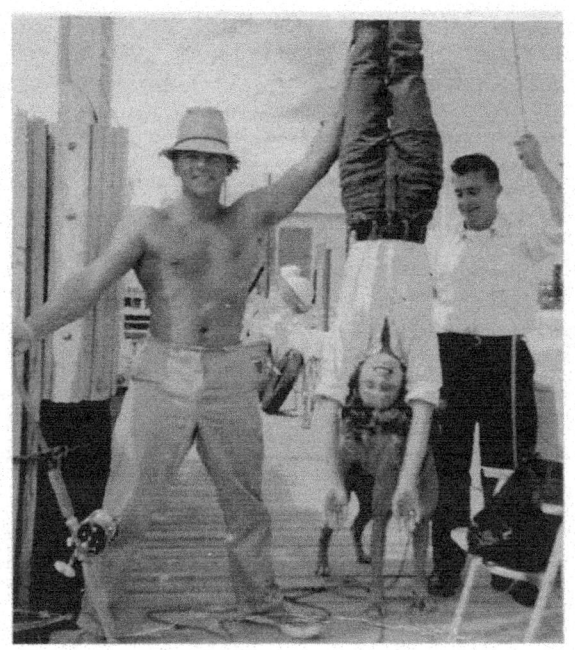

Ruth Arnstein & James Paddock

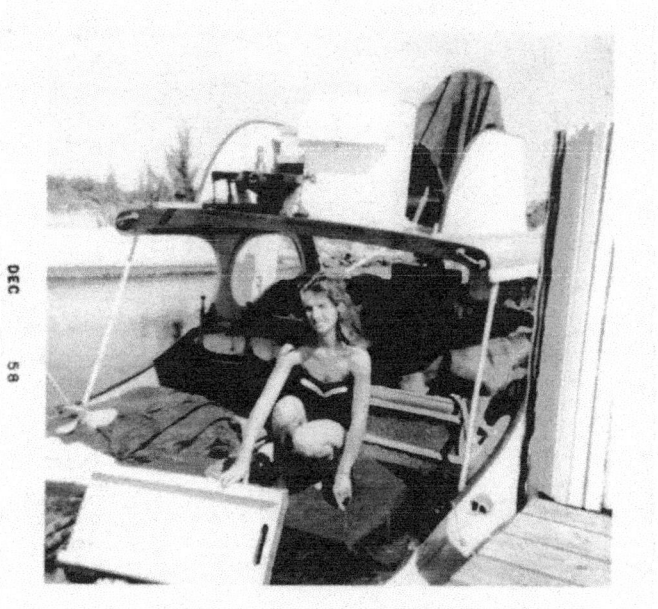

Bambino, Vaca Key, FL 1959 Ruth Paddock

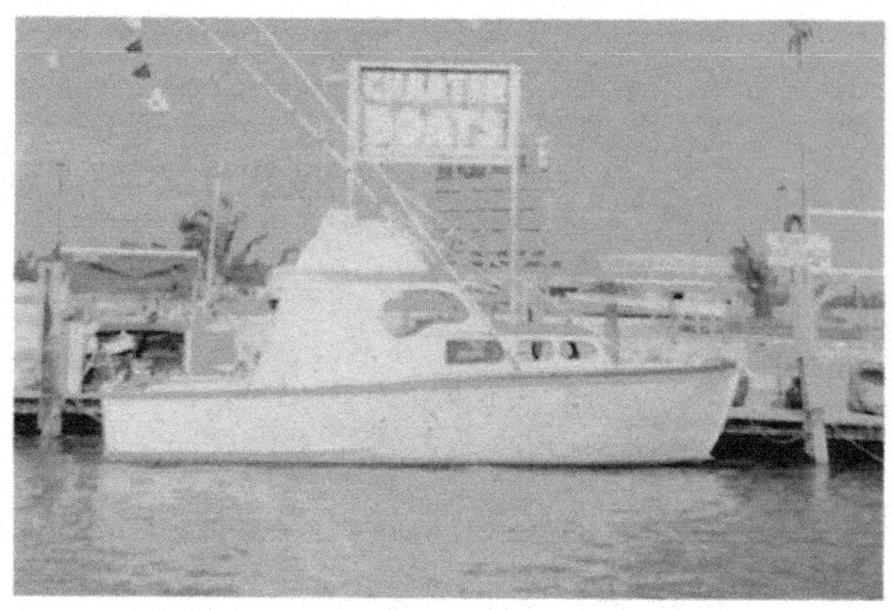

26' Norseman Sportfisherman Bambino

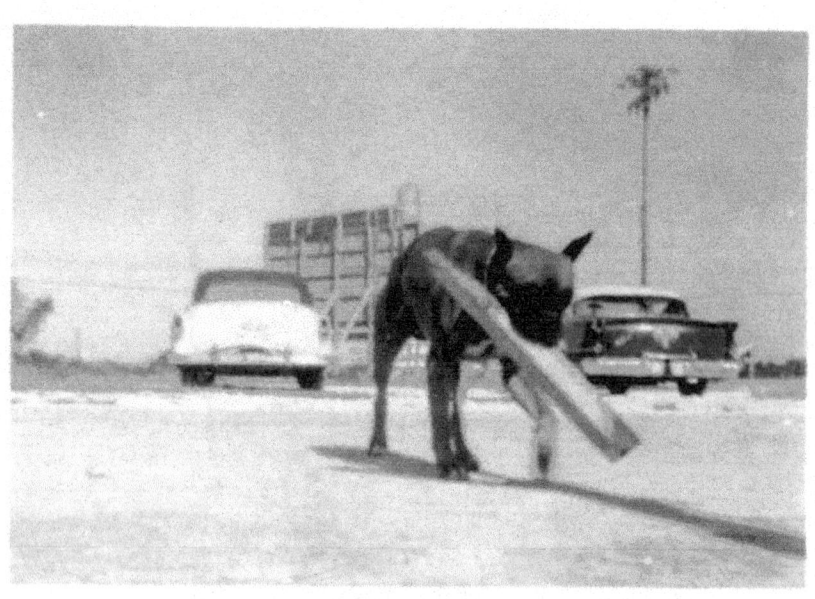

Rex – my first dog, Freeport, NY 1958, 1954 Chevy

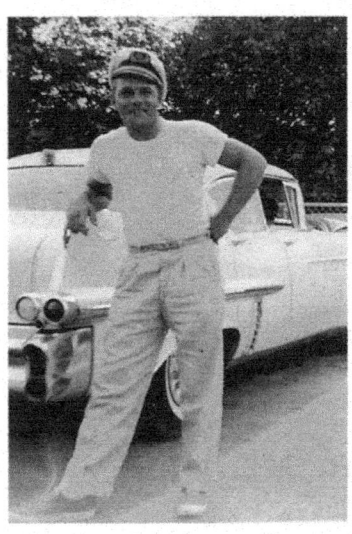

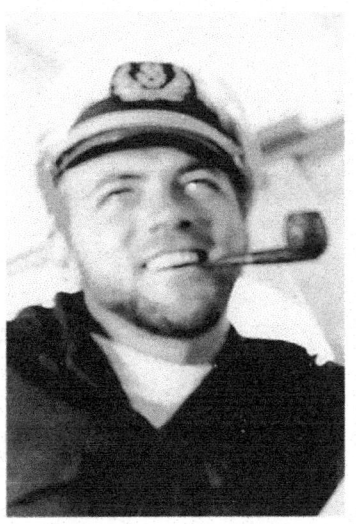

James Paddock   *James Paddock 1933-1983*

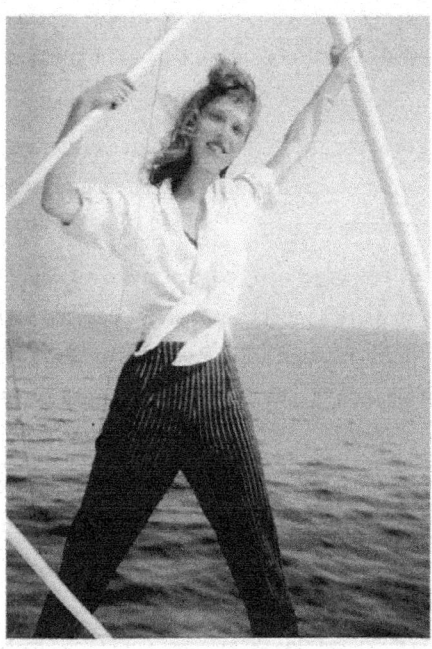

Ruth on our Bambino

CHAPTER 10:

LEAVING HOME

We planned to travel the Intercoastal Waterways or cruise outside in an unprotected ocean. On our first day, we went from Freeport, New York on the outside past lower Manhattan, the Statue of Liberty, and the Palisades of New Jersey. Landmarks of my youth fluttered across my mind, causing me to reflect, for an instant, my new choice with Jim. I did not have the time or inclination to dwell on the past. New life was moving swiftly before my eyes.

As we came closer to the shore, markers guided our way so that we would not run aground. Green lights were to our right and red to our left, and as long as we kept in the middle of the channel, we were safe.

Toms River, New Jersey, a sleepy coastal town, was our first gas stop. A friendly dockmaster greeted us as we passed the town and pulled into a slip. Rex was the happiest of the three of us to leave his new home. His little tail wagged as his generous body curved in and out in anticipation of a needed walk. Jim filled our tanks with gas and paid our fee for overnight dockage.

There was a yachting term that I soon learned, "Chief cook and bottle washer," a name given to anyone other than the Captain of the vessel. Therefore, as the chief cook, I prepared our first meal aboard. A heavy electric cord hooked to a dock outlet made the two burners electric stove operational. The icebox was beneath the stove and secured with a unique locking nautical handle. A washbasin made the galley complete.

I prepared a simple meal of hamburgers with macaroni and cheese; Kraft dinner made easy. We ate leisurely at a table on the dock listening to the birds announce the falling of night. We talked about our successful first day and the distance we would travel tomorrow. Jim stayed on the dock conversing with another boater that had stopped by while I straightened up washing our few dishes. When night had fallen and the stars were glowing, we prepared to sleep below deck. There was a bunk on each side of the cabin, and our clothing securely stowed under each bunk. Jim had to place a board and a mattress between the bunks to make a double bed. Rex had his bed beneath us. We were glad to be in a safe harbor, listening to the water lap the sides of the boat. That was my first boat-sleeping encounter.

Lying awake made me think about the enormity of this change in my lifestyle.

Having watched the skyscrapers of New York fade in the distance made me think of my not-so-distant past. I had lived with my parents and Grandmother in an apartment in Forest Hills, Queens, New York. Thinking of my Grandmother reminded me of a day, Jim and I brought our dirty laundry to my folks' apartment. Grandma was looking out the window, watching for us. She observed from the fifth-floor apartment a disagreement on the street below between Jim and me.

I was carrying the laundry bag and asked, "Jim, please take the bag for me."

"No, you carry it."

"Come on; it's heavy."

In a nasty tone, he responded, "It's your laundry; you carry it."

Grandma saw, much to her dismay, his ungentlemanly behavior. She warned me that,

"I do not think he is a good man." That was another sign, similar to the argument in Ocean City, MD. She saw that I was too smitten to see. I continued to think of home where I was never alone as they were a stay-at-home family. I was a typist/switchboard operator in Manhattan on East Second Avenue and 43rd Street during the week. I worked for US Vitamin handling the Pervinal dog supplements.

In the morning, I rode the subway, which was always a challenge. I pushed along with the crowd and stood inches away from strangers whose fingers frequently invaded my body. Not ever having to deal with this part of my life again was a blessing. A few times a week, when I could afford the parking, I drove my car across the 59th Street Bridge into the city, racing along with the cab drivers on the old cobblestone roads. The evening rush hour in the subways presented the same problems as the morning, although workers' sweat tinged the air, and the morning fragrances no longer lingered.

As a special treat on Friday, while walking home, I stopped at Jay Dee bakery along Queens Boulevard and took home a delicious seven-layer cake and four Napoleons. I wondered if I would ever eat the likes of those pastries again?

Each morning, Jim was up at dawn, whereas I lingered a bit in my new bed. I came to realize this was not advisable. Jim wanted me up when he got up; in the event I did not, ice water was my shocking awakening. The sun would greet us, shimmering across the seas. My first task was to throw off the docking lines. That required me to stand on the dock as he started the engines. Then, I released the lines, threw them on board the boat, and jumped onto the deck. When we arrived at our next docking stop, I jumped off the boat with the line, secured the bow, and then he threw me the stern rope that I fastened to the dock.

Our next stop was Cape May, New Jersey. Cape May was a bustling fishing port with larger charter boats. The US Army Engineer William F. Reynolds built the lighthouse in 1859, which stands at the southern tip of New Jersey. It has one-hundred-ninety-nine steps to the top. From the cupola, one can see twenty-four nautical miles out to sea. Enemy submarines were offshore during World War II. Thus, they doused the light from 1941 to 1945.

There was a large boathouse supplying bait, tackle, and snacks a few feet from the docks. Folks looked curiously at the sight of our packed stern. A few people stopped by to question our destination.

Leaving Cape May, we traveled to the open ocean without the protection of the Intercoastal Waterway. We headed to the expansive Chesapeake Bay at New Port News, Virginia. The bay is home to behemoth navy vessels. It was frightening to come alongside a navy ship the size of a mountain. It was hard to look up at the sailors waving to us and calling out a greeting. Our little boat was miniature next to their massive hulks of steel. We slowly made our way, avoiding any collisions with the US Navy.

We had hit some rough water before we reached the bay, and our chart had flown overboard. Now in the bay, we were at a loss to find a particular dock where we wanted to stay called Old Point Comfort. It had taken some time to navigate the bay, and now, dusk had fallen. We pulled close to a colossal vessel at anchor, and Jim hollered as loud as he could. It took quite a while for someone to show up on deck. We must have disturbed him as he appeared only in his underdrawers.

Jim declared in a loud shout, "Have you heard of Old Point Comfort?"

The response came in a very groggy voice in broken English. Leaning over the high deck, the sailor shouted, "I don't understand you."

We moved on to the next ship at anchor, and Jim called. "Do you speak English?"

A bold voice answered, "Yeah, man, we are the US Navy."

Then, a loudspeaker blasted forth: "Small craft stand clear."

Maybe they thought our outriggers were a threat. We got very explicit instructions, "Old Point Comfort is on the port quarter of your stern."

Jim took bearings, thanked him, and we went on our way.

Old Point Comfort lies at the very tip of Virginia, at Hampton Roads' mouth, which is a natural harbor. Since 1805, this lighthouse has stood at this location. There is much history connected with this area—the Revolutionary War, and then the Civil War. In 1812, the British captured the lighthouse and used its strategic location as an observation point over the ocean.

After leaving, the Chesapeake Bay, our next stop was Norfolk, Virginia. At this point, we entered the Intercoastal Waterway system again. It was thirty miles from Norfolk to the beginning of the Dismal Swamp. Virginia is the home of the swamp, although 30 percent is in North Carolina.

CHAPTER 11:

DISMAL SWAMP

The swamp begins at Deep Creek, where we encountered our first lock. The going was slow because there was NO WAKE throughout the canal. As we approached, a gate swung open slowly, allowing us to pass into the lock. The water on this side of the lock is the same elevation as the canal; the gate closed behind us, and Jim placed our engines at idle. Then, the lock operator opened the valves to let the water in, raising our Bambino to an eight-foot height, which is the water's height on the other side of the lock. He then opened the forward gate, and we continued on our way. The lock is an enclosure able to accommodate small pleasure boats. A pile-driving machine pounded the pilings into the bedrock to hold the water. The purpose of the locks was to slow down the water flow in the canal. That was a twenty-two-mile section, specifically designated as the Dismal Swamp. The lock system ended at South Mills, where the boat dropped eight feet to continue on our way. Within the locks, the waterway was very straight. Once out of the locks, the stream was wide and winding, and narrow areas brought us closer to the trees and vegetation lining the banks.

In 1728, Colonel William Byrd II surveyed the swamp between the Virginia-Carolina borders, found it repulsive, and named it the Dismal Swamp. He was born in Virginia but considered a British-American. He was a commander of the local county militias, a plantation owner, and a lawyer receiving his education in England. Colonel Byrd also was the founder of Richmond, Virginia. To me, he sounds like an aristocrat; although, he was a slave-owner.

George Washington visited this area in 1763 and suggested the draining of the Great Dismal Swamp. It would then be a navigable waterway dug for transportation. It is a thrill to know our founding fathers had been on this very spot.

Originally dug out by hand, mostly by slaves, it took twelve years to complete. There was a slimy swamp within the forestation, muck fermenting leaves, plus the danger of snakes. Hard to imagine how they finished without the machinery of today.

Along the banks, Spanish moss hung from the trees and nearly touched the water. The lacy moss gave a surreal presence. When we chanced on an open space, I could see cypress knees sticking out of the swampy water. Bald cypress trees were easier to identify with their thick trunks and gray bark. It appears as an elongated, straight tree with the crown's leaves barely visible due to its height.

Occasionally, I would see a turtle swimming near the bank. They would glide into the water, paddling about with their heads held high, and then dive into it to find food. So many trees were a habitat for birds of all kinds. Mourning Doves were present in the early morning fog.

At dusk, I asked Jim, "Can you hear the call of the horned Owls?"

He responded, "Yes, and the bullfrogs seem to answer."

The bright orange breast of the Baltimore oriole was easy to spot. Large Blue Herons with their long legs were standing in the water along the banks, and nearby a white Egret was perched on a tree limb extending over the water's edge. The chirp of sparrows, the screech of owls, and the pecking of the red-headed woodpecker accompanied us on our slow cruise in this incredible beauty. The swamp was the home to many more critters, large and small, such as raccoons, fox, otters, wild turkey, and a varied assortment of ducks; unfortunately, we did not see all these creatures.

Well-known writers, such as Harriet Beecher Stow, Henry Wadsworth Longfellow and Sir Thomas Moore all visited the swamp and were inspired by its allure. Few boats were passing in the Dismal Swamp. I took advantage of the solitude and lay on the bow topless, keeping a towel at hand, should others approach.

As we came around a bend, we spied a tugboat and requested we ride along with them. A member of the tub crew tossed a rope across, which Jim easily caught, and fastened the heavy hemp to our bow. We talked to them, from boat to tugboat, and then they invited us aboard. We were ushered into the wheelhouse and then offered dinner. During a friendly exchange of conversation, they spoke words against African-Americans. I shortened that ride by opening up my Yankee mouth. Remember, this was 1958 in the

South. Blacks were not favored. I commented in favor of them, saying, "They had a right to an education;" then, I told them, "The South belongs to them as well as it does to us. The whites should treat them with more respect."

They requested we depart. Later, Jim scolded me. He was quite annoyed since being tugged along saved us gas, but I learned no lesson; I still voice my opinion, right or wrong. Within eighteen miles, we arrived in Elizabeth City, North Carolina, on the Albemarle Sound.

Fifty-six-years later, I took a vacation with another husband to visit Elizabeth City, staying at The Pond Inn adjacent to the Albemarle Sound. Our reason was much different from my first visit. We went to see the wild horses on the beach, the Hatteras Lighthouse, and other lighthouses.

Back to the story, we were on the outer banks of North Carolina near the famous Cape Hatteras. It was late in the day with no port near. We were not aware that there had been a storm brewing; we caught the rough waters in the dark. That was a scary part of the adventure. The wind was a strong gale, and in the darkness, I could see whitecaps across the harsh waves. Jim kept the boat under control, and we made it into a safe harbor. Other than being shaken up, blown about, and salt-sprayed, we were okay.

Our next stop was Hackers Island, a community noted for generations of boat builders. The Islanders built Hatteras boats with flared hulls; they favored fishing boats as the design can endure the roughest of seas. We went to the island to have a flying bridge built on top of our boat's cabin. That way, the captain could steer the craft from a higher vantage point, giving him a better vision of the ocean.

They hauled the boat out of the water, and it was then transported on rails, also known as ways, to move it to work in the shed. Then, they went to work on the top deck, building a partial enclosure made of marine wood that would be large enough to contain a captain's chair and an additional steering wheel and throttle. At sundown, they placed a ladder along the side of our home to climb back aboard to sleep.

The Islanders were a friendly group of people, not treating us as strangers but friends. They lent us their car, and we saw a movie and visited the small village. The job took four days to complete giving the boat a more professional appearance.

Twenty years later, in Miami, I worked for a Yacht Brokerage owned by Winthrop Rockefeller. He held a Hatteras dealership. The Hatteras design followed that of the Islanders.

Our passage was smooth cruising offshore through the remainder of North Carolina, making regular gas stops, always staying in port at night. In South Carolina, we made a stop at Beaufort, a seaside village with many fishing boats.

There was an inlet leading into the Satilla River near Jekyll Island, Georgia, which we motored through in high tide and found a protected cove. Here we threw out an anchor and spent the night. When we woke, we were high and dry and had to wait for the tide to roll in again and release us.

During the trip, Jim grew a close-cropped beard, which gave him the appearance of an old sea captain. He talked with a brogue as though he was an Irishman, making me laugh. He entertained me with wild fish tales and stories about his adventures. I was learning things about him and my surroundings. *This pleasant trip was something I would never have the opportunity to repeat*, I thought.

Out of Georgia, we traveled into Florida motoring across the broad St. John's River in Jacksonville, continuing the journey offshore down to North Miami. We had survived twenty-one days together now; it was time to separate.

Jim was taking the boat the rest of the way solo.

CHAPTER 12:

FINISHING THE JOURNEY

I picked up the car in North Miami. A driver had delivered it to our destination from New York. How strange it was to be alone; I was not only devoid of companionship but also in unfamiliar surroundings.

US 1 was a direct route through the City of Miami, and then the name changed to a beautiful road known as Brickell Avenue. Stately homes lined the road backed by the blue waters of Biscayne Bay. Not one of these estates lingers, replaced by modern glass-faced edifices. Miami was in her infancy, hardly a house or business on the horizon. As I drove on, the name changed to Dixie Highway, and only one tall building appeared on the landscape. It was South Miami Hospital. Many years later, I spent a few weeks there as their patient.

I was continuing past a small mall in Cutler Ridge, a barbeque restaurant where I had lunch, farm sheds in Naranja, and on down to where the road became a single lane in each direction. Through the town of Homestead, at a traffic light before hitting the actual route to the keys, I picked up a hitchhiker. In twenty-two miles, we traveled from the Florida mainland over a drawbridge built in 1944, bypassing a well-known encampment named Gilbert's Resort with a hotel, boat, and gas dock restaurant known as Jewfish Creek. A century-old name for a bottom-feeding fish that can grow six feet long and has a large mouth. There is much speculation as to how the name came to be.

An hour and a quarter later, I deposited him at Guy Lombardo's Key Colony Beach boatel a few miles before Vaca Cut, the location where we planned to dock our boat.

Of course, when I told Jim I had picked up a rider, he once again gave me hell, "This is a tiny town, Ruth, you do something like that, and everyone will be talking."

What did I know; I came from the Big Apple.

And so, my life began in the Florida Keys.

Our adventurous trip from New York to Florida was a pleasant change from the hectic life I had been leading. Once on solid ground, I became a boat wife, the boat cleaner, the cook, and the first mate, but these tasks were not enough to keep me busy.

We continued to sleep on-board, so when there was a charter Rex and I would watch as our house went to sea. Renting a small apartment was a contentious conversion from which he always came out the victor.

Food Fair arrived in Marathon, and I put in an application, which was accepted.

I was thrilled to be able to go to work in a brand-new store. On my first day, I loaded shelves with sparkling fresh groceries. I felt like I was accomplishing something. That evening, Jim and I had a heated discussion about my employment. He thought I did not need to work; he was the man of the house and could support us. On returning home after my second day at work, I was shocked to find my clothes scattered all over the dock.

Worst of all, I found Rex missing. Gathering up my belongings, I yelled at him to tell me what he had done with my dog. How could this man be so heartless as to get rid of the dog just because I wanted to work? He had taken Rex about two miles down the road, where I found him just hanging out near an empty house close to the water, waiting for me.

Up and down the Keys coast, lighthouses populate the ocean anywhere from six to eight miles offshore. In Marathon, our closest light is Sombrero light, eight miles offshore opposite Key Colony beach. The searchlight is one-hundred-forty-two-feet high and twenty-five-feet deep, constructed before the Civil War. The coral reef runs four miles long or longer and is a threat to seafarers from the very early days when the Spanish plied the oceans. Many wrecks have occurred near the lights, and those searching for old treasure can readily be seen, especially on weekends, trying their luck at finding old Spanish coins. The Spanish coins that they may have located could have minted around 1615; Silver coins called Realest, each weighing an ounce of silver. Gold coins they named Escudos, each weighing an ounce of gold, and a Doubloon was a double coin.

Jim took me out snorkeling on the reef to see these coral reefs' underwater beauty close up. I needed a pair of flippers, goggles, and a snorkel, a mouthpiece attached to a tube extended above the water. The coral was magnificent, with so many variations in shape. Jim told me some of the names: brain coral, finger coral that reaches up nearly above the water line, bird's nest coral, and so many other colored corals, the label that he did not know. It was the most breathtaking sight to see the little blue and yellow tropical fish along with schools of tiny minnows swimming among the corals. Spiny sea urchins were walking along the bottom, and there were sand dollars, sea cucumbers, and conchs. Jim picked up a good-sized conch shell camouflaged with a rough exterior of light tan matching the ocean floor's bottom. A colloquial name for local islanders is a Conch. Thea big shelled saltwater sea snail in the gastropod Mollusk family. The conch comes to a point with a very smooth pink-colored inner lip. It is a favorite dish in the islands with the natives, and restaurants serve conch chowder, soups, and conch fritters; although without cutting one end or punching a small hole at the end of the shell, the snail will not exit. Another way to release the snail is to hang it upside down until he leaves. That is how I did it. I hung it on the clothesline. *That is an extraordinary ugly snail*, I thought.

Huge purple fans swayed in the underwater currents. A small stingray glided close to my face. Bigger fish such as nurse sharks and barracuda also inhabit the reef under the light.

Jim told me, "Do not wear any shiny jewelry as the barracuda will go after it."

Small barracuda's white meat cooked with a bit of lemon and butter is a delightful taste. I learned to eat many different kinds of fish, prepared fresh taste entirely different from the grocery store stock. Jim was most proficient in filleting the fish, and I soon learned to do the same, except I did not like to gut them. Therefore, life had its pleasant and unpleasant moments.

We were a volatile couple, and I was an impetuous young woman. I was mature and moderately spoiled, which might be an exaggeration; I was probably immature and incredibly spoiled.

We got along marvelously in the bedroom, but we could not function at all well in the living room. Finally, after a series of arguments, blowouts, and petty disagreements, numerous screaming fights, never coming to grips with the problem, Rex and I got in the car and drove to my folks in New York.

I had made no friends in the Keys, so I took full advantage of my time visiting family and girlfriends. It was December in New York, and of the four seasons, this was my least favorite. There was no doubt that he would welcome me back, and it was indeed only a temporary separation to cool things down, and soon I returned.

My 1954 Chevy had suffered a breakdown once I arrived in New York. Having spent some time in the warmer climate, I had neglected to put antifreeze in the radiator, and so I blew up the engine, much to my dismay. It was much simpler to find a car in those days. I quickly found a cheap 1949 yellow two-door Chevy. I packed my dishes in an old whiskey box, took some warm sweaters that mother had made that would have kept us warm on the water, and headed out before daybreak. I went through the toll booth on the New Jersey Turnpike, and suddenly a blue light appeared in my rearview mirror. Was I speeding? Had I not paid in the proper toll?

The highway patrol officer stepped to the car, looked quizzically at me, and said, "I thought you were a man," I had a head covering showing no hair, and I wore an oversized dark jacket.

"No, sir, I am not a man," I answered.

"I see you have a crate of whiskey in the back of the car, and it is illegal to transport it across state lines," he stated.

I explained that the dishes were in the box, and he understood without checking. Rex was an excellent passenger, but when the officer stepped to the car, he jumped up from his usual spot on the floorboards on the passenger side, very attentively onto the front passenger seat.

I made a stop to open the windows in Jacksonville as it had gotten quite warm. By the time I got to Miami, the sun was beginning to set, so I closed the front windows. For a nine year old car, it was a speedy roadster. I had made Miami in twelve hours, and now, without warning, it began to smoke. I got out, checked under the hood, and saw no problem. I drove a bit more, and smoke was still seemingly coming out of the engine. Still not seeing any trouble, I continued to the Keys, and fifteen miles from Marathon, whoosh, there were suddenly flames. I pulled Rex out; first, he was reluctant to move. Then, I pulled out the dishes, the sweaters were a total loss, and then I saw what had happened. A cigarette I had thrown out of the wing window embedded into the back seat of the car. With sirens blowing the fire department arrived. By then, the whole vehicle was ablaze. The carburetor melted, and so did the paint. Jim came to see the disaster I had wrought. He drove us to Vaca Cut, and to my surprise, he had rented a small one-room apartment. We did not have to sleep on the boat that month. I put up our first Christmas tree and celebrated the season. He did not care for Christmas, but I did. We had a live tree every year in my young life. Uncle Bruno had brought Noma lights for the tree when we lived on Riverside Drive. They were a glass tube with colored water inside that bubbled. The thought made me homesick. There are many stories regarding the Christmas tree's advent; although, Germany can receive the credit.

While I was gone, Mike Craig from California showed up at the dock asking for a job. Jim hired him as his mate. December was a good month for charters; fish were plentiful this time of the year. We were readily able to sell our fish at the fish house.

One evening Jim put thirty-pounds of amberjack in the trunk of the car to sell. It did not sell, and days later, the car began to smell fishy. When I opened the trunk, I could see the maggots crawling around on the fish. I had to take it over to Vaca Cut on the other side of where the boat lay, haul it out of the trunk and throw it into the fast running water. I wished I had a pair of gloves.

The first few months of the New Year brought few tourists. It was time to take Jim's plans to fruition.

CHAPTER 13:

ACROSS THE GULF STREAM

Jim stood on the Bambino stern, balancing a fifty-five-gallon drum. "Hey Mike," he shouted.

"Let loose of the line." Mike responded, "It's coming down, Jim. Watch out!"

Jim lowered the drum cautiously; his muscular frame strained under the weight of it. He looked like Hercules balancing the world. With a gentle thud, the drum met the deck, and Jim moved it into place. Mike agilely jumped on board and assisted him in lashing the drum securely to the deck floor.

Jim had a square jaw reflected shallow pock marks due to adolescent acne and some evidence of a motorcycle road-rash leaving a rough manly appearance. The sometimes beard hid that characteristic. Jim had a virile self-image, aware he attracted females, and he thought himself handsome. While admiring his visage in the looking glass, he intended to make me feel self-conscience about my nose to deflate my ego; he aimed to make me believe I was less of a person. Due to his dislike of shoes, his feet had calluses. He could walk on hot surfaces and pebbles with no feeling. Once, on the streets of New York, he embarrassed me by showing up with no footwear.

He always wore a captain's hat over his short blond hair; he wanted everyone to acknowledge him as a commercially licensed boat captain. He was proud of having attained his license at the age of eighteen and liked to tell people he was once the youngest sea captain. His love of the sea was in his DNA. In much later years, I discovered his ancestral past.

Jim was born in Astoria, New York, on December 29, 1933, the only child of James and Hazel Paddock. His father worked on fishing boats in New York, and Hazel worked in an office as a general office worker. Within a few years, they relocated to Florida. I do not believe Jim completed high school. He was a troublemaker and sent to Mariana, Georgia, a juvenile detention center. When back at Marathon, his home was in the Florida Keys, fishing was his sole ambition. Jim seldom communicated with his father, although he was in touch with his mother.

He had heard that fishing off the coast of Cuba was plentiful, and that is where he set his sights. Sailfish, Marlin, and the Giant Tuna were all likely to be present in the waters of Cuba. The desire to battle these enormous specimens of the deep was his current fascination. That is what started an adventure in an unfamiliar foreign port.

Mike, our fishing mate twenty years our senior, had initially come from California. He had straight black hair and deep brown eyes. Somewhat awkward and a bit stooped from an old back injury, he was a lanky, agreeable fellow with a slow, relaxed way about him and usually a soft talker. Mike had been with us for several months fishing in Marathon.

Mike was coming back on the dock now to get the suction pump onto the boat. I climbed aboard and helped Mike with the pump.

"Let's go," called Jim as he cranked up the engines.

Mike pulled our stern rope in as I walked along the gunnels to the bow to take in the line from the piling.

"Let's gas up the boat now and get an early start for Key West," Jim declared.

"Good." I said, "Then we can eat dinner there."

Jim bought one large ice chunk for the small galley icebox; we said our farewells and were off for the first part of our trip.

In early February, we had driven the fifty-eight miles from Vaca Cut, on the outskirts of Marathon, to Key West to secure official permission for this trip.

We could locate the gray two-story building with 'Customs House' etched on the top of the old stone structure after asking around. Tall windows and a wrought iron fence around the grassy front area gave it a government look. The three of us walked through the revolving doors and found the customs offices. A large wooden door with half frosted glass and gold letters displaying 'Custom Officer.'

It was a small office; the desk was a clutter of papers and forms. Knowing nothing about the procedure for leaving the country, we were a bit unsure of ourselves.

Jim spoke up, "Good afternoon Sir, we have been planning a trip to Cuba and would like to get the official papers necessary to leave the country."

Mike and I uttered not a word.

The officer looked up at Jim in disbelief.

"Are you folks aware the Cuban government is recently changing?"

"No, sir, we only wish to go to Cuba and fish," Jim told the customs officer.

"Well, young man, there is a great deal of unrest there, and I advise against making the trip."

"Yes, sir, but I do not see why because a government is changing, it would affect a fishing trip," Jim said.

Shaking his head, the officer pulled a sheet of paper from the pile and began filling out the 'Declaration of Vessel to Foreign Port.'

"Do not take any guns or ammunition with you." He advised us. "Also, you cannot take a pet." Then, he said, "Be careful over there. I hope the fishing goes well."

On the way home, I told the boys, "I know a little bit about Cuba,"

"I worked for US Vitamin, an international company dealing with Cuba. We had Cuban employees who spoke of Fulgencio Batista, a despotic leader responsible for imprisoning political figures he thought of as traitors to his government. They spoke of a rebel leader named Fidel Ernesto and "Che" Guevara.

In my research, I learned that in July 1953, Fidel Castro attacked an ammunition barracks to obtain weapons for a revolution to oust Batista from power. The attack failed. The Castro brothers went on trial and were condemned to fifteen years in prison. International pressures forced Batista in 1955 to release political prisoners, including the Castro brothers; they followed through with their plans to unseat Batista. Finally, after fighting the government army and defeating them, the rebels could remove Batista from power. I think this is all taking place now. I've been listening to the news. I hope we will be OK."

After we visited Key West, I knew we could not include Rex in our plans. I had to figure out what to do with him.

Once back home, I packed the large trunks we had used when we left Long Island, New York, four months earlier. Jim's mother, Hazel, was to store the simple household items and clothing that would be extra weight on the boat, undercover behind her house in a lean-to shed. On our way, I had the idea to ask her to keep Rex.

Jim did not think she would do it. He said, "She will store the trunks behind the house but will not keep Rex."

The house was behind the Overseas Bar & Package store on the Overseas Highway, better known as US 1. It was a small house with a living room, one-bedroom, and only furnished with necessities and located on an unpaved road. Behind the house were some other buildings where Jim's father, Jim Senior, lived with a neighbor woman Mary.

As we were in the neighborhood, I asked Jim Senior about Rex. "No, no, I have no use for a dog." I needed an alternative plan.

The next day I located a family with two children not far from our dock at Vaca Cut. I felt he would get plenty of love and attention. Rex watched as I walked away with a broken heart. Some years later, I went to see him. He had grown huge and did not recognize me. Unfortunately, the Keys have a large mosquito population, and Rex had developed heartworms. He died shortly after my visit.

Hazel took care of her mother, Gladys, who stayed home watching black and white TV. Gladys did not appear to be cognizant. Jim told me this story about Gladys.

"My father was out fishing offshore and ran out of gas. He called the house, Gladys answered. He asked her to please call one of the neighbors and see if they can bring him some gas. He said that he was out near the buoy."

Gladys' response, "Why don't you go to a gas station?"

I had met Hazel a few times; she was an earthy matter-of-fact woman. She had curly short brown hair and brown eyes. She was no more than five feet tall. Her dress was always casual, shorts, shirt, and flip-flops. I remember she could sew and made Jim his red shirts, which he wore fishing.

Shortly after I arrived in Marathon, Hazel asked if I would like to work at the Fish House where she worked heading shrimp. It was about a mile from the house, just off the highway. I agreed to accompany her. As we walked into the shed, I saw ten or twelve women fitting the definition of a Fishwife. Not complementary in the least a term I heard from my mother. The term fishwife came from the old English, referring to a loud and foul-mouthed woman. It was a word mom often called me in my impulsive teen years. Now that I was married to a fisherman, the term was almost appropriate. Fishwives were known to hack their wears shouting out the names. I had no idea that my mother was a prognosticator. The women in the fish house had their hair tied up in a scarf fastened behind their heads. Full body aprons covered skirts or shorts and short-sleeved blouses. Flip-flops were the style of footwear.

Right outside the large shed were the docks with fifty-foot shrimp trawlers with flared hulls giving them the width needed to carry the massive shrimp-laden nets. The trawlers have a cabin amidships that operates the winches that lower the nets. A mast-type structure suspends them outward from the boat. Dropping and dragging the nets along the ocean floor is how they manage to catch shrimp. Sometime during the early morning hours, the shrimp trawlers return to the docks, and come morning, the fishermen remove the shrimp from the cold storage under the deck and place them on the worktables.

The worktables are a long wooden table with a flat surface in the center. Fresh shrimp continues to arrive on the tables. Directly in front of the shrimp, there is a troth with running water on the sides of the workbench. To reach the shrimp, the workers must stand to perform their tasks. Each worker must fill the bucket on the floor beside him with beheaded shrimp. Workers were complaining about the new handling of the shrimp. Formerly, after separating the head from the body, the shrimp body was tossed in the bucket. The change was now the head was thrown in the bucket and the body sent into the troth. Therefore, the head's weight was less, and the payment, which was by weight reduced. That was a significant complaint loudly heard around the table, along with gossip of husbands, children, neighbors, and life in general.

I learned that shrimp has a sharp spike between the head and the body. Accidentally sticking this spike in your finger will make it fester for days.

It did not take me long to realize that altering the pay scale was not beneficial to the workers; I lasted about two weeks.

We had everything prepared for the trip. Jim was ready, "Let's go," he called as he cranked up the engines. Mike pulled our stern lines as I walked along the gunnels to the bow to take in the rope from the piling. Jim pulled into the gas dock, filled the tanks, and bought one large ice chunk for the small galley icebox. We were on our way from Marathon to Key West to begin our latest adventure.

On the way to Key West, Jim and I were on the flying bridge, and Mike was in the cockpit when he called up, "Slow her down some boy, I want to throw out a line and see what I can catch." During the two-hour trip, Mike had no success. Upon arriving at the dock in Key West, Mike immediately picked up his rod and reel and hurriedly jumped off the boat.

Jim had other thoughts, and he said to me, "I'm going to locate the custom's official and get us cleared for an early morning departure. Then, I'll see the dockmaster to top off the tanks, one last time, fill the fifty-five-gallon drum and the two extra gas cans. See you in a bit; how about you start dinner?"

I agreed, and soon we gathered in the stern for our last stateside meal. It was getting late, and I was tired. Therefore, I left the dishes on the deck in a bucket in the starboard stern corner. I expected to clean them when we set out in the early dawn.

Mike's earlier attempt to catch something failed. "I'm going to give it one last try," Mike announced. Jim and I walked the ten feet down the dock to join him. "I got one," he shouted, "Stay away from that piling fish," Mike was talking to the fish, which we could not yet see.

Suddenly, a flash of silver whizzed by, and Jim called excitedly, "You've got a Tarpon; take it easy. He'll give you a good fight."

Now people were gathering around to watch. Would-be anglers were murmuring advice to Mike. "Work it, boy, careful, he is moving too fast, he will spit out the hook, you know Tarpons are fighters," but Mike cautiously guided the fish to the dock and landed it safely.

Jim judged the Tarpon to be fifteen pounds a good-sized catch. After slaps on his back and praise of his prowess, we all headed home. The sun was falling in the west, and hues of pink, blue, and gray all intermingled in a sunset for which Key West is famous.

Once back at the boat, Jim busied himself plotting the course, taking readings, wind velocity, and water currents. I readied our sleeping bunks, stayed below, and fell asleep listening to the water gently lapping the sides of the boat and the whispering of the wind.

Jim's voice jolted me awake. "Get up, Ruth plans changed; we're going to leave now."

"But Jim, it's the middle of the night; it is two o'clock in the morning. I thought you said dawn," I asked him groggily.

"I did. Can't you feel the wind coming around? It feels like there is a storm brewing. I need you to throw off the lines."

Jim was now revving up the engines of our twenty-six-feet fishing boat. "Mike, you get the bowline and let Ruth get the stern."

"I hear you; I'm going to do it," I called out.

Jim maneuvered the Bambino out of the docking slip and into the harbor. The water that had been a glassy calm some hours earlier was now choppy and showing whitecaps. Salty spray dampened us as we headed toward the Straits of Florida, and as soon as we reached open water, the sea baptized us with a crashing wall of water straight across our stern.

Jim announced, "We are in a head sea, one of the most dangerous kind of water. If we are not careful, we can capsize."

Mike and I exchanged glances.

"Oh! We are in for it. Are you ready, Mike?" I quipped. "Me, oh sure, I love to swim with sharks."

We were now well away from the protection of land. Huge waves were curling over our heads, thundering, splashing on the bow with a mighty force. The vessel tossed about, from one wall of water into the next. Up and down she went.

Looking out to sea, just over the horizon to the north, the glow from the lights of Key West disappeared, and far in the distance to the east, the lights of Miami tinted the sky. In a few moments, all vanished, and there was nothing to see but a vast thrashing ocean visible only by our navigational lights.

The waves were breaking straight over our bow, and we looked like drowned rats and felt even worse. Sailor that I was, this kind of sea was not for me. It was not long before I was nauseous; Jim looked my way and laughed.

"Now Ruth, you aren't seasick, are you?"

I gave him a weak smile, thinking, *can I get off? I feel terrible.*

A twenty-six-feet boat did not belong in a storm like this; she moaned and sputtered as she climbed still another wall of water, and her propellers whirled in unbinding air. We did not talk; we watched, listening in shock at the sound, and there to the port side as if motionless, the water appeared like a fortress daring us to conquer her. Then, the giant wave crashed directly into us and was gone, sloshing along the deck. I could feel the boat lurch over to starboard, and then snap back.

"Another one likes that, and we may swim the rest of the way to Cuba." Jim blurted out.

"Let's put some more gas in her now, so we don't run dry."

Suddenly he shut down both engines, and the sound of the wind was clear; it cried and whined while it churned the salty brine.

In the cockpit, before leaving, Jim and Mike had lashed a fifty-five-gallon gasoline drum. It was to use for refueling on the high seas. Now was the time to use it. Mike handed Jim a full five-gallon can; Jim crawled out on the narrow gunnels fighting to stay on board as I held my breath while he poured the gas into the small opening for the starboard engine. Jim hollered.

"This can is empty – hand over the next, start pumping, Mike, it will take three more cans for this tank, and then I'll get the port side."

The evening before, I neglected to wash the dishes, and now with the engines off, I could hear the clear sound of the metal dishes banging against the bucket that I placed in the stern. I had nearly forgotten about them and vaguely wished in my nauseated state that I had washed them.

Mike pumped the gas and passed it again. I felt sicker than before with the gas fumes rising and the constant rocking of the boat in the troth. They were working feverishly to complete this task when unexpectedly Mike called, "Jim, something has happened; I'm not getting any more gas up through the pump."

Jim was now in the cockpit; both men examined the pump.

"Let's unscrew it, Mike; I think the pipe came loose inside."

They tried to loosen it with their hands. However, it was either cross-threaded or rusty. "Hey Ruth, look alive; get me the large wrench."

I sighed; I was in no shape for an emergency. I went down to the cabin where I figured it would be and fumbled around, not finding it.

"It's under the console under the wheel," Jim called out, exasperated. I thought why he did not say that before, now I had to walk across the deck, feel around for this wrench, which I found quickly, and then back across the deck and lurched forward to hand it to him. Using the tool, he loosened the pump fitting; he could hardly see inside the drum; sure enough, the pipe had become unattached due to the rough sea.

"The opening is too small for any of us to get our hand in the hole," Mike said. "Ruth," Jim ordered, "Get a hanger." Again, I slowly moved to the cabin; I had to hold on as I made my way across the short distance; I knew where they were, found them quickly, and passed one off to Mike. Jim bent it, stuck it in the hole, trying to hook the pipe. The combination of fumes rising through the hole in the drum and tossing sea were beginning to affect even my staunch captain and mate. Mike had to stop and hang over the side to breathe some fresher air, and then Jim too needed a good breath of ocean air.

Again, Jim requested, "We need a light; it's under the port bunk." I went below; I could hear them probing around in the drum and muttering curses to one another. I produced the light, and Mike held it while Jim explored, then Jim held it while Mike tried, and at last, he had success. Skillfully Mike brought the hanger over the hole and lifted it.

"I've got it," Mike shouted over the roar of the wind. Mike reached for the top of the suction pump, and together, they securely screwed the pipe onto the pump.

Now Mike was able to fill the cans again and continue to hand them off to Jim. He completed filling the tank and jumped back into the cockpit. Mike handed a full can to Jim, and then Jim challenged me.

"Come on, Ruthie; it's your turn." I looked at him with amazement.

I took the can, struggled out on the narrow gunnel, and emptied it into the port tank, straining with the weight of the can while hanging onto the side of the boat.

The action of the waves bouncing against the hull caused saltwater to trickle down my face into my eyes, making it difficult to see. I thought, *damn him, he thinks I can't do this, well I'll show him*, and I finished emptying the can; extremely pleased with myself, I climbed back into the cockpit. I wanted to kill him.

"See, I knew you could do it." Jim teased with a smirk on his face

"You son-of-a-bitch; did you want me to fall in the water? You knew how hard that would be for me, you bastard; you would like to see me over the side; you always say you will feed me to the sharks. That was your great opportunity, so sorry it didn't work."

At last, the final can emptied as dawn showed her face toward the east. Jim stepped to the stern for a moment, and to my dread, he planted his foot squarely into the bucket of dirty dishes. As poorly as I was feeling, I had to try hard to conceal a laugh. He stood for a bare instant, bent down, jerked the bucket off his foot, and with a mighty heave tossed it overboard.

"Why did you leave them there?" He spat out the words.

"Why would I want to wash dishes when Mike is on the dock catching Tarpon? Why did you throw them overboard?"

He started the engines, took a quick reckoning on the compass, and declared, "We are way off course; the Gulf Stream is doing a good seven to eight knots. I figure we drifted about seven miles off course. We are going to have to fight our way against the drift. Another five hours, and we should see some land."

Jim was feeling the strain of his fight against the ocean. He turned to Mike, "Do you think you can take the wheel for a while, Mike?"

"Sure, Jim." Mike stood firmly at the console, took hold of the controls, and again, a tremendous wave swept over us.

"Hold tight, Mike, don't panic, that's it, ease her out gently," Jim's calm voice advising Mike, knowing he had been nervous – he had never run the boat in waters such as these.

"No more like that please, I don't want to be responsible for sinking us. I didn't realize this little boat could be that hard to hold." Jim just gave a knowing smile, nodding his head. Mike had a very short stint at the wheel, and Jim took over again.

My seasickness had made me feel a bit lightheaded, and the engines' groan was like a lullaby. In my drowsy state, I wrote this poem:

Ocean characteristics change

They rage they roar, ravaged by wind

Then become calm

Rain pelts down, forming tiny pools in the massive sea

Dangerous whirlwinds,

Waterspouts appear from nowhere, threatening mariners

Tides flow – the moon glows over a glassy sea,

Sailors.

I dozed fitfully with the sound of the boy's voices waking me now and again from my light slumber. Jim's voice sounded distant.

"Do you feel the sea changing direction?" Jim declared. I became more alert to the boat's movement, the sea was still rough, but it had lost its drive. I heard him say, "Keep your eyes open." Jim sounded like a fifteenth-century Columbus.

"Do you see that haze on the horizon? That means there is land close." The haze began to take shape; we had been on the boat for fifteen hours and struggled for not quite ninety-four miles. Peering out of the windshield and standing side by side, each of us wanted to be the first to yell.

"Land Ho," Jim was first.

"I see it, I see it," Mike and I sang.

CHAPTER 14:

CUBA

The pearl green water was now a light chop as the haze on the horizon began to take shape. Seagulls were circling, screeching as they thrust headlong into the water, searching for prey. Emerging with a fish squirming in their beaks, the seagull swallowed the tiny silverfish, diving again for more.

Jim noted, "See in the distance, half a dozen rowboats scattered farther away from the island. The masts of their boats are laid across the boat when they fish. They use the put-puts on the stern when they follow fish into deeper water. At day's end, they raise the mast to sail home. Strangely, these small boats would not be so far offshore; if a storm came up, they would be in trouble. The fishing must be better out here."

Suddenly, a shot rang out. Mike pointed. "It's over in that direction," He exclaimed, pointing excitedly.

I noticed one of the fishing boats had broken away from the others and was heading our way, arms waving wildly, screaming, "Banditos, Banditos." He was signaling us to move away. Just then, there was another shattering sound seeming to cut across our bow.

The man in the small rowboat was still screaming hysterically, "Banditos. Go away, go away."

"Let's get out of here," Mike said in an excited voice.

"I didn't come to Cuba to die; I only want to fish. Hurry Jim, move this boat."

Jim had been taking the shortest route toward the inlet to the port of Havana. This way would have saved an hour of boating by cruising perpendicular to the shore. Now our approach would have to change. He pushed the throttle forward with great urgency heading back out toward the sea, then reversing course to turn into the bay following the channel markers to the port entrance.

Steadily advancing, we could see Cuba was a verdant tropical land cast out in the middle of the ocean. Moro Castle, the legendary fortress completed in 1660 to protect Havana's city from buccaneers, became ever more visible.

Castillo de los Tres Reyes del Morro Castle is a striking lighthouse surrounded by a large high rock jetty standing tall at the harbor entrance. As we slowly glided past her massive old black charred walls, I had visions of cannons peering out to sea aimed at the galleons and brigantines that might attack, although the castle's eyes no longer scanned the bay.

Finding a suitable slip at dockside was an easy task as we were the only floating vessel in the harbor. The empty concrete dock was a large, poorly lit shed against which we lay horizontally.

Almost immediately, six men hurriedly approached our vessel. Their loud voices were audible from a distance; as they came closer, the Spanish swelled into a crescendo while they gesticulated, pointing down at us. The first thing I noticed was that they were carrying guns, big black guns. Each man shouldered his weapon in a threatening manner, ready to use it. They were dressed in camouflage clothing, berets, and boots and appeared extremely malevolent. Suddenly all was quiet as a tall, broad-shouldered, dark-skinned man stepped from the group. He dressed in a loud sports shirt, pants, and a white yachtsman's cap. His small mustache accentuated his Latin air.

"You must have come a long way?" He spoke with a heavy accent.

"Yes, we have come out of Key West, Florida. It was a long trip with terribly rough seas. Please, sir, we believe your officials must clear us?" Jim spoke very cautiously.

"Yes, Capitan, you must have your papers checked. No foreigner can set foot on Cuban soil until checked. I will get the Officials. Please wait here." He spoke the words with authority. Turning toward one of the men he gave, what appeared to be an order in Spanish. The man acknowledged with a nod and quickly ran toward the street, easily seen from the boat.

While we waited, the man identified himself.

"I am a cab driver; my name is Carlos; none of these men can speak English. If you need my services, I will help you. You are the first American boat in the Havana harbor since our revolution. You know Fidel Castro has taken over the country, Batista is gone now. He flew to the Dominican Republic, saying he took millions of dollars with him, stealing from his people, and murdered many. Castro and his rebels have fought hard against the Government of Batista. We are going to be a new country now with Castro." We all shook our heads in response to this statement.

The other men languidly leaned against the building on the other side of the dock, never taking their eyes off from us, their rifles still in the ready position.

Jim posed a question to Carlos, "Down the coast, as we came into the bay, people were shooting out toward the sea. Do you know what that was?"

"Oh yes, Castro takes his men up into the hills for target practice every afternoon. That was what you heard."

We could hear voices and heavy footfalls coming down the dock. Carlos looked at us and announced, "The Officials come now; I will be your interpreter, OK?"

As soon as the officials approached the boat, Carlos spoke to them in Spanish; then he turned to Jim, "You are the Capitan?"

"Yes."

"Do you have any papers?"

Jim looked at me, and I went below, brought the papers forward, and handed them to Jim, who gave them to Carlos.

"This is what I have," Jim said.

"Can they come aboard?" Carlos spoke to the officials. "These men are the Custom's Officials," he informed us.

We could not figure out why they wanted to come aboard, but soon we knew what they were after. Two Officials, also dressed in camouflage and carrying pistols at their hips, jumped on deck with their heavy boots. They moved about searching the console cabinet, below deck under the bunks, the galley area, and even checked the head apparently in search of weapons. They muttered to each other with sideways glances at the three of us.

I felt as though we were guilty of something. Then, the Officials climbed off onto the dock. I spoke to Carlos, who translated, "All your papers are in order. The charge is four dollars American money. Do not leave your boat yet; the Immigration Officers come right away."

Within a few minutes, three other men arrived, dressed in the same garb and paying no attention to Carlos and not requesting permission; they just jumped on board with their heavy boots. Poking about, not as thoroughly as the first group, one of the men spoke in broken English.

"I am the Immigration Officer." "How many, three?" pointing at us

We all nodded our heads in agreement. Did they think we were hiding somebody?

"Papers?" he said, putting out his hand. Jim handed him the same papers as the group had received before. The official looked at them all too quickly.

"OK, three dollars American money."

Jim paid them, and they climbed off the boat, speaking loudly in Spanish. Not a word did we understand. Thinking we could now set foot on solid ground, we were shocked when another group arrived and spoke to Carlos. Different from the previous groups, these men were in official-looking uniforms. They were much more polite and talked to Carlos, who once again translated for them.

"These men say the first officials were not the right officials, and now these men have come to clear you. They want to come aboard." And so they did, they checked through the boat, checked the papers, and Carlos, still standing on the dock, announced, "Their fee is five dollars American money." I looked at Mike, putting my hand over my mouth so no one would hear me, "I sure hope they don't send the rest of their friends."

"Shush, they may hear you and do just that." After they were all gone save for Carlos and two of his cronies, Jim jokingly said, "Quick, jump on the dock, hold onto your money and run like hell before any more 'Officials' come racing down here."

He made mock gestures as if leaping off the boat and then, more seriously,

"When we are ready to go to town, I don't think we should all leave at once; I don't trust all these unfriendly faces."

I agreed and offered to cook up a bit of Dinty Moore canned beef stew dinner. We had to eat in shifts as only two dishes and one fork remained as the rest was at the bottom of the Gulf Stream. Before they left, Jim asked me, "You do know where the gun is, don't you?"

"Yes, but don't worry, Jim; there wouldn't be any trouble."

Carlos had hung around the dock and now stepped up, offering to show the boys the life of nighttime Cuba. When they left, the other remaining men on the dock followed them. They did not think I was a threat and left me alone on the boat. I was exhausted. I needed to get some sleep.

The racket above deck woke me suddenly from a sound, dreamless sleep, and it took me a few seconds to realize where I was. The loud voices belonged to my boys, but I could not quite figure out what was all the commotion. When I emerged from below, they fell silent and stood looking down at me.

"Where were you?" Jim asked angrily.

"Where was I? Where do you think I was, out on the town? I was sleeping." I was mad—what a dumb question.

"Why weren't you out on the deck?"

"Why should I be? All was quiet here."

"How do you know? You were asleep."

"Jim, what's the matter with you?"

Then, I realized they were both drunk. As I looked at Jim and Mike in the reflecting light from the building across the dock, I could see they were so drunk they were having trouble standing up. Mike was trying to say something,

"Jim, I've got to get some sleep."

He slurred, and then I saw a woman trying to hide behind Mike. She stepped a bit to the side and half smiled at me. I was not smiling. What did they think they were going to do with her? Oh! I knew what, but how?

Mike went below, and the woman stayed on the dock, standing close to Jim.

Ah, I realized she was not with Mike but with Jim. Suddenly he looked down at me, "What do you want?" Jim said slurring his words.

"What do you want with that woman?" I said in an agitated tone.

"I think she can sleep on the boat."

"And where do I sleep?"

"You don't need to sleep, I did all the work today, and you weren't even conscious of half of it. Seasick woman, you do not deserve to sleep. I've got this sexy lady, and she needs to spend the night here."

That was it, he was drunk, and there was no way I was spending the night on the boat with another woman. Jim began to get louder, and the louder he got, the more abusive he became.

"Everyone can hear you, Jim." I was embarrassed that he was acting up.

"So what, so they hear me. They do not know what in the hell I am saying anyway. Hey, garble, garble, yack, yack, I can't understand them, they can't understand me."

Then, the lights of a car shone down the dock, and moments later, Carlos came hurriedly walking along.

"Can I be of assistance?"

"Yes, Carlos, I would like to go to the airport. Can you take me?" I said shyly.

Carlos was quick to answer.

"Yes, lady, I will take you." It took me a moment to gather up a few clothes.

In the car, Carlos began to explain, "I am sorry; I took them to the 'Nacional de Cuba' hotel. They drank Cuban rum, which is very strong. Do you know about the 'Nacional Hotel'? It is famous for gambling, and many Americans used to come here. We had notorious gangsters such as Lucky Luciana and Myer Lansky. Do you know them?"

"I have heard about them."

He drove straight to the airport twenty miles away. When I went to the ticket counter, the agent asked for my birth certificate. I did not realize in my haste that I would need to have it to get back home.

"No, I don't have it with me," I said quietly.

"This is the last plane this evening. Tomorrow there will be another. You can come back," the ticket agent informed me.

I explained to Carlos that I would have to come back tomorrow. He offered to give me a grand tour of Havana before returning to the boat. We saw some charming old and modern buildings and drove down some excellent roads in the city proper. He bought me some Cuban coffee. Wow, was that strong. Cubans are straightforward in the area of casual lovemaking right on the street, kissing and hugging with no qualms. Americans are less demonstrative. When Carlos came to a corner, he blew his horn and then went on. I inquired about this strange procedure, and his answer was, "Whoever reaches the corner first and blows his horn has the right of way; in Cuba, this is how they do it."

We arrived back at the boat. Mike met me at the stern, "Jim has gone to a hotel, don't worry; she is not on board."

I went below to relax and immediately noticed the jacket my mother had made for me was missing. It had hung just above the bunk.

"Mike, do you have any idea what happened to my jacket?" I could tell he did not want to tell me,

"Jim gave it to the girl."

Oh, I was so angry. How could Jim do that? It was not bad enough that he went off with the girl. Jim had no respect for me. That he takes me to a foreign port, leaves me, and on top of that gives her my clothes. The morning could not come soon enough.

In the morning, I was still angry and delighted that I did not have to see him as Carlos arrived early to take me back to the airport.

The trip, which the day before had taken us fifteen hours, took me 45 minutes.

I got a job at Jones Shutter Products, which made striking panels accented in the middle with flowers. The smell of resin permeated the small plant. It was not displeasing to me.

I stayed stateside for three weeks until I got a call from my mother, "Ruth, Jim has called; he said he was sorry and wants you to come back to Cuba. Of course, I gave him your phone number at work." Well, that was a shock. The next call was from him. He was all apologetic, smooth-talking me into returning.

"Come on, Ruthie, you know I was drunk; I'm so sorry. You know I love to have you with me. I love you. You have to come back; this is a beautiful country. Come on."

My nature is to forgive; besides, I wanted to see Cuba.

I flew into Jose Marti Airport in Varadero Beach, which is some eighty miles from Havana. I deplaned at the tarmac, walked to the terminal that had a chain-link fence separating the passengers from the welcoming crowd. I could see Jim, and Mike on the other side, waving to me. The officials inspected my luggage. I had a carton of cigarettes, and they felt it suspiciously expecting to find contraband. A female customs official beckoned me to follow her into the ladies' room where she frisked me; not finding anything, she released me into the waiting crowd.

Both men were so happy to see me embracing me, kissing me, and giving me big hugs. They were both bubbling over with stories to tell. They told me, "After you left, we obtained a traveling visa and proceeded down the coast of Cuba. We entered Matanzas Harbor, and although we had papers stating we could travel freely, they ignored the order. They put us under an armed guard during the forty-eight hours that we stayed in port." Jim was anxious to tell me every detail.

"The day we were to leave Matanzas, the water conditions were not favorable, although the locals said it was safe enough for passage. You should have seen this place; it has a narrow outlet to the open sea with high sea walls on either side. On rough days, it was treacherous to maneuver a small craft through this outlet." Mike interrupted Jim's tale.

"Ruth, believe me, the Cubans knew it was a bad day, and they would not acknowledge the fact. I think they wanted to see us hit the seawall. Jim can maneuver in any situation, but events did not go so smoothly. Tell her, Jim."

"Before leaving, we bought another fifty-five-gallon drum, which we lashed to the flying bridge. In the raging water, it was so rough you would have been sick. Well, the cord got loose, and the drum came crashing down into the cockpit missing Mike by a hair. We almost lost it."

Mike took up the story, "Our little boat was almost smashed into the walls. The rough sea loosened some planking, and we took on quite a bit of water. By sheer good fortune and Jim's handling of the boat, we made it back into Matanzas Harbor."

Now it was Jim's turn again, "When we showed up at the dock, the men that told us it was safe to travel were standing there laughing at us. I got the definite feeling that being American was not very popular with the Cubans. Conditions improved the next day, and we headed for Varadero Beach."

A taxi ride from the airport deposited us at the Yacht Club. The marine facilities were all entirely modern, and the surrounding grounds appeared well kept. Jim felt it was a friendly atmosphere at first and decided to stay and try to make a living. First impressions are not always correct, and after investigating, he found that if they were to run a charter boat fishing business in Cuba, he would have to pay the government a certain amount of what the boat cost when it was new. In Florida, it was only necessary to pay for a fishing license.

After a while, it was evident the dock officials were not concerned about keeping up the atmosphere of camaraderie. That is what made him decide I should come back and enjoy the lovely surroundings. When the money ran out, and it became impossible for us to stay, we would go home.

I decided I would make the best of it and enjoy all that I could while there. The following day Jim showed me the unbelievable huge bathrooms of the club. I estimated them to be forty feet long. The men's bathroom was in light baby blue tiles; the women were tiled pink with sixteen cubical, each containing a bidet.

That afternoon, Jim recounted another experience, "I had taken the head man of the Police Department out fishing to make friends with him. The next day they arrested the man because he had allied himself with Batista. That did not put me in a good position with everyone else, and from then on, they suspected we were rebels against Castro. They kept us against our will and under surveillance."

As I wandered around the Yacht Basin, I noticed the officials never took their eyes off either the boat or us. These men dressed the same as the men that had initially come aboard the charter boat when we were in Havana. I tried to speak to them, and I could see they understood my English but enjoyed making a fool out of me and having me repeat myself repeatedly until I looked like I was playing a game of charades with them. Mike was again relating other experiences Jim and he encountered in the small city.

"We were in a restaurant and bar we had been patronizing. One evening there was a dispute between a Cuban soldier and a civilian. To emphatically make his point, the soldier took the butt of his rifle, slamming it on the floor, and it went off and shot a hole in the ceiling. We left quickly for fear the incapable hands holding the weapon might accidentally fire a wild shot at us. These soldiers were all very young."

After hearing that story, I suggested we eat our meals onboard.

An American Cup sailing yacht docked close to our fishing boat at the Yacht Club. The crew seldom spoke to us.

The conventional mode of travel was a bicycle. Occasionally, I rode the two miles into town on a rented bike to do the marketing. I stopped at the local bakery and bought a sweet and a container of milk. I was able to say those few items in Spanish. Before returning to the Bambino with my scant load of rice, coffee, and Cuban bread, I investigated Varadero Beach. It is a pristine white stretch of sugar sand. I marveled at the clear blue-green sparkling water. The glistening white sand was a peaceful pleasure that I have never forgotten and have often wished for the solitude I enjoyed that day.

The once famous National Hotel, filled during the season before the revolution, now was empty of tourists. The white sands stretched bare.

We traveled up and down the coast around the vicinity of Varadero. The landscape was strikingly unspoiled. I could see large homes built on many of the cliffs that came straight out of the water. We swam in the calm, warm water of this scenic paradise. We also fished frequently, but much to our dismay, we found very few species in the waters around that part of Cuba. The commercial anglers in the area were successful in catching fish by throwing out large quantities of bait. Sportfishing used rod and reel with fish bait on one hook. We did hear that fishing at the southern end of the island was good, but we could not travel there to find out.

I wanted to see more of Cuba. The boys had been to the market town of Cárdenas, and they decided to show it to me. The only way for us to travel was by bus. The bus was old and full of people holding onto various-sized parcels. On top of the bus were crates of chickens. It was a very loud bus with the birds squeaking and the excited conversation of the occupants.

The road was very narrow, with bicyclists all over the street, and the driver was incessantly honking his horn. Along the wayside, sugar cane, pineapple, and tobacco were growing. The houses that lined the road were no more than shacks with pigs, goats, and chickens at every home.

In Cárdenas itself, there were horse-drawn carriages on the main road and few cars. Many children wandered about the streets, not in play, but trying to earn money as shoeshine boys. The side streets were cobblestoned, and one area was dedicated entirely to marketing goods from wristwatches to oranges. I bought Jim a lighter "Made in Japan."

Our limited funds did not last long. Three weeks after my arrival, we decided to return home. Early in the morning, the day of our departure, Jim and Mike left again for Cardenas to pick up our official papers to leave the country. We had planned to stop off at Cay Sol Bank, a small island north of Cuba, to do some fishing before returning to the Florida Keys. Somehow, the officials heard of our plans. The Cuban officials feared that we would pick up some Cubans along the coastline or out in the water trying to flee Cuba illegally. They refused to issue us clearance for any other port.

When the boys returned after a delay of two hours, we prepared to cast off immediately. Why they kept them became clear when before we could get our engines started, a uniformed camouflage-clad man came to the boat and informed us we could not leave yet. He would not tell us why we had to delay our departure.

Finally, after five hours of waiting, we were able to depart.

The Cubans were not taking any chances with us. To make sure we would not go to our initially planned stop, they had brought a fully armed naval vessel up the coast from Havana. This trip usually takes five hours, the exact time of our delay. The naval vessels stayed behind us but had us in her sights for twelve miles out, into international waters. They made sure we were going straight to the United States.

An ocean of glass, a clear night offering a cosmic display of vast galaxies winking far above us made us realize we are just a spec upon the universe—a small boat cast upon an enormous expanse of ocean. The water was so calm that we each took five-hour shifts at the wheel. Instead of steering with the compass, we navigated according to the stars.

CHAPTER 15:

RETURNING HOME

The Bambino, with Captain Jim at the helm, glided into homeport at Vaca Key. He docked in our former dockage space.

"Jim, you know full well that we should have gone into Key West to clear customs and immigration. Now we can't set foot on land until they clear us." I commented.

The yellow flag, flying from our starboard outrigger, was a declaration that we had just arrived from a foreign port.

"I'm going up to the bait and tackle shop, just a few steps away, to use the pay-phone to call Key West and request an officer come to us."

Turning to Mike, I said, "You know he is going to get dressed down. It wouldn't surprise me if customs charged an extra port entry fee."

"You know him, Ruthie; he was trying to save gas and time by coming here instead of Key West."

"I understand that, but I like to play by the rules, and I feel we should have docked back at Key West."

Giving up on my useless argument, I sat down on the fighting chair in the stern, surveying the sights of home. My only regret was the loss of Rex, who was not standing on the dock in his usual excited greeting, wagging that little stub of a tail his body bent nearly in two. I would always miss him.

Looking at the dockside view from this lower angle as the tide was out, I saw the three fishing boats alongside the dock. Jim had built a good-sized box to store gear and shared it with the other boatmen on the relatively small dock. I used to sit on the box and watch him as he performed repairs on our boat. The fledgling bait and tackle shop stood between us and another dock on the other side. To our left was Vaca Cut, where at high tide, the water rushed through the cut. It was accessible from the gulf side and a fishing spot for locals.

I could feel the whisper of a soft, warm, southern breeze across the exceptionally calm waters. It was barely dawn; the sun was shedding a gentle glow across the horizon. As I sat contemplating and gazing out toward the East, the glow gradually became a fiery red ball slowly lifting above the horizon. The water became a shimmering seascape, lighting up a perfect Key's day. It is a delightful, refreshing feeling, taking pleasure in nature, sun, sky, and clear waters. I loved the sea, and it had provided me with the adventure of my life from the stormy beginning to calmer seas.

Mike came over to me and sat in the other fighting chair. He said, "I wonder how long Jim will be. I want to get off the boat."

"Oh, Mike, it's a lovely day, can't you tell the difference here? Cuba was beautiful, but I feel they had more humidity, and the air was most oppressive. Maybe the oppression I felt was what was happening there."

"Ruthie, as you know, Fidel Castro, has embraced Communism. He has already punished and killed those who were in the Batista government. Castro will continue to put more constraints on the people. He would not let them leave; he will take their belongings and run the country down. I fear that they are such close neighbors. The future of Cuba will continue to be a mystery." (This story took place in 1959. We know the answer to the mystery now, and all that took place.)

"Yes, Mike, I agree, and I feel so badly for the people. We saw so much poverty, and this will undoubtedly get worse."

Mike said, "Here comes Jim; he is walking across the dock. I wonder what happened?"

Jim's response, "Sorry it took so long, they gave me a lecture about coming here, but they are on the way. What have you guys been talking about?"

Mike answered, "The plight of the Cuban people."

"I think we could discuss that for a long time. I am sorry now that we were not able to do what we set out to do. Now, we are home and in the same predicament as before.

There's more competition at this location, making it harder to make a buck. I talked with the men in the shop, and they said the business was slow, more half-day charters than a full day. I want to look for another place. There is a new start-up location in North Key Largo called Ocean Reef Club. One of the men at the bait and tackle store told me."

CHAPTER 16:

OCEAN REEF CLUB

Rising to the ever-present sun's rays heating the water from the night's chill, I prepared for our trip north along the Upper Keys coastline. I untied the boat lines in the bow, and Jim did the same in the stern as we slowly glided away from our home port.

It took us over half a day cruising along the Florida Keys coast to reach our new dock site. North Key Largo is the first key within the archipelago of islands that constitute the Florida Keys. The Ocean Reef Club is a peninsula twelve miles east of the main island. It is a real estate developer's dream to make this limestone landmass into a deluxe golf and fishing resort.

As we approached, we could see the large glass in front of the Clubhouse. During the time we spent at the Club, I would only enter the building on one occasion. Designed in a stylish motif, the Club had colorful fish mounted on the walls and photographs of several documented world catches. My errand concluded; I passed through the overstocked bar with plush gold carpeting and exited never to return. Jim was not an employee of the Club. He was a freelance sports fisherman, brought in for the convenience of the guests.

Jim immediately spotted the dock.

"I see the dockmaster waving us in," I said.

"We do not look very professional with our belongings packed in the stern of the boat," Jim said as he waved hello to the dockmaster. Although our possessions were not as many as had been on our virgin voyage from New York, nonetheless, we still did not look like an elite fishing boat worthy of the Club.

As Jim began to maneuver our Norseman closer to the dock, he whispered, "Wonder what spot he will give us? See Ruth, there is enough room for two boats, and it looks like the dockmaster is directing our boat into the second spot. I guess the other boat is out. That's a good sign; people must be chartering."

The surroundings were spacious enough to accommodate several yachts plus a few amenities at the dockside. There was a rough wooden table for filleting and scaling the day's catch, a picnic table with benches, and a small metal shed for minor repairs and stowing gear.

A sign on a pole over the unoccupied dock read, "Tommy Gifford's Stormy."

"Tommy is a well-known name among fishermen. I have heard the name many times along the docks. I'll be pleased to meet him." Jim said.

This time the dockmaster heard his comment and said, "You're right; he catches those big fish with his kite."

We saw the dock-master's name clipped to his shirt, 'Frank-Dock master.'

Jim and I looked at each other. I whispered, "A kite, what is that about?"

"I have no idea. Guess we will find out."

"Hey Frank, when is Tommy expected back into port?"

"Oh, half-day charters only last till three; he'll be in soon."

"I may as well take you to see where you're going to live," Frank said as he climbed on his golf cart and motioned us to ride on the back seat. A few houses spread across acres of flat sandy limestone. Most of Key Largo was of limestone and coral rock, but some native trees and shrubs were evident. The homes we passed were vacation homes. We were traveling away from the water toward the resort's back.

Our guide showed us to a modest three-room cabin with a living room that, fortunately, had a TV and two chairs and a couch for Mike. The kitchen had a nice clean refrigerator and stove with plenty of cabinet space for our few kitchen accessories. The bedroom contained a double bed and the only bathroom in the house.

I asked Frank, "What's that shed over to the left?" It was a huge wooden building with double doors.

He answered, "That is the carpenter's shed, and his cabin is a bit further back over to the left, hard to see through the thick foliage. You will see him in the morning when he comes to work. Now look here, young lady, just behind the house, is a wash house."

I looked, and there was a screened enclosure; I saw an old wringer-type machine, and to the right was a nice size clothesline. Wow, I thought that type of device was outdated. My mom used to wash on one of those when I was about eight. It was in the kitchen of our eighth-floor apartment in New York. When she put the clothes in the wringer, sometimes the sheets would form a big bubble of water and squirt it all over her and the floor. Grandma would help mop it up.

"Be careful, Ruthie, don't run; you will slip," Grandma said in a commanding voice. Mom had strung lines all through the kitchen, and I would play peek-a-boo around the clothes. It made me think of Mom getting the sheets caught in the wringer and Grandma help pull them loose. So now, I would have the same experience with the sheets spewing water all over me.

"Thank you for pointing that out," I said, rather pleased. At our last location, I had to go to a Laundromat; this was an upgrade. I felt the house was sufficient for Jim, Mike, and me. I had one more question, "Who lives in the lot behind us with the nice lawn?"

"That's the Gifford house. You will share the wash house with them and other staff on the grounds."

The only person I ever saw was Esther Gifford at the wash-house, and at the line and no other person.

"Well, it's time to get back to the dock. I will assign you a golf cart you can use to unload your things. Come along now."

We had left Mike at the boat; it was time to collect him and our things and take them to our new house. We had always slept aboard, except for a few months at Christmas, when we rented a tourist cabin. *That would be a pleasant change*, I thought. I wonder how long we will stay here. When we got back to the dock, the Stormy had returned with a sailfish and a sizeable colorful dolphin.

"Hi, Tommy, I'm so glad to meet you; I've heard a lot about you. I've heard you fish with a kite. Can you tell me about that?" Jim introduced himself and talked for a bit while Mike loaded our things on the borrowed golf cart. As they were still talking and looking over each other's boats, Mike and I left for the house.

I noted Tommy was a weathered, five-three, stocky, sixty-four-year-old fisherman with knurled hands and a floppy hat with a chin strap. He wore a tan shirt with sleeves to the elbows and a pair of baggy shorts.

Jim became fast friends with Tommy. He learned about kite fishing and how to make a kite. Sitting on the floor in the living room, needle and thread in hand, stitching a sizeable silky scarf that I had worn on my head. We had a cat Tag, and he decided he was going to help in this endeavor. Unfortunately, Jim did not see it that way; he tossed the cat across the room, which was the last time Tag went to him. Tag stayed faithful to me and always came scampering across the grass when I called.

Each morning, Mike and Jim left for the docks hoping to snag a charter. If not, there were always repairs to do to the boat. While Mike was with us, I seldom went out on the Bambino. He could handle the mate's job better than I could.

Jim did well with the kite fishing. The Miami Herald came to the Club and scheduled a day of fishing. They took pictures of him reeling in a good-sized sailfish and wrote an excellent article for the paper. A few weeks later, they came back, made a picture of my sunburned face and floppy hat, and called me the fish lady. I caught a filefish that day; it is an unusual-looking fish with its flat body and sandpaper skin.

For a time, we had a little mutt dog I called Chopper. He was light brown with floppy ears. He got along fine with Tag, the cat, but I could not get him to stop chewing things. I sprinkled red pepper around, but it did not faze him. I had never had a puppy and did not know how to raise one. Yes, I had Rex; he was a Boxer, but I got him when he was already full-grown and the chewing phase was over. Poor little dog, he chewed our record collection. That was it. Back to the pound he went. I had feelings of remorse; I hope a more experienced owner got the little critter.

Dave, the carpenter, came to work every morning. He stopped in for a cup of coffee most mornings. He told me how the place was growing and when a house sold.

One morning Dave unexpectedly said, "You do know this place is anti-Semitic?" I could not figure out why he popped up with this comment. Perhaps, it was because I was not wearing the identifying sign of a Christian cross around my neck. I said nothing further to advance this conversation; I was not about to admit I was Jewish. There are times in my life I have not come out and revealed my birth religion. I never found it a necessity to proclaim unless directly asked, amid folks, telling jokes specifically geared to Jews, then I would say, "You know I am Jewish." I never was a follower and always felt one scrutinized Jewish people more critically. That has gone on for generations since the Spanish Inquisition.

Currently, Ocean Reef Club has a chapel, 'Our Community Many Congregations.'

One lucky morning I heard a knock on the door. I opened the door, and there stood a woman who worked for the resort. She had a little job for me. I had a typewriter and was happy to type the labels she brought me. I noticed the material contained literature about the resort aimed at possible new owners. I wondered if one of my mailings would produce a sale. Then, perhaps, they would see fit to give me a percentage; a good thought, highly unlikely.

After a few months, we bought a blue 1951 trunk-less jalopy that had seen better days. I had to learn how to drive it; I had never driven a standard transmission. A few lessons from Jim gave me the basic idea of how to operate it. I jerked down the rougher roads until I was able to get the hang of it. Now I could travel the twelve miles to town, down a well-paved road. The old car lacked an inspection sticker, and tag renewal required inspection. We drove to Sweetwater, a suburb of Miami. From North Miami to the Keys, this was the place to go if you owned a junk heap.

Pulling up to the window, the inspector questioned us, "What happened to your trunk?"

Jim quick to answer, "It flew off in Lake Surprise."

He squinted at us with a perplexed look, but he passed us. Lake Surprise is an extensive body of water just off the Overseas Highway in Key Largo. I used to go there to catch pinfish for bait. I took a rod, reel, bucket, some worms in a plastic container, and a net to scoop the fish from the lake as I was bringing my catch back alive. I positioned myself at the edge of the lake, casting into the calm waters. The chance of the trunk flying into the lake was a long shot, but the inspector did not know that.

On one of my outings, I was driving past the Angler's Club, with blooming purple bougainvillea at the entrance, and I got up the nerve to enter through the decorated iron gate and go into the main lodge. No one seemed to be present. Hanging on the wall was this quote, "The Assyrian tablet of 2000 BC says, 'The Gods do not subtract from the allotted span of men's lives the hours spent fishing.'" President Herbert Hoover, it was said, frequented this fish camp. As I turned, a tall man, dressed in casual attire, shorts, a collared T-shirt with the alligator to the left; he wore topsides and carried a creel basket in which to place his catch. He stood in the doorway, observing me. Approaching, wow, I thought I was in big trouble trespassing, he smiled.

"What can I do for you, young lady?"

"Well, Sir, on my occasional trips to town, you see, I pass your lovely flowered gate, and my curiosity got the better of me. I live at the Ocean Reef Club, and I realize

I'm a trespasser but was interested in seeing this place as the rumor is that President Hoover visits here."

"You are quite right, but the president has not been here of late. He has been sick."

President Hoover took office in 1929, at the time of the financial collapse and the beginning of the Great Depression. His term only lasted till 1933, four years, but has lived twenty-seven years to current date 1959, the longest of any president after leaving office." He passed in 1964. "Thank you for telling me all this; I'll be on my way now."

Further down the road was a three-cabin fish camp. Mom and Dad came to visit and stayed at this camp. Dad was an avid angler. We took them out fishing; Mom caught a sailfish, and Dad caught a few yellowtails and a grouper. He was delighted, and Mom sent her fish away to be mounted. That fish ended up on their living room wall; she was so proud. This fish camp had ramps to off-load a boat and put her on the ways. Before they left, we put the boat up in the air at the fish camp to scrape off barnacles and repaint.

Since I spent a lot of time by myself in my little cabin, it left me time to write some of the things I was experiencing. Here is one of the stories:

Unbelievable Life and Red Wine Passage, written on September 1, 1959

Driving down our twelve-mile access road, we spied two narrow abandoned pathways hidden by dense foliage. Planes fly overhead in an endless search to beat time, but in a remote area in the center of North Key Largo, time stands still. Each road seemed like a fascinating expedition. Each path began with cracked and broken pavements. Choosing the closest path to town we curiously, and cautiously stepped gingerly over broken holes and branches that had bowed their way into the road. Peering through the closely entwined leaves and twigs, we saw an opening in the brush; there were three dilapidated shacks, relics of times gone. Also, in this mosquito-infested territory was a deteriorating makeshift garage. It contained a Model-T-Ford in a rundown condition. To the left of the building, the rusted-out remains of another motor car leaned humbly decaying.

Looking ahead into this forest of leaves, and insects a human-made boardwalk of rotting unbalanced planks extended to the gateway of still another clearing. Upon approaching this spot, a large unfinished hull of approximately twenty feet protruded grotesquely into view. The spines had bits of the old canvas hanging from them. No decking remained; therefore, the keel was visible, and two torn upholstered seats still clung to the bulkhead. That seemed entirely out of place in these surroundings. There was no discernible boat trailer on site, and the water was not close. At the other end of this clearing, two aged shacks stood with their doors flung wide.

We suddenly realized, to our astonishment, that human life dwelled here.

"Good afternoon," Jim said, a bit surprised, "we happened upon this trail and followed it. We don't mean to be disturbing you."

"No worries, I just live here in de wood, isn't got no people, just stay here. My name it be Captain Tom Lowe. I be sixty-eight-years."

"How long have you been living here?" I inquired.

"Been here de past sixty years, no lectric, no one come. No water cept from rain."

He is a light Negro cast, with white stubble upon his chin and a full head of coal-black kinky hair. His eyes are bloodshot, spread far apart the wide bridge of his flat nose. His lips are big, and when he laughs, he displays a set of yellow pointed teeth. He was six feet tall and of medium build.

He slowly turned about and headed toward what seemed to be his dwelling, which contained a constantly smoldering stove. Through the years, it has caused the entire interior of the house to become black as soot. It is dark, dismal, and depressingly hot from the ever-constant burning embers. Tacked to the walls are old newspapers; the stove smoke has made them illegible.

Bugs are flying everywhere; I had to brush across my face to keep the tiny ones from getting into my eyes.

Captain Tom's dress identically resembles his living quarters' color and condition – dark, dirty, and unkempt. The old man of the woods appears physically strong with his slightly hunched over back and sturdy stance. From the way he speaks, I would say he indulged in the self-conversation since he talks fluently and comprehensively. He showed us some papers, and we could see he could read and write. He spoke of his childhood and showed us some books, plus an official document signed by Woodrow Wilson.

Jim said, "Thanks for showing us around. Hope we didn't bother you."

He just shook his head and said, "Naw, you'll come back."

As we left him, we wondered if anyone was aware he was living there.

The second pathway's approach revealed a maze of mangrove trees with roots anchored in the brackish water. Their broad, waxy leaves formed an opaque, nearly impenetrable entryway. These plants grow all along the southern coasts, not only in North America but also in South America, the Islands, and many countries overseas with shore-lines. They survive in saltwater and frequently mix with freshwater, thus making brackish water. Our egress was securely blocked at this path as the one prior was; we did notice a difference, though. The water is hardly moving through the upright roots, appeared red.

These were red mangroves; nowhere had I read that the water was tinged red wine color. We continued and saw a wooden bridge; only its charred base was jutting grotesquely from the Red Sea. Many sunlit and darkened hours passed since efforts to establish a passageway, failing to beat this hostile environment.

Months later, we returned to the old man in the woods. He was no longer there. His cabin vandalized, one of the shacks burned, and the hull smashed to smithereens. We searched about the property like junior investigators. We had all the knowledge of Perry Mason. Everything carried tinges of dark blotches, deciding they were not blood, only dampness laid upon the ground from the heavy dew. Sure not to disturb anything, although our footprints had already done the damage, our next stop was at the Monroe County substation.

The uniformed inspector looked up from his newspaper as we entered, "So what do you folks want?"

After we explained, he told us, "A month ago, old Tom Lowe walked in here just as you are doing. He said he was 'done wit de woods. Some nasty young white boys,' that is how he put it. 'They came into my place and ran through, knocking my things over and setting a fire. Scared me, I hid in the house behind my bed. I did't wit this city people coming into my home. Best I move on.'"

The officer assured us they had relocated him, and he was safe.

Back in our car, I said, "At least he is OK. That place was in shambles already; it is sad to think that we have hoodlums here. What did they think they would find – gold, silver, and treasure? You know, these Keys are full of treasure; maybe they thought the old man buried cannonballs or doubloons. Ah, there was not anything of value there. Poor old Tom Lowe."

Mike had brought prohibited marijuana into our lives. That was an evening pastime, enjoyed by the three of us. As our original stock dwindled, I sewed some pot seeds on the seldom-used airstrip on the resort. Venturing out to pluck some leaves, I discovered a large mower had chopped them up into an unrecognizable pile of grass. What a shame; they had grown taller than I had. The munchies always prompted Jim to ask me to bake a cake late at night. I had no objection to that. I can eat cake anytime. Entertainment in the evening consisted of *I Love Lucy*, Rod Serling's *Twilight Zone*, *Perry Mason*, *Milton Berl*, a variety of shows. The TV was a must; there was nothing else to do. At least in Marathon, there was a movie theater.

I was at home when suddenly a siren sound penetrated the still air. I drove down to the dock to see Mike lying on a gurney rolled into an ambulance.

"What happened," I questioned an anxious Jim.

"We were putting a green sailfish into the boat. Mike had gaffed him, but the way he was lifting him into the boat, the fish turned his head and stabbed Mike in the groin. I think he is OK, but for safety's sake, we called the hospital. Let's you and I follow the ambulance so that we can bring him home." Mike was OK but had become disgruntled.

Then, there was the day that the two boys headed into town by the Greyhound Bus. I took them to the station. Jim told me, "There will be no need for you to pick us up."

Strange, I thought, yet I went on my way and gave it no further thought as I did some grocery shopping in Key Largo's under-supplied store. After five, I heard a car pull up at our door. Looking out, I was shocked to see a late model green and white Plymouth driven by Jim. How in the hell was this possible; we had no money to buy a car?

"What is this?" I questioned in an agitated tone. "Where the hell did you get this car?"

"We stole it," was his response, a slight smirk on his unshaven face.

"What are you going to do with it?"

"What do you think, drive it?"

"It's stolen; I will not drive a stolen car," I answered. However, within a few days, I was driving it just around the Club. Instead of shifting, it had push buttons, but the ignition lock was hanging below the dashboard, and I was not comfortable handling a stolen car. It did not even take a month for the boys to dispose of it. They drove it into Lake Surprise.

Mike slowly drifted out of our lives as quickly as he had drifted onto our dock at Vaca Key situated a few feet from busy US 1. People driving by frequently stopped to chat; Mike was one of these people. There seemed to be a connection between him and Jim, and he hired him on the spot. Now that we were in a new location, the town was further away, and he lacked transportation; he decided to head for a city. We never heard from him again. I think he intended to take the stolen car, but on second thought, he must have reconsidered.

After a fishing day, Jim returned home with a large bird. He called it a frigate bird, but upon researching, I found no bird by that name. The birds hang around fishing boats, hoping to grab lunch, which is what this bird did. Jim snared him accidentally with fish bait, and the hook lodged in the bird's face. After he unhooked it, he thought I would like to see the bird. The bird's wingtips, when extended, spread from wall to wall in the kitchen, where it flew on top of the refrigerator and spent the night. The cat took one look at that bird and spent the night under our bed. Jim released it in the early morning.

In the late summer, Gar Wood, a well-healed angler and investor with Fin-nor fishing reels (considered the Rolls Royce of reels), came to our cabin to talk to Jim about captaining his boat on a fishing trip to the Bahamas. I cooked fresh Florida Crayfish, which Jim caught by hand earlier in the day.

Jim was thrilled, and after Gar left, he said, "This is a good moneymaking deal for me. I can probably pick up some other jobs that way." I was pleased too. The Club was not busy in the summer, and I thought it would be an excellent opportunity for him.

After returning from Bimini, all he could talk about was the boat and Pat, the girl that Gar had with him. "She laid in the sun, on the forward deck with no clothes," Jim told me.

"I guess you enjoyed that?" I said.

"Well, no need to be jealous, I didn't touch her, but she wears a lot of makeup and knows nothing about fishing."

"I never knew you to like makeup. Why do you always make a face when I put lipstick on?"

"You never wear it, and it looks strange to me."

"Well, no matter, she is a pretty girl," Jim said.

There were a few more fishing trips with Gar and the girl. Jim was excited about the fact that Gar wanted to fish in South America. He told me, "Off the coast of Peru from sport fishing boats are where they catch all the big black Marlins. They have contests to determine who catches the biggest one. An American caught it, and it weighed seven hundred and two pounds. Do you know that Earnest Hemmingway fished in Peru, and that is where he got the idea for the *Old Man in the Sea*? I have always wanted to do that. That was why we went to Cuba, which is known for big fish. I missed that chance because of Castro, and now I think this is my chance."

"No, I read the book but did not know that is where he got the idea. I thought he was fishing in Cuba," I commented.

All he talked about was the chance to catch the big fish, and I believe in catching the girl too. Our relationship began to suffer, until one day he said, "Let's take a ride into Miami; I want you to meet someone."

I had a feeling of foreboding; I felt things were about to change, and change they did.

CHAPTER 17:

_____

DECEIVED

The elevator ascended to the sixth floor of an upper-class condominium on Miami Beach. Jim was taking me to meet a girl, a girl that would be responsible for my undoing. Pat very politely ushered us into her home.

She was beautiful in a classy way. Dark hair cut short, massacred brown eyes, red lips, five-one, and one-hundred-and-five shapely pounds. In a relationship with Gar Wood, she was a paramour to a married millionaire inventor and a speedboat enthusiast.

He kept her in a stylish apartment, elegantly furnished. The mustard-colored couch had futuristic matching chairs with striped pillows, and there were coffee and end tables with matching lamps. There was floor to ceiling drawn sage drapes to give the room a sensual appeal with its indirect dim lighting.

Jim, the fisherman, had fortuitously met Pat while fishing on her lover's boat. Jim said, rather bravely, as he did not know what would happen, "Ruth, this is Pat, the gal I have told you about."

I politely responded even though I wanted to scratch her eyes out. "Hello, Pat, nice to meet you. You have a lovely place here." I felt shy in front of her, embarrassed and shocked. I was trembling inside with rage; a feeling of sickness overwhelmed me. I was determined not to let it show. One of the few times in my life, I was tongue-tied.

Whatever I had to say, or could have said, would not have changed the events that were to follow. It was awkward standing there. There was no reason to stay; Jim had introduced me to Pat, which was all we came to do.

"Nice meeting you. We have some errands to run," I said. Pat nodded, and I quickly exited.

Jim followed within minutes.

Back in the car, I was trying to gather my senses after the encounter. I was still shaken. I now had to figure out what my next move would be.

"Ruth, I am going to put the Bambino in dry dock. I want to sell her." He had it all figured out for me.

"Isn't this sort of sudden?"

"No, not really, I've been talking to Pat, and she wants to accompany me up north when I take Gar's boat to New Jersey for the summer."

"You're taking Gar's boat up north; does he know you are taking his bimbo too?'

"Sarcastic, always sarcastic, no, he trusts her."

"He trusts her? And I thought I could trust you?"

"Let's not get into it again. We've been talking about splitting up for months."

"So that's if you put the boat in dry dock, and I go where? What the hell are you going to do with me?"

"What do you mean, what am I going to do with you? You can stay on the boat."

"Well, isn't that nice of you!" I flippantly answered.

Before the boat went into dry dock, we formed an amicable truce. At my bidding, we went to see an attorney together. I felt it would be best to sever our relationship legally, even though we had not begun it legally. Many, many years later, I found out that Jim was married before he met me, so had he agreed to marry me, he would have been a bigamist.

Packed on the boat were our paltry belongings along with me; the boat went into dry dock. Jim departed with the prostitute. I should have learned my lesson from the Cuban floozy. He seems to have an affinity for sluts.

The day I was alone on board left me an emotional wreck. I angrily cried, chastised myself for my stupidity. I hated him and loved him. Had visions of his liaison with Pat, hated her, oh, how I hated her. She stole my man.

The following day, I left the boat and drove to New York with his new mate Chuck. He was six-foot tall, blond, blue eyes, slim build, and a good dresser. To save money, we rented a room with one bed.

The warmth of his body gave me comfort, and temptation won over my moral sense, and we slept together. When we reached New York, he went to New Jersey to meet Jim, and I went to my parent's home in Queens, where I spent the summer.

I had a brief job at Bobker Bearings in Long Island City. Then, I applied at Girl Friday and was placed at the Shell Oil Company. Here I met Mickey, a long-time employee. We spent our lunchtime together while I chatted about Jim. I was heartsick, and she was a compassionate friend with whom I am still in touch.

By July fourth, an anniversary of sorts, I was ready to get back on the merry-go-round and called Jim. I had no idea what kind of a greeting I would receive. After a few months of separation, I missed him.

"Hi, Ruth," he sounded upbeat and pleased to hear from me.

I asked, "What's up? How are you and Pat getting along?"

"How are you doing? Pat, well, she turned out to be a neurotic woman. She freaks out when her Tampax cord hits her leg. She goes all nutty. She clings to me, won't go out on her own. I can't take it anymore. I've got to bring Gar's boat back to Miami; you want to come?"

I thought for a brief moment. That was my chance to get back to Florida. "Sure, where will you leave from?"

I joined him and Chuck on the boat in Freeport, Long Island, New York. "Hi, Chuck, how was your summer?"

"It was OK, Ruth." There was no sign of our previous tryst.

Going thru the Dismal Swamp a second time I was sitting on the tuna-tower in Indian fashion, arms folded, legs crossed, Jim hit a sandbar somewhere in South Carolina. I went flying off the tower, bounced on top of the cabin and then the deck, and landed in ankle-deep water. The Coast Guard took me to the hospital. The tendons in my collarbone had broken, and they attempted to do nothing.

"Are you Ok, Ruth?

"I believe something snapped."

The nurse inquired, "Are you pregnant?"

"No, no, why?"

"In case you are, you may abort, and we can save the baby."

"No, no, I'm not pregnant."

Later Jim came to see me, and despite any discomfort I was experiencing he closed the door and we made love.

As my left bra strap slides off my shoulder today, I am reminded daily of this accident.

Finally, the boat repaired, and the propellers straightened, we took off for Florida. Chuck was exhibiting suspicious behavior, and I realized an affair was going on right under my nose. I had no clue Chuck was bisexual. Once again, Jim deceived me. A huge argument ensued; bitter words and accusations spilled out of me. Jim was no slouch either; he was cunning and spiteful. It came to a boiling point, and I exited the boat in Titusville, Florida, and took a Greyhound bus to Miami.

CHAPTER 18:

_____

MY WILDER SIDE

When I arrived in Miami, I stayed at the Royalton Hotel downtown and called a doctor. He told me he could do nothing for the tendons in my clavicle. He said the healing process had already begun.

Nowhere to live, I contacted a friend, Art. He sent me over to the Travelers Hotel in northwest 36th Street to a fellow named Phil. He offered me a cabana just off the pool. It had a jalousie wooden door, a bench to sleep on, and a rod to hang a few clothes. Only my clothes, which I had managed to salvage from the boat, were with me. As I went out applying for jobs, I would iron my dresses to look like an ordinary person living in a traditional house.

I submitted a job application to Southern Bell. After fulfilling all the requirements, I was hired on as an overseas operator. Supposedly, this job's qualifications were a bit stiffer than just becoming a 'number please' operator.

It was the beginning of the Communist takeover of Cuba. Spanish-speaking operators were behind me. I had to sit straight, with legs flat on the floor and with no crossing of legs. I was inserting a pair of phone cords into a jack to connect on a manual switchboard. I was able to make contact with all the islands of the Caribbean and Europe. That required four sets of cords, crisscrossing one another.

The din in the room was constant. English, Spanish, Dutch, French, and Portuguese conjured up an image of the Tower of Babble. Names such as Tegucigalpa,

Honduras, Caracas, Venezuela, and Montevideo, Uruguay brought about the desire to travel to these places.

It was a Saturday afternoon when Art showed up poolside. He was talking to Phil when I came around the corner.

Casually, I walked up and said, "Hi, Art."

"Hi, are you ready to move?"

"Move, sure where?" My heart skipped a beat; moving sounded good.

"The house I own, over near Southwest 8th Street, just became vacant. If you want it, at no charge for a while, you can have it," Art announced.

"No charge, I like that. I'll take it."

The house hardly had any furniture, except a bed upstairs and a couch in the living room. There was no electricity in the house. At night when I came home, on the bus, from work at Southern Bell in downtown Miami, I read until dark; the candle did not allow enough light for extended reading. Art would come by occasionally to be sure I was still there.

Because I was trying to get my life on track, the last person I needed to hear from was Jim Paddock. Once again, my mother was the go-between. He asked me to come to Deerfield Beach, where he lived in a small apartment with a girl. I went, probably against my better judgment; I met the girl and had not the vaguest remembrance of how she looked. He told me, "One night, she fell asleep on the couch with a cigarette and burned it up. The fire department came to put out the flames, and luckily, she was not hurt."

We talked for a few hours, excluding her from any conversation. I think Jim wanted a threesome, and I refused. I had to stay the night as it was too late to drive home. Early in the morning, I headed down to US 1 for my job. I arrived late, and that was not my first time. They were sticklers for punctuality, and they had previously corrected me for not keeping my feet on the floor. I now suffered the consequences for my indiscretion, and they fired me.

While staying at Art's house, after losing probably the best job opportunity I would ever have, I got a job at Hartley's Department Store in downtown Miami. It was November 8, 1960, a memorable day for me, as it was the first time I had voted. I felt I had attained adulthood voting for John F. Kennedy, my choice for President of the United States. I was thrilled to be able to accomplish this single act of voicing my opinion. For years, I had joined the discussion at home with Nicky, a Republican, and Mom, a Democrat. When I came home, a few people were sitting on my couch, friends of Art, and by candlelight, we talked about Kennedy.

In 1961, Art rented my space in his house, and I moved to a bungalow off Southwest 8th Street. I was still working at Hartley's. On days off, I spent time in Miami Beach and befriended a lifeguard, John Stevens. He had lost his place, moved in with me, and slept on my couch. I had a soft heart for helping out people in a jam. The homeowner got wind of it and asked me to leave.

Moving over to Miami Beach seemed like a good idea as I was spending more time on the beach. While I was apartment hunting late one afternoon, the Miami Beach police pulled me over. I had two friends in the car: Paul Richards from Chester, Pennsylvania, and a fellow he had picked up along the way. Paul did not have the proper ID, and I opened up my mouth to defend him. The officer told me to shut up, and I replied, "Drop dead." That got me a ride to the Jailhouse. An officer read my rights to me, fingerprinted, photographed, and placed me in a tiny holding cell just like any convict.

I thought I could get out of the mess by saying, "I know the Captain."

It only took moments for an over six-foot, redheaded police officer to open the cell door and let me know, "You don't know me."

"Well, no, I don't know you, but I know your brother Art."

"That will go nowhere in this police department. Don't ever say you know me," the officer was angry. That was a stupid move.

After a time, a bail bondsman showed up, and for twenty-five dollars, they released me. I arrived late at court. The judge chastised, me and then credited me with time served. Either the court or the bondsman kept my money. That cost me twelve-dollars-and-fifty-cent a word.

I found a nice size place on 46th street and with John, and now Paul, who had asked if he could make my home his too; it became party central. Beach lifeguards sometimes stopped by with girlfriends and beer and ended up sleeping on the floor. It was hard to keep the noise contained, which contributed to why I sought another place to live.

Aside from constant evictions, my job record was looking pitiful. Getting jobs was no problem; holding them was another? A somewhat upscale hotel, the Beau Rivage on the north beach, hired and fired me. Venetian Isle Motel decided they didn't want me either. I had spoken to a guest, and that was prohibited. My confidence and self-esteem were suffering. I was the culprit to blame; too much nightlife.

Homeless once again, I found a house for rent on Lennox Avenue, right where the downtown bus stopped. I was now working for Alvin's Women Apparel. I shared the Lennox Avenue house with Ricky Masters, a drag queen I met at a café I frequented on

Park Avenue. He was working as a chef, and for a few weeks, I worked there too. I also met a Miami Beach detective, Al Harp, who became my benefactor with benefits. It was only later that he mentioned his wife, Estelle.

More on that later in the gun shop story.

Ricky would be waiting for me at our house as I exited the bus. He cooked me dinner, and on the nights he went to the gay bar, I watched him change from an attractive young man into a classy female. We had an arrangement; when either of us had company, the other stayed in their part of the house. One night, I had a visitor.

Miami Beach was a tourist Mecca during the 1960s. Many young people came to the beach to find work at the hotels. Acquaintances were casual, short-lived, and numerous. The Tiki bar was a hangout on the beach where the lifeguards patronized, and I did too. I had one unforgettable night when I drank too much. It was after closing, and I staggered from the bar to the curb outside, where I sat and threw-up. Embarrassed even today, I learned a lesson and seldom imbibed liquor. I was single, looking for fun and friends, and this is how I hooked up with this odd assortment of out-of-towners. No one was permanent. We all were moving through the river of life, experiencing in our youth, which would not occur again. Too soon, the vitality of youth will fade, and we will recollect our days of glory.

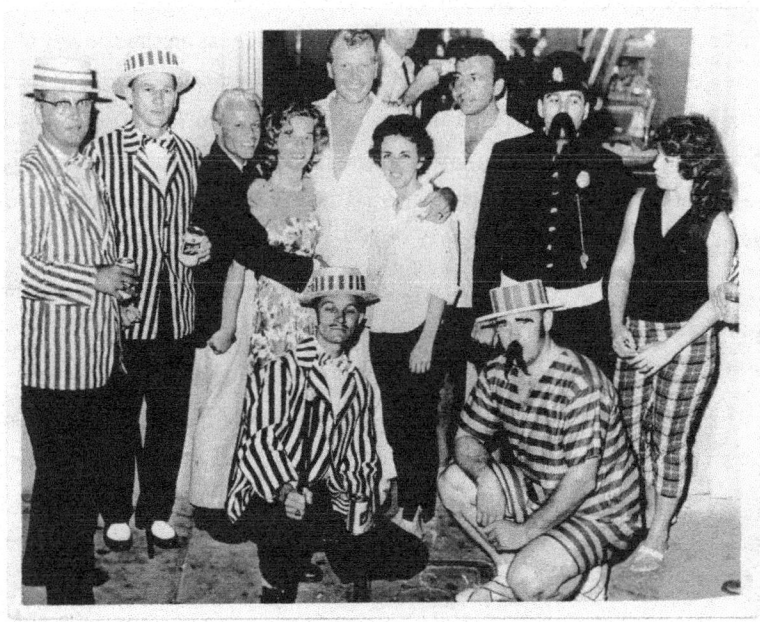

CHAPTER 19:

PREGNANT AND ALONE

My visitor Jim showed up in September 1961. My mother, his constant informant, told him how to reach me. The sexual attraction I had for this man was hard to contain. We made love, and on June 24, 1962, my son, Jerry, was born.

I had been working at the Biscayne Osteopathic Hospital. Richard Swanson, a resident doctor, and I became friendly. He needed to get to Texas and had no way of getting there. He had to take his Comprehensive Osteopathic Medical Licensing Examination to practice medicine in Texas. I offered to rent a car, and off to Texas, we went. Caught speeding along a Texas highway, I paid the fine to the police officer immediately. What chance did that money have of getting into the town coffers? I dropped my friend off in Dallas and took a Greyhound bus home.

When I returned, I had no job, and my roommate Ricky had walked out, stealing my sewing machine. Unable to keep the place and not wish to trust another roommate, I had a month to relocate.

I had luckily met Beverly Poe, a barmaid at Art's bar in the Carillon Hotel. Bev had long brown hair cascading down her back. We became instant friends. She told me she had rented a place on West Avenue with her five-year-old daughter Jennifer, and her mother, Gladys. Sadly, she said, "My mother has a tumor in her stomach and is scheduled for an operation."

A few days later, I accompanied Bev to the hospital. The staff mistakenly took both Bev and I as her daughters. That made me privy to her mother's personal information.

Bev was working on the day the doctors revealed, "During the operation, we discovered a cauliflower-shaped growth, and when handled, the petals fell away. It is impossible to remove: the tumor is inoperable."

With no other choice, Bev returned home with Gladys to live out her days.

Two blocks from the Morton Towers where Pat, Jim Paddock's lover, once lived, oddly enough, her number was 833 West Avenue. That was my new residence number. Strangely, the numbers were the same, but had no resemblance to each other. My building was a relic of old Miami Beach's weekend getaways. It most likely was built in the 1920s as a small walk-up hotel; it had a dozen rooms on the second floor, one I rented. Beverly's family lived down the hall.

There was a Murphy bed, invented circa 1876, as a space saver in small apartments. This innovative-hinged sleeping apparatus folded up and stored vertically on the wall. The bathroom was huge compared to the kitchen, which I was only capable of walking into sideways to reach the ancient gas stove. But, the rent was a remarkable sixty dollars during the off-season and forty dollars during the summer.

For nine months, I lived in a dark green painted room. I had four months of morning sickness and hardly gained any weight. I was ninety-eight pounds when I got pregnant and one-hundred-nineteen pounds at full term. I was alone and lonely. I had trouble sleeping and took purple sleeping pills. In the 1960s, the Thalidomide disaster sleeping pills caused children to be born without or shortened limbs; this drug could not have been what they prescribed.

I had friends, but none of them came to visit. Al came only late in the afternoons after work, but never on weekends. That was the worst time, and I took to writing sad papers about how I felt. I tried to hold down a job at Kelly Girls, but the morning discomfort ended that for me. I tried a few more times, but I think the sideways glances at my finger, minus a wedding band, discouraged employment.

Fortunately, I had Al, who was compassionate about my condition. When he opened up a bar in the Cadillac Hotel on Collins Avenue, he put me to work behind the bar, and I closed out at night. It was a large room with a band and dancing. One night, I talked to and danced with a kid named Jerry, who was so sweet. His actions must have influenced me to call my son after him. Eventually, Al had to introduce me to his wife, Estelle. I tried to be as cool as possible, but I'm sure she knew there was more to my presence. I told her that we were the briefest of acquaintances and that my tummy had nothing to do with her husband. I tried not to listen when their voices rose in the hallway. When it became apparent that my time was near, Al put me up in a rooming house across the street near the hotel. One shocking morning soon after, I awoke, and as I stood, my water broke.

Al had arranged for a police officer to pick me up and deliver me to the hospital.

The delivery was not easy. After hours of labor, I was taken to the floor above for x-rays to ensure the baby would fit through the small opening I was offering. Wheeling me back to the labor floor the nurse inquired how I was doing. I told her, "I am still in intense pain." The doctors administered pain medication to reduce the pain, and finally, eighteen-hours later, my boy child was born to an unwed mother. Fret not, Jerry; you may now join the ranks along with Confucius, Leonardo Da Vinci, Alexander Hamilton, and Lawrence of Arabia, all unwed mothers. My darling, innocent baby, never let the circumstances of your birth deter your ambitions. It had been a laborious birth, but he had all his fingers, toes, and a pink splotch on his left cheek from the forceps delivery. He did not cry until the nurse smacked his foot to wake him up.

Jerry and I had a two-day stay at Baptist Memorial, and then Al whisked us to a room in the back of the Cadillac Hotel. I had no desire to breastfeed and painfully swelled up. Packing my breasts in ice was my only relief.

I strung a line to dry diapers, and I had a diaper delivery service set up by Al. The formula and all the essentials were available in this unlikely nursery. The hotel supplied the crib.

After five days, my mother showed up to see her only-ever grandchild. Every letter from my mother for the nine months of my pregnancy had expressed doubt that I could not take care of a baby without a husband. She unconditionally fell in love with Jerry, and I believe she chastised herself for questioning my ability. I'll grant you my pregnancy was unexpected, but I had the strength of my convictions. Giving my baby up was never a thought. I wanted a boy, and I got what I wanted.

I know Nicky influenced my mother. Born in 1882, he carried the Victorian belief that a pregnant woman having a child out of wedlock was a 'shame' to the family. They placed the woman in a 'house of shame' in those years, and suitable parents adopted her baby.

Mom went back to New York, and I moved a few blocks away to Indian Creek Drive.

Baby Jerry and I were getting along famously. He was eating his Gerber baby food like a champion. I found a sitter and went to work at Les Violins, a fancy Latin Supper Club and bar, as the evening barmaid. It was in downtown Miami, near the Venetian Causeway.

Jerry was four weeks old, and I was feeling nervous and teary. I developed a rash, of all places, on my eyelids. I had to wear sunglasses to hide them. Every night I came to work, the bar manager instructed me to go to the restaurant and eat dinner. It was their way of showing appreciation for their help. They usually fed me steak or lobster with all the toppings.

One afternoon at home, I had an unexpected visitor. It was Mary Paddock, Jim's stepmother. She came to see the baby and reported that the baby looked just like Jim, Jr.

Her visit prompted a call from Jim, and I took Jerry downtown to see him. Jim saw Jerry once when he was three months old. He was staying at the Howard Johnson's Hotel in the city. I left Jerry with him while I ran an errand. Upon returning, Jerry had soiled all over his father. He acknowledged the baby but had no intention to stay around.

I had not heard from Jim for a long time. One day, he came to town, called me at work, and asked if I would like to accompany him to the Keys on a boat delivery. After we drove back to Miami, I took him to our house to meet his eleven-year-old son. Jim sat in the living room; I called Jerry and introduced him to his dad. Jerry was not impressed, and we never heard from Jim again.

When Jerry turned fifty, I did a massive Ancestry.com search for his ancestors. They were whalers off the coast of Massachusetts in the 1600s, supplying oil to light the lamps and exporting it to Europe. There was a Paddock island named for them in Boston Harbor, now called Peddock Island. I do not know if Jim even knew this as he never spoke of family.

One of his great, great, great grandfathers married a woman who was the daughter of a Mayflower passenger, making all following descendants qualify as Mayflower descendants. One stipulation to claim this distinguished honor is to supply evidence of your ancestors. I was able to find all ancestors except Jerry's father, who, by all accounts, is dead with no records. According to my diligent research, he died in Costa Rica at the age of approximately forty-eight.

I chanced upon the man who was a radio and TV commentator and a client on Jim's boat Stormy. As we spoke, he said, "I had fished with Jim Paddock a couple of times. The last time I saw Jim on his boat, Stormy, he brought a dark woman aboard and collapsed on the forward bunk. I had to bring the boat back to the dock. I was unaccustomed to handling that boat. It was an uphill battle for me. I will compliment Jim on his fishing expertise but must voice my disgust at his rude behavior. I know of Jim's amazing fishing feats. I know of articles and books that quote him." He gave me names of the magazines and books with passages Jim wrote and others about him. I located and collected them for Jerry.

One of the articles spoke of his fishing knowledge and that Jim Paddock passed. By noting the date of the magazine, I determined when he might have died.

I can only assume he died of a drug overdose or drowned. I will never know.

Postpartum had a hold of me, and I could not hold down the job and even found it challenging to deal with Jerry. He was now three months old. I had no choice but to leave Miami and seek help up north from family.

In September, we arrived in New York at my mom's home in Forest Hills, Queens. That evening, my mother's cousin, whom I called Aunt Gretel, and her husband, Uncle Ludwig, were visiting. I was appalled when Mom began to inform Gretel that the baby belonged to someone else. She was ashamed to tell her he was mine.

The get-together was to remember my eighty-six year old grandmother. It saddened me that she had passed without the knowledge of her great-grandson. I held deep feelings for my grandmother and knew she would understand my situation. She was outspoken and would have expressed her dissatisfaction with the way Nicky behaved toward my baby and me.

Nicky would not let us stay in the apartment. My dad came to get me, and we went to his home in Irvington, New Jersey. He gave me a room on the third floor with a window overlooking the roof. The squirrels would come on the roof, and visit and Jerry would laugh and point at them.

Margot's cousin Edith lived on the second floor with her two children, Benno and Jane. Janie was about eleven and loved to come up and feed Jerry and play with him. Benno was a bit shy and spent his days watching television. More about Jane later.

While home with baby Jerry, Dad found me a job typing envelopes paying one-half cent per piece. He would deliver the finished job and bring more home.

Years before, in downtown New York I had a job in an old building walk-up stuffing envelopes. It was a mail-order business sending pretty girls to G.I.s like Betty Grable's famous 1943 pin-up picture. Along with Betty were more revealing photos that I felt were inappropriate. I learned how to flip envelopes so the closure flap would fall over the envelope. A lesson learned, but not a long-lived job.

In a local paper, I found a job in another town. It was with a writer who needed some typing done. I took Jerry in his carriage, rode a bus, and walked a few blocks to his house. Snow showed up one day, and it became too difficult and cold to take Jerry out. I gave up the job.

Living with Dad and Margot was the best thing that could have happened. Dad was elated to be a grandfather. On weekends, we drove to Phoenicia, New York, where they had purchased a hundred year old farmhouse. They were remodeling it to have it ready when he retired.

Dad would take Jerry into the quaint mountain town and proudly introduce him to the shopkeepers. I was so pleased to see him displaying his grandson.

After six months, I recovered from post-partum blues and was ready to take Jerry back to Florida.

Beverly and her family had moved into a two-story apartment on Alcazar Avenue in Coral Gables. It was an old pink Spanish-style building. They had designed the building in a circle with an interior courtyard with a bench surrounding a currently broken water fountain. The four corners of the tower had one-half of a second story, and we called that the crow's nest, where Jerry and I moved in temporarily.

One morning I felt a growth under my arm. After consulting with a doctor, he decided I needed a biopsy. Leaving Jerry with Bev for a few days, I went to the hospital and hoped it would amount to nothing. He cut under my arm to remove the node and unknowingly damaged a nerve in my arm. That left portion of my upper arm stayed numb for years. The operation was successful. The doctor decided I was allergic to cats, which caused the problem.

Beverly's mother was still with her, but her health was failing rapidly. Beverly came up with a plan to take care of her mother. She married Charlie Daugherty, who came from a local Miami family and had a plot at Woodlawn Cemetery. That would enable her to bury her mother in dignity. After her mother passed, Beverly moved out to live with Charlie. There was no love, and the marriage was not a success.

I moved into an available vacancy in the next-door apartment at 395 Alcazar Avenue. The Alcazar apartment was called an efficiency apartment with one bedroom, a living room/ kitchen with a bamboo pull-up shade to block off the kitchen, and down the hall, a bath where I washed Jerry's diapers and clothes in the tub until I became more solvent and patronized the Laundromat.

I worked for Howard Johnson's, and before leaving for work in my white uniform I brought Jerry outdoors and sat on the bench, watching him play before taking him to the sitter.

My waitress-fountain job began at three o'clock and ended at ten. I was able to pick Jerry up from the sitter, who was across the courtyard in another building. I would carry him home sleeping and put him to bed. It was a perfect job for me at that time.

The following morning, when I reported for work, the manager told me, "You are fired."

"What have I done?"

"You stole a tip from one of the other girls."

"There is no way I did that; she is lying."

"There is nothing I can do," he said.

I drove to downtown Miami, to the main headquarters of Howard Johnson, and begged for my job.

"There is nothing I can do."

That was bullshit; I never stole a tip. I was mad. The hell with waitressing; I would get a real job and applied in a Girl Friday Office. This work was more up my alley.

In 1963, and for a few months into 1964, I worked for the American Publishing Company. They sent out booklets to folks that desired to become postal employees. There was an IBM Executive typewriter. I didn't know how to work it, but I conned my boss into believing I knew how. I knew nothing about the proportional spacing, but I figured it out. The boss tried to chase me around the desk and asked me to his place at lunchtime. I held the job without complying; I needed to work.

He always kept the radio turned on. On Thursday, November 22, 1963, I heard the devastating news of our president's death. I called my mother; I knew they only listened to the newscast at five. He let me go home. I picked up Jerry and tried, with the television on, to explain the tragedy to my boy. I stayed glued to the small screen. I knew I was watching history unfold. All the dignitaries, Oswald, and then no Oswald, the police headquarters' commotion, and the sympathy I felt for Jackie and her young family overwhelmed me. One emotion after another played out on national television. It was a horrible weekend. I kept wondering how the sun could shine the next morning. I left that job and found employment elsewhere, working for Kelly Girls for a time until I found a decent paying job. Each time I changed jobs, my pay was a little higher.

Al stopped by once to give me the sad news that his oldest son had passed away from a brain tumor. He was all broken up. He gave up the bar and went back to being a full-time detective until he retired. It was 1974, a chance encounter I saw Al on Bird Road; he was walking a little dog. We spoke a few words acting like strangers. Later, I heard he passed away.

Hurricane Cleo slammed into Miami on August 27, 1964. All night the winds blew, and rain pounded the roof. It rattled the second-floor shutters while Jerry slept, and I listened. After the blow, we rode around to see all the downed branches. Delicately circling any wires live or not, we drove out to Matheson Hammock, our public swimming hole. It was a deserted beach. Not a swimming day, just a training experience so Jerry would know how dangerous hurricanes could be. Trees were disturbed, leaves scattered, and sand blown on the road. I drove around puddles, careful not to fall into a hole.

When I was in the kitchen, Jerry crawled out of his crib and got into my purse. He found my lipstick and smeared it all over his face and the mirror. I could not keep the little devil in his crib. A friend gave me a baby bouncer. I could see his moving toddler legs protruding from the holes in the seat, reaching to the floor and impulsively pushing against the floor. The Alcazar was a sufficient apartment, with one bedroom, a living room/kitchen with a bamboo roll-up shade to block off the kitchen, and a hallway to the bath. I washed Jerry's diapers and clothes in the tub until I became more solvent and patronized the Laundromat.

I didn't roll-down the shade for two months. When I did, I was disgusted and astounded. The shade was alive with hundreds of crawling German roaches. They were so happy in there that they never came out. I felt creepy all night. The following day, I took Jerry to Esmeralda, my new sitter and neighbor. I then bought a bug bomb, lowered the shade, and set the bomb off. That evening, before picking Jerry up, I vacuumed the littered floor with a borrowed cleaner from Brenda, an office girl at Manufacturers Mutual Insurance.

Soon we had new neighbors. Two and sometimes three college graduates moved in from the University of Miami. Ted Trowbridge, one of the boys, and I became good friends.

The aqua Chevy was our transport while Jerry was still small enough to sit in a seat hooked onto the front cushion. I came to a sudden stop, and Jerry swung backward. The car had no back seat, and there was a spare tire exposed on the floor. The sudden stop moved his seat forward and back, throwing him into the rear. How his head did not hit the rim of the tire, I'll never know?

One day Ted had a job interview and no car. I offered him the use of my Chevrolet. He took me to work, and then he used the car for the remainder of the day. Thanking me profusely, we became almost lifelong friends.

Nearly every night before Jerry had to go to bed, Ted came over to play with him. He would get him all excited, hiding and laughing, and then go home, leaving me with a wild child.

The college boys came over one night and helped me hang wallpaper. The exterior walls were eight-feet high, whereas the back sloped down, making it easier to reach. My Cuban neighbors gave me some food they received in their refugee packages. When the Cubans began arriving in Miami, the Freedom Tower was their first stop in downtown Miami, which stands seventeen stories above the city and the bay. That is what they saw as their boats pulled into the Miami harbor. It was the reception area for Cuban exiles from Castro's Island from 1962 until 1974. Today the building is a museum. They did not eat the oatmeal or the two-pound chunk of American cheese. I cooked the oatmeal up for the boys at ten-thirty at night, and it was so thick that the spoon stood erect in the pot. We had many laughs. The wallpaper job partially completed was never finished.

When Ted married, he and his bride Carol asked me to be a bridesmaid. My mother bought my turquoise dress as she knew I would enjoy the experience. She figured I wouldn't have another opportunity again as I was getting older. Also, I could not afford to buy a dress.

Jerry celebrated his one-year birthday with Esmeralda, her daughter, and a friend or two of mine. He walked on his birthday, frequently dragging his blanket behind. As he grew, he rode his tricycle up and down the street.

We were outgrowing our small-size living quarters. I had thoughts of clotheslines, a garden, and a larger play area for Jerry. Beverly and Ted had moved away, and I heard of plans to demolish the building. It became a Burger King. It had not been the easiest of times, but I was carrying away fond memories.

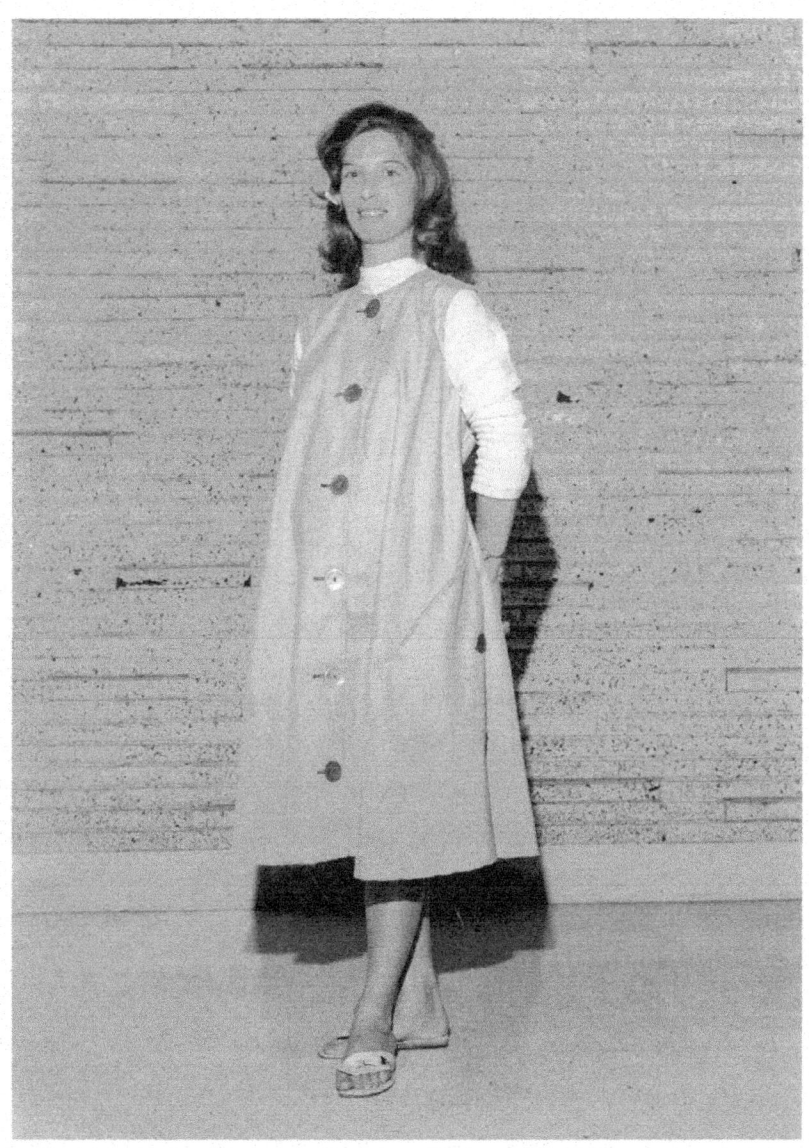

Ruth, pregnant April 1962"

PART THREE

CHAPTER 20:

ROGER AND JERRY

Saturday was Jerry, my three-year-old son's day to romp in the outside world away from our city street. With no destination in mind on that seldom chilly day, I headed west on the Tamiami Trail on the west side of Miami. I wanted to drive until something sparked our interest.

About twenty miles out, a hidden brown building appeared. The front door stood open, and a man sat on the ground holding up the building, or maybe it was the other way around. He dressed in jeans and a T-shirt advertising an airboat ride. He was clean-shaven with brown hair, a slim fellow about twenty-four years old and six feet one inch tall. As we approached he let out a friendly, "Hi, how are you folks doing today?" he said while he checked out this woman and a small child.

Not a shy boy, Jerry asked, "What are you doing?"

"I'm sitting here having a smoke. It's a slow day."

"What do you mean, slow day?"

"Not too many people came out to ride on airboats today."

"What's inside?" Jerry inquired.

"Oh, it's your regular country store, a few drinks, some souvenirs, fishing tackle, and of course the airboats outside."

"Jerry, we can walk around; there does not seem to be much more here to amuse us." We were just hanging around, and it was getting awkward.

"Hay," I looked in the direction of the current proprietor and said, "By the way, what is your name?"

"I'm Roger Blohm, new to Florida from New Jersey. I have not yet found a place to stay, and the accommodations in this wayside shop are nil."

I introduced myself and said, "You already know this is Jerry. I didn't see a sign out-front; does this place have a name?"

"This place is Coopertown, population about six. Jerry, have you ever seen an alligator?" Roger inquired.

"An alligator, no."

Roger took us behind the shop and down a path to a watery place surrounded by saw-grass. Taking Jerry's baby hand, he pointed to the middle of the swamp where two eyes were staring at us.

"Oh, Mom, look an alligator. Can we get closer?"

Roger quickly put his hand up, saying, "No, no closer, alligators can run eleven miles an hour on land and sometimes faster. In the water, they are quicker and can swim twenty-miles an hour. I'll tell you what; if you want to see more alligators, we can go out in an airboat."

"Can you take one of those out, Roger?" I asked, thinking it was a huge responsibility.

"Sure; that is what I do; come on, the boats are over there."

We were his only non-paying clients. Airboats are flat, aluminum bottom, open boats capable of gliding through the shallow water. Cutting through saw grass and marshes, they can travel at sixty miles an hour. Their propulsion, surrounded by a cage, protects the propeller from objects flying into them. Aircraft propellers are the power that moves the boats, with either aircraft or automobile engines mounted on the back. We sat on an elevated seat so that we could watch in front and avoid debris. Roger traveled at a safe speed so we could see the alligators. It was powerful engine noise, and it bruised Jerry's tender ears.

"Jerry, let me tell you about these Gators. They are prehistoric. Do you know about dinosaurs?"

"Yes, I know Tyrannosaurus Rex."

"Well, the Gator has been around for one hundred eighty million years, so he can be called a dinosaur. One Gator can live fifty years and can grow to nine feet long. Look, there is one across the water. He is sunning himself now; as he sees us he will slide into the water."

"Mom, look, look, he is big. Wow, Splash! There he goes."

Although the noise was daunting, the vast, untamed wilderness was exhilarating. To absorb all the mysteries of animals and plants in one day was futile. Instead, I concentrated on the abundant stag-horn ferns reaching out in multiple directions from the mother host tree.

Orchards poked their yellow and purple heads through the thin blades of sawgrass. Their tall, delicate stems were gyrating from the water's action beneath their tender roots.

It was time to turn back; Roger had proven to be an informative guide. As I was walking back to our car I thought I would offer the fellow a place to stay. He wouldn't be the first man I picked up at the spur of the moment. He seemed harmless enough; I didn't think he would cut our heads off.

I asked, "Roger, since you have no place yet, would you like to come and stay with us?"

He was quick to respond, "If you think you have room, yes, I would like to stay."

I had a white Ford, and Roger followed me in his Oldsmobile. I brought Roger into my two-bedroom, first-floor apartment in South Miami.

Within the first week, Roger was able to locate a job. That was good as I knew he would contribute to our household. Although I was working, women's salaries were not equal to men's.

Roger and I were getting on well, and most importantly, Jerry liked him. Roger expressed the idea that someday we may marry. I was not ready yet.

One weekend Sarah, a friend from my work, Jerry, and I got together at her Mom's home. Meeting Sarah's mother was the most fortuitous get-together of Jerry's young life. Mrs. Goodwin noted that Jerry's speech was not as understandable as a three-year-olds should be. I had no trouble understanding him, but she said he had hearing loss, and therefore was not speaking accurately. Mrs. Goodwin was correct. Clogged Eustachian tubes affecting his middle ear distorted his hearing. Jerry spent one night in the hospital to remove his adenoids and tonsils and then came home to recover. Jerry's speech improved radically within a few months.

Roger tended to Jerry as I took his car a few miles away to fill a prescription. I parked in front of the pharmacy. When I returned to the car and shifted it into reverse, I heard a frightening thud. I had snapped the drive shaft. The three-inch steel drive shaft piece, much to Roger's dismay, became a paperweight.

Roger bought an old panel truck, thinking ahead to have a handyman business that he could do on the weekends, picking up odd carpentry jobs and plumbing. He joined the South Miami Moose Lodge and did work on their property. Aside from private Moose meetings, which he could not talk about, they also had social nights on Saturday evenings. There were dances once a month, and Roger and I would go. We practiced the foxtrot at home as he wanted our dancing to be perfect. Roger was a good dancer, never held me close, just the proper length away from his body. Holding my hand, he turned me around and never missed a step. He would get annoyed if I made a misstep. I hired a babysitter for these nights. Roger took her home after, and I found out he made a pass at her. To attract her attention, later he threw pebbles at her window. That was a warning sign; I should have paid attention.

The other big event at the Moose was bingo. The ladies were experienced players, whereas I was a novice. I can recall winning one game and not be a fan of bingo; I stayed home. It did not seem worth it to get a sitter. They also had a bar, and most of the people were drinkers, including Roger. He preferred a bit of beer and no hard drinks. I was not a drinker and found it challenging to fit in.

Within three months, we moved out of the apartment to a rental house on 44th Street. It did not take long to see the termites flying about the place. Only tenting the house would get rid of them. That would be up to the owners; otherwise, they were not leaving. The termites didn't bother us; they were only eating up the house.

The house was two bedrooms with one bath and a small backyard. It was enough room for the three of us, but we were thinking of expanding the family. That never happened. We lived there for about a year-and-a-half.

Across the street, there was a light-yellow house with green awnings and night-blooming cactus towering up higher than the roof. When it went up for sale, we bought it.

I never wanted to move across the street again and carry all of our belongings over to a new house. Roger did all the heavy lifting along with a few friends.

While making a move to keep Jerry out of the way, I took him to a local church for summer classes to give him some of that good old religion, Presbyterian style. As he came down the stairs after school, I noticed how pigeon-toed he was, practically tripping over his own feet.

The Orthopedic doctor fitted him for a brace wrapping around his waist with aircraft rubber cables running down his legs and attached with metal to the bottom of his shoes. It did not slow him down one bit. He ran, rode his bike, and slept in it. He was so active that he broke the shoe attachment. The cobbler that repaired it said, "Never in all the years since I have worked on these braces have I had a child break them." To say he was a wild, super energetic kid was an understatement.

Alexander Day school, his nursery school, asked me one day, "Jerry is so active I hate to ask you, but do you keep him restrained or locked in a closet?"

"Of course not; he is very active." After nursery school, he came home and ran around the house. I felt maybe that he was too active. He began taking Ritalin, which was supposed to calm him down. He remained on it for a year, and then I took him off. I repeated it in first grade again, and then he asked me to stop giving it to him, which I did.

After we bought the house across the street, Roger purchased two original wagon wheels; he cemented at the Ixora hedge's edge to dress-up the walkway. At the entrance on the left-hand side of the front yard, he installed a lamppost. Jerry and I planted a sweet potato, and the leaves climbed up the post.

Roger planted a banyan tree in the middle of the backyard, which grew tall enough for Jerry to climb. There was a lime tree way in the back, and on the left side of the yard; the previous owners had planted fifteen different varieties of rose bushes. I acquired an education on how to cut, fertilize, and propagate them. Roger didn't do any work with them.

In time Roger, an animal and plant enthusiast, sectioned off the back portion of the yard and planted a vegetable garden. Roger knew all about plants. He knew how to improve the soil with metal shavings. He collected these from mechanical shops and showed Jerry how to sprinkle them in the garden. We all walked a cow pasture and collected dung. It was not messy as it had been in the sun and dried out. Roger and Jerry took the patties, spread them around the garden, and then dug them into the soil. He did the same with the chicken residue, which we collected at a chicken ranch. Jerry did not want to do the chicken ranch again. The noise of the chickens and the smells were atrocious. Roger and Jerry spent hours planting vegetables, which we harvested and ate. After we parted, this strip of land became overgrown and the habitat for unwanted critters.

One day, Roger came home with a baby raccoon that he found on the side of the road and built him a wood and wire cage with a tree inside so he could climb. We named him Bandit. As he grew, he became too wild for me to handle, and one day he chewed his way out of the cage and disappeared. Roger had more success with the turtle's Jerry and I had collected along roadways. Seven varieties lounged in the pond that he built them.

Roger was a good dad. As he formed the turtle pond and put together cages, Jerry was by his side learning. They put together a rabbit cage, and we had baby rabbits, but I will not tell you what the male did. If more babies were born, they had to stay away from the buck.

Our most exotic feathered pet was a pheasant. I did not know the bird's medical problem, but I had to feed the bird with a dropper. When doing so, the pheasant choked and died. Oh! I had killed him. I sat there with the dead bird in my lap, crying. What terrible thing had I done? Roger finally came home and took care of the beautifully feathered bird.

On July 5, we drove to Daytona Raceway for the Independence Day car races. There was a great deal of excitement and noise. Roger explained the flag system to Jerry, but although Jerry enjoyed the cars going round and round, the noise bothered him.

Many an evening, Roger would come home with a couple of buddies from the Homestead Bar that was a few blocks from the house. They sat around drinking beer, and occasionally Roger took out his guitar and sang some Country and Western songs.

Roger changed jobs frequently. He felt that if he worked for himself, he would be happier. He rented a warehouse next to the Miami River. He pictured himself as a boat engine mechanic. For company, he took Crystal along, Jerry's black and white dog. She was not a prudent dog and got pregnant. My fault rather than hers since I had neglected to have her spayed. Roger ended up having no success with boats. Instead, he rented a 76 gas station and put his mechanical skills to work.

Roger surprised us by buying a twenty-four-foot inboard cabin cruiser with two sleeping bunks. He checked out docking facilities along the river, but that was not practical, so he looked to Goulds, a railway stop of the Florida East Coast railway. Rog found a wide street with a canal running beside; way down that street, it exited to the bay. He built a dock out of four-inch-thick Styrofoam blocks and added a wooden deck. He hooked it to a protruding pipe along the bank, tied the boat up, and it stayed there long after our use of it. Jerry and I only remember going out to sea three times. Once on a rough day, we were out in the bay, and poor six-year-old Jerry was so sick he didn't care about fishing, just wanted to go home.

After we were together a year and a half, on September 20, 1966, a Justice of the Peace married Roger and me. There was no rah, rah, rah, or throwing of rice. We decided to take our honeymoon later. I looked forward to this union with optimism. I thought that getting married would lend stability to our relationship. I had doubts about Roger's beer-drinking habit but figured I would get accustomed to it. My immediate family members were not drinkers, and exposure to this kind of life was new.

Roger was a good father figure, and to cement the bond, I prepared adoption papers. That way, I could make Jerry's name match mine. Jerry was beginning his school years, so it was an opportune time to accomplish the change. I made every effort to contact Jerry's father for permission, but the filing went through with no answer. Jerry was now Jerry Blohm, which he is still.

For Christmas of 1969, we flew to Newark, New Jersey. Herman, Roger's father, had anxiously awaited our arrival. We drove to Cranford, where Betty, his mother, greeted us warmly. This home was Roger's childhood home; his parents had lived here since they married. His parents and I got along well.

Herman told me, "I have worked at the Singer Sewing Machine Factory all my life. Betty always stayed home and took care of the children. Do you know Roger has an older sister?"

"No, I do not know that. Roger has never spoken of her."

"Her name is Cynthia. She lives in Texas with her Army husband. We seldom see them. Our family is not close."

"In case Roger did not tell you, he adopted Jerry."

"That makes me very happy." Herman put his arm around me, thanking me. Then, he turned to his son with a big smile and hugged him.

Aside from introducing me to his family, we wanted to show Jerry snow. After snowball fights and sleigh riding, Christmas presents, and a delightful visit, I was ready to go back to Miami.

In 1970, it was time to fulfill our promise to each other to go on our honeymoon. My mother came to watch Jerry, and we flew to Montego Bay, Jamaica, and stayed in Ocho Rios, the gem of the Caribbean. Green mountains gently touch the sea as it washes over the sandy beaches below. We had time to ourselves, talking about the future, expressing our love.

The Rio Grande rafting trip was the highlight of our journey. Our guide steered the raft from the stern while we sat in luxury on the open raft. It was a romantic scene. Along the shores, native women, barely clad, washed clothes in the calm waters; their naked children were playing happily. We had a great time on the trip. I hoped it would last, and the closeness I felt would linger. I wanted my dad to meet my new husband. One long summer weekend, we drove north to upstate New York to attend an antique auction that brings folks out of state. People are always looking for that treasure their grandparents valued.

My dad lived in a hundred year old farmhouse in the neighborhood near the auction house. About six o'clock, the crowds began to gather at the old barn. The auctioneer projected his strong voice over the gathered assembly, "Now, if you plan to bid on an item, be sure I see you nod your head or raise your hand. Have your money ready. We collect at pick-up. Now let's get to selling. We have some kitchen items first ... "

In his auctioneer tone, he yodeled along to a quiet, attentive audience. Suddenly, he sees a little hand go up, "So, young man, do you see something that has caught your fancy."

And Roger turned around then to see that the young man was Jerry. He was out of his seat, hands on the kid, and out the door as the auctioneer was chortling, "Guess that boy was out of order, no money kid, no bidding." He went on calling one piece after another.

The after-auction days we spent with Dad and family. Roger cut the grass for Dad and kept busy hammering in nails to hang up his tools. It was always great to see Dad as visits were seldom between New York and Florida.

We hauled a loaded trailer back to Miami, including a few of the best items, which were two super-sized copper kettles that Roger got when we divorced. I felt Roger was drifting away, staying longer at the bar and going to bed earlier, avoiding me. Roger was always dedicated to Jerry and the kids in the neighborhood, spending his free time showing them how to use a hammer properly and how to handle a drill.

One day I received an unsolicited call from an unknown woman. She told me, "Roger is bringing roses to a woman in the beauty parlor across from the gas station. I thought you might like to know."

I was stunned: how dare he cut our roses and give them to another woman? That was the second clue that I had a cheating husband. I realized that expecting a permanent relationship might have been a dream. When it became apparent that Roger had liaisons with other women, the emotional attachment I felt a few months earlier was dwindling. There was no such conversation to say, "If you do it again," because it was not an open topic.

The most damaging hurt I felt was when I had requested Roger bring home a homemade chicken soup from the Cantonese restaurant. I was sick in bed with a fever. When he failed to show up, I got out of bed and drove the six blocks to his 76 Gas Station. He was standing, key in hand, at the door, and pressed against his back was a woman of about fifty. There was no question of her intent. They separated upon my exiting my car. Not one to accept things calmly or in stride, I burst into the shop and proceeded to tear down shelves – knocking over cans and disrupting all moveable items while unleashing obscenities. I cannot recall eating my soup that night.

After a year, Roger tired of the gas station and put his truck to work as a handyman. This job suited him better than the previous ones. He was a workaholic. Now he worked long hours and still kept up the yard and cut the bushes with the hedge clippers I bought for Father's Day. He taught Jerry how to cut the grass. Even though he was still small, he could push a mower.

Seldom did Roger relax unless he was playing his Gibson guitar and drinking beer. After work or on the weekend, I would sit and listen to Roger working different chords and singing country tunes. He had a mellow voice. He lined up a few performing dates, but that did not go anywhere. Those were the only times we sat together, enjoying each other's company. Jerry was growing up with country music, and it followed him throughout his life. It reminds him of the man I truly believe he loved.

Jerry had received a new bike for Christmas. One New Year's Day, the three of us, each on our bicycles, rode around the neighborhood-wishing folks a Happy New Year.

We had been eying the neighbor's house as it had a garage. When it went up for sale, we immediately bid on it. They accepted our bid, and we bought the house and prized garage. We rented the home to an older couple that had no use for the garage. Roger wanted a place to work. I wanted a place to put the kiln for the ceramics I was making. It also provided space for the Cub Scouts. Roger did all the electrical work to move the wiring so that the bill would come to our house and the tenants would not feel responsible for the electric bill. After we divorced, for spite, he tore out the connection.

We did the scout meetings in the garage. For one of their merit badges, I taught the kids how to make Christmas trees and snowmen. Roger instructed them through their other badge requirements and took them away for a weekend camping. Over the years, Jerry has remained friends with some of the boys who were in his pack.

Mom bought another house across the street. We rented to a family that did not pay the rent. Eviction notices later, they moved. It was in this house, while I was on a ladder hanging curtains Jerry repeatedly came and nagged me. While still on the ladder in a fit of temper and desperation I hit him with the curtain rod. I caught him on his side, ripping some skin, but causing no severe damage. He went directly to our neighbor Maggie for sympathy as he was playing with her son Michelangelo. She gave me hell for hitting Jerry.

Janette and her husband were in a rough place in their marriage. Always fighting, she wanted to remove the gun her husband kept in their house. On a whim, she gave it to Roger to hole up. One night, angry and drinking, he used her gun to shoot up our garage.

I called the police; they took the weapon and Roger away. The next day I picked him up at the Jailhouse. I did not file any charges.

We had also bought a house on a neighboring street that I had planned to rent to Jeanette. I did rent it, but not to her. I saw to it that Roger got that house in our divorce settlement. As the house was just a few blocks away, Jerry would ride his bike over to see his dad. The divorce did not change his feelings.

Roger's habit of spending time at the bar, and drinking, also got him in trouble with the law. Twice on the way home, he paused at the side of the road and peed. One officer caught him each time and carted him off to jail. The following morning, I had to pick him up.

One afternoon I had left work, and Roger showed up a bit tipsy. An office friend called to tell me he had been there, looking for me and dropped his cigarettes all over the floor. When he came home, I mentioned the incident. It did not go over well. He looked disheveled, and when I told him to glance in the mirror, he put his fist through the glass.

It was no mystery to Jerry, at eleven; he knew we were having problems. We were standing in the bathroom picking up the shards of glass when he said, "Mom, I understand if you and Dad break-up. It would be better than fighting."

That same night Roger went to hit me. A bottle of aftershave, named Decision, it was a long container; I picked it up and swung it in Roger's direction. I made contact. He slid down the bedpost to the floor. I looked at him lying on the floor, walked into the living room, and sat on the couch. I thought that maybe I had killed him. A few minutes later, he walked out, went outside, and got in his vehicle. He never came home that night. The next day, he returned and as we stood in the garden area, he told me he passed out twice in the truck.

Every Tuesday was bowling night. Roger dressed neatly, was always on time, and came home late. Frankie was a girl on his team. She was friends with the garage neighbors, so I had an opportunity to meet her, a short, chubby, unattractive twenty-something girl. Frankie was having an affair with my husband. She won, she married him, and I didn't want him anymore. It was a no-fault divorce, and I prepared the papers; September 24, 1973, was the end.

Not to leave you hanging, Crystal had a male puppy Bull that looked like a bear. When he matured, he became mean. Bull bit the garbage man over the fence in the butt and an older woman on the leg as she walked down the street. Jerry, attempting to stop him on his rampages, grabbed his collar, thinking he could hold him. Instead, Bull dragged Jerry through the cherry hedge. We had to euthanize him.

Now, as embarrassing as it is, I must divulge Roger was an alcoholic. Jerry recalls Black Label bottles aplenty. I was an enabler; I bought the Bush beer.

Roger had no sex drive; I only bring this up because he remarried three more times. He did not know what he was looking for in life, he never found it, either in work or women. He died alone in a hospital in 2009 of a lump in his throat, undoubtedly cancer. He was a smoker.

In February 1971, I became a secretary to three yacht brokers at Bertram Yacht Company. I remained there for five years. Why I left the job; I will tell you in a following story.

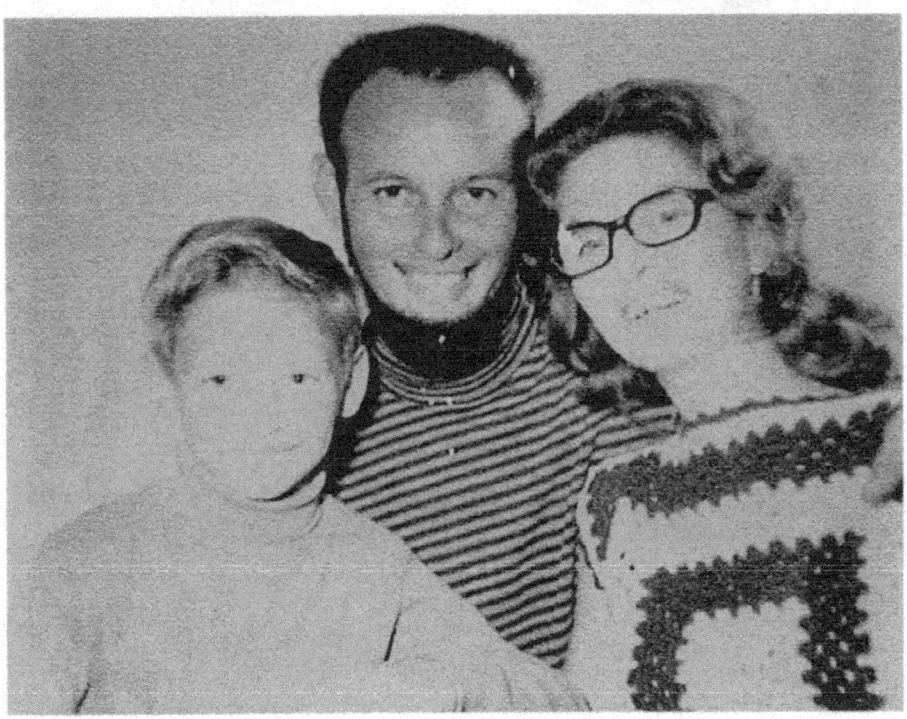

1969 Jerry, Roger & Ruth Blohm (Second Husband)

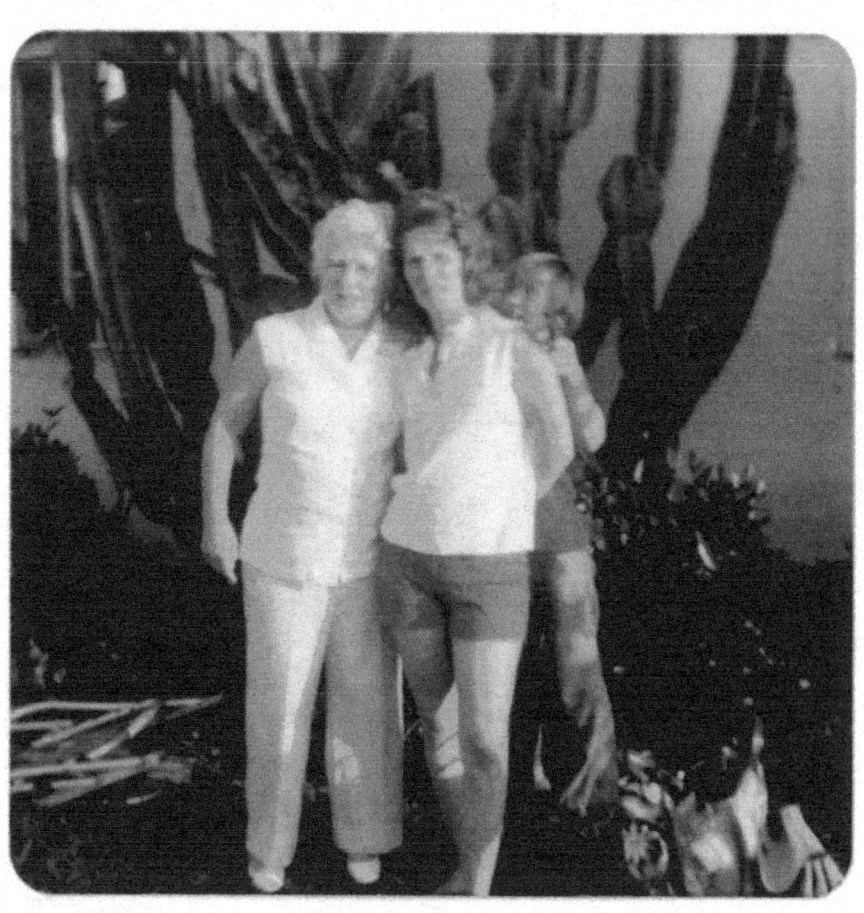

CHAPTER 21:

_____

JANE

My dad played a minor role in my earlier life, but he was my rock after Jerry was born. He moved me onto the third floor of the duplex he shared with his wife Margot and her cousin Edith in Irvington, New Jersey.

Edith raised her two children, Benno and Jane, as a single parent after her husband, Max, died, and my dad became the father figure for the kids.

Jane was an eleven-year-old girl. Every day after school, Jane made her way to my apartment to feed and play with Jerry. She was sweet and caring and disappointed when I announced my departure.

One summer, Edith and Jane came to spend their vacation visiting Roger and me in Miami. Jane had grown to be a lovely woman of seventeen. They played at being tourists as I drove them to the Miami Seaquarium and walked on the beach. Both Jane and Jerry had changed over the years, but each felt tenderness toward one another. After a short but memorable visit, Edith and Jane returned to New Jersey.

Jane finished her schooling and worked in a delicatessen until she met a local police Officer Frank. Although advised not to marry him, she did not listen.

My dad filled me in with the details of Jane's relationship and marriage. He felt strongly that this was not a good merger. He feared for her, deeply concerned for her welfare.

Within the first year of marriage, she had a girl Sarah, and soon after, a boy, Hank, named after my father.

Jane and Frank were having problems in their marriage. Frank was possessive, insisting she obeys his rules. That did not sit well with Jane, an independent young woman.

When Frank was at work, Jane packed her things, and before she could get out the door, Frank arrived home. Seeing what she planned, an argument ensued, and Frank shot her dead.

Frank did a short stint in jail and went home to live with his mother. The courts gave custody of the children to Frank's mother. Edith had to go to court to request visitation, which seldom occurred during their growing years.

Sarah grew up to become a teacher. She visited Edith infrequently and did not stay in touch with her maternal grandmother.

The last she heard of Hank was that a hunting accident took his life.

The dreadful outcome of Jane's premature death hurt my dad emotionally. The unfairness of the punishment and Edith's inability to see her grandchildren caused my father to have a heart condition from which he eventually died.

Benno, Edith, Frank, Jane, Groom's Mother, and Sister.

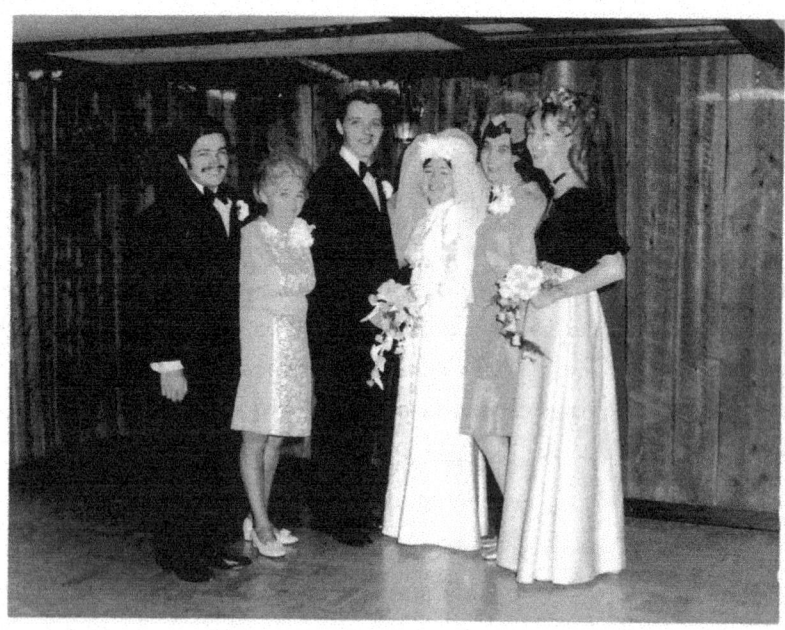

CHAPTER 22:

A FRESH START

My first day at work for Richard Bertram Yacht Sales was Tuesday, February 1971. I don't know why, but my mother said, "Tuesday is a good day to begin a job." It worked for me; I stayed there for five years. I never held a job for so long.

I was one of four girls in a secretarial pool for twelve yacht brokers. One day Dick Bertram requested I become his secretary. I felt flattered. Then, I found out it was not an extraordinary honor; he changed girls frequently.

Dick Bertram was prominent in the powerboat industry for racing his deep V-shaped hull design speedboat 'Lucky Moppie.' *Sports Illustrated* referred to him as "one of the finest ocean racers anywhere." He designed the Bertram yacht, which is a sleek, high-quality, luxury sportfishing yacht. Riding on his fame and fortune, he opened a brokerage office.

The company had established a well-known name among the rich and the very rich such as Aristotle Onassis, Aga Kahn, Prince Bertille of Sweden, Winthrop Rockefeller, and King Hussein of Jordan, whose yacht I had a hand in outfitting. Some years later, I worked for Winthrop in his Allied Marine Yacht sales, where we sold Hatteras Yachts.

Carol Cappiello was the new boat sales secretary. She was a redhead, born in New York but raised in Mississippi. Carol taught me her job, and had it not been that Charles was about to be born, she would have stayed. I asked her frequently when she was due, she said,

"You asked me only because you wanted my job, and then you kicked me out of the office." Through some spiritual phenomena manifested in the universe's synchronicity, Carol and I, two entirely different personalities, built a friendship, which is still flourishing after fifty years. *Well past any of my marital disasters.*

Margot Drummond was in the listing department. Her job was to keep track of yachts that yacht brokers listed for sale. It was a taxing job answering to the demands of the brokers.

She was a beautiful wavy-haired blond German gal about five-six. Her German accent and her efficiency attracted Meredith Drummond's attention, one of the many sales staff.

I had barely been on the job for a month when a wedding took place between Margot and Meredith. I was invited to their home to participate in the celebration, although I knew neither of the participants well. We developed a lasting friendship, and forty-nine years later, Margot and I are still friends.

Sadly, Margot passed away in September 2020 from a heart attack.

Gail Jones was a secretary with shoulder-length, natural blond hair, blue eyes, and five foot four inches tall with a trim figure. Gail painted complicated fantasy pictures with fairies, butterflies, and swirly designs in an array of colors. On weekends, she displayed her art at street shows.

We took our homemade lunches at our favorite spot under the 37th Street Bridge. It was a nice setup with tables and chairs. We went down the docks passing a few hired captains sanding, painting, or washing their boats. They nodded and called hello to us. We went past my office window. During a long workday as a new boat sales secretary, I had the good fortune to face these luxurious cabin cruisers and imagine foreign shores, ocean breezes, and perhaps, meeting an exotic lover. *Get back to work, Ruth, no more dreaming.*

"So, Ruth, I've just completed a few new paintings. This weekend there is an art show at the University of Miami connected to the Lowe Art Museum. I'm going to be showing there. I wondered if you have anything planned. Can you meet me at the show and spot me when I take a break?"

"Sure, Gail, I'm fond of art shows, and that will give me a chance to see your new work. I can take a look around and see what's going on in the art scene."

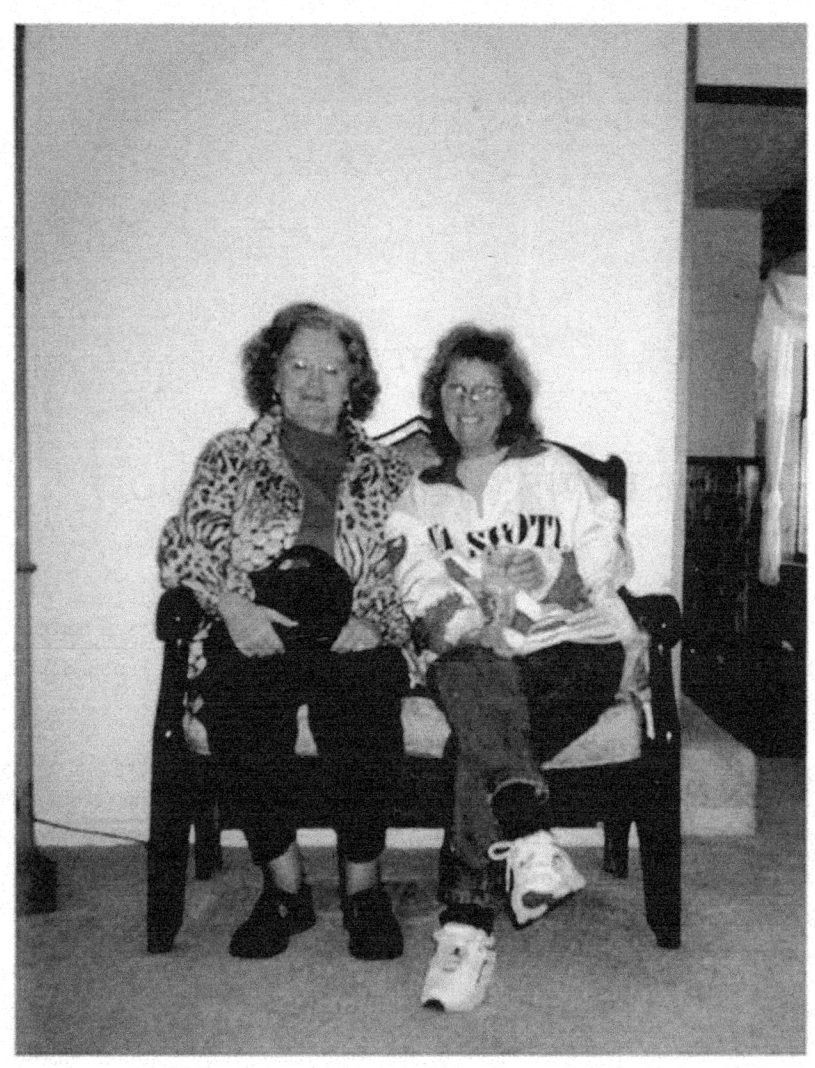

Carol Berndt and Ruh

CHAPTER 23:

THE LOWE MUSEUM ART SHOW

It was mid-afternoon in May on a balmy, sunny Florida spring day. I had parked at the wrong end of the show area. As I was walking across the grass, I spotted a sculpture display.

The sun seemed to reflect off his pieces. The item that caught my eye was a seagull on three pilings joined together. It stood about seven inches tall placed on a white rock. I had embroidered a pelican on pilings years before; it seemed like an odd coincidence. Had I the money, I would have bought it. Had I a crystal ball, I could have glimpsed the future, and it would have told me to buy it now, or my life will change drastically.

I stopped to chat with the artist as I scanned the area for Gail. Cutting the conversation short, I told him, "I've come to help a friend out, and I'm running late. I like your work, so I'll be back." He probably thought he had a sale. When he handed me his business card, it showed a New York address. The card reads James Boylan. I introduced myself and took off feeling a bit giddy. I liked this fellow. He had a certain charisma. A bit flirtatious, but I felt some chemistry. The flirting was mild. No gorgeous slim woman had a chance to escape his clutches. First, a hug, and then the quintessential question, "Would you model for me?" and the girl would say, "How?" His reply, "in the nude," and she would answer, "NO."

"Gee, this may be my lucky day I told Gail. I met a sculptor on my way to you."

"What's he like?"

"I figure him to be short, about five-nine. Sparkling blue eyes and a come-hither smile. I did notice his teeth aren't perfect." His teeth were horrible. A few years later, they came out, and he got false ones, which he hated and had them out more than in his mouth. "He's a bit heavyset but not fat, and some muscles."

On the return to my car, I stopped at his booth again. He began the conversation with,

"Well, I'm glad you came back. You said you liked my work, so let me tell you about it. The artwork is silver solder with a frame of copper wire."

He was a man with little or no business sense. He used braided wire, which he unwound and straightened. I ordered a large spool of copper wire wholesale. He purchased individual rolls of solder. I got it wholesale in large quantities.

"I want to explain the woman at the center of my display. Of course, you saw her?"

"Yes, of course, she would be hard to miss."

"Well, I'm married to her; it is my wife, Irene. She is a redhead and a fighter of a woman. When she reaches the pinnacle of her battles, she appears grotesquely changed. I'm tired of fighting with her. She dissolves my creativity and drains my energy."

Energy became a reason to hug another female. It sounded like bullshit to me. WARNING SIGN. He wanted me to know that divorce plans were already on his agenda.

"I'm sure you are curious about the mushroom," he exclaimed.

"It looks like the A-bomb," I noted.

"That is what it is. It's the atomic bomb, and the people you see are running away. They are miniature to express the enormity of the bomb."

"That is a rather sinister topic for an artist," I said.

"Art can be conveyed in many ways, gleeful or morbid. It should provoke thought and feelings." He wore his feelings on his sleeve. Contrary to my belief, I don't think you should put it all out there. That grew into plenty of contentious issues. "We are the conscience of the world. Dali and Pollack expressed their art in entirely different styles. From Salvador Dali, there was distortion. From Jackson Pollock, it was what you imagined."

"But it is such a destructive force," I said, referring to the bomb. "Some of your other works display a lighter subject matter. Are you fascinated with war?"

"Somewhat, I was a sailor serving during the Korean War; I signed up when I was seventeen. I never served in Korea, but in 1953, my ship docked in Cuba at the beginning of the Cuban revolution. As a young man, I was enchanted with the revolution's idea and attempted to join Castro and Che Guevara. That got me in big trouble."

"What happened?" I asked.

"The Navy frowns on enlisted men going over the hill."

"What does going over the hill mean?" I inquired

"It's against Navy regulations for a serviceman to leave his unit without permission. It is called AWOL, Absence without leave. They sent a few MPs, Military Police, to find me. I was confined to my billet till we reached port."

"Of course, at that time, you had no idea what corruption Castro would inflict on the Cuban population and how it would impact Miami in particular. Perhaps, your adventure was intriguing, but your punishment could not have been pleasant."

We then progressed down the list of more of his work.

"And why the knight, what does that express, except that it is a well-done piece?" I asked.

He answered. "That is Don Quixote, Man of La Mancha." He went on to tell me whom The Don was. "Quixote is a nobleman without a title who goes out into the world to revive chivalry. He does not see the world realistically and feels he is living out the story of a knight."

Jim had a similar problem. Of course, he did not see it that way. He was not always in the realm of reality. Years ago, I had seen the play on Broadway when I was in college; I knew the subject.

Then, there was a child holding the bridle of a horse and another child playing with a ball.

That showed some consistency. Jim continued to tell me, "A happy young child at play is one of my favorite topics. We all have a child within, and I try to characterize the innocence of children."

"When I saw other works of art here, I noticed that most artists stay within a certain theme. You seem to cover a gamut of topics. It is haphazard and discombobulating," I said.

His response was, "I have many interests and try to express them all."

"I don't mean to belittle your artistic ideas; I just thought I would mention it."

Then, he asked, "Are you seeing anyone now?"

"No, I haven't met anybody lately. It's hard to work all day, and then go out at night as I have a young child." And so, I gave him my phone number and headed home to my son Jerry.

Before I left, he pointed out a poem he had written; it is entitled *An Artist's Thoughts*. It was typed on a three-by-five-index card reading, "A Jim Boylan Original."

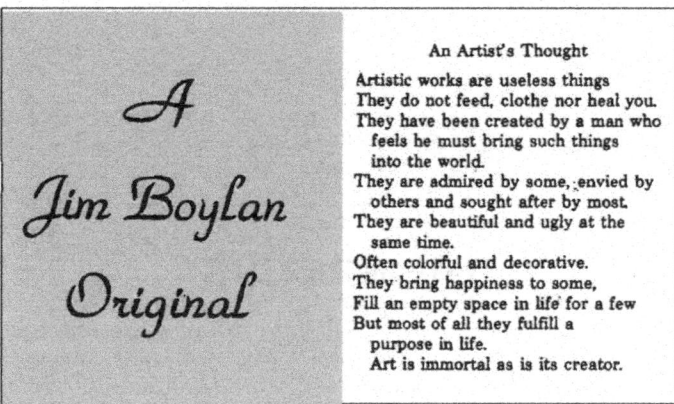

An Artist's Thought

Artistic works are useless things
They do not feed, clothe nor heal you.
They have been created by a man who
   feels he must bring such things
   into the world.
They are admired by some, envied by
   others and sought after by most.
They are beautiful and ugly at the
   same time.
Often colorful and decorative.
They bring happiness to some,
Fill an empty space in life for a few
But most of all they fulfill a
   purpose in life.
Art is immortal as is its creator.

In the future, I would have them printed on a three and a quarter by two-inch silver card, which I designed. He hung the poem from all his sculptures.

I had dated a little. I did not drink, so I never did the bar scene. The men I had met were mundane. They talked about their work or ex-wives; Jim could at least carry on a conversation about other topics.

When I got home, I mentioned to both my Mom, who was watching Jerry for the day that I had met an artist. Jerry seemed to perk up at the comment.

CHAPTER 24:

THE MEETING

It took Jim a few weeks to give me a call. It was seven-thirty on a workweek evening. I was pulling weeds in my garden when the phone rang.

"Hi, Ruth, I've been busy doing a few art shows in the next county, so I couldn't call." He seemed so enthused to meet me; I thought he would have called sooner. Cell phones were in their infancy; a call required a phone booth, and a dime, and perhaps a quarter or two from the next county over.

He said, "I was thinking about you. Would you like to come over to the beach and spend the evening? I'm a bit limited on gas and don't know my way around town very well. Where did you say you live?"

"I don't live far from where we met."

He was way north on Miami Beach, and my home was in South Miami. I answered, "I have to take Jerry to the neighbors, and it may take me a while." I had to shower and dress, dirty and sweaty from the garden.

When I got there, he was still cleaning out his living quarters, which consisted of an old blue and white Ford Econoline van. He had outfitted it for living on the salary of a starving artist.

The conversation began:

"Hi, you made it here that quickly?" Then, after looking closely at me, he asked, "How old are you?" That was a delicate question to begin a date.

"And how old are you?" He was four years older than I was and looked younger; maybe it was the long hair. It was time to prove our ages, so we took out our driver's licenses, and each of us had been truthful.

We laughed a bit at that, and then he began with no hesitation to spill out his entire narrative.

"Before I left New York, unbeknownst to me, my oldest son James got into the van and only announced his presence when we reached New Jersey. That disclosure was too late for me to turn back."

"Where is James now?"

"I asked him to leave for a few hours." I did not get to see James on this occasion.

He gave me a detailed, thorough explanation of all the improvements he had made to his truck. "I made a bench on each side of the interior of the van, which I covered with carpet. These hatch covers lift, and that is how they convert into a bed for sleeping." Was this a romantic overture? He had a shyness about him, almost like a little boy. He would use the little boy trait to nullify a situation. I could fall for him.

After his presentation, we took a walk on the beach. Darkness had fallen, and the ocean water had a soothing effect as it lapped gently ashore. There was a sparkle in the water, and I gave him a lesson on what caused that.

"The light you see is made by the bioluminescent plant and animal life. Disturbance in the water makes the light stronger." We sat on the sand with our toes in the water; it was a mild night. He wanted to complete his story, so I listened quietly.

"I have a twelve-year-old son, Timothy, an eight-year-old daughter Suzette, a fifteen-year-old daughter, Annette, and a daughter Stella who has a son and husband, Paul. Stella is only sixteen. She needed to marry. Plus, James, at eighteen, makes five."

"Wow, that's a lot of kids. Are the younger children all up north?"

"Yes," he said, "It's challenging to travel without another adult and do the shows with the kids. They are with their mother."

He referred to wanting to have his kids with him. I wondered how he would handle that situation. He said, "Where we live in New York, kids act tough. I would rather bring my kids up in a better environment." *Was I getting a message?*

We then walked back to the van, and with expected anticipation, we had our first kiss. It felt good to hug him, and soon, we were petting heavily. Then, we struggled on the carpeted bed, discovering that we could be well suited for each other.

We arranged for Jim to come to my house after completing a show and sending his son James back to New York. It may have been a sudden decision, but I wanted to get to know him better. If we were to start a relationship, I wanted it to be permanent.

The next week, he parked his old blue Ford Econoline van on the easement in front of my house. That was early summer 1975.

He was doing his work in the house and asked me, "I work easier when I have a TV. Maybe you could pick one up." I did, and when a month later the bill came, I asked him, "Can you give me some money for the bill?"

"I thought it was a gift," he said. That is not what I intended, and I had to swallow the bill. I think I would be fair in saying he manipulated me. The incident put him in an awful mood that lasted until morning. Money discussions usually produced the same results. He had no money, so any thought of financial help was pretty much down the drain. When there was an art show, I usually received some help, but I was footing the bills.

Carol said, "You were under his spell; you just didn't see what was happening."

Jim was concerned about his kids up north. He called home frequently. We had just begun settling in when speaking with his daughter Stella, she told him that his wife had left for a few days, and there was no food in the house. Irene went to be with her boyfriend James, whom she eventually married. Both James' had been friends since boyhood. That was his way of life, but he wanted no more of it.

The news greatly troubled him. As he made the van ready to bring Suzette and Timothy here, I was assessing my situation. I was using the extra bedroom, which was perfect for a little girl, but I had my needlepoint and rug hooking along with an office arrangement there. Jim also sculpted in that room. I moved my things to a corner of the living room.

I told him, "You will have to move your work into the garage next door."

I worked my ceramic hobby and poured clay molds of Christmas trees, birds, and a Miami Dolphins football player. I also decorated porcelain dishes. Then, I painted them and fired them in my kiln. My mother owned the house and garage.

Before he left, he affectionately took me in his arms and told me he cared for me. He said, "As time goes by, we will become as one. I love you." I had the thought, *was this too soon? Was I a vehicle, so he could house his children?* Nevertheless, I was feeling tenderness for him. I knew I would miss him.

I had other thoughts regarding Jerry. Thinking of my childhood, I could have been happier if I were not an only child. I thought Jerry could benefit from having siblings. Like his other friends, a father figure in the home would be suitable for a boy.

The fact that the children were going to accompany him back to Florida lit a fire under me. I now had to outfit the bedroom for a young child. There was no bed.

Jerry and I hunted a bed in a used store. We rounded up a dresser and chair, making the room into a presentable child sleeping quarter. As for Timothy, we found a single bed that would fit into Jerry's area. It was exciting: we were ready for a new family.

I gave some thought to the size of the house. When I was married previously, this house was adequate for the three of us, but now there would be five. There was only one bathroom with three small bedrooms. By mid-1976, we moved into a larger three-bedroom house with two bathrooms, and we divided a former remodeled garage into a bedroom for the two of us.

CHAPTER 25:

_____

THE ARRIVAL

Jerry and I watched with expectation as Jim's signature vehicle rounded the corner. With jubilation, two redheaded children exited the van. His eight-year-old daughter Suzette was a skinny redhead. It didn't take me long to figure out that she was a spoiled brat. Jim favored her over the boys. It was never her fault. Her long hair was a maze of knots, and she was continually pulling up her oversized jeans. There was a vast difference between the boys separated in age by four months. Tim was a roly-poly who thought the world revolved around the TV, and my Jerry was a short blond, athletic, skinny kid.

Dirty and uncombed, they were awed as they entered the house. Jerry immediately latched onto Tim taking him to their shared room. Suzette looked around with some tribulation until Jim took her to her new room. She was not pleased to be there alone. She insisted on a light. Daddy fixed one for her, and that quieted her. Eventually, she got used to sleeping alone.

It was not long before Suzette came to me and let me comb the knots out of her long locks. She told me, "I imagined you in a grass skirt."

I told her, "You are confusing me with a Hawaiian princess." We giggled, and that helped break the ice. The blending of the family was a relatively smooth transition despite the differences. No Mom and Dad, in the beginning, we were just first names.

With some success, Jim and I tried to make love quietly in my antique four-poster rope bed. Loving wasn't the only thing we did. Jim was a talker; he liked to tell stories of the past.

"I was seventeen and joined the Navy early with my mother's permission. It was 1949, June 14, Flag Day, and I was at the Statue of Liberty. There was a Girl Scout troupe there, and one of the girls was holding an American flag; I signed the dowel of that flag."

I, in turn, told him, "In 1949, I was eleven and at the Statue of Liberty with my Girl Scout troop. I remember a good-looking sailor signed the dowel of my flag. I kept that for a long time. That is a freaky coincidence that it could have been you."

It took some time to obtain school records for his kids and enrolled them in the South Florida system. Finally, accomplished, and then it was summertime.

I had intended to take a vacation from July 25 to August 22. Before we met, I decided to take a wagon train ride in Wyoming with Jerry after Jim brought his two children to Florida, which squashed my plans. I have regretted not going on that trip. We made alternative arrangements to drive out west. It would be a getting-to-know-trip and a visit to pre-picked sites that Jerry and I would have seen.

Over the years, Jerry and I had made fair use of our weekends. We had traveled to many different venues. We had a tent, which he and I could erect in minutes; comfortable foam- covered mattresses, camp cookware, a Coleman lantern, and a small chess set. Everything we needed for overnight camping.

Our first trip was to Ft. Myers to see Thomas Edison's home and learn about his inventions. We visited an overstocked seashell business just up the road. In the same general area was Marco Island, where we walked on the beach and collected starfish, sand dollars, and shells for a home project to remember our day; we made a display in a frame of all the seashells.

As we became comfortable with our travels, we ventured further from home. Cypress Botanical Gardens and water ski shows are near Winter Haven. Homosassa Springs Wildlife in Citrus County, Florida, State Park is where we glided on clear waters in a glass-bottom boat. This park was magnificent, one of the best we visited.

Bok Singing Tower and Gardens in Haynes City was probably the most restful and peaceful place we encountered. In Lake Wales, we discovered Spook Hill. A forgotten law of gravity and the car rolls uphill perfectly on its own.

We had gone to Michigan, where I almost lost Jerry after he slid down the towering Sleeping Bear Dunes, which contain tiny particles of light tan sand.

We visited Mammoth Cave in Kentucky, saw Niagara Falls and Washington, DC. There were still more places, but let me get back to the escapades of our new family trip.

CHAPTER 26:

OUR VACATION TRIP

Jim was outfitting his van with additional side windows so that the kids could view the scenery as we traveled, which was a useless endeavor. They wanted to crowd up to the front to be with us and look out of the windshield.

This vacation was nothing like the one I had planned. It turned out to be almost three weeks of controversy. Suzette was the fire that lit up the boys, and Jim and I argued about the kids.

We made stops at a few towns on the way through Florida. We buzzed through Mississippi putting Biloxi, and Gulfport behind us. At a KOA in Slidell, Louisiana, the kids were to sleep in the tent, and we made ready to crash in the van. We camped in the primitive area where we heard bullfrogs, and crickets, and other weird sounds. The slow-moving fog and delicate lacy Spanish moss hung from the live oak trees conjuring creepy imagery in the imaginative kid's minds. Scared and frightened, they ran to the door of the van, terrified of the night. They spent the night in the truck while we camped in the tent. It was easier to make love in the tent as there was a bit more room. That sleeping arrangement followed through most of the entire trip. I enjoyed this extra physical attention, which undoubtedly turned my head, causing me to ignore his other traits. Even after a few weeks, I still felt the exuberant feeling when first falling in love.

In New Orleans, we took a two-and-a-half-hour excursion on the Natchez steam wheel paddleboat along with our vehicle down the Mississippi. The large red blades at the stern churned up the muddy river bottom. We allowed the boys to get closer to the stern, but Jim would not permit Suzette, who pitched such a fit that he had to hold her tight as she squirmed to find freedom.

Once back on terra firma, we walked Bourbon Street in the heart of the French Quarter. We heard music coming out of every bar, which we could not enter. We stopped for PO-boy sandwiches, and as we ate in an open-air café, we saw only the side of a boat glide past. I did my best to try to explain to the kids that New Orleans was three to six feet below sea level and the levees keep the water from the city.

While riding in a horse-drawn carriage and seeing the houses with arches, court-yards, intricate wrought-iron balconies, and porches, it occurred to me that although the early residents of New Orleans were French, the Spanish architectural influence was omnipresent.

To pay a war debt in 1763, the French turned the town over to the Spanish, who occupied it until 1803. Through a series of treaties, the land reverted to the French, and on April 30, 1803, in Paris, Robert Livingston and James Monroe signed the Louisiana Purchase Treaty for fifteen million dollars.

Our next stop was San Antonio, Texas, and the Alamo. Jim and I had a terrible feud over the kids making our very own Alamo. Jim took his two in one direction, and I moved Jerry along another passageway. It might have been the most disturbing disagreement on the trip. We finally made it up, but my parenting was being questioned and not for the last time. I did not care much for his criticism and argued my point. Jim always felt the kids were trying to come between us. He was not about to let them have the upper hand.

We drove through Austin toward New Mexico's Carlsbad Caverns. We saw fields of oil wells dotting the landscape. The pump jacks going up and down were boring into the surface, oil from below. We passed a closed gas station, and shortly after, we ran out of gas. Ironic to see all this out of reach oil as the van chocked for lack of gas before running out. The first time this happened, we made it into a service station. That was the second time. Jim had never brought up the fact that there was no gas gauge in the van. His inabil-ity to keep track of the mileage and consumption of gas left us in precarious situations.

We only traveled as far as Malaga, New Mexico, at one building gas station with one pump and a sign on the door that read, "Closed for the night." We slept in the van, and shortly after sunrise, a man appeared, filled our tank, and off we went.

It was exciting to arrive at Carlsbad Caverns, which appeared to be a large hole in the earth with a paved walkway entrance. Throughout the cave, the cement path wound down to what felt like the bottom of the planet. The cavern is one thousand feet deep. Our children found it impossible to keep their hands off the walls as I reminded them they were forbidden to touch the cave walls' natural beauty. I heard the ranger's warning of expulsion from a distance if we could not control our young children. Once we reached the bottom, we were in a large chamber with stalagmites growing from the ground up and stalactites hanging from the ceiling. The cave was awe-inspiring in size, having the most extensive underground chamber in the United States. Although we saw only half, we had walked three miles. Thousands of bats leave the cave at sunset to eat insects and return at dawn.

After we left, we drove down to the Guadalupe Mountains National Park. That was an open area where our children could burn off some excess energy.

The next day, leaving our car in El Paso, we walked across the international bridge, or border crossing over the Rio Grande's thin strip, paying two cents per person to enter Juarez, Mexico. Below, standing in the shallow water, the children of Mexico begged for coins by holding up a broomstick with a makeshift V-shaped cardboard collection receptacle to catch the pennies people threw to them.

Shops lined Juarez Avenue, and all the shop keepers stood in front of their shops to attract the customers before their competitors were able to snatch them away. The knives tempted Jerry and Tim cared more for belt buckles. The prices were ridiculously low, but when Jerry realized he could bargain, he tried. At one point in the middle of the negotiations, he decided he did not want the product and walked out. The merchant chased him down the street, and he had to complete the purchase. The market was another place we visited and left our US dollars there too. We crossed back over to El Pasco; going through customs, we had to declare all the belts, knick-knacks, knives, rings, bracelets, scarves, blouses, a dress, and cigarettes we bought.

We picked up the car, and Immigration stopped us on the road heading for Alamogordo, New Mexico. They were satisfied that we had not tried to bring any illegal Mexicans into the country.

While on the road, our morning breakfast usually took place at a truck stop or local café. Figuring out what the kids would eat was ordinarily my bailiwick. On this one morning, while I was putting my contact lenses on in the women's room, Jim did the honors. When I arrived at the table, the little darlings were sitting still waiting for their food. They never sat that way for me. I was incensed. I got up, said not a word, and walked out, heading for the highway. Truck drivers tooted at me and called out of cab windows. It was a broad, expansive four-lane road. I had no idea where I was going and just needed to burn off some steam. The further I walked, the madder I became. Why was he not following me? When I waltzed back to the cafe gas station, Jim was on the phone with my mother, trying to figure out what he would do with three children and no woman.

He explained, "How could I follow you? I had no conception what direction you had taken. Not only did you upset all of us, but also, unfortunately, not knowing you well enough, I had no idea if you were coming back. Your mother assured me you were."

We headed across New Mexico and outside Albuquerque, Jim's van broke down again.

Think of all the time we lost because of his broken-down van. I kept my mouth shut, but I had enough. This time we took the truck to an AAMCO station. It was the transmission.

We received a loaner and visited Old Town in Albuquerque. We ate lunch in a very picturesque place with a historical background as far back as 1609. We walked around the town and then it was time to go back and get our broken-down van. Within ten blocks, we blew out the new transmission stuck in front of a Best Western where we spent the night. The next morning we called AAMCO, who came and got the van. While they replaced the transmission, we received a loaner again. We spent most of the day in the downtown area buying Indian jewelry. We went back for the van, but it ran very poorly, and they suggested we take it to Stony's garage.

The shop was not a jazzy gas station, and with no place to go without our van, time spent at the location was a disaster. The kids were running around distracting old Stony, so Jim positioned each boy in a designated corner seat. There was an old-school backseat bus bench, which Jim, Suzette, and I occupied while the van was in repair. The boys complained, she moaned and groaned, and the van ended up not fixed. That evening we limped up a hill with our barely operating van. Halfway up, we ran out of gas. I spotted a cop. Jumping out of the truck, I approached him and requested, "Officer, we are out of gas. Is there any way you could get us some, otherwise we are stuck here on your hill?"

I explained, "We have been in Stony's garage all day." The officer gave a knowing nod. "Sorry we ran it out of gas; it has no gauge. After two days of being stuck waiting for a vacuum advance delivery, this whole mess is delaying our forward progress."

The officer was most helpful. After he brought the gas, he also gave us a jump for our dead battery. Stress had gotten the better of me. I began to yell at the kids; this caused a three-hour delay as Jim felt it necessary to talk it out again. Let's have action, not talk. I yelled to relieve frustration. He complained about their behavior and on and on. For me, it was too much talk. We had to take the sick van and find a place for the night. It was a ten-thirty dinner, and then parking at a KOA. We all slept in the truck.

The next morning the children and I slept in while Jim took the van back to Stony. We went swimming, and in an hour-and-a-half he returned as a passenger in Stony's car to bring us back to the garage, which we were quite familiar with by now. More time spent on the problem and interrupted by an old wrinkled Indian fellow selling, of all things, Indian jewelry. Jim bought a turquoise ring for himself and one for me. The kids bought rings and earrings, and the aged native told us of a park where we could buy more Navajo and Zuni treasures. After all the incompetence and still more adjustments to our ride, we left with no more clanking and grinding.

The Native American Acoma Indians lived sixty miles west of Albuquerque atop a three- hundred-sixty-five-foot mesa. They have lived in this village for eight hundred years. After three tries, our reliable vehicle was unable to ascend to the Pueblo in Sky City. By the time we arrived, I would venture to say the Acoma tribe did not want any company. Disappointed, we drove to Grants and the Bluewater State National Park. We pitched our tent in the dark while the kids slept in the van.

The next day we located the Park Ranger, who sold Indian jewelry. Jim loved to bargain and thought he could get the 'better of the deal.' That took hours of negation. We came away with authentic silver, turquoise, and coral inlaid cuff bracelets and a-half-dozen more pieces.

Down the road, we found out what a good deal we had gotten.

On our way to the Petrified Forest, which is two-hundred-thirty square miles of desert, we ran out of gas. The boys had to push the van off the highway down a slight hill to a gas station. Suzette was very perturbed as Jim would not permit her to join the boys as the truck rolled under boy power and my help. She made her brother the target of her dissatisfaction by inflicting scratches that drew blood on his back.

Trying to make this vacation not only fascinating but also educational, I informed the kids. "Two hundred twenty-five million years ago dinosaurs inhabited this area. The Triassic period is the name given to that time."

"Are there any dinosaurs now?" Suzette inquired.

"No, silly," Jerry said in his big boy attitude.

"Fossils of dinosaurs are here," I explained.

"What is a fossil?" asked Suzette.

Tim spoke next, "They are the bones of the dead dinosaurs that died a long, long time ago."

"What about these fallen trees?" Jerry wanted to know.

"A long, long time ago, after the ice age, the water flooded this area. The trees fell because the water soaked their roots, and they dislodged and fell into the water and became buried by rocks and dirt. After many millions of years, as the water receded, the wet wood of the trees separated, allowing stones and dirt to seep into the wood and eventually make them hard."

"Can we touch the trees," Jerry wanted to know. Jim stopped the van, and the kids got out and felt the trees.

"They are so hard," Suzette said as she bent down.

Jim addressed Tim in a stern voice. "Tim, I don't believe that you can hurt them, these trees are harder than granite, but you shouldn't kick them."

"You know I put some of my sculptures on pieces of granite?" Jim said.

"Yes, Dad, I know," said Tim.

Back in the van, Jim said, "Read the sign, kids," as he removed a petrified rock from Jerry's hand.

"You see, it is against the law to pick any up. What if everyone that came here wanted to take a rock home, there eventually won't be any rocks and so no Petrified Forest," Jim informed everyone.

As we left, the Ranger checked us out. Luckily, Jim had made Jerry throw the rock away.

"Now, kids, when I do my next dinosaurs, I'll put some trees next to them."

"OK, Dad," Tim said.

"Do it, Daddy," Suzette exclaimed.

Our next stop was the Painted Desert, which was fantastic with red, orange, pink, white, and lavender colors. Mesas stand high above the colorful sand. We could see how the shifting of winds changes the landscape daily, leaving swirls and waves with highs and lows in the ever-shifting sands.

In 1540, Francisco Vazquez de Coronado, on his quest to find gold in the Seven Cities of Cibola, passed through this tremendous natural land and named it 'El Desierto Pintado' (The Painted Desert).

His Pained Desert was a far different landscape than the one we had just left. "It's like a rainbow," Suzette observed.

Jim was preoccupied, seeming to meditate as he looked at the magnificent scene. In places, it looked as though someone had painted lines in the sand in white, red, black, and gold colors. The same color themes prevailed at both locations.

"You know Ruthie; I don't usually sculpt landscapes; I wish I were a painter right now I could make a beautiful picture. But I could do a piece with a landscape of rolling hills and a mesa with a child looking out over the view," he said in a slow manner giving me the impression he was considering it.

"Daddy, I want to see that piece," Suzette exclaimed. I knew he would make the piece for her. She undoubtedly was his favorite over the boys.

At last, we were on our way to the Grand Canyon. Water was a precious commodity in this part of the country, and therefore, we had to buy the water we needed. I told the kids, "At home, water is a natural resource. Even though, when we do not get enough rain, we have to conserve our water." After buying our water supply, we found a campsite; set up for the night; built a campfire as the nights are chilly. And in the morning, after breakfast, we trucked to the canyon. It was, without a doubt, a magnificent sight. We were all in awe at the enormous size.

"Here's a little information for you guys," I said. "The canyon is two-hundred seventy-seven miles long and eighteen miles wide. It is a mile deep, making it the deepest canyon in the world. Five to six million years ago the Colorado River began to carve its way down the canyon. If you look over the edge, you will see the river way down below." Suzette had been hanging back, and when she heard what I said, she came charging forward, scaring Jim to death, thinking she would go over the edge. Looking at Suzette in a worried fatherly way, he spoke, "While we are here looking at this canyon, I want to protect you and hold on to you."

"OK, Daddy, you can hold my hand."

We saw the canyon from different angles along the south side, which was just as impressive as the north side.

We took a four-hour horseback ride through the hills surrounding the canyon. Jim rode a spirited brown horse named Chum-head. My horse White-slim gave me a good trip. Comical names for horses. Suzette had a smaller brown and white animal called Tonto. That sounded more western. The guide led her most of the way, although she rode alone for a while and did well. Jerry had a high-stepping brown horse called Charlie Brown. Tim's horse Pie-face was a slow, plodding, dark brown and white animal. Tim had trouble with his saddle and had to keep dismounting and adjusting the strap. The girdle was too loose, and Tim fell off the horse. Later Jerry's horse took off at a gallop, and Tim's horse followed. The sudden movement jolted him and threw him off his horse. I wish I had a picture of Tim's hard-luck fall. Just imagine the rider sitting on his horse, suddenly as his horse bolts forward, he is ejected not to the side, but the back, remaining in the same position in midair as though he sat astride his horse with his legs spread in the shape of a horseshoe.

We broke camp early on the morning of August 13, 1975, heading for Wyoming.

On scenic Route 89, we entered Panguitch, Utah. Like most western cities, it was a Wild West town back in 1864 when Danish settlers were members belonging to the Latter-Day Saints Church. The population of the city has remained small. It is now the gateway to Bryce Canyon National Park. We did not go there. After dinner, we bedded the kids down for the night and kept driving. He had to get his night driving in; I was so enjoying the daylight.

Forty-three miles outside Salt Lake City in Provo, Utah, we ran out of gas at ten-thirty at night. Jim stayed in the truck while the kids slept on the bunks in the back. I walked across the highway to the open door of a Holiday Inn to inquire where I could get a can of gas. A pimply teen waiter offered to take me. He seemed to drive in a scattered pattern out of the suburban streets and into a darker wooded section with no visible homes; thoughts of misdeeds circulated in my suspicious sleepy head. Finally, there was a gas station way out in the night in Provo. He filled our can, and we made our way back to the empty gas tank of our van parked on the side of the road. Jim was dozing in the driver's seat during my misadventure as a drunken man passed the truck, expelling grunting sounds that startled him awake.

Off we went again in the dead of night. I dozed on and off until we reached Coalville, Utah, at 4:00 a.m. Looking at my Utah map today, Provo is forty-three miles from Salt Lake City. Coalville is forty-seven miles from Salt Lake City, but it is sixty miles from Provo to Coalville. Why did it take, from, let us say, 11:00 a.m. (by the time we filled the tank) to 4:00 a.m. to arrive in Coalville? I think he got lost; it should have taken about an hour. Therefore, assuming we left the Grand Canyon at 10:00 a.m. when we broke camp till 4:00 a.m. when we arrived in Coalville, Jim had driven a total of eighteen hours. Jim's driving endurance was incredible.

We jumped on Highway 80, and shortly we stopped at a large billboard proclaiming, 'Welcome to Big Wonderful Wyoming.' We all ran to the sign for pictures.

Just before we reached the best part of our trip, I wanted a little adventure and suggested to Jim, "See this little line on the map?"

"I see it. It doesn't look like it goes anywhere," Jim said as he glanced at the map.

"Why don't we take it? We haven't done any off the road; we should do something different."

"I know you are more adventurous than I am. What are you getting us into?" Jim questioned.

He made the turn, for about one-quarter-of-a mile, the road was rough gravel, and then it became dirt. Later, it became a tiny sliver of a road in less than a mile, "Look, Ruth just ahead of us is a big dip, and in the middle is a large puddle. I hope the shocks can handle this."

Cautiously, he moved the van slowly down the big dip. The kids had all come forward, and when we hit bottom, there were squeals and Oh's.

"Dad, are we OK?" Tim spoke up.

"Daddy, I almost hit my head," Suzette proclaimed. "Mom, are we stuck?"

"No, we're just in a puddle," I said with a confident attitude.

This sliver was a downhill muddy cow pasture path, and suddenly before us stood the most massive white and brown horned bull I had ever seen.

"Oh, wow, look at him; I want to get out and pet him."

In a chorus, "Ruth, Mom, you're crazy."

"Look at those horns," I said, admiring the beast and took a picture through the windshield.

"You stay put," Jim said in a commanding tone.

"I love cows. Look at those gentle eyes; he wouldn't hurt a flea."

"Well, you are nuts; he may not hurt a fly, but he may hurt you, and for all, I know he may think we are a big cow and ram into us. I wouldn't trust an animal that size, and now we can't move until he does." The kids laughed nervously, and I kept watching the big animal. Finally, he meandered across the path, and we proceeded on our journey.

I said, "Maybe we'll see a buffalo next." No one commented and just shook their collective heads. We did see deer and chipmunks, a large mottled colored rabbit, and other animals moving so fast we could not identify them. We had to figure out our position as the trail wound round about the mountain ridges. Fortunately, we did not run out of gas again, though the fear was present.

It was late in the afternoon when we arrived at Jackson Hole, which is a western tourist town loaded with people. We bought more food supplies and headed out to the less populated park area.

Jim took the wrong road, and we turned about. Just by happenstance, we reached the campsites.

It was almost dark, of course. We unpacked out cooking gear, sleeping bags, and duffels with our clothing and the most essential, our tents. We could see the snow-capped mountains all around right from the campsite. We built a fire, made dinner, and bedded down.

On that first morning, I slept late, cuddled warm as could be in my sleeping bag in the nude. I saw no reason to change my regular sleeping habit. As I peered out, the boys and Suzette scuttled about setting up the camp. A wood chopping area, a rack for pots and pans, a site for the water, and Jim made a unique sink for me.

The Park Ranger stopped by and said, "You folks have done some work here; this is the best campsite I have ever seen." Jim graciously thanked him.

We played with sticks in the woods, pretending we were shooting at one another. We cooked on a grill, slept on the ground, and suffered the August chilly weather. After our cookout dinner, we sat around the fire, and Jim told stories. I walked to the laundry shack. The camp personnel had to do our wash as the water was scarce.

Additionally, we had to pay for showers. Jim and I met some other campers, and once the kids were in bed, we went to their site and listened to music. The jagged Rocky Mountains made me think of those rugged individuals that settled the west.

On day three, we piled into the van with breakfast out of the way, and it did not start. Jim plugged into the only available outlet, in the women's room, with our battery charger. While we waited in the rain, Jim said, "Since we have some time, I think I'll chop some wood for the campfire tonight." I was not sure if I saw the sense in that as the wet wood would make lighting the fire troublesome. "We could buy some dry wood." He did not listen to me and chopped away. We then picked up our wash and drove up to Yellowstone National Park, where we had lunch in a picnic area.

Located in Montana, Idaho, and Wyoming, Yellowstone was the first national park in the United States and possibly the world's first national park. President Ulysses S. Grant signed it into law on March 1, 1872. We looked at the geothermal pools of hot water, and at precisely five-ten on this day, and every other day Old Faithful shot up to the sky as the rain came down. Half the world's geothermal features are in Yellowstone. Jim drove about seventy-seven miles around the park, which spans an area of three thousand four hundred sixty-eight square miles; we saw geysers, many pools of hot boiling water bubbling up through the ground, and an abundant forest where pines, Douglas fir, spruce, and blue spruce grew.

Yellowstone was the end of the National Parks part of the trip. On a very wordy wooden information sign, I read aloud, "Native Americans have lived at Yellowstone for eleven thousand years." In twelve years, I moved four times. "Can you imagine that they live right near an active supervolcano that is considered the largest one on the continent? It has erupted several times in the last two million years."

"We don't want to be here when it does that the next time," Jim said. He encouraged me to read on, but attention spans were limited.

My last bit of information was, "Life began fifty-five million years ago during the Eocene Epoch." I felt I was reading to myself as they fiddled around, ready to leave.

I thought about beginning our trip from Florida and ending in Wyoming; the kids now had an idea of the vastness and the differences in our great country.

Our new family was disappointed that the National Parks part of the trip was over. They talked about what they had seen, but soon got bored. The only thing we could do was make up a game. The trinkets they bought had lost their appeal. There was little left to amuse them, so the quibbling started. By the time we got to Denver, nerves frayed, and Jim's patience was gone. Without notice, he pulled off the road and asked, "I want you to come with me."

"Where are we going?"

"Let's get away from the kids; we need to talk. There is a place we can sit on the hill and watch the van."

"Ok," I said. "I'm coming." Turning to the kids, I said, "Please, just behave, we will not be long, and we can see you."

Jim was a talker and liked to rehash things repeatedly. I do not care to do that. Say what you have to say. What is the sense of talking about it? That is what he did on this lovely hill overlooking Denver.

"You are catering to the kids; you always do," he began.

"The kids are going to grow up and go away. We are going to live our lives together," he continued.

"Yes, Jim, we will live our lives together, but the kids are going to be in it. Do you feel that they are such a disruptive force that you can't live with them?"

"They want to rule you. Tim and Jerry want their way. Jerry gets everything he wants."

"No, not everything he wants. He has been an only child for twelve years. This is a new experience for him. It takes getting used to; he now has to share his room, toys, and friends. Maybe to you, that is easy, but I feel that twelve and thirteen-year-old boys may want their privacy. Your kids have been brought up differently from mine."

"You think your kid is better than mine, Ruth."

"No, Jim, I did not say that. But you cater to every whim of Suzette, and she is spoiled."

"Well, she is the only girl; the boys pick on her and make fun of her."

"Suzette is a sensitive child; this is all new to her. She'll get used to having two older brothers. The boys tease her to see if they get a rise out of her, and she always does."

"Don't worry, if we bring them up right, they'll know who the boss is." My words of wisdom.

That went on for an hour. We could not agree on how to handle the children. In time, he made it clear once they reached eighteen, they needed to get out on their own. I think he was jealous of the attention I gave to them, and he wanted all my attention. Finally, although we did not resolve it, we needed to get on the road.

We took US 70 out of Denver and over to Kansas, where we muddled our way on secondary roads to Dodge City, Oklahoma. Jim wanted to experience Dodge City as the legendary Wild West town seen on TV. He told the children, "This is the famous Dodge City, where Wyatt Earp and Bat Masterson were Sheriffs protecting the town. You kids know the TV shows 'Dodge City'?"

They all chimed in, "Of course, we do, and we watch it every week. Why was this town so special?" Tim asked.

Jim answered with, "Dodge City had a railroad, and the Cowboys came in driving the cattle from the range to the train station."

Suzette wanted to know, "Where were they taking the cattle?"

Jim explained, and all eyes were on him, "This was a frontier town in the late 1800s, and the town was not very developed, so the cattle had to go by rail to the big cities in the north to feed the people."

Then, Jerry asked, "What made the town so wild?"

Again, Jim had their attention, "Once the men came in from the range driving cattle from Texas cattle ranches, they were hot and tired. There was a bar in town, and they went to drink and gamble. Then, the fights broke out, and so did the guns. Gunfighters came from near and far. They gambled and drank, and then they had to prove they were better than the other man."

"OK, let's move on to the museum. There you can see the guns and clothes they wore." I said.

The kids were interested in all the paraphernalia, the wanted posters, and most of all, the wax dummies of Billy the Kid, Jessie James, and Calamity Jane. Soon the boys were pulling dollar bills out of their pockets, buying souvenirs. There were guns in big glass cases, which the boys pored over.

Suzette was somewhat bored and said, "Come on, Daddy, I want to go."

"Wait a minute Suzette; we are going up to the Boot Hill Cemetery in a little while. Just hold up a bit." It did not mollify her, and she hung onto Jim's hand, trying to pull him away.

The cemetery was nothing special, only one gravestone of a person unfamiliar to us. The kids ran to the van, and we were off down the road east through Kansas.

We arrived in Wichita late at night. Next, we headed for Oklahoma City. The kids slept through Arkansas and Tennessee. Going south just outside of Knoxville, we picked up US 75 and went right through Georgia, going south to Jacksonville, Florida, and onto US 95 to Miami.

"So, Jim, we're almost home. Just about four-and-a-half hours with no traffic, we should be there. It was quite a trip," I said, and he agreed.

The vehicular breakdowns were a test of my patience. I had stuck it out due to my tenacious character. When I had an exuberant feeling of falling in love, in the beginning, I felt everything was rosy; I learned it was not so. What we see and what we think is not always what is. I learned that Jim was still right, regardless of the issue. He felt he knew everything and tried to sway others and me toward his direction. Jim was lazy and to top it off he was moody. He had tunnel vision and could only do one thing at a time. I found him to be insecure, thus making even grocery shopping a twosome. My independence took a terrible dive. I felt I passed an invisible test with him and the kids during the trip. Had I deserted him, his children would not have had a chance. He had nowhere to go, no money. The children would have ended up back in New York with their mother. She had made it clear to me I could do a better job raising them, and so I stuck it out from 1976 when we married to 2006 when the divorce finalized. Between that time and now, there are multiple stories to tell.

As I tell these stories and look at myself from the outside as a stranger looking in at someone else, I did not make the right life choices; I made too many quick decisions without thinking.

The summer with Jim's children extended to the school year and beyond. Tim and Suzette seldom spoke of or to their mother. She had told Jim we were better equipped to take care of her kids.

After the vacation, I continued to work at Bertram. Jim stayed home working on his sculptures, getting ready for winter shows. There was a benefit to him being home; the kids had an adult around when they came back from school."

Jim, I said, "It is evident that with the three kids we are going to need a larger vehicle for the shows." Therefore, the Econoline Van was retired for a Winnebago. It was now our new transportation and sleeping quarters for the shows out of town. It became my job to load the sculptures into the vehicle after I came home from a full day at the office. He was putting the final changes on his work instead of planning and being ready. I would get the boys to lend a hand if they were home.

On most evenings, he cooked dinner and left a mess in the kitchen. Jim was an imaginative cook. He liked to make the plates look appealing by adding foods with color. It was his artistic ability showing. It was my job, along with Suzette's, to clean up and load the dishwasher. Other than a few shows, we were planning our wedding.

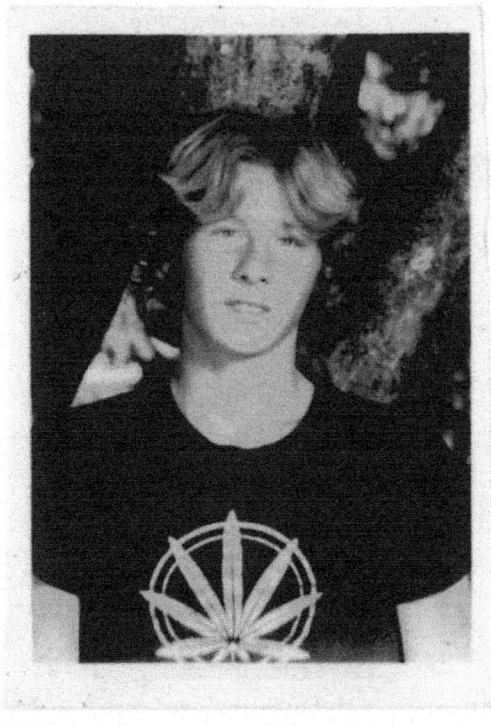

Timothy Boylan Jr High 1976

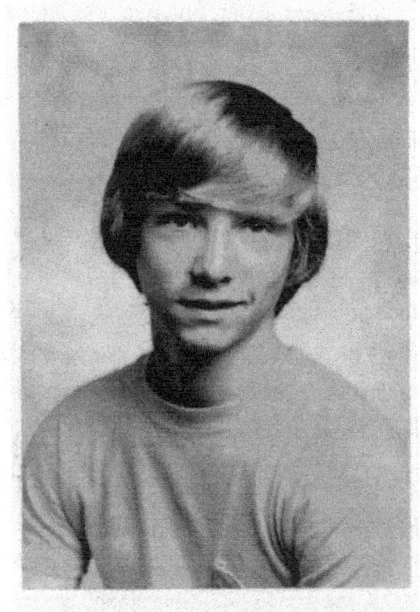

Jerry Blohm Jr High 1976

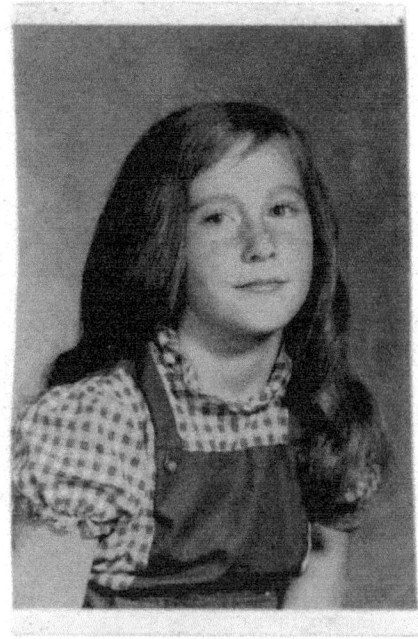

Suzette Boylan 9 yrs old Elementary 1976

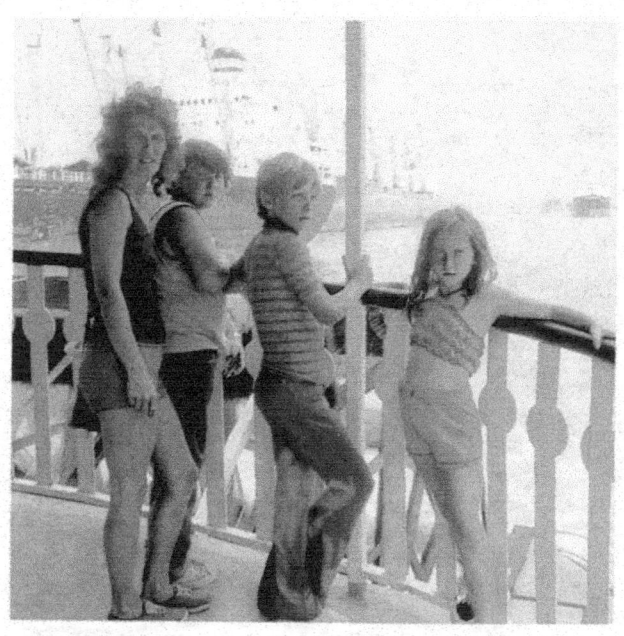

Boylan 1975, Jerry 13 yrs old, Tim 13 yrs old, Suzette 8 yrs old, Ruth 38 yrs old Mississippi River on the Natches steamwheel paddleboat

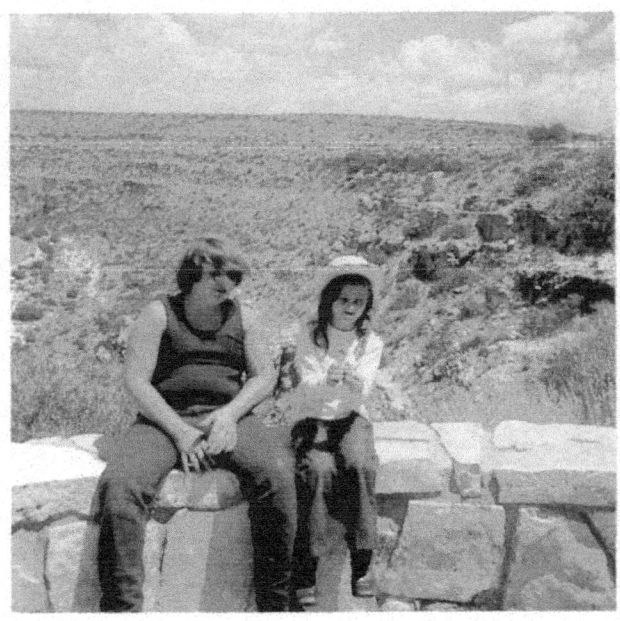

New Mexico 1975 Tim 13 yrs old, Suzette 8 yrs old

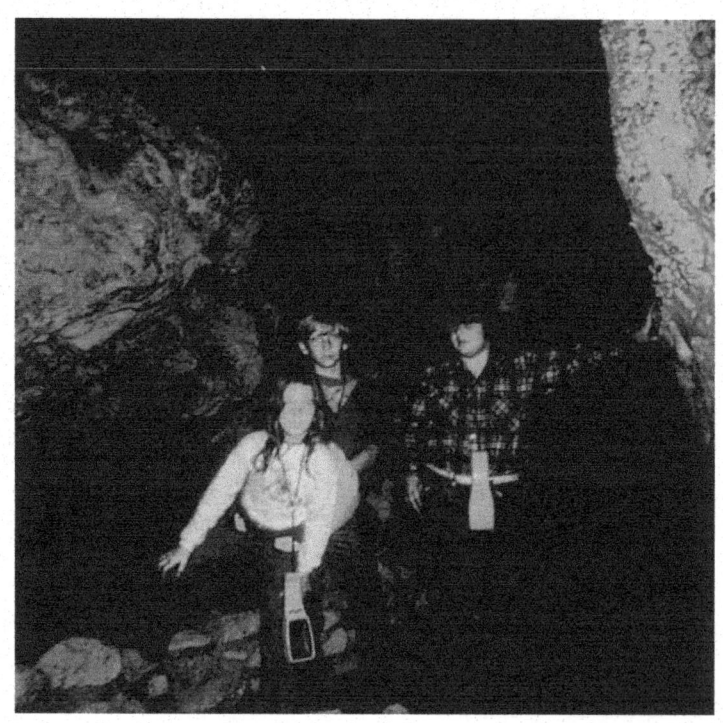

Suzette, Jerry & Tim Boylan 1975 Carlsbad Caverns, New Mexico

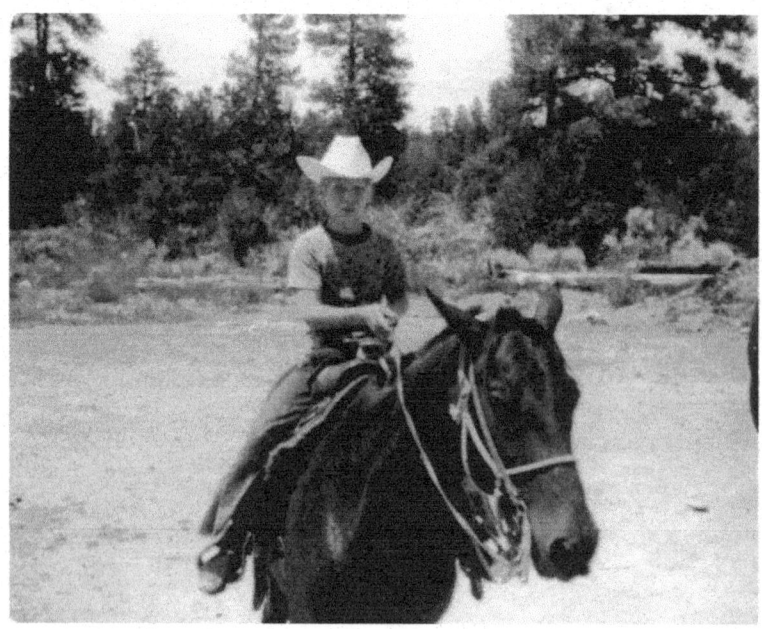

Grand Canyon 1975 Jerry Blohm

CHAPTER 27:

_____

THE WEDDING

On April 3, 1976, Jim and I married at the Plymouth Congregational Church in Coconut Grove, Florida, during the Lenten season. Built in 1917, it is fashioned after a Mexican Spanish mission constructed of limestone rock and wood beams. I decorated every other pew with bouquets of carnations.

This marriage was number three for me. *Number one was common law. I was ahead of my time; this became fashionable fifteen years later. My number two marriage was a Justice of the Peace.* For Jim, this was number three if you want to count the union that the Italian father had annulled. Jim had married Carmella on a dare. That caused her father great dissatisfaction, but when Jim plucked fruit from the fig tree, Papa considered it a devilish sin. Thus, the marriage to Carmella ended. At every art show, Jim searched the faces of the women for Carmella.

We first contemplated marriage in the Catholic Church. With my Catholic school attendance and familiarity with the religion, when Jim suggested we marry in the church, I had no objection—converting to Christianity would take years, but papal consent would be possible. Marriage counseling by the church was an option.

Father Augustine ushered us into a classroom. He questioned the religion of my previous marriage partner. I had no idea what Roger's faith was, but his father, Herman, was visiting and agreed to inform the priest that Roger was a Methodist. Therefore, as he was not Catholic, the church did not recognize this marriage. Father Augustine continued with the lessons, and at every turn, Jim questioned or disagreed with the teachings.

Father Augustine was a new disciple, and after three weeks of constant disagreement, he discharged us. And so we came to marry in a Congregational Church.

Our ceremony should be guaranteed to last a lifetime.

I felt self-conscious as an older bride and the focal point of the wedding. I did love Jim. He wanted to get married more than I did. I figured we could continue to live in sin, but there were the children to consider. In the end, it was better to make it a permanent arrangement.

I wore an off-white satin wedding dress decorated with tiny pearls, a high collar, long lacy sleeves, and a flowing train, and Jim wore a white tuxedo and bow tie. Jerry and Timothy suited up in black tuxedos with carnation boutonnieres and bow ties. Suzette looked lovely in a short sleeve, light color aquamarine, full-length gown matching the bridesmaids. My mother donned a floor-length sleeveless, white dress, and my mother-in-law had a full length, long sleeve, pale turquoise gown.

Ted stood in for my dad, who could not make the trip from New York. No doubt to my mother's delight. Years later, Ted got me a job where he worked.

I had a maid-of-honor, and he the best man. Two more groomsmen and two additional bridesmaids comprised the wedding entourage.

We stepped into the secluded tropical garden landscape with colorful orchids and palms after the ceremony for pictures.

To my surprise, Carol and Charlie were married in the same church five years earlier.

We did it up royally by having a reception at Sweden House with all the friends I could think to invite. Food, entertainment, photographers, a band, dancing, throwing the bouquet, and retrieving the garter from my leg were all part of the festivities.

Our wedding party helped transfer the many gifts to the house. We would open them upon our return from our honeymoon.

Suzie, Jim's mom, agreed to stay and take care of the kids. Poor woman; the boys found a turtle and filled the only tub in the house with water for it. I heard no other stories, but she was glad to see our return.

We honeymooned on the island of St Martin. On one side, it's French. I loved French cuisine, especially the French onion soup. On the other, it's called Dutch St. Maarten, where gambling tables are a way of life. Jim was a greedy gambler. I knew nothing of this vice. He gambled all the money. Only American money was acceptable to pay the fee to escape the Caribbean Island.

Had it not been for the quarter I found under the seat on the plane, we wouldn't have had a pickup at the airport.

Our plane made a stop in Puerto Rico. We had to go through customs and declare our fresh fruit. It was disappointing that the Puerto Rican Food and Drug Administration saw fit to confiscate my tangerines. We were able to keep our other gifts.

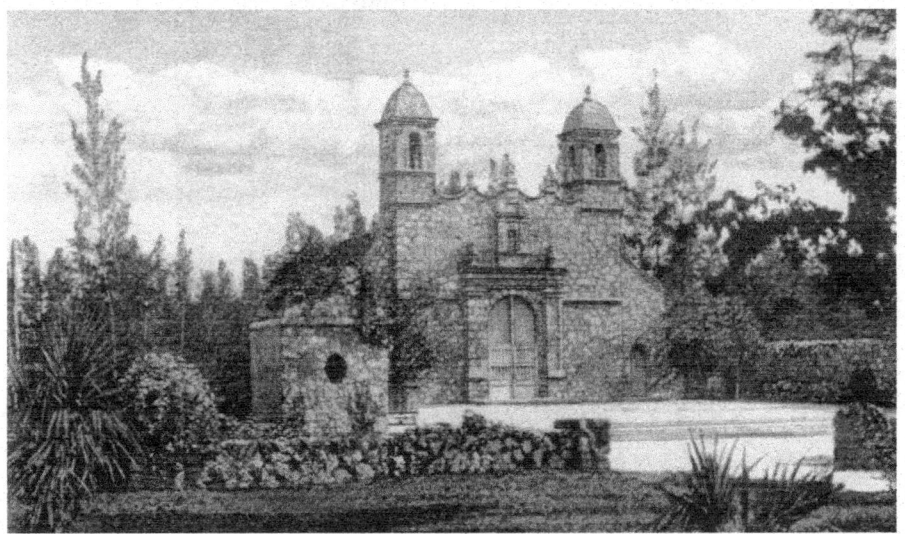

Plymouth Congregational Church

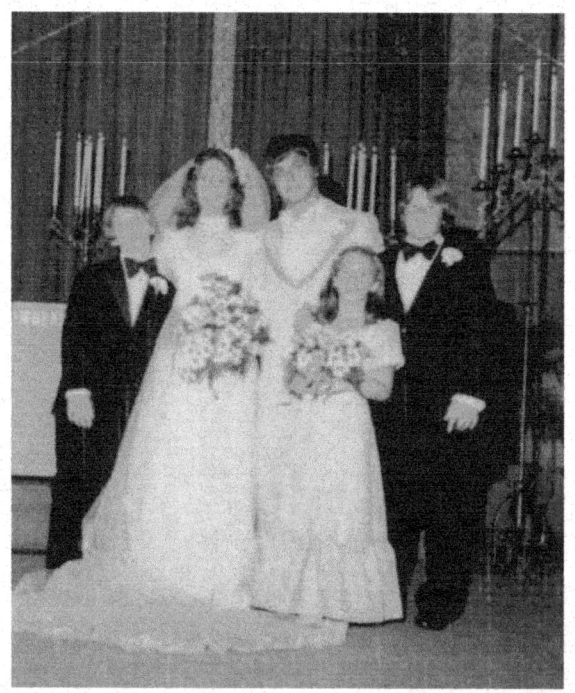

Jerry, Ruth & Jim Boylan, Suzette and Timothy April 3rd 1976, Wedding Day

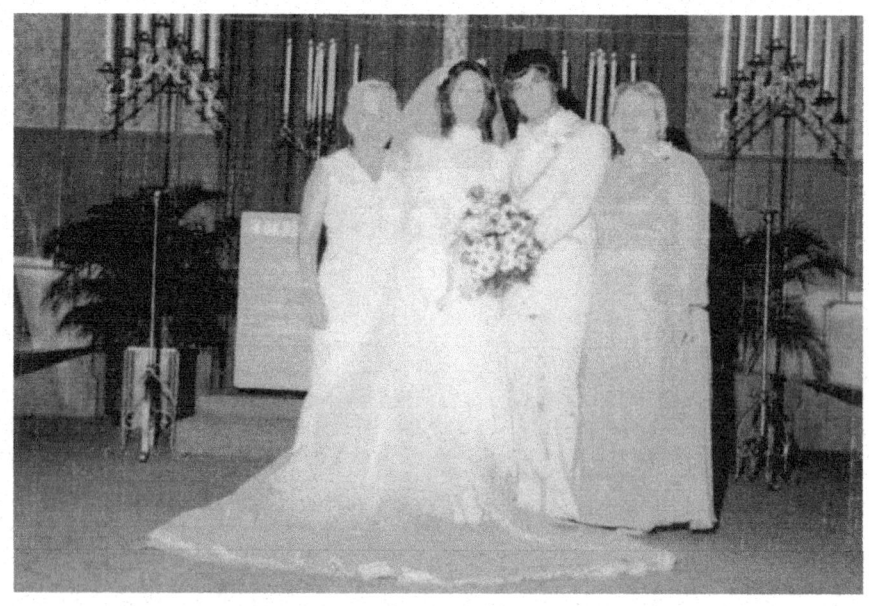

Regina Arnstein, Ruth Boylan, Jim Boylan, Susie Boylan Wedding Day"

CHAPTER 28:

_____

MARRIED WITH CHILDREN AND ANIMALS

After the honeymoon, we lived in my small home from April until December. I looked for a house in our neighborhood as I wanted to keep the kids in the same school. I found a larger home eight blocks away, which was within walking distance of the high school and elementary.

I was the only person bringing in a steady salary, and my new sculptor husband couldn't prove any income. We needed a co-signer to complete the deal, and my mother stepped up and signed her life away.

The house came with two amenities – a bar with a Schlitz globe and a pool table. Each child had a bedroom. Suzette got the master with a private bathroom, suitable for the only other female in the house, and the boys shared a bath. We transformed an expansive Florida room by splitting it in half to make our bedroom. The rest of the room became the family room.

Conveniently, there was a room in the back, perfect for Jim's workshop. We put in sliding glass doors so he could look out at the oak tree where I hung my potted plants on its spreading limbs. During hurricane season, these became missiles. Everyone had to join in to move them into the house. They also were a problem at mowing time; the boys had to duck around the hanging stag-horn ferns. These plants were a hobby for me and annoyed Jim. He had to have all my attention.

Eventually, we installed a swimming pool in the backyard. Boy, was that a fiasco. Instead of a rectangular pool, Jim wanted it shaped with a curve and softer corners. The wood had to be wet and then formed into a curved contour. He felt only he knew how to do this, and he carried on and fussed during the process.

One weekend, we took off in our Winnebago camper to go to an art show. Sometimes we just took Suzette and left Tim and Jerry at home under the watchful eye of a neighbor.

The next morning at home, I heard something that resembled a kitten crying. Questioning my son, this is the story I heard.

"Mom, we were out riding our bikes, and on the corner, down the street, the dozers were clearing a lot. They had knocked a tree down and out waddled baby raccoons. The dozer operator must not have seen the raccoon up in the tree. It was sad; the momma died. I saved one, and Donna; (school friends for years) you know Donna, Mom, she rescued another."

When Dingy was a kit, he would fit in the round sink in the bathroom. He would swat at the water as I washed him after each meal. He slept in bed with me, in the morning went out, and played in the tree to return in the evening. Dingy was fierce when it came to stealing a burger off my plate. A tiny hand reached up, grabbed the food, moved away from me, and growled while devouring it.

One afternoon a stray cat appeared on my doorstep. With a cat already in residence, we did not want another. Therefore, I made a trip to the pound to offer the unwanted stray cat; simultaneously, a woman arrived with a Basset Hound. She wanted to turn him in, and instead, I took him, and she took the cat. When I came home, Jim was shocked because he was sure the dog would hurt Dingy. Instead, they got along famously, running around under the pool table and wrestling on the floor.

After eight months, Dingy found out he was a boy and went off to raise a family. I hoped he would return, with family in tow; however, he never returned.

The Basset Hound was not an ideal dog. He dug all around the border of the fence, trying to get out. He howled in the morning every time a child left for school, which was enough for me to turn him over to a Basset Hound rescue organization.

Fritz, the cat, came from the Bertram Ship Yard, and she found residence in the small house, and then the new home. When we first moved into the new home, I called out, "Fritz," within minutes, a male voice answered. That was how I met our next-door neighbor. Next was a Siamese cat I found on the street; she was not well and soon passed away. Noel and his wife Joy had a place in the Everglades. They were making a move and wanted to pass their cat lady onto us. She was a long-haired black and white cat. We left her at home, where she sat in the center of our circle driveway under a Marginata tree.

At the Coral Gables Art show, a Japanese paper artist who practiced Kirigami's art had picture cuttings of geisha girls and colorful birds, representing long life, riches, health, and love. He gifted us his blue plumed, squawking parrot named Blue. When each child left for school, that parrot screamed. It was unfortunate; I had a scatterbrain day when I hung Blue in his cage, in the tree, to clean it. That way, not all the birdseed dropped onto the floor. Leaving Blue outside, I took the bottom of the cage into the house, and wow, when I returned, no bird. It was an accident. I don't think anyone believed me.

As for the Double Yellow-headed Amazon parrot, Pedro, the back-fence neighbor called the law on us because she thought he was a child, calling out, locked in the house. He would say,

"Pedro wants a cracker and screeched and screamed." He was not my bird. He bit me, but Jim could handle him. We also had a ferret, and Suzette's guinea pig, which made a habit of leaving his cage and jumping into the pool.

One afternoon, my mother visited. Without realizing it, she opened the door, and the ferret ran out. The neighbor's dog bit him; that called for a Veterinarian visit with stitches. Days later, Mitzie, my dog, a leftover from my previous marriage, was bitten by the same dog. I rushed her to the Veterinary clinic, stood to watch as they sewed her up and fainted dead away.

CHAPTER 29:

_____

THE ART SHOW CIRCUIT

When first we met, Jim's blue and white Ford Econoline van was his sole convey-ance for sleeping and carrying his sculptures to the numerous art exhibitions where he displayed his works. Shortly after we were together, I bought a Winnebago motor home. It comfortably slept all of us. It was a home on wheels. He had no credit, but I had my house, which I mortgaged for the purchase. Just a few more years, I would have had the home paid off. Now I was back in debt for love.

Jim's art shows were the only way he made any money. Not all artists, I learned, only plied their art exclusively. Many worked nine to five jobs. Jim did not. In the future, when he did have a job, he did not sculpt. He had a one-track mind. Sculpt, no work; work, no sculpt. However, he did interrupt work to make dinner most of the time.

Before an artist can participate in a juried show, he must apply with pictures of his work and his display racks along with the appropriate fees. This process takes weeks and, in some cases, months. He put together this arduous task, but once I became a permanent staff member, I took the pictures and forwarded the applications.

The famous Village Art show at Washington Square in Manhattan automatically accepted Jim as a long-time previous participant. That giant spring-summer event took place at the end of the school year. I had to give up my job so that I too might go to New York with the three kids for that exhibition. Bertram's had been fair to me for the three-week trip out west, but there was no way they would hold my job for the entire summer.

That put me in the motor home with three hungry children. I was always responsible for breakfast at home, but now I was the cook. That was unfamiliar territory. One pleasant day in Florida, New York, we parked in a public campground giving us electricity. The area was a dairy farm country, and down the lane, we purchased fresh milk. Back at our home on wheels, I prepared the best warm hot chocolate any of us ever drank. It seemed right after breakfast, and the dishes stowed away; it was time for the kids to eat again. The chore of making sandwiches and Mac and cheese was not the hardship I made it out to be. Office work suited me better.

We were on our way to Buffalo, New York, where Jim won best in the show. He received a red ribbon and a few dollars. As we were pulling out of town, something snapped in the motor home, and we put the money into repairing the break. Money was a scarce commodity during that summer trip. After the show, we visited my dad and Margot in Phoenicia in the Catskill Mountains in New York. Being fed by Margot's cooking for two days was a refreshing change from my meal preparation. Across from their home, a rocky creek idles among the mountains. The kids and I walked the rocks; I missed a rock and dipped my foot in the icy water limping back to the house only to have my father laugh at my clumsiness.

Next, we pulled into Yonkers, New York. It was a rainy day, and Jim assembled with a few artists who teased Jim about their lousy weather. Jim stepped into a phone booth, telling them, "I'll get this taken care of; I'll call God and request a sunny day." Within minutes, the sun shone. We set up our display. He placed a red velvet cloth on the table, and I brought out the sculptures, which he spaced a foot apart. Shortly after a white spot appeared under each piece of art, I had cleaned the bottom coral pieces with Clorox, and it bleached out the red. Jim sat down, frowned at me, and began writing a note. It said, "I feel your services are no longer needed. Consider yourself fired."

Mystic, Connecticut, was our next stop. A hurricane was brewing, and the boys taped up the windows and did not take it off soon enough for it to require laborious scraping. Jim put his coffee pot on, sat down only in his ragged shorts, and went to work. It was late in the evening, and after dinner, the kids went to sleep while I read and saw Jim watch his TV and put his pieces together.

The storm blew over, and we had a decent show, mainly because my sister-in-law bought a large piece of a boy on a lake fishing. Grace was Eugene's wife (do you remember him? He was Nicky's son who walked the neighborhood in East Orange during the air raids.) Eugene had worked for Electric Boat in Mystic. He passed from lymphatic cancer in about 1975. Grace remained in Mystic, raising their adopted children, Nanette and Douglas. This artwork was a reminder of the death of Douglas drowning in a local lake one winter.

Mystic's seaport afforded many places for the boys to entertain themselves, while Suzette and I had a lunch of potato pancakes with applesauce in a delicatessen. We walked the charming streets and viewed the many art shops with nautical paintings.

After that show, we rode down to see his mother, Susie, in Southington, Connecticut. Jay, Jim's brother-in-law, gave us less than a warm welcome. During our stay, we seldom saw Jay. Before we left, he told us, "Well, it was fine you came to see your mother, but I suggest you not visit again."

Jay was from Arkansas, a mid-westerner with a drawl, speaking slowly, dragging out his words. He worked in a factory all his life without an ounce of artistic appreciation. He disliked his brother-in-law, was distant with his mother-in-law, and married to Rosemary, Jim's older sister, with whom he had three children.

Our last show that summer was at Fernandina Beach, Florida. They knew how to put on a party. Coming around to each booth with pirate garb, they captured me and placed me in a cell.

The organizers brought out jail on wheels. Dressed as pirates, they arrested people and put them behind bars with other laughing people requesting a ransom. The boys had a ball with Suzette tagging along with them. It was a fun show with good sales of Jim's nautical pieces.

Gasparilla Festival of the Arts is a two-day event held in Tampa in March. Artists were vying for fifteen thousand dollars, should they win Best in Show. Artists from around the country and abroad attended that festival. Walking around the fairgrounds, I reveled at the talents of excellent creative people and their compositions.

Most weekends with one or all three of the kids, we did shows. Coconut Grove, Florida, was a local show with excellent sales. My mother sat and watched the people and marveled at our sales.

Then, there was Las Olas in Ft. Lauderdale that was considered an ultimate show where the rich came to look and buy.

Out of town, we had the Indialantic show on a blistering hot day. Lovebugs swarmed, landing on car grills and sun-screened bathing-suited art show guests. Jim ogled at those walking the boardwalk. After the show, I leaped into the ocean, removing my bikini and waving it over my head. Do you think I upset Jim? I put the suit back on before I exited the water, refreshed.

At New Smyrna, I came across an artist that used a similar technique as Jim. His work showed more wire, whereas Jim had coated over the wire to make the shape.

Virginia Beach's seaside extravaganza in 1977 featured countless drawings, craftworks of pottery, jewelry, and string art along the sandy beach. Behind us was the boardwalk where attendees could observe the show. It was here that I heard that art fairs attracted more people than football games. Unbelievable! That was a two-day show, so as darkness crept over the ocean Jim closed the doors of his display. It consisted of three doors that folded in, making a shelter for the sculptures. It had been a long day in the sun, and sales had been excellent.

Virginia Beach, a tourist town, offered a wide array of restaurants. Just off the beach, we chose Carousel, a French-Vietnamese place with an exceptional fare. He cooked. She was the maître d'. Upon leaving, we realized the wind had kicked up. Checking our display from the boardwalk and seeing that it was standing, we noticed that some roofs had blown off and merchandise scattered by the winds, but we were safe.

Parker Playhouse in Ft. Lauderdale displayed a few of Jim's sculptures. Late one evening, our phone rang; it was a gentleman who had been to a show and saw a piece he wished to buy. It was a hobo sitting on a park bench. We hustled out to Lauderdale and handed the work over to the customer.

Months later, Liberace appeared at the Parker Playhouse. My mother, Jim, and I enjoyed the show, and afterward, we went backstage. Jim gave him a sculpture of a grand piano with candelabra. This piece rests in the Liberace museum in Las Vegas. Liberace invited my mother to Palm Springs, but she never went.

Jim had taken no art classes. He studied the human shape, creating life-like subjects in a smaller form. To me, not an art connoisseur, his work showed creativity and originality. He had talent. He was meticulously fabricating intricately designed pricy boathouses that sold well. He also made golfers, anglers, mermaids, and children at play.

Well before Jim, I did an event on Watson Island in Miami. It was in support of the Mexican lettuce growers. I showed porcelain jewelry I fired in my kiln. I had also made plaques depicting 1776 Revolutionary soldiers in commemoration of the war. In a few years, it would be our country's 200th birthday.

My attraction to art shows continued. In 2014, I attended the South Miami show along with Carol. I tripped over a curb and fell splat into the street in front of several vendors, breaking my right hip. Instead of sending an ambulance, the fire department arrived. Spread out on the road, much to Carol's chagrin; the ambulance came and took me away.

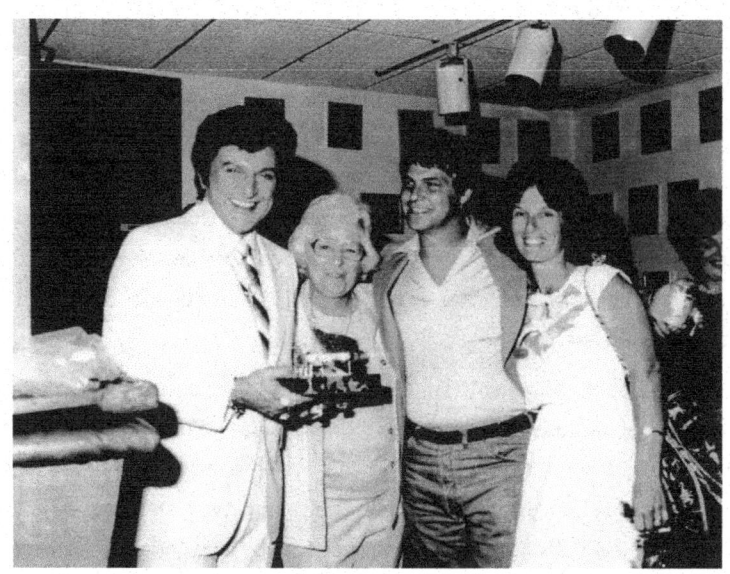

Liberace accepting a sculpture made by Jim Boylan. Liberace, Regina Arnstein, Jim Boylan and Ruth Boylan

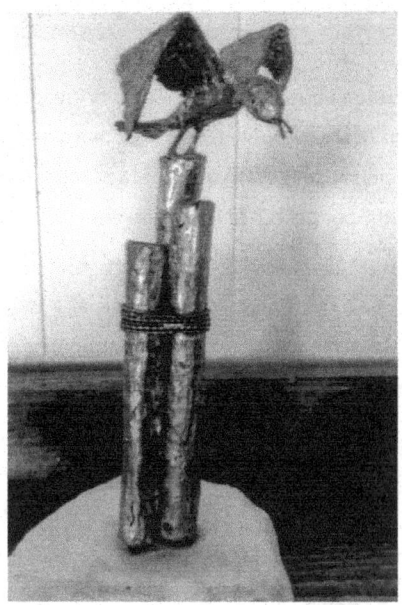

Jim Boylan sculpture

CHAPTER 30:

_____

JIM BOYLAN'S CHILDREN

James – 1957 -- Stella – 1959 -- Annette – 1960 -- Timothy - 1962 -- Suzette – 1967
Jerry – 1962

Annette

In 1975–1976, establishing a hierarchy with Jim's older daughter Annette was a continual battle in the first year. What instantly comes to mind was the day Annette, who was visiting, disagreed with my parenting of Suzette. Suzette insisted she did not need a shower, and I attempted to persuade her she did. There was one small bathroom in the house; it was not a place for three females. Annette did not like what she saw and started to beat me up. She outdid me by three-inches, a slim girl of sixteen, Irish strong, New York-bred; I was no match for her. She won, but not in the end; we sent her back to New York on the next plane.

During the bathroom confrontation, Jim was in the garage, working on his sculpture pieces for the weekend show. I ran the short distance to the garage in a confused, teary, angry state. Making an effort not to scream, I said, "Annette beat me up."

"What do you mean she beat you up?" He was puzzled and concerned.

As I explained the basic details of the disagreement and fight, he became angry.

"Annette always was protective of her sister, but that type of behavior does not belong in this house. I will not condone such an attitude toward you. I do hate to send her back to Irene, but I fear there is little choice. I'll tell her she must leave."

Annette had a second chance with us after she called to say, "I am not getting along with Mom (Irene). Can I come back, Daddy?" (She always referred to him as Daddy.) The relationship with her mother, Irene, was rocky. She knew she would get more needed care from her dad.

Her first disclosure to us was, "I am having female problems." Jim and I took her to a doctor, who proclaimed, "Your daughter will never get pregnant." That sounded great; she had enough trouble taking care of herself. She did poorly in school, had difficulty in the lower grades, and, although not slow, acted immaturely. At eighteen, she had not finished high school, and Here's Help, an accredited Miami-Dade Program, had adult classes to remedy that situation. Their focus was GED and work-related education to give her the tools to make a living wage and feel competent to live in a place on her own. We encouraged her to attend school, which she did willingly.

Annette did not feel the need for education; instead, she was more inclined to find a boyfriend. Andrew, a boy from the Dominican Republic, was her mate of choice. He was well mannered, an attractive teen, speaking English fluently, and seemed to care for Annette. If a marriage took place, I do not recall.

One day, she turned up at our house, letting us know they were bound for the Dominican Republic. Three months later, a call came from Annette, "Daddy, he beat me up. I want to come home. I am at the Naval Base now. Can I come home? Can you make my flight reservation? I have no money."

Of course, she came home pregnant. Seven months later, twin boys, Andrew and Joseph, were born. However, that was not the end. She tied back up with him, got pregnant again, this time with a girl, Evie. Eventually, she went back up north to her mother. After that, Annette only called, but she did not return.

James, Jr.

This next tail is sad, but well worth the telling. A weekend in 1979, James, Jr. came to the house and wanted us to take his two-month-old baby girl for a few days. He and Lorie were going camping in the Everglades in Monroe County, Florida, and didn't want to take the baby. Right away, no thought required, we said no. That was no doubt the best decision we ever made. On Sunday, James, Jr. called and said the baby was dead. She had died of sudden infant death syndrome. He had no money to bury her.

They had gone into Naples with the child in search of a funeral home. Later, they checked into a motel for the night. The following morning, Lori awakened in fright, knocked on the neighbor's door announcing hysterically, "My baby is dead." The innocent woman, with no knowledge of the situation, immediately phoned the police. Soon, the area was swarming with officers, fire, and ambulance services. The city dispatched a helicopter to assist, and it flew above the skies over the motel.

Jim and I immediately drove to Naples and made our way to the funeral home, and with James, Jr. arranged for the service. Then, Jim and I went to the cemetery to choose a plot. We paid all the expenses for the funeral and the cemetery plot.

By the time the funeral was in place, the funeral home had heard of the morning incident. They arranged for police protection during the service should any commotion arise.

After the service, James Jr. picked up the tiny casket and placed it into the hearse. At the gravesite, he once again carried the baby to the burial site. It was a heart-wrenching experience.

Irene had flown in from New York. In a quiet moment in the afternoon, as we leaned against the outside wall of the funeral home, she said, "Ruth, I think you have better parenting skills with Timothy and Suzette. You are doing a better job than I can." The gist of the conversation was to make sure I was keeping her children.

We paid for the ticket for Irene to return to New York. At the airport James, dramatically, declared to his parents, "My life is over; I am going to walk into the ocean and drown."

Irene responded, "James, you better get a grip on yourself; this was not your fault."

James and Lori did not stay together. He hooked up with an older woman Beverly who helped raise his son James. He became a long-distance truck driver, and the last I heard, he lived in Mississippi.

Unfortunately, James, Jr. passed away on December 5, 2019, of a heartache.

Stella

Stella and I never became close. She was a grown woman with an infant son when Jim and I married. Stella is short and has brown hair with a great body taking after her fraternal grandmother, Susie.

Susie was living with her daughter, Jim's older sister, Rosemarie. When Susie became ill, she requested her son bring her to our home in Miami.

Stella willingly helped pack her Grandmother Susie's belongings when we moved Susie from Connecticut to Florida.

In 1987, Susie suffered a diabetic stroke.

Stella helped care for her grandmother and was with us when in 1988, Susie passed. After the funeral, she went back to New York.

Suzette

There was a little girl, who had a little curl,

Right in the middle of her forehead.

When she was good,

She was very good indeed,

But when she was bad, she was horrid.

Henry Wadsworth Longfellow

I think this poem speaks volumes about Suzette, although she had no-curl, but the reddest of red hair.

She was a slight little girl with gorgeous long red hair inherited from her mother and a temper to match. Her hair attracted unwanted attention, which made her feel self-conscience. As a child, she was shy and determined to get her way, although she displayed a sensitive and caring nature. She was moody at times and manipulative.

Jim was the father of five children; God forbid they were all to live with us. Suzette and Tim were the youngest ones, and I was their temporary mother for the summer. By the time school began, I had found I was the full-time mom of three growing children.

Making girlfriends in the new neighborhood was impossible as there were only boys. She would play alone in her bathroom, like little girls do, washing her dolls. She hung around with her brothers and the other boys when they let her.

February was the month when Suzette on the 19th and Tim on the 22nd each had a birthday. Their mother, Irene, sent packages for all three children via the post office. There was heightened drama when the mail-lady rang the doorbell. We all ran to answer it, and upon opening the door, our old fifteen-pound brown female Scottie mutt Mitzie ran out too, frightening the postal lady. To get away from the dog, she sought refuge on the hood of my Dodge Colt parked in the circular driveway. With a mace spray canister in hand, she sprayed the dog while pounding her boots on the hood of my car. That was the first in a series of accidents my new car endured.

Suzette had begun to show an interest in gymnastics. We enrolled her in a class where she did, I thought, exceptionally well, working on the parallel bars and the balance beam. If she felt she did something wrong or fell off, she would get discouraged. She was hard on herself. Then, she would get moody and say, "I want to quit." With encouragement, she continued for a few more months, but she was displeased. She had learned and performed on the mat doing handstands, cartwheels, front handsprings, and forward somersaults. Frequently, on a happy day, she would bounce around the yard showing off her acrobatic skills.

After graduating from elementary school, Suzette moved on to attend South Miami Jr. High. Instead of making friends with girls her age, she hooked up with an older classmate Carla who lived with her father. Her mother was in prison for neglecting a child who died. Soon they were skipping school together.

The two girls went to Carla's home and called the police, concocting a story that a black man tried to break into the house. When the police arrived, he told the girls, "This is a serious crime. Reporting something that is not true could get an innocent man injured."

We wanted to keep her away from Carla, and when the school suggested transferring her to Here's Help, a school for problem teens, we agreed. She was the youngest person in the class. Her peer group kids were fifteen, sixteen, and seventeen. Besides her regular studies, she attended two after school days in peer counseling groups; we were required to show up for parent counseling classes once a week.

Academically, she was doing fine, but at home, a wrong word uttered by the boys could throw her into a mild tantrum.

We were eating corn cobs for dinner, served on the corn cob plates I made years before.

Something said, and suddenly the plate flew across the floor, broken into pieces. Suzette stormed away into her room.

At Here's Help, Suzette passed all her classes and should have been placed into the eighth grade, but the school was conducting an experimental summer program to keep kids off the streets. Her attendance at these classes would have no bearing on her promotion. We made every effort to get her to these additional classes. She missed a few classes, and then at the end, she missed four sessions. We were shocked when notified that she hadn't passed the eighth grade. When she heard the news, she was so disappointed and felt it was unfair.

We invited the guidance counselor and all the kids to a pool party at our house to commemorate the end of school. The counselor felt she was doing well and was ready to go back to her school.

In the fall, Suzette went back to South Miami Jr. High. She found it hard to accept that she ended up with twelve-year-olds in the seventh grade. Suzette connected with a little girl in her class. I was hoping that if she had a friend, it might make her feel better about school. I would drive her there, and Cathy's mother brought her home. That didn't last long. She liked their pool more than she liked Cathy, a more attentive child.

That was the time we began to notice a change in our daughter. We saw her physical development for her age, but at the same time, she was still a child. Puberty had set in, and I thought her raging hormones caused her inability to cope with life. The land of limbo between child and teen was taking its toll on this sweet little girl and giving us a sulking, moody teenager.

Once we settled one problem, there was another. We were not aware that Suzette was skipping school. One day, a truant officer picked Suzette up and took her to juvenile hall. Both Jim and I went to court, and embarrassed, we stood before Judge Faust.

I told the judge, "I had no idea my daughter was not attending school. Please, can I take her home? We will insist she must go to school." The judge was sympathetic. We appeared to be good parents, dressed well, and showed that we were an educated couple.

Turning to Suzette, the judge said, "I don't want to see you back in my courtroom again, young lady. Listen to your parents. You mean the world to them. These are good parents to take time off work to be here for you."

Suzette hung her head down contritely and answered politely. "Yes, ma'am." She was scared.

We wanted her to know that we loved her and were willing to give her a second chance.

We stopped off at a restaurant to treat her to a nice meal and show her we trusted her. She behaved well; no smart answers, and promised to change and go to school. The meal over, she requested to go to the ladies' room, where she crawled out of the window and ran off. She manipulated her dad and me into believing she would reform. Later that day, she returned home with no explanation.

She went back to school for a few weeks; everything proceeded along, as it should be, until one evening, Suzette didn't appear for dinner. We all started making phone calls. Finally, Tim got a lead from a young boy up the street, who said, "After school, she went to the home of a boy in her class."

He told Tim where he lived, and I followed up by going to the boy's home. She knew I was there, and so did the boy's mother, but she denied me entrance into the house and would not release our daughter. Suzette refused to come out. I called the police, and they came to the house.

The police officer told me, "I can't go into the house and take her out if the parent there will not let you in."

Suzette refused to leave. What was I to do? Jim came back to the house with me and talked to her from the front yard, threatening to send her back to juvenile. That garnered a response, and she slowly came down the steps.

Her punishment was to stay home after school for a week.

On an afternoon trip to Sears in the parking lot, another car struck us in a hit and run accident. It was the second in a series of dents my Dodge Colt suffered. Also, to complicate things more, Suzette told me she stole a pair of earrings. I was aghast and said as gently as I could, "Why would you do that? You know that is shoplifting; you could go to jail."

"I wanted them. No one was looking, and these were just on the counter, so I took the earrings. These aren't expensive."

"Expensive is not the point; you don't just pick something up in a department store and walk out with it. Let me see them. Look, you have to have pierced ears for these."

"Well, I didn't look at them that closely."

"So, now what are you going to do? You know you have to go back to the store and give them back," I told her sternly. She and I walked back into the store, found a salesperson, and returned them.

I think the incident was embarrassing enough that she did not do it again.

Once again, life was settling into a routine. All were attending school. At least I thought they were, and Suzette was enjoying the pool with Jim after school.

Then, the next thing to surface was Tim told his dad that Suzette was smoking. That was grand of him as he turned her on to it. Jerry was the only one in the house that did not smoke. At least not packaged cigarettes. She always wanted to do what her older brother was doing.

One Sunday morning, Jim and I had gone out riding our motorcycle with a forty-year-old-and-over-group called the Sundowners Motorcycle Club. Jerry and Suzette were in the house with Grandma.

Upon our return, Grandma informed us, "I was in the kitchen, and suddenly I smelled smoke and ran back toward the bedrooms. When I went into Suzette's room, I saw the mattress was smoldering. I called her, and she took some time to answer me. She was under her bed, hiding. She had dropped her lighted cigarette on the mattress, and it caught fire. I got all excited and called for Jerry, and he and I threw the mattress out the door."

I do not think Suzette tried to get into trouble. I felt part of her problem might have been that she was not with her mother. When I asked her, "Do you want to go back to New York and live with your mom?" She always gave me a negative response. "No, I love you guys."

We did not ignore her, and she was getting plenty of attention and love even though we corrected her for her misdeeds. I think she was unable to communicate her feelings, and it caused emotional stress. She could not express herself to us in any other way except misbehaving.

Suzette and I got along fine. After dinner, on most evenings, we would clean the kitchen together. She handed me the plates, and I would load the dishwasher.

Suzette had stayed after school, and on my way home from work I picked her up. We made a stop at the Sundry store for some after school sweets. The car to the right of us was an old Cadillac with big tail fins driven by an elderly man. We must have been driving an invisible car because he turned his wheel right into our right rear door as he backed up. That was accident number three. We were fine, only the car suffered.

A few days later, when I arrived home in the evening, it was a pleasure to see Jim had cooked our meal. Now my job was to set our glass and chrome table for dinner. Hoping there would be no drama, I called all the kids to the table. He had placed Pedro, our double yellow-headed Amazon parrot, on his perch. Pedro was an integral part of our family. The boys showed up, but no Suzette. In times like these, Pedro was a distraction. During dinner, he would repeat his name and say, "Pedro wants a cracker." He walked back and forth on his perch, dancing and fluffing his feathers. It made us all laugh. In a bit over an hour, after we worried where she could be, she showed up. This behavior was becoming more frequent. More conversations, more promises from Suzette. More of the same.

"Why can't I do what I want? It is still light out."

Jim spoke up, "Now listen, you know we have rules, and you must come in for dinner…"

"I wasn't hungry," she snipped.

I said, "So, where did you eat that you weren't hungry at six?"

"I ate nowhere; I just ate. What difference does it make? Why do you care? I'm home now."

She stormed off to her room. What does one do with behavior like this? Her disobedience was becoming more frequent.

Three days later, Suzette was out the door, ready to leave early for school. At about eleven, a call came from her school that she was not in attendance. I let Jim know, but I stayed at work. She stayed gone the entire day, and in the evening, we reported our daughter missing to the Police Department. They classified her as a runaway and informed us there were four hundred runaways in our county. We made frantic phone calls to all her school friends and enlisted the help of our boys. No one seemed to know her whereabouts. A phone call came for Tim from a boy that said he had seen her at Key Biscayne. That rang a bell. Paul was a friend of Tim's who had come to our house. I knew she liked him, and I knew he lived on Key Biscayne. Of course, at her age, she was boy crazy.

At 9:00 p.m., we headed for the Key. We checked at the closed Seaquarium, the Marine station, and the beach. A Park Ranger took us around to the hangouts for runaways. We had no success. In the morning, a concerned parent phoned, suggesting I go back to the Key and check at the toll booths, the lifeguard stands, and at the end of the Key at Cape Florida lighthouse. We checked schools, Tropical Park, Dadeland Shopping Center, the bus station and called the eight-hundred numbers for runaways. We stopped at Pizza shops, gas stations, and seven-eleven's; we were out of options and exhausted. Our phone rang in the early evening; a young man told us our daughter was on the street corner in North Miami Beach near the Wild Horse Saloon. Like good parents, we hopped in our car and collected her.

By now, we had lost control of the situation. Not only was Suzette running away, but Tim also was not going to school. It was time to get some help from a professional person. We went to see a female blind psychiatrist with the three children. After three visits, Jim declared, "I am not happy with this woman. I cannot understand how a blind person can be objective. I do not believe she has any experience with family counseling." He felt he was the brunt of her comments. I disagreed with him, but said nary a word.

I do not want to put all the blame on Suzette. The boys did their share too.

One evening, Tim and Jerry climbed out of their bedroom windows and met a group of their pals on the street. One of their girlfriends was spending the night at another friend's house while the mother was out of town. That is where they were going until Jim apprehended them. We called the parents of the girls and boys who were involved in this illicit event. That night we dealt with some upset girls fearing their parent's wrath.

"Oh, please, Mr. Boylan, don't call my parents. They are going to kill me," one of the girls cried nearly on her knees.

Each evening was a concern. Each evening I wondered, will we all be having dinner, or will one be missing? It is hard for me not to stress how many times she took off and how disturbing every incident was to us. It seems Suzette was under arrest one more time and placed in Juvenile Hall. I cannot remember the exact incident, but this next one is clear in my mind.

We were getting ready for bed, and the phone rang. It was 10:30 p.m. Suzette's voice sounded, "Mom, can you come and get me? A friend brought me here, and then he left. I can't get home."

Accident number four. The woman insisted to the officer that Jim was driving. I was driving. It took quite some time to unravel this discrepancy. After a long delay with the police, we finally picked Suzette up from a house full of boys, drugs, and Quaaludes.

She told us, "There were four boys and two girls, and they were all older. They wanted me to smoke pot and do drugs and other things," she was crying and trying to catch her breath. We talked some, but it was best to take her home.

I would have been the dumbest mother alive if I did not think my daughter was sexually active. At thirteen, she looked like sixteen. I had proposed the question to Jim about birth control pills, and his response was, "Then she will think we are giving her permission."

"That would be better than to get pregnant."

He ignored my pleas. It may have been too late already as shortly after this 'evening out,' Suzette informed me that she was pregnant.

I told her, "I was not raising a child of a thirteen-year-old. I convinced her to have an abortion."

I knew this did not sit well with her, but eventually, she realized the final consequences of having a baby at her age.

In 1982, we decided to start a business locally instead of going out of town for the art shows. We opened up a gun shop just a few blocks from the house.

Suzette had just turned fourteen.

Jim brought his gun home from the shop and hid it under our mattress for safe keeping.

He had taken the time to explain to Suzette and the boys the traumatic effect of a bullet. He used a milk carton and showed her how a bullet entered with a small hole and how it exited with a large one. Our bedroom was off-limits, but one day when we were out, Suzette went into our bedroom, stole the gun, and gave it to a boy. Thank goodness, before any damage occurred, we got it back. Again, we restricted her to the home.

Here is another small incident that sticks in my mind. We were arranging a little party with our motorcycle friends. On the corner of the bar, I had placed a cut-glass bell Jerry had sent from Germany for my collection. During the afternoon, unexpectedly, there was a crash, and it lay smashed on the floor. Suzette never admitted touching it.

Suzette's return to the seventh grade was going poorly. I checked with the Mast Academy on Key Biscayne. It featured marine biology, swimming, and maritime studies. They agreed to take her. I felt this would be an excellent opportunity, a new school, and a fresh start. She seemed to accept the challenge, but I noticed my car missing from the driveway the morning she was to start classes. Suzette stole the car keys, and late that night, a knock on the door let us know the whereabouts of our daughter.

"Good evening, we have just apprehended your daughter. We have her in the back of the patrol car. She has driven your car into a telephone pole. Do you want her?"

"No, we do not." We felt obligated to exhibit 'tough love.' That was her third appearance in court.

Appearing before Judge Faust again, "Hello, Mrs. Boylan. I see Suzette has gotten into trouble once more. I understand you are concerned about her well-being. Stealing a car is a significant offense. I do not want to keep her in custody. I do not feel that will do her any good, and it is not my recommendation, at this time, to release the child in your custody. She has been in my courtroom three times, and that makes her a repeat offender. I am suggesting we place her in a protected counseling environment at Coral Reef Hospital. They have a good temporary program, and I feel it will benefit both you and Suzette."

We went to see her three times a week. It was a breath of fresh air to know she was safe. We did not need to correct her in this environment. We played UNO, a family card game that she enjoyed. We laughed, but did not talk much as that embarrassed her in front of the staff, which was present. The location was an adult facility. They were giving her counseling, but they could not do any long-term residence program. We needed to find an in-house school program with group counseling classes; that would be best for her future development.

That put us out on the road, checking a place that would be suitable. In the early eighties, in many communities, boarding schools for troubled kids was not available. People objected to having them in their neighborhoods. Tampa, Florida, was the first place we checked. They were not interested in accepting Suzette.

Highland Hospital in Asheville, NC, was our next choice. Here Zelda Fitzgerald, F. Scott Fitzgerald's wife, perished in a fire that consumed the hospital in 1947/48. After a year of reconstruction, it was an impressive old structure appropriate in size but not in location.

Highway Two Forty was visible from the property, and we were sure Suzette would find her way down to it and escape.

Our next place was Sheppard Pratt in Townsend, Maryland, near The Beltway. It is a facility on the leading edge known for the treatment of adolescent mental and behavioral disorders. We met with the staff and agreed she fit the program. One of the stipulations was that we appear twice a month for counseling sessions with her present. She was with patients her age and received clinical programs and behavior therapy.

During her confinement, it was hard for me to retain a full-time job. Jartran Truck Rental fired me, but the insurance lingered. It covered hospital expenses. I sold Creepy Crawlers, a swimming pool cleaner, and worked for a job recruitment agency. Jim kept the shop open.

On a pleasant day in South Florida, we took our motorcycle to Maryland without thinking it through. The weather changed to a northern climate, and I froze on that bike.

Suzette spent six months at the hospital. The staff felt she was ready to come home. I flew into Dulles International, rented a car, and picked up a not so happy teenager. Her behavior on the plane showed me her attitude was no different.

Once she returned home from Maryland, Suzette went back to school.

I had a friend Janette that I met when Jerry was six years old. She took in children for after-school care. Janette was an intelligent woman but a troubled person. On many evenings, we talked at length. She phoned me often and discussed her problems. This particular night she had said, "I don't want to bother you anymore."

My response, "You never bother me."

The next day I left the shop to pick up some guns and never thought any more about our conversation. That evening I got a call from her sister Kay informing me she had hung herself. How would I have gathered, from that exchange, what was really on her mind?

James, her eldest son, lived in a halfway house. Kay requested we get him and bring him home. I know this was more than she could handle. She was disabled. Janette left a boy Arnold about eleven, and a girl Janny a daughter of nine-plus, Anthony, who was away at college and was on his way home.

We brought James to our house because he did not wish to stay at his mother's place. Suzette immediately latched onto him. I should have known better. He was eighteen, just the kind of boy she liked.

We all went to the sparsely attended funeral. It was an open coffin, and I could not bring myself to look at her. After the funeral, Suzette and James stole two valuable oil paintings right off our wall. They had hung in my mom's former home in Germany. Then, Suzette and James traveled to New York to her mother's house. Irene did not allow James to stay in the main part of the house. She told him, "Either get out of my house or stay in the attic away from my daughter." He did not linger long and soon became a memory for Suzette.

That was still not the end of Suzette's problems. In New York, she was caught driving drunk. Hence, she was incarcerated and had to spend six months in a rehabilitation center. She wrote me notes from there telling me how much she loved her dad and me. She was sorry she had not listened to us. She wanted to come back and prove to us she had changed.

A note she wrote on November 27, 1984, read –

Mom, I hope this birthday is a happy one. And, with each year may they get happier. I hope you had a nice Thanksgiving. I'm sorry I haven't gotten in touch sooner. But things have been a little uppity. I'm also sad about Siegfried. I cared about him. (My mother had been caring for Siegfried, this ninety-year-old man). Tell dad that I miss him and that I love you and him both. I hope you're both feeling young and cheerful. Happy Birthday once again.

Love, Suzette.

Your Daughter

Once she met Wilfred (she called him Willie), life seemed to turn around for her. They rented a house, and his family loved her. She gave birth to Jennifer and was a good mother. She took some nursing classes and had a job taking care of patients.

On June 29, 1998, Suzette received a new computer from Jim. She loved to work on the computer and wanted to make me a website. She wrote to us saying, "This is terrific. I can't believe you guys did this for me. I can't thank you enough. Thank you about a thousand times."

On July 4, 1998, she wrote, "I love you. Happy 4th of July."

This letter appeared on my computer on July 6th, 1998.

At 12:30 a.m. on July 5, 1998, our phone rang. I answered it. It was Wilfred, "Suzette is dead," he cried into the phone. She was thirty-one years old.

She had been hiding beer around the house and began to drink on July 4th when she suspected Wilfred had another woman on his boat that afternoon. She then drove to her mother's husband's home, where her stepfather, Jim, lived to get more beer, and she died in a single-car accident on the way home, not wearing her seat belt. She hit a curb at a high rate of speed and was thrown through the windshield.

Jerry flew from Miami to North Carolina to accompany us to New York. This funeral was dreadful; emotions were unchecked as the family wept uncontrollably. Jennifer did not come to the funeral; she stayed with Willie's sister. Jennifer was eight years old, the same age as Suzette when she came to live with me. She refused to talk about her mother.

I met Suzette's friend Verna. (She was her mother's friend.) I told Verna, "Do you remember when Suzette, Willie, and Jennifer came to visit us in North Carolina?"

"Yes, I remember. Irene was pretty out of it by then."

"It was at that time Irene died, November 30, 1995. It was my Birthday. Suzette had said people died on the birthday of someone they liked."

"Poor Irene," she said. "I think Suzette just needed to get away from her mother. She knew the end was near."

Well, I did not know until that time that Suzette was sleeping with Jennifer. I remarked to her that she needed to stop sleeping with her. The terrible shame is that she had not listened to me. Of course, no one ever thought this tragic death would happen.

Through Verna's sadness, she was most compassionate to me. I would not have managed through that funeral without her friendship. We wrote back and forth for a few months, and then she unexpectedly passed on September 19, 1998. Her father had just committed suicide. She was still mourning Irene after three years, and now the death of Suzette. She wrote that she visited the cemetery three times. How tragic, she must have died of a broken heart.

As bad as the funeral was, the burial was even worse. Annette wanted to throw herself on top of the coffin. There were tons of flowers. Walking away was hard.

In time, Willie married Katherine, and they had an autistic son. Nine years later, I received a call from Jennifer. "Last night, my father died in a motorcycle accident. He had been drinking. He never stopped mourning my mother."

June 5, 1998, we had sent Suzette some pictures, and they brought back memories. She wrote a letter to us on the computer she loved –

> *It made me realize that those days were the best years of my life. Not just the ones where you brought me to go and see Mom (Irene), but when I was so young, I didn't know what I had … until I lost it. And Mom, I see how come Daddy could love you so much for taking in Timothy and Me … I don't know if I could do what and put up with and what you did. You're special! I'm very lucky to have both of you in my life. I know this now; I hope it isn't too late. I'm not perfect; I don't claim to be. Just want you to know that everything you tried to teach me then has finally sunk in my brain. I just wish it did then. You guys were right; there is no rush to grow up, enjoy your childhood. Well, I wish I did! I'm not going to keep thinking this. Just going to apply it in my life now. I know you don't agree with everything I do. I'm sorry for that. Just might be my way now … I just wanted to tell you how grateful I am that you guys were so giving and loving. I love you, Daddy and Mom.*

Suzette was overly sensitive and caring, and she had a jealous streak. The appreciation came too late.

She loved animals, and she loved me, and always said, "Mom, you have to take it easy and take care of yourself."

It took me years before I could place a picture of Suzette, Willie, and Jennifer on my dresser. Today, I look at them and wonder what would have been?

Jerry graduated from high school and went into the Air Force. Tim had done poorly with school attendance, and just quit school. Instead, he joined the Peace Corps. Kentucky is where they shipped him.

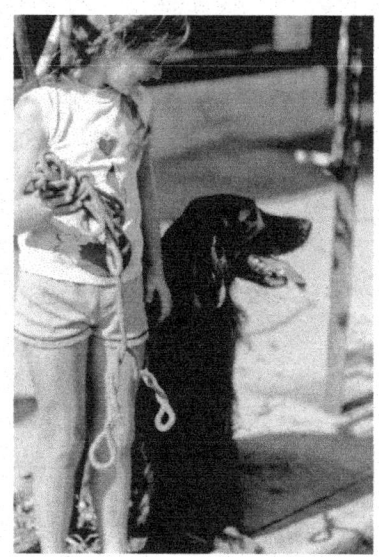

Coconut Grove 1975 Suzette Boylan 8 yrs old"

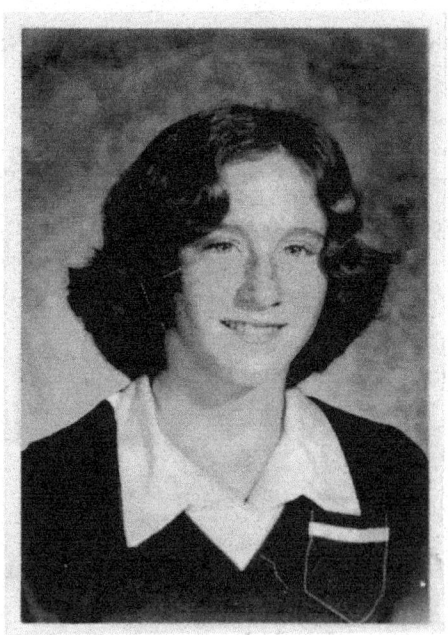

Suzette Boylan 1980 7th Grade 13 yrs old"

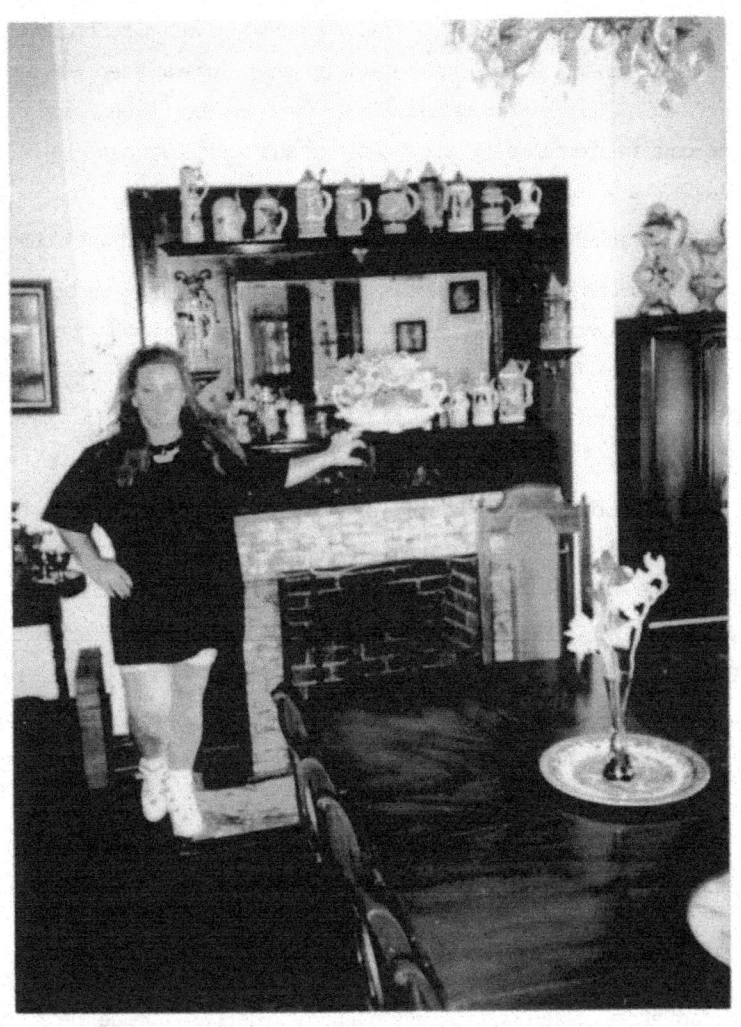

Marshall House Marshall, NC Suzette Boylan 1994 – 27 yrs old"

Jerry and Timothy

My mother always wanted a girl, and she ended up with me. She was Regina, which stands for a queen, and she made me the princess. She was adept with her Singer sewing machine making my dresses and knitting many sweaters for me. Grandma taught me the delicate art of embroidery, also how to knit and crochet. As a girl, I should have learned to clean and cook. I failed in both of these endeavors.

I always wanted a boy and was fortunate in that regard. When I was a child, I said,

"I would love to have a family with six children." I did not know the complications that would present. Once Jerry was a reality, I considered getting him a brother or ... Then, through no hardship on my part, a boy, Timothy, and a little girl, Suzette, were thrust upon my doorstep.

Was I prepared? No. But, there they were, flesh and blood, ready to call me Mom.

Jerry's bedroom was too small for two thirteen year olds. Therefore, we required a larger home. Tim and Jerry knew that moving day would allow them to choose which room in the new house would be theirs. Timothy scored the newly painted white room gaining three open corner windows. Jerry had no choice but to take the brown paneled smaller bedroom; he did not return home in time, although he was pleased with his cozy area.

As I said, I wanted a boy, and now there were two. Girls are harder to rear, in my opinion, and Suzette was more challenging in many ways. So, now you ask what complications arose with my newly acquired extended family.

Number one. The grocery bill increased threefold. It mattered not whether the child was slim or roly-poly. Growing boys consumed unimagined quantities of food. Styles changed, sizes increased, and of course, bills mounted.

Number two. The refrigerator attracted Jerry possibly more than it attracted Tim, who ate more at dinner. Jerry was always in a hurry to get back outside. He opened the fridge door and stared inside, expecting the next event. Then, he spoke to the items on the shelf, deciding what to grab for himself, not mindful of others. I was overly conscious of the door opening frequently and my joy of defrosting the fridge. *That was before frost-free refrigerators.*

Number three. There were more kids in and out of the house. That caused more dirt and sweeping. Except for the day, the washing machine flooded the Florida room, and we were expecting company. I had no complaints while their friends Curt and Joey helped mop up the water. Cleaning the pool, cutting the grass, and taking out the garbage was now divided chores. Tim or Jerry would say, "I did it yesterday."

Were their memories faulty at a young age? Funny, they could never get it straight whose job it was on that particular day.

Our yard had a large spreading oak tree where I hung stag-horn ferns and other plants.

They swung about waist high; therefore, Jim passed the task to the boys.

Number four. Irene, Suzette and Tim's mother, believed that each child should get a gift if one child had a birthday. I didn't see it that way, but I had to go along with it. Then, I had to think of all the Christmas presents I now had to purchase.

Number five. There were only one TV and two different tastes. *Were Suzette's requests ever honored? She tended to accept her brother's choices.*

One night, after bedtime, Tim came back, plopped down in a beanbag chair, and flicked on the TV. Once the sound became apparent to me, I dashed into the Florida room, and raising my voice, told Tim, "What do you think you're doing?"

"I wasn't tired. Figured I would watch TV."

"You have got to be kidding; it's your bedtime."

"Oh, come on, Mummy, just a bit more."

Wow, I was impulsive back then; I ripped the cord from the wall and cut the plug off.

Tim went to bed, and I taped the plug back on.

Tim also wandered out of his room nearly every night, wanting a drink of water. He could not seem to recall that water also ran out of the bathroom faucets.

Number six. The boys were simpler to rear than Suzette was, although they got into trouble too. What set them off in the bathroom one Saturday to cause the old soap dish attached to the wall to shatter? No one would tell me. It was fists flying, feet dangerously slipping on the floor, and Suzette's high-pitched voice above their voices adding to the commotion. I ushered the fight to the front yard, where they had less likelihood of hurting themselves. It ended as a draw; no one won. Conflicts of this nature were uncommon.

Number seven. Before our family multiplied, we needed Grandma to make a fourth in Monopoly, Risk, and cards, and Jim always wanted to win at Scrabble. The games lead to adrenaline kicking in, especially with Jerry and me, the two competitive allies. Tim was not as aggressive, and Suzette watched. These were exciting games.

Number eight. Jim had a habit of checking on the boys. One day after school, he checked on Tim, and to his amazement, he found a female in Tim's closet.

Number nine. The boys were of the age that they could remain alone at home. We took Suzette away for an art show. Upon returning and pulling into the circular driveway, Jim immediately noticed his red Toyota parked peculiarly with the lawn mower angled toward it. Jerry had made an effort to hide the damage to the passenger door. He had taken the car to a friend's house. Backing down their driveway, Jerry slammed into a pile of rocks, destroying the car door. His punishment was that he had to pay for a new door.

Staying at the house alone, these boys took advantage of our trust. In the bar, we kept a small stash of liquor, Christmas gifts I received at work and would have remained there for years had the boys not helped themselves to the contents. It is still questionable how many girls slept in our waterbed and with whom.

Number ten. Tim spent countless midnight Saturdays becoming acquainted with British humor. He went to the movie theater with his friends to see the *Rocky Horror Picture Show*. Audience participation among the devotees was the norm. Fans acted out parts and dressed up as the actors. They shouted comments, flicked lighters, and shot water guns at the screen, all in response to scenes from this classic film. A cult had developed.

Number eleven. Jerry and his friends headed to Coral Gables and the Biltmore Hotel. The hotel first opened in 1926 and closed after three years. Reopened and rede-signed in 1929, the hotel built in Mediterranean Revival style featured Moorish and Spanish influences. It was the tallest building in Florida, towers ninety-three feet over the fledgling city of Coral Gables. During the jazz age of 1920 through 1930, it was the stomping grounds of South Florida's elite. Called the 'American Riviera' where big bands entertained and Hollywood personalities such as Judy Garland, Ginger Rogers, and Bing Crosby appeared. The Duke and Duchess of Windsor and Franklin D. Roosevelt graced the halls and Al Capone, who ran a speakeasy on the floors above.

All the glitz and glamour ended with World War II, and the hotel became the Army Air Force Regional Hospital and Veteran's Administration until 1968. In 1973, it sold, and renovations did not begin for ten years. It was during this time that Jerry and his friends entered the building. The security guard heard the boys and called the police, who arrived, arresting the boys for trespassing. They handcuffed them and placed them in the back of the police car. Billy Henning, a friend, had a bag of pot in his pocket. As they walked into the police station, Billy managed to extract the pot from his pocket and drop it on the top of a hedge at the station entrance. It was gone when the police released them.

We received a call from the Coral Gables Police. Upon seeing Jerry, Jim was furious and reached across the table to swat him. Our neighbor Wayne, a police officer, corrected Jim, and said, "Take that home; you cannot discipline him here."

Somewhat embarrassed, Jim backed down.

Jerry gave me a one-inch crystal ball that he had stolen as a remembrance of the event. He now keeps it in his 'adolescent remembrance box' and all the other items he collected during the early part of his life.

Number twelve. One day, Tim went into Jerry's room and stole a red-topped gym sock with pot inside. Loud voices brought us into the fray. Jim felt involving the police would put the fear of the law into our delinquents. We were sure that had discouraged their pot use, until on July 4th the kids climbed to the roof to observe the fireworks show at the Junior High a few blocks away. Instead, we had our very own fireworks when Suzette found pot growing on the roof.

Number thirteen. In the beginning, Tim attended school. But when he was in high school, I frequently received calls at work from the vice-principal. He was not showing up regularly for classes and eventually dropped out.

Timothy enrolled in the Peace Corps. They sent him to Kentucky, and he came home with Jeannie Sizemore. On Thanksgiving in our new house, Jeannie left the table for the bathroom. When she did not return, I followed to see if she was all right. She was sobbing, "My family back home was so poor they could only buy a small bird. Each of us could only have a small piece of turkey." At my urging, she dried her eyes and came back to the table.

"Jeannie, that is sad, but here you may have as much turkey as you want."

Number fourteen. In the summer of Timothy's seventeenth year, I got him a job at American Marine Canvas. He learned everything he could about making boat cushions, curtains, and Bimini tops for yachts.

That was the best job and the only job Tim had. It grew into a marine business for him, fashioning canvas products. He has a shop near the Miami River.

He has not remained close to his other siblings.

Number fifteen. In a shop behind the building where I worked was a marine mechanic. In the summer of Jerry's seventeenth year, he went to work for the mechanic. That was not his forte.

After high school, Jerry enlisted in the Air Force. He spent time in Germany, returning to Pease Strategic Air Command base in Portsmouth, New Hampshire. He received an honorable discharge, although he left before he completed his four years.

In 1988, he graduated from the University of Florida with a BA in Journalism. Today, he is married with three adorable children and lives in Miami.

Jerry and his partners are owners of Miami Prop Rentals and 3D foam carving and fabrication in a thirty-thousand-square-foot building. They rent props for commercials and movies and construct set designs for events and films.

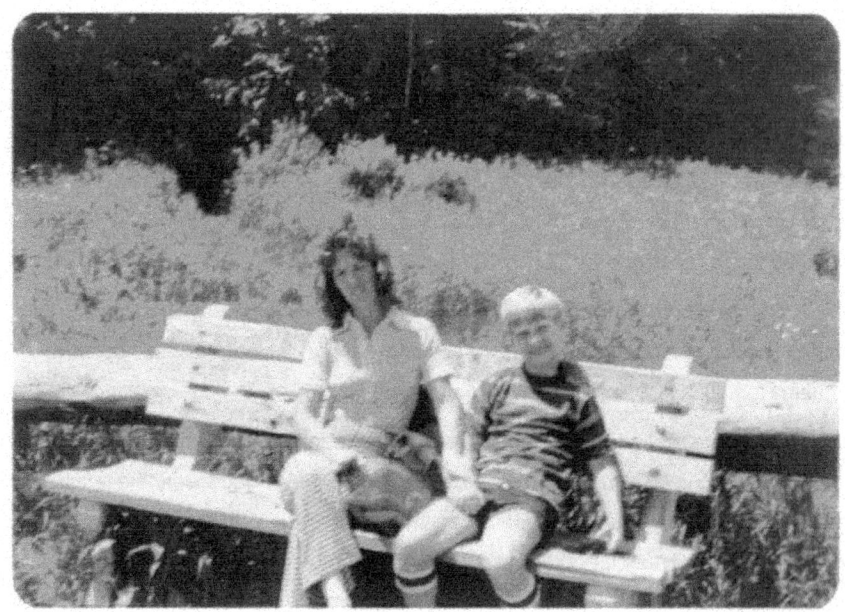

Jerry Blohm 12 yrs old, Ruth Blohm 37 yrs old

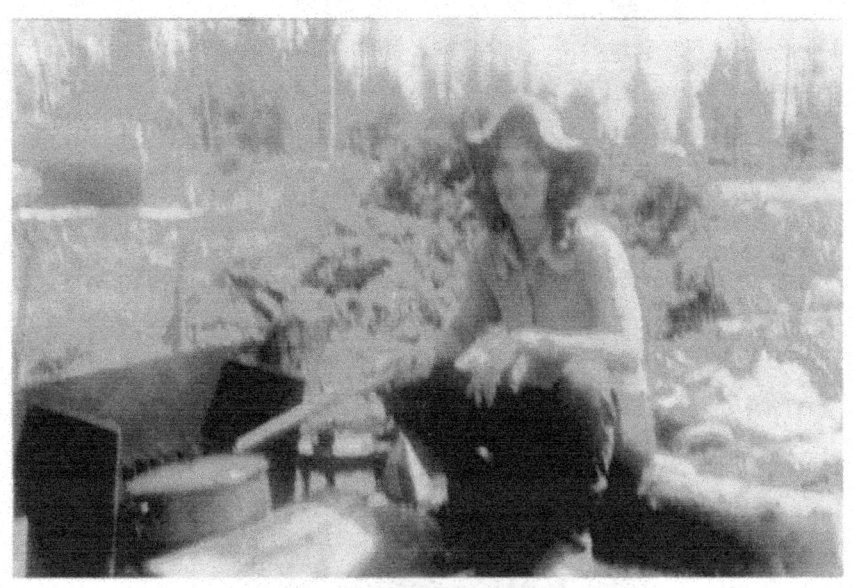

1975 Summer – Wyoming Trip, Ruth Boylan 37"

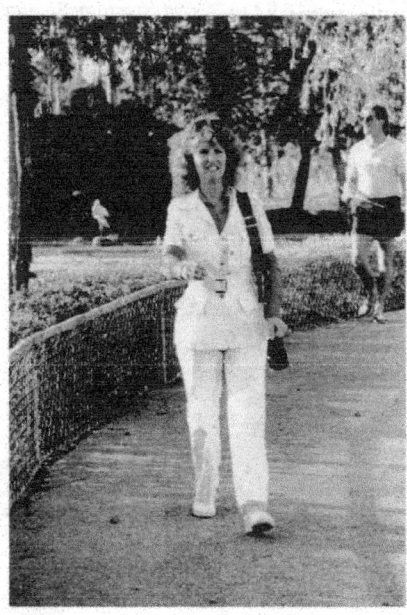

Miami – Old Parrot Jungle, Ruth Boylan 43 yrs old

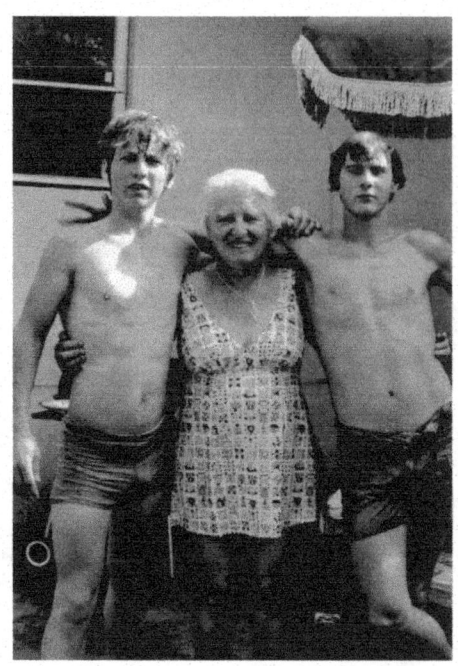

Gina 79, Jerry 16 and Tim 16 6735 SW 54 St Miami FL Just out of the pool

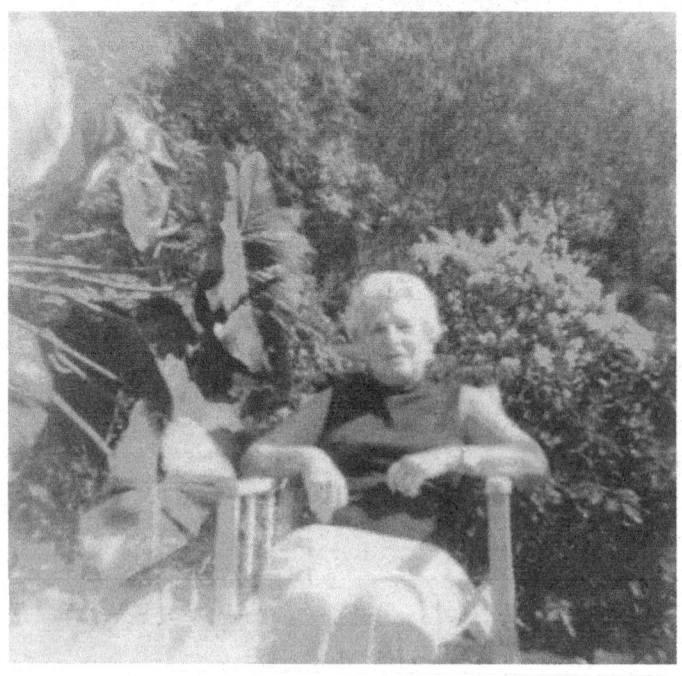

Regina "Gina" Arnstein in Margate FL

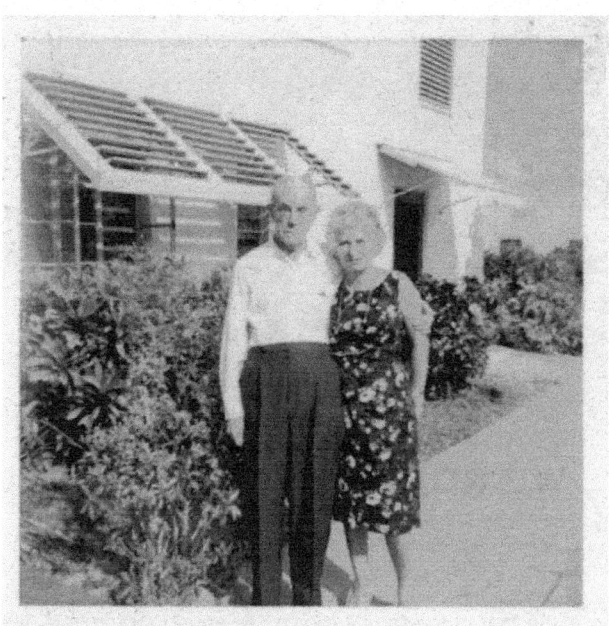

Nicky and Gina Arnstein Margate, FL

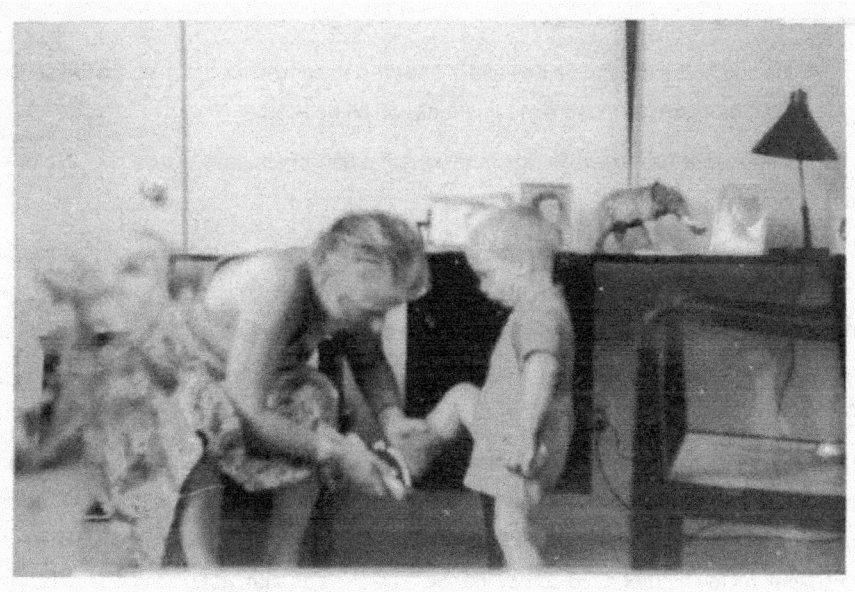

*Jerry 2 yrs old, with Grandma Gina in Margate, FL. Picture behind Jerry's head is
Ruth Arnstein*

CHAPTER 35:

_____

WE RODE MOTORCYCLES

Jerry was the first in the family to acquire an old motorcycle. He had a job in Coconut Grove parking cars at a restaurant a few miles away. Getting there on his cycle was better than his bicycle. He managed the old bike successfully until he slid down the alley near work and injured himself.

He had his heart set on a Kawasaki, and we helped him buy it. It was in good shape for a used motorcycle and had a red gas tank, which he liked.

We bought Tim a new Honda, and we got a new chain drive, Kawasaki, in black, although Jim wanted a red one.

When in the motorcycle shop, I sat on a display bike; dismounting, I knocked it over along with three other cycles. The one that had the most damage, and the damage was minor, was the black one. He forced us to buy the damaged bike. The shop owner was so upset that I thought he would have a heart attack.

On Sundays, Jim and I rode with the Sundowners Motorcycle Club. They were a group of over fifty folks except for Marilyn, the couple's daughter. Bill and Fran were in their sixties. Ten or more of us gathered in a grocery store parking lot to ride to different locations for breakfast. I remember the Miami to Florida Keys trip on a warm typical Florida day. I took off my helmet amid comments of, "You can't do that; put it back on." I did, but it felt so good with the wind blowing through my long hair; I wanted to break the law just once and feel as I did when I was a teen. The scenery seemed to pop out brilliantly when on the bike. It brought me closer to nature than in a car.

Tim remembers the day he rode with the group. Suzette rode on the back of her Dad's motorcycle while I rode with Tim. He didn't have a backrest, so I had to keep my arms wrapped around his waist. Our destination was a restaurant near John Pennekamp State Park in Key Largo. At the entrance to the park was a speed-bump Tim did not notice, and we flew over it, raising me six inches above the seat, laughing all the way.

Jim and I had done a scuba dive off a boat at Pennykamp some years before. It was during our training that we learned how to use scuba equipment. I had done free diving in my past life and seen coral reefs, but Jim had not. Instructed to stay together, I swam around, much to his dismay. He tried to talk underwater as he panicked, looking for me. He was scared to death of sharks. We never saw a giant shark, although a nurse shark was hanging around us. We also never dove in seawater again. As ridiculous as this may sound, he wanted to clean our pool.

I had a desire to be the master of my motorcycle. A friend stopped by and asked, "I have an old Yamaha bike I don't want. No money, I just bought a new one, you can have this one." Wow, my wish became fulfilled. Up to the schoolyard, we went with the new motorbike. I knew little about starting the bike with my foot, turning on the gas with the handlebar, and most importantly, braking. It would not survive due to my ignorance. Jim failed to have the patience to watch me repeatedly slam into the fence as my hand and foot coordination did not cooperate. I was doomed forever to ride on the back of his bike.

At eight in the morning, Jim and I, with eight other motorcyclists, left Miami heading for Brookhaven, Florida, three hundred miles away along State Road 441. It was an easy day's drive. We arrived in Brookhaven, a small pleasant village, where we had lunch at a picnic area under a mass of leafy trees.

I rode up on the back of Marilyn's BMW, and Suzette rode with Jim. On the ride home, we switched up. 441 was a truck route. There was no problem until the updraft from a truck knocked one of our riders off the road. Marilyn with Suzette was ahead of us, and as we caught up, we saw a passenger in the sand at the side of the road. She had red hair, and Jim immediately assumed it was Suzette. It was not. Everyone went home, but we stayed with the couple waiting for the ambulance. Ralph's wife was frightened and a bit bruised, otherwise fine. His motorcycle took most of the beating.

When we went to various art shows in our motor home, we saw gangs of motorcycle riders minus helmets with bandanas, leather jackets, and pants along the highways. Sometimes these were the one-present Hells Angels, at least their dress appeared as such, or they could have been doctors and lawyers riding Harleys and Choppers.

On one of our trips, a group of us rode to Monroe Station in the Everglades in Monroe County that stretched from the Dry Tortugas, which is seventy miles west of Key West and includes Everglades City. We took Tamiami Trail, which leads into the twenty-six miles of Loop Road, where Monroe Station sat for approximately seventy-five years. In 2013, a fire destroyed the Station, which had been on the National Historic Register. It was a favorite ride for many in Miami motorcycle circles. Here some of the one-presenters spent time drinking beer and being rowdy. There were rough-looking bearded fellows with bandana headgear and their biker chicks wearing leather outfits. They drove Harley's and Choppers with jolly roger banners flying from their rides. I looked over their machines with interest, and Jim hustled me away, afraid I would cause a stir.

On a balmy Sunday, with Suzette and the boys, we went over the Rickenbacker Causeway Bridge to Key Biscayne. Many beaches line the key on the Miami side, and across the causeway, we could see the Sunfish boats with colorful sails skimming along on the ocean side. Virginia Beach lies on the Bayside, somewhat hidden from road traffic. Jim and I were the lead bike, and the family followed. A man came walking up from the beach. He was hard to see until he got closer to us, and we saw he wore a tie and nothing else. Jim nearly turned his bike over in the sand, trying to depart before Suzette got a glimpse of him. It was a gay nude beach.

The Daytona Beach Motorcycle rallies were coveted events that if you had a motor-cycle, you should at least attend one time. Tim decided to stay home and take care of the animals. Jim, Jerry, Suzette, and me, with some of our group, joined hundreds of bikers as we drove down the main streets of Daytona Beach. Marilyn and I coupled on her BMW, and Jim and Suzette rode together while Jerry soloed. We stayed on the beach, pitched a tent for Jim, Suzette, and me while Jerry had his tent. We ate meals with our group, played horseshoes, badminton, and built campfires along the famous beach. Joined with friends, sang songs, and told stories. It was a boisterous, loud crowd full of fun.

Our longest ride went from Miami to Towsen, Maryland, when Suzette was at Shepherd Pratt Hospital. We took off on a beautiful warm day and headed north. Naturally, in October, the weather was colder than we experienced in South Florida. Our first stop was for warmer clothing. Our second stop was for more warm clothing. I huddled behind Jim, who had the windshield in front of him for protection, whereas I was more open to the wind. I insisted we stop for the night; our appointment at the hospital was not until the morning. We signed in, and behind us was an African-American couple. I could not believe what I heard.

"We do not have any rooms. Down the road, you'll find a place."

I was incensed. That was Maryland close to Washington, DC. It was 1987. How could people act that way toward someone of a different color? Born in New Jersey and living in New York, I never experienced anything like that. I wanted to say, "They have rooms." Jim moved me along, fearing I would open my mouth. I had gotten in trouble years ago for the same feelings.

I did some reading about the section of Towson where we were going. The Ridgley Plantation in Towson, where tobacco grew, had slaves. Today they will refrain from speaking of that place. Although this took place around 1850 and the Emancipation Proclamation of 1863 brought freedom, it was now one hundred thirty-seven years later, emotions still perpetuated.

While in Maryland with Suzette, the hospital let us take her out for a picnic. We stopped in a local grocery, and while Jim selected cold cuts at the counter, I picked up chips.

Suddenly, I recalled Suzette liked ham. I ran up to Jim and asked him to order a quarter pound of ham. Oh my, you would have thought I asked for a rattlesnake. How did I know they were a kosher grocery?

On the way home, one of our saddlebags opened. Clothing littered the highway, and Jim turned around to retrieve it. Truckers tooted at us, and motorist peered strangely amused.

The motorcycle needed repair, and we sold it before leaving Miami for North Carolina. I loved riding on the bike; it was a shame we ran out of time, running the gun shop, and could not fix the machine.

Today, Jerry has a Harley, which he brought to North Carolina with a group of friends.

They visited the Biltmore House and invited me to tag along. I could not get on Jerry's bike, but instead, I rode with Graylin, his friend since grammar school, and his partner. I got assistance the first time from Big Bill, who picked me up and placed me on the seat. After that, I was able to do it alone. We rode around the estate, and then back to their hotel on the other side of town. I was thrilled to experience the joy of riding on a motorcycle again. Jerry stands behind Mercedes pregnant with Jacob, Josie, Joslyn in the carriage, and I am left.

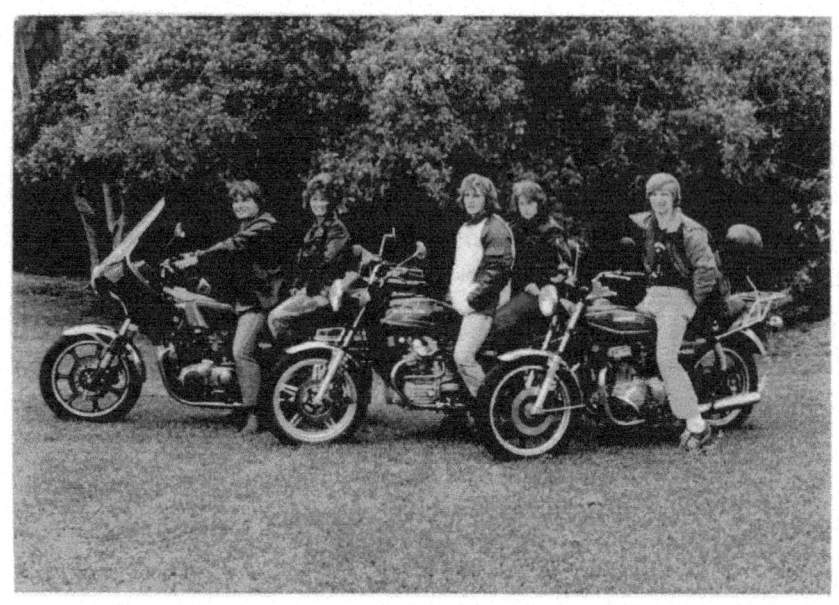

1979 Boylan Family on motorcycles Jim, Ruthm Time, Suzette and Jerry

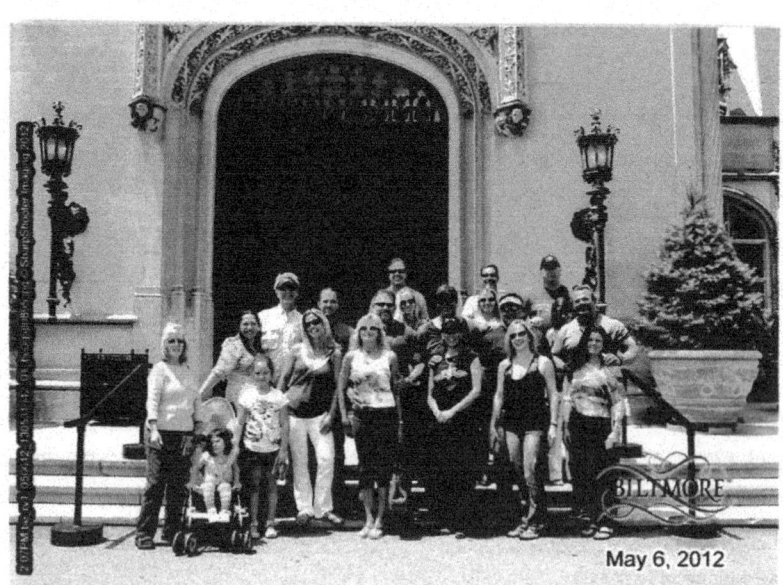

May 6, 2012

CHAPTER 36:

RACCOON GUN SHOP

In the late seventies and early eighties, Miami experienced crimes, riots, drugs, home invasions, and the Cuban migration. My husband wanted to protect the family, and we bought a gun. I learned how to handle it going to the range and firing our new thirty-eight caliber Smith & Wesson pistol.

Purchasing manufactured bullets was an expense. Using reloaded ammunition was less. Jim was not satisfied with the quality of these loads. That is what prompted him to make reloads. Word got out, and we began selling the reloaded shells. We soon found out we could not conduct business in a residential neighborhood. We started to look for a suitable location.

My mother chanced upon a commercial rental three blocks from our house. It was a corner storefront in a four-store mall. Probably the smallest gun shop in Miami. There was a dividing wall separating the front from the back. Jim built a platform over the rear of the store to make reloads and repair weapons. In front of the store, he constructed a rack to hang rifles. We purchased two used glass counters to display semi-automatic handguns and pistols.

Before we could sell firearms, we needed a license from the Bureau of Alcohol, Tobacco, and Firearms, which was free along with the paperwork. Customers had to fill out and sign a federally numbered form, which I understand today is more involved, affirming the following brief questions:

Have you ever been under indictment or convicted of a felony?

Are you a fugitive from justice?

Unlawful user of marijuana or controlled substances or committed to a mental institution?

Are you a US citizen?

My job was to record the gun deliveries in a bound record book, with the customer's name and purchase address. The gun shop kept that information until we went out of business. Then, we forwarded our record books to the Bureau of Alcohol, Tobacco, Firearms and Explosives (ATF). I also kept track of stock inventory, sales, deposits and kept the books.

We needed a Miami-Dade County license who upped their charges from a double-figure amount to a triple-figure amount. So, what was twenty-five dollars originally was now two hundred fifty dollars, just making it harder for the ordinary citizen to conduct business legally.

We set up some accounts to purchase our supplies with Southern Gun as our primary supplier of weapons and ammunition. Most often, the merchandise came in by UPS, requiring a check. More often than not, I kited him a bank check, and more often, the payment arrived at the bank before my funds, causing me sleepless nights worrying about the twenty-five-dollar Non-Sufficient Funds bank would charge to my account.

There were times I drove to Southern Gun to collect our supplies. Speeding along the highway in my truck, firearms on the seat next to me, gave me a feeling of power. In a city infamous for crime, I was a minor gun purveyor.

On one occasion, as I stopped at the pick-up area, a woman was with a child. She was speaking Spanish to the child, and I commented that she should speak English. That comment caused a significant stir, and my salesman, a Latin man called Arturo, was called downstairs to deal with me. We had become friends, and he said, "Ruthie, you know how these people are. You cannot say that."

"Art, if they don't teach their children English now, in the next twenty years, this will be a Spanish state."

"I know that, but it is something we can do nothing about."

I left, and when I got to the shop, Jim knew the whole story. Art told him, "Don't let Ruth come down to that area of the warehouse again."

As an American whose family came to this country and learned English, I felt it was the new arrivals' responsibility to teach the children our language. My stepfather would not allow me to speak German because he did not want me to have a German accent.

"You are an American; you should sound like an American."

Jim took longer to get ready in the morning. Therefore, I opened the store. Except for one morning when he did indeed open the shop. Next to the gun shop was a full-service hardware store with wheel barrels, red lawn mowers, and shiny new galvanized metal garbage cans on display. He placed our opening moneybag on top of the garbage cans, so he was hands-free to open the door and turn off the alarm.

When I arrived later, I inquired, "I don't see any money in the cash register. Did you forget to put it in the drawer?"

Without a word, he ran to the door and looked for the bag. It was gone. The high school was a block from our shop; I didn't have to wonder who took the bag. A school bus driver found it on his bus, empty except for the papers inside.

We had a sign above the store reading Raccoon Gun Shop. To draw more attention, I figured that we could have a raccoon painted there as the building's side was plain. High school kids wandered into the shop occasionally. I asked, "Do you know of someone that can paint?" They replied, "Yes."

Within a few days, we had a group of kids demonstrating their talents by painting an artistic, vivid, animated raccoon announcing Raccoon Gun Shop. He had a fluffy black and white striped tail, wrapped around a full body of gray-brown fur surrounded by yellow, red, and blue designs. Did we collect traffic from the freestanding Farm Store next-door, or were people only thinking of milk and ice cream?

When the concealed carry permit law came into effect in Florida, before we began giving National Rifle Association (NRA) approved classes, we had to qualify and pass a class ourselves. We charged seventy-five dollars. There were four to five student-customers per class. We taught the NRA gun safety classes with gun history first, and then took our students to a safe area in the Everglades and taught them how to handle a gun properly. They had to go to the police department with a certificate in hand and apply for the concealed weapon (CCW) permit. Other than working late and ordering dinners, these classes were profitable. A TV station did a two-minute segment of our classes.

Mike appeared at our door, touting his window-washing business. From then on, he cleaned our windows. Mike wanted a carry permit and took our class. Then, he introduced us to a group that shot pistols and long guns on Sunday afternoons.

We got involved with real guns in competition shooting. I stood at the marked spot and aimed my adjusted light trigger forty-five handgun at steel targets. I shot against an opponent and came away with a ribbon.

Another customer introduced us to a paintball competition. We dressed in camouflage and went out to the Everglades, where this sport was underway. In the old game of capture the flag, two teams always hid in the woods for protection. One day I took a paintball in the chin. That hurt; I wouldn't say I liked that. The game was fun

A few doors down from our shop was a Cuban pizzeria where I went each day to get my slice of non-gourmet pizza. The day the slight dark older woman walked into the store, I was busy munching my pizza slice with extra cheese served on a paper plate. I had placed the plate atop the handgun display case, allowing me a counter to lean on.

The woman wore a faded blue dress with vertical stripes. Her hair was black with some grey, cut short, and wavy. In her hand was a plain brown paper bag from which she pulled a small thirty-two caliber revolver.

"What can I do for you today?" I asked her after I placed my slice back on the plate.

She handed me the gun and said, "It isn't loaded. I'm looking for bullets, um, I, I don't know what it takes."

I looked at the gun. It was old, with most of the bluing rubbed off. Without thinking, facing the window of the shop, I pulled the trigger. After all, the lady said her gun wasn't loaded. BANG! Her weapon was loaded. I forgot all my safety training. I never checked the cylinder. I blew an eight-inch hole in the front plate glass window, just left of my desk. My ears were ringing, and the look on her face was that of dread. She purchased a box of bullets, and Jim showed her how to use the gun safely.

We were not a busy shop, so when customers realized they could hang around and talk, Jim was a willing conversationalist. Customers and school kids stopped by; one student was a curly-haired, good looking, light-complexioned, well-mannered black boy. His father was Eugene Mercury Morris, the former running back for the Miami Dolphins. Mercury came to buy a gun for which he paid by check. Unfortunately, the check bounced. The news media covered the incident, and I was on TV. That was my fifteen minutes of fame. Eventually, we got the gun back. Jerry told us, "Mercury lives down the block from the middle school. He comes and plays basketball with us in the schoolyard. All the kids like him." Interesting information. I framed the check and hung it on the wall.

Edwin, an African-American who lived blocks away, peddled gold chains and old used guns. He talked to Jim for hours, telling tall tales and trying to trade his possessions for money or goods.

Andre Dawson, a six-foot-plus slim African-American, who played baseball for the National League Montreal Expos, came to our little shop a few times. Once he came with his brother and bought a firearm. Upon mentioning this to Jerry, he told me, "Mrs. Dawson is my science teacher."

I had come to know Mrs. Dawson the day Jerry and I went to the school to speak with her. Jerry had stolen glass flasks from her class to make bongs for smoking pot. Jim had discovered them in Jerry's closet. (Privacy is not sacred when a teen.) Jerry was embarrassed. He liked Mrs. Dawson and didn't want to look bad in her eyes. She was pleased he came forward and promised not to tell the class.

Mr. Biando was a math teacher at the high school. He liked to come in and talk guns with Jim and kids with me. His favorite story he related to exchanges with the kids was, "No, what word did you not understand?" No means no, not maybe or I'll think about it.

Some parents could not say no, but teachers can. Mr. Biando liked guns, he told us, "I was standing in front of the hall mirror wearing my cowboy holster, acting like a western cowboy with two guns in my hands when my wife walked in." Embarrassing!

The South Miami Police wandered into the store frequently. Blue-eyed, friendly Police Officer Ed Schultz sat on a stool in front of the counter. I liked speaking with him until one day Officer Juan came and told us terrible news; he said, "Ed was strangled yesterday in the Sunset Movie Theater by a girl." Remembering Officer Schultz is a sign above US 1: "Sunset Drive – Ed Schultz."

Jon Wyatt was also a South Miami Police Officer that I knew from my job at Bertram's. He was a yacht electrician. I had called upon him one day to fix a breaker problem I was having at my house. The problem was in the back of the house. Jerry, at eleven, was always interested in how a repairman fixed issues. Jon also arrived at our store one night when we had a burglary. Sometime later, it came out that Jon was relieved of his position. Accused of sexually assaulting his young cousin, he went to prison.

Located on busy Miller Road; therefore, I would know when Eddie Webster was on his way to the shop. He was proud of his remodeled older Ford with the back bed made of lacquered-slatted wood, which he fabricated. He was a hunter and a cigar smoker with the stogie hanging out of his mouth showing pictures of his recent deer kills. I had to turn my head away. We sold guns for personal protection, not to shoot innocent animals. As far as the cigar was concerned, "Eddie, please leave that cigar outside. Sorry, since I was a child I disliked cigar smoke."

He obliged by placing it on our black protection railings' horizontal crossbar covering the outside store window.

Randy Cason came into the shop looking like *Serpico*. He was short, and his longer than police-style hair cut was uncombed. Serving in the Miami Police Department, Randy used one of the first cell phones made of heavy plastic with an antenna sticking up. It was a strange-looking contraption. Randy thought it was cool. He and I hit it off when I was able to find a holster he wanted. He chatted with Jim about converting semi-automatic handguns to automatic. A *Miami Herald* news article let us know why Randy's appearance at the shop ceased. The headline reads,

"City of Miami Police Officer Randall Cason arrested for converting a handgun to automatic."

Randy had a longhaired friend Charlie, whom he would bring into the shop. While Randy was doing time, Charlie was doing his wife. Upon Randy's release, Charlie could not face his friend with his betrayal; he went into the woods and killed himself.

Not many of my gun shop stories are pleasant. One is downright bazaar. A tall, well-built blond man visited us to purchase a weapon. His story went like this, "My brother and I are buying guns, and we are taking them to Central Florida and burying them at different intervals so we will be ready when the invasion comes."

Willie Pope was a ray of sunshine. He was a six-foot-three, muscular, attractive, black ex-football player; his mother cooked dinners every weekend for a market in another part of town. Willie would bring me this delicious soul food of sweet potato pie, roast, and green beans.

An acquaintance came to tell us, "I was just at the animal shelter and saw a Doberman scheduled for Euthanasia. I cannot take him and wondered if you want a dog." Jim and I looked at each other. We closed the shop, and within an hour, we owned a Doberman; I named him Oby for oblivion. He was a fantastic dog, a protector.

One eventful day, a familiar woman entered the shop with a man. At first, I could not place her until she said, "You are Ruth." Quizzically, I answered, "Yes."

"I am Estelle." I almost fell over. Twenty-four years ago, I had dated her now-dead husband when I was pregnant with Jerry. She had some nasty words for me that I had to listen to until finally, she left the shop. That was a story I had not told Jim, who wanted to know everything about my past. I had a lousy afternoon.

I had not told Jim about other people that came before him, and one afternoon, as we sat in front of our house yard selling, a former boyfriend unexpectedly showed up.

"Hi, Ruth, it is so nice to see you." We chatted a minute; I tried to keep the conversation to a minimum. After he left, Jim was full of questions. Did he have to know everything about my wicked past?

Peter, an Englishman with a tale to tell of an evening he went to start his car and it would not start, so he shot it. Peter came for the reloads, "Your reloads are the best in town. I go to other shops, and they are nowhere near your quality."

Making reloads were a multi-phased job. The old brass needed to be tumbled for twenty-four hours to bring back the shine and clean out the gunpowder. The reloading process began removing the old primer, replacing a new one, reshaping the brass, loading the powder, and seating the bullet. Then, we placed them in ammunition boxes, and then put them on the shelf for sale.

Jerry was home from the Air Force, and before heading out to college in Gainesville, he gathered a few of his buddies. It would be a day of borrowed guns and shooting in the Everglades. All used weapons. We never shot new firearms. During the afternoon, a Forest Ranger arrested the boys and confiscated the guns. Oh, yes, we got the boys out of jail, and we got our weapons back too.

The House of Bijan on Rodeo Drive in Beverly Hills sent us a letter requesting our license. Any gun delivery from one shop to another, each must submit their Federal Firearms license. They wanted to fill an order they had from a customer in Miami. I sent the license, and a phone call followed, "How much do you charge for this service?"

"Twenty-five dollars," I responded.

Then, a call came advising, "Federal Express will deliver the gun."

Naturally, we opened the package. A polished veneer synthetic plastic case containing a velveteen pouch encased the gun along with the *Robb Report* magazine. As the House of Bijan was a total unknown, the magazine was enlightening. It is a menswear boutique, to quote the article, "The Mediterranean courtyard leads kings and presidents into the most expensive store in the world where they come to pick up their twelve-hundred-dollar neckties."

The gun sold for ten thousand dollars. It was a thirty-eight caliber Smith & Wesson handgun with a glossy blue finish, a gold cylinder, a gold hammer guard, and gold on the top strap.

We saw the man approach the shop, dressed in a suit and tie, not a regular customer, so we knew he came for the gun. He was a friendly chap, the CEO of a bank. The second gun we received went to another Miamian who was not as pleasant as the first man was.

I could have kicked myself for charging only twenty-five dollars for the transfer. I have no idea why they chose to deliver the guns to our shop.

On an evening after five, a working black man entered the shop. He carried a check he requested cashed. He was not a customer, and Jim refused. The man said, "I need to buy groceries for the kids and am out of money. Please, can you help me out?"

I agreed to cash it. The next day the bank notified me that the check was no good.

"These checks have been circulating about town. He stole the checkbook from the company."

I rounded up my son and his biggest friend and drove them in my red Dodge pick-up truck to the man's house in the black part of South Miami. I pulled into his drive-way and told

Jerry and Curt to stand by the truck. I knocked on the door. He came to the door shirtless, and I saw a child standing near him. He immediately recognized me, "You gave me a bad check last night. I'd like to have my money."

He reached into his pocket and pulled out the cash. I took it and left. Later on that afternoon, Bill Fatool, a South Miami Police Officer with whom we had become friendly, stopped by the shop. After I told him the story, he said, "You're lucky Ruthie that he did not kill you. Do not ever do that again."

Burglarized three times in the ten years that we had the shop, we never saw the guns again, and the perpetrators never arrested. We had an alarm system that called in the middle of the night, of course, and jerked us out of bed. Dressed in night clothes, we drove to the shop and met by breaking glass, busted countertops, iron bars yanked from the front of the store, and once a police officer almost shot Jim thinking he was the criminal. Jim was barefoot; how could he have thought we were burglars?

When we first opened, we did not run a metal cord through the rifles' trigger guards on the rack. After the first burglary, we knew better. Like jewelry stores that remove the product and place them in a safe, we did not do that regrettably. We had no safe. We closed the shop in 1991.

The next paragraphs will explain how we came to close the shop and end up in Marshall, North Carolina.

It was a slow day at the gun shop, and this harried man came through the door with a pile of booklets under his arm. He began to pour out his tale of woe regarding his son. The boy had gotten involved with marijuana, and Judd, the father, had spoken to their minister. He had advised Judd to move the family to North Carolina's mountains, and Judd carried under his arm real-estate pamphlets he had collected. He said, "I don't need these anymore; I have found a place in Lake Lure where we will move soon."

That was weird, Jim and I had been discussing a move, and North Carolina was on the top of our list. Jim had an old friend from New York living in Saluda, North Carolina, and he wanted us to relocate. What was still weirder, Judd had not been in our shop before, and we never saw him again.

We began looking through the booklets, and property in Madison County caught our eye.

I checked om the weather, population, and business opportunities. I figured if George Vanderbilt put his house in Asheville, that was good enough for us. We called the realtor and set a date to see the land. No, it was not near his friend Gordon, but it was on the same side of the state.

We drove up, looked at the land, and made a quick decision to purchase it. It was fifty-three acres on Little Pine. Then, we went into Marshall and stopped at Penland and Sons. We spoke to George Penland, who quickly got around to telling us, "I have a house for sale; it is up the hill." We could not figure out how to get up on the hill and look at the house, but Jim and George shook hands, which meant we were buying a house after months of negotiations. Please read on.

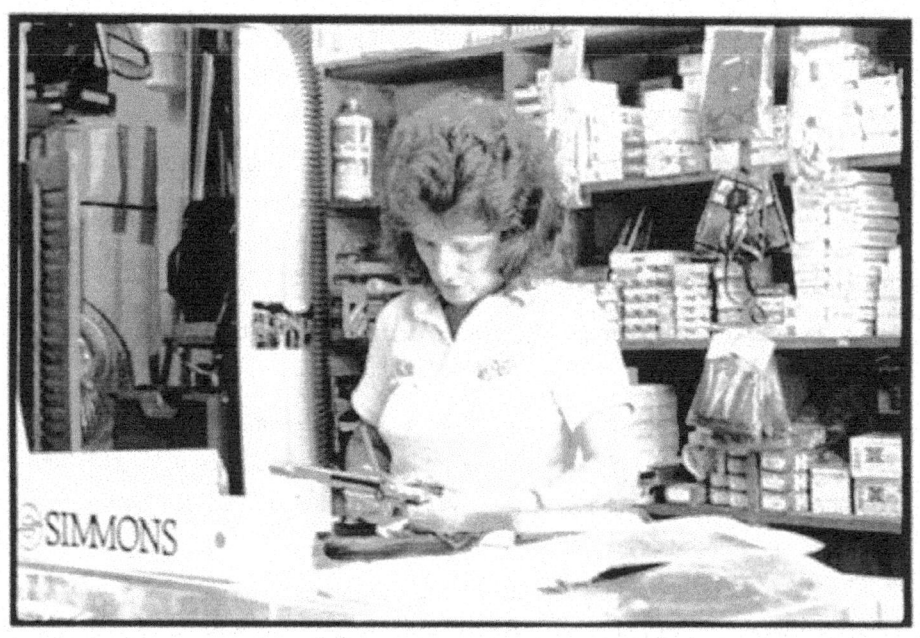

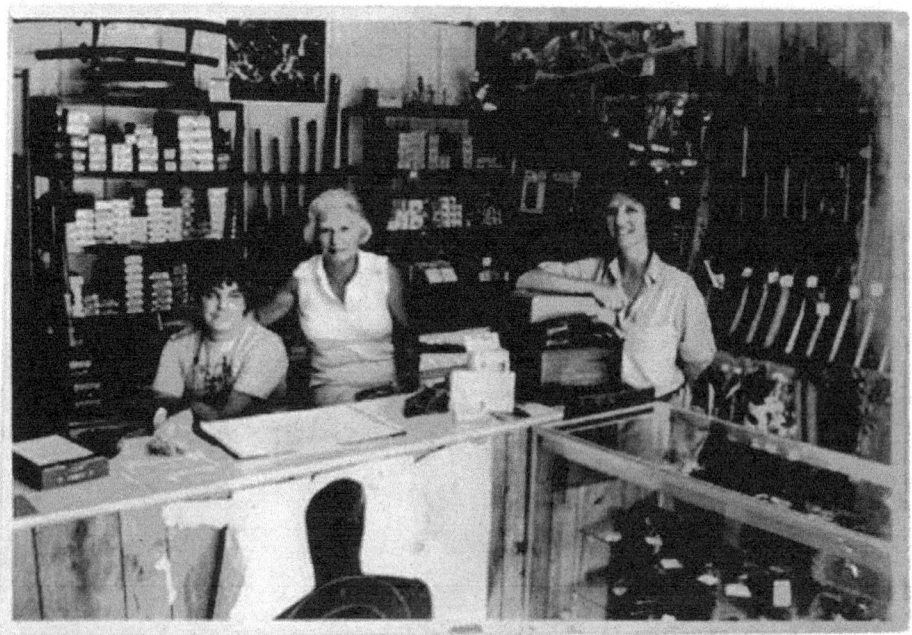

Raccoon Gun Shop Jim, my mom and Ruth

PART FOUR

CHAPTER 37:

_____

MARSHALL HOUSE BED & BREAKFAST

Labor Day weekend, September 1988, we closed on the 1903 pebbledash mansion above the French Broad River overlooking the hamlet of Marshall tucked away in the Appalachian Mountains.

We had bought the largest house in Marshall that had eleven bedrooms, eight functional living spaces, and two original bathrooms. I considered the prominence of the house and was curious who had occupied it. I researched and spoke with the locals; I found that the house would qualify for a listing on the National Register of Historic Places. It was indeed more than fifty years old, eighty-eight at the time of purchase. A glance was sufficient evidence of its architectural value, and one of the former owners was a man of importance.

We submitted our listing and received the honor of having our house listed on the Register of Historic Places.

We stayed in a downstairs bedroom for the first night at the Inn; we named it the Grand Room, the house's largest room. An ugly chandelier hung from the ceiling. We replaced it with a crystal one we purchased second-hand in Miami. I was nearly asleep when I heard a noise coming from the tinkle of breaking glass. The next day, we heard that two people broke into the Madison County Courthouse a few feet away from our house. They were seeking to erase evidence accidentally burning the courtroom drapes.

When in Miami, we purchased large items such as mirrors, chandeliers, china cabinets, a desk, and pictures from yard sales and antique shops. We bought knickknacks, clocks, teapots, dishes, and silverware, and kitchen appliances. In each of the nine rentable rooms, the last owners, The Penlands left behind dressers, nightstands, tables, and chairs. Also left was the entire dining room with an extensive buffet, serving cabinet, china cabinet, dining table, and chairs. We returned their furnishings after we left the house twenty-eight years later.

Still, in Miami, running a business, we now owned a large house in the mountains. At first, it was not possible to leave Miami. I ran an ad for a housekeeper, and Ann answered and came for an interview. She claimed she had done this type of work before, so mistaken, I thought she was a good pick. After a few weeks, Ann decided not to stay, and as salary wrote a check for two hundred fifty dollars out of our bank account. She had not earned that amount, and there was not enough money in the bank to cover it. That was mistake number one.

Mistake number two: I hired a woman named Susan as our second housekeeper. She was a slight acquaintance from Miami. Suddenly, after a few weeks, she had a case pending in Texas and had to tend to a court proceeding, never to return to the house. Our spies spotted her on Main Street with a local man, and later I learned she was involved in a drug case. Upon leaving the house, she took a full-size mattress. Unbelievable.

It became necessary to hire a third woman. I should have realized that in my desperation to put someone in charge of the house, I was making bad choices.

Along came Shirley, a well-mannered, educated, and experienced woman. We spoke about the opportunities offered in the house and her expected salary. I told her, "We are just beginning; funds are slim."

Shirley faced me and said, "I would love to work here, but I must make a salary, and you are working on a shoestring." With that, the lovely lady departed.

Number three is supposed to be a lucky number, so I knew I had achieved success with Linda. She had been working at the hardware store next to our gun shop in Miami. I approached Linda with a proposition, "Linda, how would you like to work in our bed and breakfast in North Carolina?"

"What a wonderful offer. You know I have a young child, and this would be great that I can be home with her. I accept the offer." Unbeknownst, she brought along a girlfriend, also with a child. These two girls were man hunting.

George Penland, from whom we purchased the house, phoned one evening and told us,

"Your house is like the Little Whore House in Texas." The women were trouble; there was no doubt. They inappropriately placed beer cans outside on the roof edge in a second-floor bedroom, blatantly displaying beer in a dry county. A slighted beau stole an old-fashioned doctor's carriage we had placed in the front yard.

A month after I moved to Marshall, Denny, our local police officer, drove me to a barn hiding our carriage. I collected it and returned it to its former location.

As Jim stayed in Miami, I was alone to do the work in the house. There were two blocked-off fireplaces in the living room and grand room. There was not only plaster, but also bricks. As I struggled, to my amazement, soot poured out. The oil furnace in the basement vented through the chimney, causing the accumulation of carbon. We installed a propane-burning furnace, which we vented through a basement window.

The house needed a new roof, and George Penland recommended a roofer. I hired this fellow who thought he was Elvis Presley. He also thought I could make more money if I had a massage parlor in the house.

The house stood in plain view of the town and, for years, hidden behind towering Balsam trees. The pine needles from the trees had played a part in destroying the roof. With the help of my neighbor, Dennis Rector, who worked for French Broad Electric, he brought a crew and giant trucks to cut down three trees that blocked the house's view.

I had taken care of the most pressing problems. Americans were now coming to the mountains, vacationing, and whitewater rafting and hiking. They knocked at my door for a night's stay and breakfast, and off they would go with a hug and a thank you.

I never expected to be the proprietress of a historic Victorian relic in a southern town in Western North Carolina. I was that gal that lived in the big apple, and southerners were a distinctly different group that drank sweet tea.

These were a few of the guests: a nun in shorts on vacation drank coke for break-fast; a man that climbed microwave towers that sent signals to the railroad; doctors, nurses, teachers, and a veteran who came into the kitchen and cooked breakfast. A chef from New Orleans who was watching me and told me, "You don't break eggs on the edge of a dish; you crack them open on the counter."

There were female soccer coaches and a couple of people that wrote in the guest book,

"Best speeding ticket I ever had! It brought us to Marshall House for a great stay." "Thanks so much for your fast hospitality. Our wedding vows meant so much to you, letting us use your B & B instead of an office."

Then, the letters arrived with notes of thanks. "Ruth, thanks for the warm hospitality and the fabulous 'innkeeper stories.' We loved sharing ours with you too. Your terrific critters were so much fun – we made so many new four-legged friends. I will see you again – for sure."

A rabbi who felt I did not know about my religion and sent me a book, *1,201 questions and answers about Judaism.*

Carol from New Jersey repeatedly came with her Dachshund. At that time, Comfort Inn in Mars Hill did not take dogs, so our house, she said, was perfect for her needs. A Boston Terrier accompanied Carol on one of her many trips. From innkeeper to a friend, we exchanged family stories. I would sit in her room, at her request, and speak of more than the weather. Carol was a gardener and brought a tray of impatience, which she planted in the driveway. Her main reason to travel from New Jersey to North Carolina was that she had an attorney son in town. On Thanksgiving, Carol spent the day with her family. Upon arriving back at our house, I noticed she walked with a limp. At dinner, she had suffered a stroke. Sadly, that was her last visit to our home.

The Baily's from Kentucky wanted me to promote cross-country skiing. They were also pet lovers. One of my cats climbed into a tree across the way, and Ann insisted her husband Mark climb up and rescue the cat. He did it, reiterating that if the cat got up the tree, the cat could get down from the tree.

Kathy from Florida, who has been my friend since first staying at the house, visited often.

Carol, my friend, for years used to come frequently in the beginning. Living in Asheville, her son Michael had gotten sick and stayed with me until Carol and her husband came to take him back to Miami. Carol's visits coincided with the fall season, her favorite chillier time of the year. In 2017, Tony and I had sold the Marshall House, and Carol and Kathy came to our new house to celebrate my big birthday.

For a few years, Margot, my step-mother, and her cousin Edith had their German yardman drive them down during fall color season.

Pete Hanley visited, and a few years later, he returned with his bicycle, which he had ridden from Columbia, South Carolina. He wished to keep it in the house for the night and stood it in the hallway near the front door. The next day he rode his bike onward to Tennessee.

The house was an attraction that was visited often, with folks just coming up to look at it. I would answer their questions, and then they would be on their way. A frequent question posed,

"Do you have a ghost?" They wanted me to say, "Yes." However, I could not say it was so. One time, I thought perhaps there was a presence that knocked a ceiling light fixture down in Room 8 where I was working. Some people claimed to see an apparition; one man saw a redheaded person at the foot of his bed. Another saw a woman dressed in a long white dress, but none of these "ghosts" appeared to haunt me. I think it all depends on what you believe.

The Elementary school brought their fifth-grade class to see the house. I gave them a lecture about the courthouse and the area and the old house's history. Other parents of home-school children came, as a class, to develop social skills.

Olan Mills Portrait Studio has set up shop at the house for two years. I met so many local folks that they would remind me they had been in the house when I saw them on the street.

Paying guests were beginning to arrive from Florida, Atlanta, Michigan, Washington, DC, and California. As word spread, tourists from Germany, England, and France came to Marshall and our house. I wanted to entertain them with stories of the area and the mansion they chose to spend their time in.

During breakfast and after the guests spoke to each other, I told them I had a reservoir of stories I could tell about the courthouse built by the same man that built this house and a civil war story. After breakfast, they usually wandered out to the porch. Then, I gave them a brochure about traveling around the county. When I saw them look across the river and get a little restless, I explained they were looking at the cotton mill that operated back in the early 1900s. I disappeared, allowing them time to chat and make their plans. Back in the house, I would go to clear the dining room and clean up the dishes.

After everyone left, it was time for me to dash upstairs, capture the sheets, throw them over the rail, run back down, and throw them in the washer. Go back upstairs, make up the beds with the second set of sheets and back down to change the washer to the dryer. Go upstairs with the clean sheets, store them away until next time, and clean the rooms. Now go down, put the dishes away, check the dining room and living room, and keep going like the energizer bunny. If they stayed for two nights, I only made the beds over and waited to do the sheets the next day.

During the week, I was Cinderella. I swept the cinders; I vacuumed the floors that miraculously grew dust.

Clean, clean was my mantra of the day. Polished the furniture, and scrubbed the hearth, cleaned the kitchen, and dusted the dining room. I was feeling like a sailor on the H.M.S. Pinafore.

In the evening, when the guests reappeared and wanted to hear more, I related Jim White's story, who was the first owner.

Alfie was a goat, who I bought one spring to take care of the growth on the hill. As I cleaned the front yard, I temporarily tied Alfie to the carriage. That was the same doctor's carriage I retrieved. A light rain was falling; he did not like the rain and suddenly bolted, taking carriage and goat five-feet down a bank in front of the house. The goat was fine; the carriage met with an unfortunate end.

Days later, Alfie and I were walking across the porch; he was on a long chain, and when he darted, he pulled the chain and flipped me over onto the porch. He became frisky and placed his hoof upon my shoulder, leaving a mark, which remained after he was gone. Frisky did not work out well if you were a goat, living on the edge of a hill, and had a chain wrapped around your neck and jumped, imagine the outcome. I was devastated. George Penland was the early morning crier with the dreadful news. While serving breakfast that morning to a Jamaican couple whose daughter was attending Mars Hill College, I delicately expressed how distraught I felt over my loss. That evening they presented me with a stuffed bleating lamb.

After breakfast, my friend Everett arrived with his pick-up truck. He placed Alfie in the back, covered him with a blanket so I could not see him, and delivered him to an appropriate area.

In spring 1991, I met a gal named Terry Thompson, who approached me about music on Monday evenings during the summer. Terry also told me about an H & R Block job, which I held onto for twelve years. Musicians gathered on the fifty foot porch and in winter in front of the reception room's massive stone fireplace. Guitars, banjoes, base, fiddlers played Old Rocky Top, and the Devil went down to Georgia. Songstresses sang Irish and Scottish ballads, and those that could clog clogged to the music on the front veranda. I felt privileged to have these warm, friendly folks pick their instruments in my home.

Robbie was a relative newcomer to the area, and we had become fast friends. Jim had remained in Florida selling our house and disposing of the gun shop and only arrived in the latter part of 1992. It was Robbie's idea on music Monday that Jim and I would partake in a mountain marriage ceremony complete with Vince Heffner, the Baptist minister. One of the musicians appeared with a rifle advising Jim, "You will make her a respectable lady and marry her." Dressed in an old long orange stretchy Halloween outfit stuffed with a pillow, I proceeded down the steps. My teeth blackened and barefoot, trying not to laugh. Vince stood below, bible in hand, and a gang of folks at the bottom of the stairs cheering us. Everett Boone laughed so hard he slid down the wall that had been supporting him, collapsed on the floor, legs stuck out before him.

On yet another music evening, Robbie and I decided to pull up the old green carpet on the stairs. Many years ago, Ma Penland had the carpet professionally installed. It probably was in the mid-fifties, and many a foot had trodden upon this now threadbare runner. Pulling it up was no easy feat. Dust flew covering us; the rug lay in pieces after two hours of our labor until some hardy beer-drinking, bottle clutching men toted it out the front door, leaving our stairs in need of refinishing. The ladies returned from the front porch once the dust settled. The men went back to playing, patting themselves on the shoulder; sure, the advice they passed on to us had assisted the process.

In November, one of the musicians recognized a local guest arriving with his family during one music night. He told me, "Be careful; I know that man, he is bad news." In the morning, the man and his family had breakfast and left. Later that day, he was picked-up on bad check warrants.

"Former Sheriff Helps Man Wanted on Check Charges." It was so kind of the paper to mention that he stayed at my house.

On quiet evenings, I sat with my ledger book at the six-chair dining room table, looking into the living room. I dreamed what it would have been like in 1903 when they built the house. Imagine the ladies, sitting in the tea house, dressed in long skirts, reclining on white wicker chairs. They poured a freshly brewed cup of tea from a lovely porcelain teapot resting on the table covered with a lace cloth.

Picture a carriage approaching the house, driving under the porte cochere, and discharging its passengers. The men would be sitting around the potbellied stove, smoking and discussing the events of the day, while the women were in their living room, away from the smoke and men's conversations.

Around seven o'clock on an October eve, there was a knock on the door. A small man wearing a light tan hat cocked back on his head, dressed in jeans that were too long for him, and rolled up over the top of his boots, a red plaid shirt, and a can of beer. Slightly stumbling into the reception room, he said, "I know George Penland; I used to babysit for him."

"George doesn't own the house anymore."

"I'm JB Tweed; just give him a call and tell him I'm here."

I did just that with no answer. "I'm so sorry, George Penland is not home," I reported to Mr. Tweed.

"Oh, that's OK; he'll come and pay you when he gets home; he knows me." And with that, JB sat down in a chair to wait for George. George paid, and with time and abstinence, JB came to stay. A cantankerous old gent who would tell me one day, "That is the worst meal you ever cooked." And the next day, he would compliment me for the most fabulous meal I had cooked. He was humorous, told stories about the old days in Marshall, and said those stories repeatedly. He smoked unfiltered cigarettes, didn't like to shave, and hated showers. JB, although brought up in Hot Springs, did not stay there. At first, he lived in Marshall, where his uncle ER Tweed owned the clothing store, which is now Penland and Sons. Instead, he went to Detroit, Michigan, where he found work in the Boroughs Factory. After retiring, he did as many others did from this area and returned to their hometowns. He joined the men in Penland's store.

JB had no transportation one day; he requested our Baptist Minister Vince Hefner drive him into Asheville. Of course, Vince did not stick around, and JB had no way of getting home. He took a cab, which arrived at my door around ten o'clock that night, requesting forty dollars for the ride. I was shocked; JB was as drunk as a man could be.

I phoned Vince the next day telling him, "What were you thinking? Please don't be so agreeable next time." I believe I said a few other words, but nothing to compromise our friendship.

Not all memories of JB are prized. There was the day I picked him up outside the Jailhouse in Asheville, after his arrest for public intoxication.

On an April day, while I was preparing JB's dinner, I heard a bang from the room above. Suspecting the worst, I sent my husband Jim to check; JB never came to dinner again; under his arm was the *Reader's Digest Condensed Book of Roots* he wanted me to read. JB was seventy-five; his funeral was at the pauper's cemetery near the highway with few attendees. His sister, who lived in Charlotte, wanted nothing to do with her brother. She was still upset because, as a child, he had pushed her in the mud when she wore her new dress. She could not understand how I could tolerate him. I cared for JB and treasured his anecdotes. He was a sensitive, lonely, older man, and he held me in high regard. As a younger man, he had been a drinker. One day we came home, and JB was on the second floor calling down something incoherent to us. He managed to sneak in a six-pack and drank it all.

Robbie used to say, "JB is a hoot."

My interest in the town and my desire to keep my house at the forefront of every-one's mind motivated me to join the Madison County Chamber of Commerce. I volunteered as the secretary, and then treasurer of the Tourism Development Committee. I ran for town council and received forty-seven votes, not realizing I had to be a locally born candidate. I joined the Depot committee and became the secretary, recording the minutes. I received grant money from the Tennessee Valley Authority (TVA) to fix up the caboose at the Depot, and then a clerk in the Marshall town office stole the money. I joined the Madison County Art's Council designing rock jewelry and participated in shows, which I still do. I worked for Helpmate and Communities in Schools keeping their books. I was on the committee of Handmade in America – Hometown revitalization assessment.

I was the Jewish girl that ran the largest Christmas Parade Marshall had ever seen for five years. To act as a judge, I recruited Howie, a friend and the only Jewish man in town, to judge the best-decorated float. Once we put a Santa float together, and Jim dressed as Santa Claus.

One year, I rented a convertible and selected Everett Barnett, the parade's Grand Marshall, the only black man in town. Everett was a small, slim man, maybe five-foot-two-inch tall, brought up in Marshall with his siblings. His mother cleaned homes and worked for Bessie Lee Penland a long time ago. He was the only one in the family that chose to remain in Marshall. He was a house painter and a gardener, planting flowers at the Depot and around town. Everett was a favorite of the town, and they created an Everett Barnett Day and gifted him a lawnmower. Daily at Penland and Sons, George Penland, attorney Edwin Mashburn, whose office was next door, and Everett could be found sitting toward the back of the store chatting. All knew JB, and he walked into town to spend time at the back of the store too.

Everett Barnett lived up the hill above my house. When he came to town, he often stopped at my door with typed stories about our little village. When he passed away, his service took place in the church at the end of town, where black folks worship every other Sunday. How surprised Everette, a quiet, humble man, would have been to see the church jammed all seats taken with standing room only, and many others stood outside to show their respects.

I joined a group out of Asheville called the Micro-Management Development Center. At the first meeting, they put six people together, attempting to find better ways to start their projects and get money to establish their businesses. Don Stevens was a writer; Esther Trump was a crafty person; another woman wanted to learn how to start her business and a female artist, who wanted to learn about the Internet. It was a business model from Bangladesh, which began in India in 1961. It grew into the Bangladesh Institute of Management Studies. We met at different locals, and when Don Stevens, an aspiring author, came to the house, he said, "When I walked in the door at Marshall House, I thought this is a writer's house."

The *News-Record & Sentinel* newspaper picked up the story,

"Author Debuts his First Novel at Book Birthing. He calls it a fable to the path of rebirth." It went on to say, "He asked for a home-cooked feast for a gathering of friends and family." That is what we gave him, including mountain music from well-known musicians. We had at least twenty-five people at tables scattered in every room on the first floor except the bedroom. I asked the teenage neighbor Karen to help with the serving. Robbie and I ran our legs off from the kitchen to the tables. It was a success, although I have never heard from Don again.

In the early nineties, while Jim was still in Miami, I mentioned that I was planning to make lunch at the house. He immediately said, "But you can't cook."

"I know that, but I can read." I wanted folks in town to know the Marshall House was open for business. With only one restaurant in town, maybe I could attract business by preparing food. I had no license to serve anything other than breakfast muffins, although I made muffins, eggs, bacon, pancakes, and French toast. The way around having luncheons was to charge a one-time fee calling it a private club. I shopped on Wednesday; all day Thursday, I spent in the kitchen preparing homemade everything. With occasional help from Robbie, we made lettuce salads, carrot salad suggested by Barbara Penland. Claudia recommended cucumbers in sour cream, coleslaw, ambrosia with mandarin oranges and pineapples. There was cheese, tuna, egg and chicken salads, and cold macaroni salad that was a favorite, plus a bowl of fruit. On Friday, I set up the dining room. I lit a fire under the two stainless steel servers to keep the food warm. I heated pigs in a blanket, chicken, meatballs, ham, and beans. The ham and beans caused a loud unexpected blowup from a male patron complaining there was not enough ham. It upset one of the women, who pulled me aside, saying, "What a nerve; I'm so sorry. I think it was just fine." Louise ran the library in town and enjoyed cabbage rolls only fixed once and Kielbasa with sauerkraut and apples. There were rolls with restaurant butter and large-flowered bowls containing the food. I made chocolate and vanilla pudding pie topped with real whipped cream and fresh chocolate chip cookies, which were a smash. I almost forgot the sweet ice tea. It costs four dollars per person for a meal. Marshall came up the hill to eat a buffet luncheon on china dishes and silverware in the dining room or on the veranda, on the tables set with tablecloths cloths overlooking the mountains, river, and town. It made a hit for six months. A local portrait painter, Ron, heard about lunch and requested a meal. His meal was free, as Ron became my dishwasher and found a romantic connection with one of the customers. After the luncheon, I served the remaining food to the weekend guests. When Jim arrived from Miami, he acted like a big shot, wore jewelry and a tank top, and drove my customers off.

There was Ruth, the wife of the owner of our local oil company, who requested I prepare a luncheon for her daughter's wedding reception. A local attorney Steve married his wife again in front of the stone fireplace in the reception room. I heard it did not work out. Mattie, a paralegal for her husband's law practice, had me put together a party for her stock-market exit swan song. For two years, a lovely genteel neighbor invited her family to our house for Thanksgiving dinner. Jim cooked a traditional meal, and I served her guests. She also brought her bridge group to the house a few times. I was so careful not to make mistakes and become embarrassed. The ladies were so proper, the upper crust of our Marshall society; they were the bank president's wives, a hardware store owner, a merchandise distributor, the library director, a retired schoolteacher, and a store owner.

Sometimes I did not get the upper crust of society looking for rooms. There were times social services dropped undesirables on my doorstep. The winter months were the slowest, so I began to rent to permanent guests, local folks who had a job, and some who didn't. Several men out on probation and needed to stay close to Marshall were sure to pay their rent on time and with their best behavior, as they knew I would report any wrongdoings. There were the ones that rented and did not have a car that caused me the most consternation. When they rented the room, I told them, "You need to have a ride and do not beg rides from other guests." Of course, that was not the case; every person always begged for a ride from another. Then, there were the ones that worked but could not manage their money, so they paid their rent late, or not at all, always with a promise to catch up. A few never caught up. I issued a few warrants, and one ultimately paid.

One day a package arrived from FedEx for a tenant, and it remained on my desk for a few days. It came from California, filled with marijuana. No – I never smelled it. I called the police, he went to jail and then to a halfway house. Authorities determined he was not right.

Susie and Kim were schemers. Susie swore she had a big check coming from Canada. It never arrived, and I received no payment. She had a large brown and white blind hunting dog. Her excuse about moving was, "What will I do with Mission?" Finally, she joined up with another tenant and left. It turned out that arrangement did not work out, but she never returned. She placed Mission in the pound and left town. Mission found a good home where she could run around out of danger. Susie's conversations seemed always laced with unimaginable unlikely family events. I would be chasing rainbows to collect her debt.

Kim, too, waited for the money, which never came. I took her to court but lost. I was unprepared, so she walked away from that charge. Kim was a conniving, lying, evil woman. She was hooked on pills and got her son involved in the same. She had a rental house, which caught fire. It was due to a dryer malfunction. She claimed she lost everything, but the truth is she stashed all her belongings in a safe place before the burn.

Bob was a tenant who stayed in a room next to the stairs. Early one morning, he slipped down the stairs covered in oil. I gathered all the folks together and determined that Kim's boy had spread the oil because the mother was unhappy with Bob. Bob felt she did it because he caught Kim pilfering through his medications. After she moved out, she moved into a trailer and was found dead of an overdose. Her son lost his life in a car accident. It was a sad ending for a boy who had a chance in life and chose the wrong parent with whom to align.

A local man that rented a few times came to the house with some questionable women. He wanted separate rooms for them and one for himself. One girl left the next day; the other professed her dissatisfaction and departed. Upon cleaning the room, I found a large number of prophylactics in the dresser drawer. He kept calling to rent, and I turned him down.

A mentally disabled girl, who was twenty years old, and seldom bathed, stayed at her parents' request. She kept her cat in her room, and when I found out she was not feeding it daily, and she was not feeding herself regularly either, I requested she leave. I was called again to house her and denied her a room.

Another woman kept a caged rabbit in her room and burned incense. While she was in the kitchen, it toppled onto her dresser, setting some papers ablaze. A passerby saw the blaze from town and called the fire department. She got the rabbit out successfully, but the burning smell stayed for hours. She joined the Army and became an explosive expert.

On a winter morning, as I peered from the kitchen window, I saw smoke. As I descended the steps to the basement, I saw fire. I woke all the guests, hurried them into the yard, and called the fire department. A water heater had caught fire.

A man drank heavily, caused no problem, but urinated in a jug, throwing the contents out the window. Then, the young pregnant girl peed in an old-fashioned washbasin that stood in the room. She placed it under the bed, unbeknownst to me. When I pushed my mop under the bed, I knocked it over.

Otis, the dog, belonged to a tenant; he slept on my couch during the day. Part Pitbull never frightened anyone, and he and my Lucky dog were great friends.

Donald lived on the third floor and brought a Dalmatian puppy home. Nice guy, he ended up getting arrested for drugs, and the Dalmatian went to another resident who moved on and kept the dog. For a short time, a mother and daughter came with their blind Saint Bernard. He and my dog Tar sat on the landing of the stairs.

Then, there was the Indian woman who only paid rent when the casino paid profits to reservation residents. I had to move her out and carry her many clothes down three flights of stairs with help while the local police officer watched as she loaded up her car. No gentle words resounded that evening.

A girl in Room 8 stayed a while, and then she disappeared for a week. She felt if she was not there, she did not have to pay rent. I moved her out, but she left her massive quantity of clothes. I gave them to our second-hand shop on Main Street.

Late one evening, a woman loaded with bags of clothes took a room. Shortly, I received a phone call from the Sheriff's office, asking if she was at my house. They requested, "That girl has an arrest warrant. She is a shoplifter. We cannot keep her in our jail; please keep her overnight; we will pick her up in the morning."

There were a few instances involving cars. One girl had borrowed money against her car, and a truck arrived to repossess it. A man left his older yellow BMW parked in the yard and never returned. I had to go to court to prove my case, so I could get it removed. I finally was able to sell it.

Some years later, I rented to another older man called Alfie. He is no relation to my goat, only the similarity of names. Schooled in horticulture, he knows every term, common and scientific. He plants flowers around town and tends the garden. He is a part Tuscarora Indian and comes from Louisiana. A devoted member of Alcoholics Anonymous (AA) for twenty years cooked his food, and many evenings we talked and ate together. He is an intelligent and insightful man with whom I often discussed my problems. He loves animals and gives his time to the Friends of Animals Organization. The town council gave him an award for beautifying the town. Alfie is a sixties throwback with blond shoulder-length hair, blue eyes suffering from macro degeneration, and depleted hearing. The ladies swarm around him. His room in the house was on the third floor. He never complained, but when he was able to secure an apartment on Main Street, I did not feel guilty about moving. Whenever I see him in town, I shout hello to my friend Alfie.

Approximately, seven guests over the years became fast friends. So many people came through my door that I was able to help in some way. I will miss this. Bed and

Breakfasts have the reputation of being hard on relationships. Although I had a few house-keepers for short times, many of their marriages failed be it due to the constant care and devotion to the paying guests, the steady work, or misunderstanding of their partner. That, too, was my case. I shed the one I arrived with and chose a man with more understanding and a greater desire to help me. He also was a long-time renter. Life is unpredictable.

The stairs that gave an extra charm to the house had become a burden. My sickness in 2002 (next story) moved me down to the Grand room. I felt I was stealing from myself by living in it, but I had no choice. I had outlived my ability to care for this grand mansion. It was time to pass it on to younger legs and brighter ideas. At the end of 2015, an interested couple came to see the house and purchased it.

Slowly we started to search for a new place. My experience had ended, and so the next chapter began. On January 18, 2016, Tony and I vacated and moved into a house overlooking the Appalachian range's mountain peaks.

I have been back to the old house on a few occasions. The downstairs remains the same, but the second floor is very different. Changes include mainly reducing the eight bedrooms to four, each with a bath. The rooms are now larger, more like the original layout. A wall in the backyard blocks the encroaching hill, and the porch has a welcoming appeal. The old house is no longer mine. I felt a part of history in the old place, and I have a pinch of remorse to leave her.

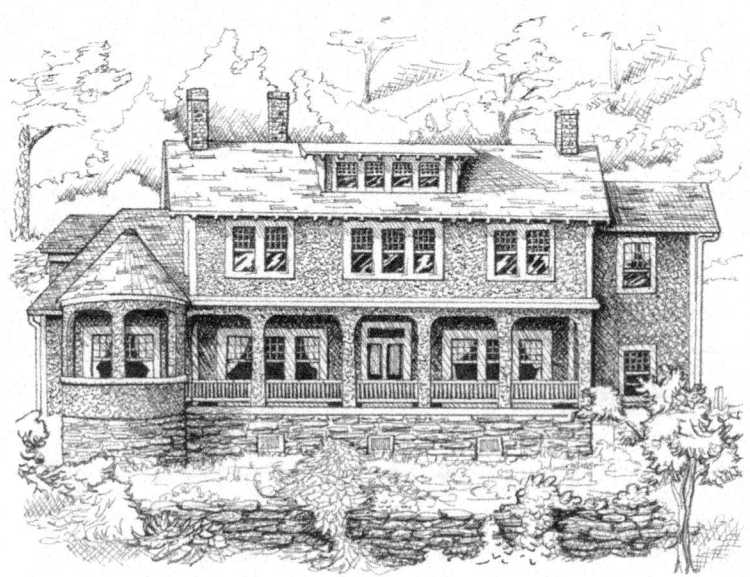

Pen & Ink Drawing of the Marshal House by Russ Daniels

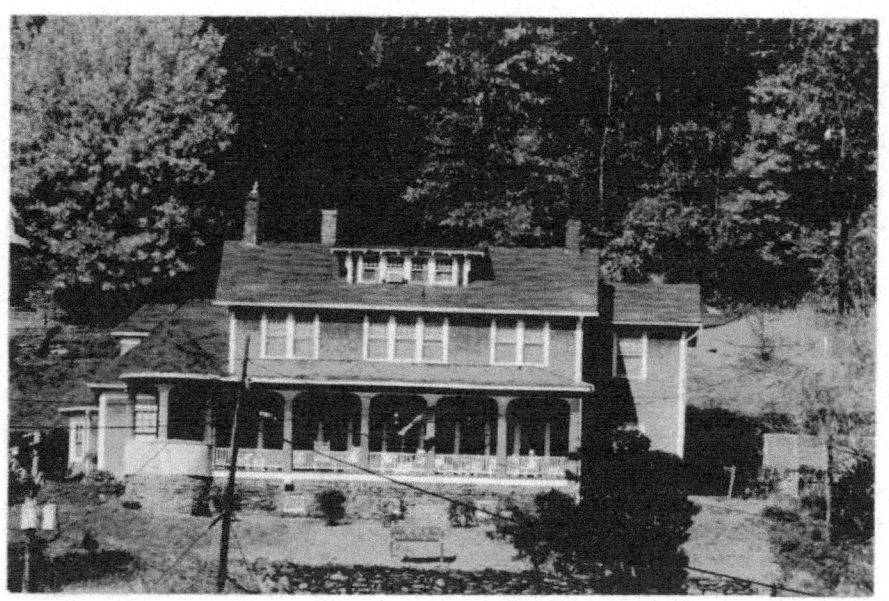

Marshall House B&B 1903 home

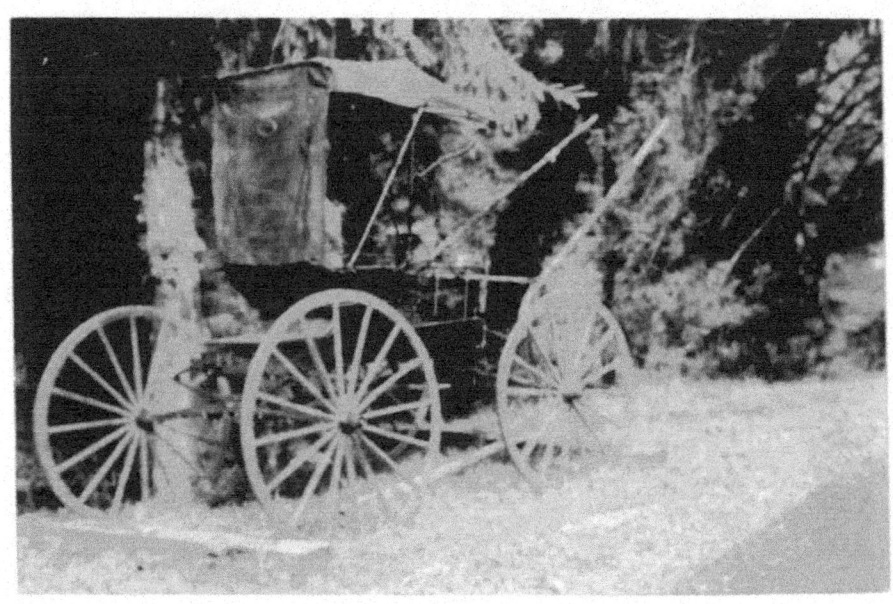

Doctor's Carriage

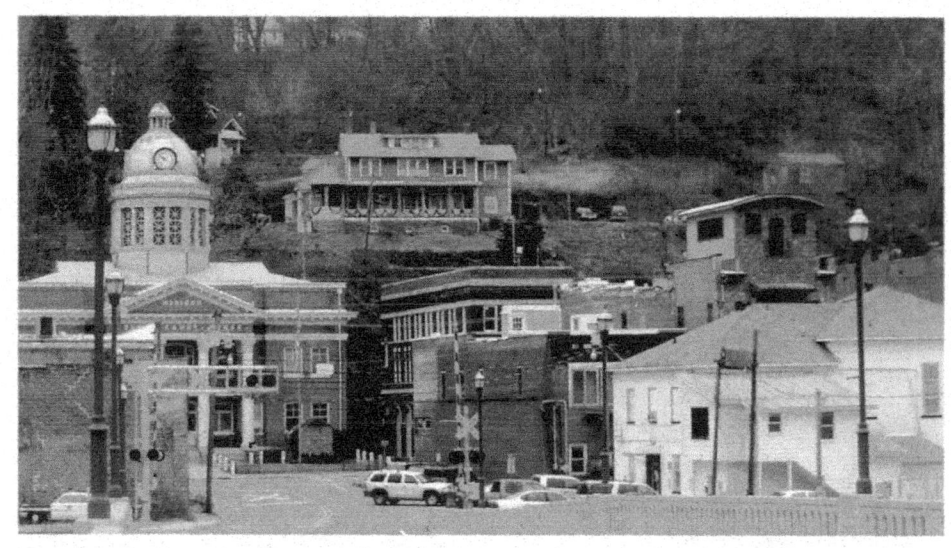

Town of Marshall, NC

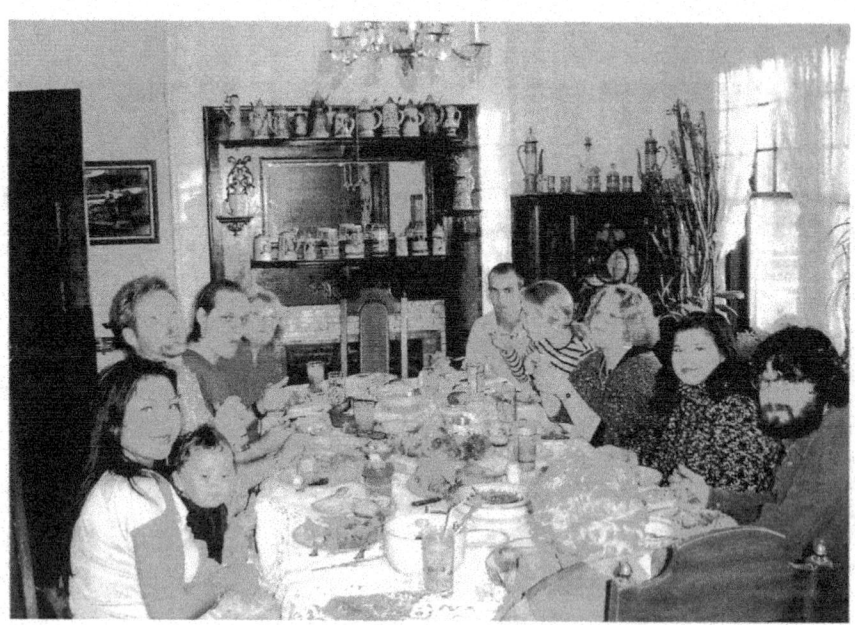

Josie's first real Thanksgiving

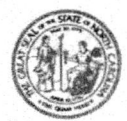

North Carolina Department of Cultural Resources

James G. Martin, Governor
Patric Dorsey, Secretary

Division of Archives and History
William S. Price, Jr., Director

January 30, 1990

Mr. and Mrs. Jim Boylan
5 Hill Street
P. O. Box 865
Marshall, N C 28753

Re: Certificate of Entry in the National Register of Historic Places for
        James H. White House, Marshall, Madison County
        December 21, 1989

Dear Mr. and Mrs. Boylan:

Please accept the enclosed certificate which states that the above-referenced
property has been entered in the National Register of Historic Places. You are
most fortunate to own and preserve a property that justly deserves this honor.

The National Register has been called "a roll call of the tangible reminders of
the history of the United States." It is, therefore, a pleasure for the
Division of Archives and History to participate in this program and thereby
make our nation aware of North Carolina's rich cultural heritage.

In order that we may keep our records up to date, it would be very helpful if
you would notify us of any changes in ownership or of any major alteration of
the property, including moving, destruction, remodeling, or restoration. We
appreciate your efforts and your cooperation in preserving the best of our past
for posterity.

Sincerely,

William S. Price, Jr.
State Historic Preservation Officer

WSP,Jr./mlr

Enclosure

C: The Honorable Anita R. Ward, Mayor, Town of Marshall

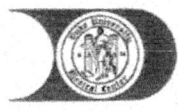 **DUKE UNIVERSITY MEDICAL CENTER**

Hyperbaric Center

November 14, 1990

Ruth Boylan
The Marshall House
S. Hill Street
P.O. Box 865
Marshall, NC 28753

Dear Ruth:

I wanted to write and thank you for a delightful stay at your Inn. I have stayed in numerous Bed and Breakfasts all over the US and Europe, but I enjoyed the Marshall House more than most. I have written to the author of The Complete Guide to Bed & Breakfasts, which I usually travel with, asking that she include the Marshall House in her directory.

I encourage you to "keep up the good work" as Marshall House has an awful lot going for it.

The house is historically unique in design. It is very comfortable and set in a truly picturesque little town, a "real" American small town. There is nothing artificial or touristy about either the town of Marshall, the house, or even its properties. For city people daily facing the assaults and false pretenses of our modern world, the Marshall House is true to its slogan, "a place to relax!"

The fact that it isn't perfect is part of the charm. I'd much rather stay in plastered rooms with a small crack in the ceiling than rooms in supposedly historic places, obviously extensively rebuilt with modern materials.

The Marshall House and the city of Marshall are like a visit to the recent past, a quieter, more peaceful time so hard to find at most Bed and Breakfasts.

We thoroughly enjoyed ourselves!

Sincerely,

Chris Wachholz
Box 3823
DUMC
Durham, NC 27710

P.S. Please keep us informed of events like the Fortune Teller weekend.

/pd

| F. G. Hall Laboratory | 684-5514 | Diver's Alert Network | 684-2948 |
| Oxygen Transport Laboratory | 684-8908 | Clinical Hyperbaric Oxygen Therapy | 684-6726 |

Box 3823, Durham, North Carolina 27710

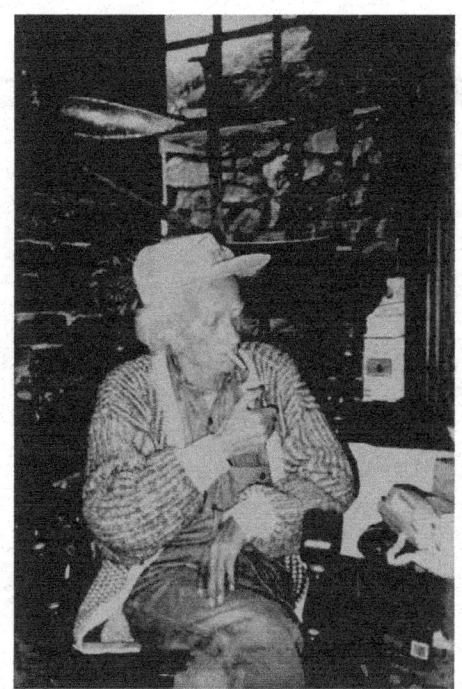

J.B. Tweed

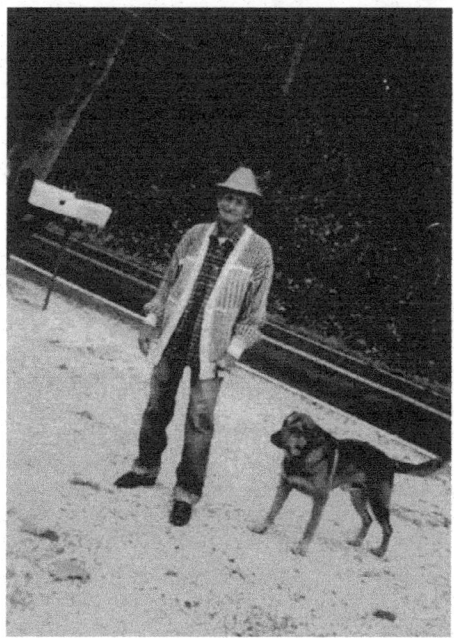

J.B. Tweed

Stop and smell the flowers

Town of Marshall names May 1 Alfie Booth Day

By Melissa Dean
melissa@newsrecordandsentinel.com

April showers may bring May flowers, but one man helps grow them.

The Town of Marshall has designated May 1 Alfie Booth Day, in honor of the local master gardener.

"It's overwhelming," Booth said. "I have been so well accepted in this town and treated well by the people.. how unbelievable."

The 66-year-old master gardener will be honored as a thank you for donating his time and knowledge to beautifying downtown through gardens and landscaping.

"He tends the plants up and down the street so we thought it would be fun to have a day to recognize him," said Rev. Melissa Upchurch, who helped organize the day. "He beautifies the town and has such a giving spirit."

Celebrations for Alfie Booth Day will begin with a presentation for Alfie in at Town Hall at 9 a.m., but it won't stop there.

Look out for all sorts of fun surprises throughout the day as Marshall shops and restaurants join forces with local specials like Zumas' Alfalfie salad.

The Louisiana born, Asheville-bred master gardener moved to Marshall just over three years ago after visual disabilities stopped him from working.

"I just wanted a small town where I could get involved in the community," said Booth.

Since moving to Marshall, Booth has donated countless hours of his time to taking his passion to the streets of Marshall through projects with the local Presbyterian Church and The Depot.

The 66-year-old holds degrees in horticulture and fine arts- a collaboration that he takes to his projects.

"My approach to gardening, as opposed to landscape architecture, is more from a fine arts background," he said.

His canvas-the ground; his paint- the seeds.

Over the last year, that canvas has been behind a local attorney's office on North Main Street, where Booth has transformed the area from a tangled web of invasive weeds and brush to what will soon be a beautiful piece of radiant art.

Using giant sunflowers, hi-

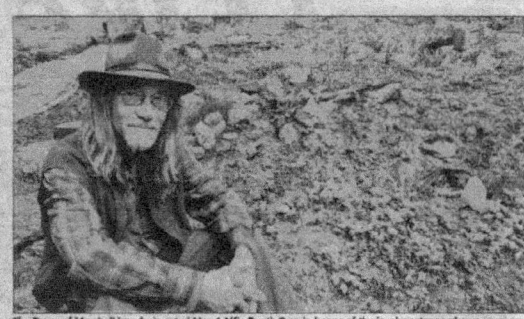

The Town of Marshall has designated May 1 Alfie Booth Day, in honor of the local master gardener. PHOTO BY MELISSA DEAN/THE NEWS-RECORD & SENTINEL

biscus and angel trumpets, he hopes come summertime the area will be transformed into a children's garden.

Though a master gardener with over four decades experience in organic gardening-Booth credits his undertaking to another infamous gardener – the late Everett Barnett.

"Everybody always spoke so highly of him and he planted all

around town," said Booth. "I just saw myself picking up where Everett left off."

Everett tended to gardens and landscape in Marshall before decades.

And while Booth's education and passion has led him to becoming a master gardener, he says what he loves most about what he does it that there is always something new to learn.

"They call it a master gardener, but I don't think there are any master gardeners, we are all apprentices," he said.

When asked how he felt to have his day kick-off the month known for flowers, he answered as any good gardener would-

"I'll be showing my appreciation back to the town when all those eight feet sunflowers bloom."

Alfie Booth

_____

CHAPTER 38

DISASTROUS LETTER

The high school reunion letter triggered an old buried memory.

It had been years since I reminisced about my first love. Curiosity spiked. I looked him up and wrote him a short note. Carrying on a busy life, once the letter hit the mailbox, I forgot about it.

Months went by, and one day, a post arrived. Oh, dear, my husband saw it, and I told him what I had done. The repercussions of this epistle lasted well into the night. Had life been peachy keen, I probably would not have even considered writing the message. But, as in all relationships, sometimes one needs a little excitement.

The letter brought about a phone call, and from that first phone call, it generated a call per day.

We rehashed:

"Do you remember our first drive-in? What was that movie?" I asked.

He didn't remember it any better than I had, but we remembered other things that went on in the car that night.

He asked, "Do you remember the dance?"

"Yes," I responded.

Then, he continued, "You wore a black velvet top and a full skirt with a crinoline that whirled about when we danced. You liked to do the Lindy to Bill Haley and the Commits

– 'Twelve O'clock Rock' and I was terrible at that, although I could dip you relatively low while your long hair swept the floor."

I reminded him, "I used to see you on Friday nights at your Civil Air Patrol meetings. I was a softie for a uniform; you looked so grown up."

There was more; he sent me tapes of the day's music, the popular radio programs, and a forgotten tape I had made for him. That embarrassed me. I had forgotten about it, foolish to talk all about those private encounters. This evoked thoughts that dipped down to the emotions I felt when I was "dumped."

I realized that he was living in the past.

I desperately wanted to marry this man and was devastated when he told me he was marrying another. I managed to get over the shock and moved on. I had a life with lots of ups and downs, but it wasn't staid. I had more adventures, excitement, and love, which I would never have experienced had I tied the knot with him.

Unfortunately, he claimed his love for me had never died. Well, my heart was not so open. After all, he had espoused to another woman.

"Oh, but you and I would have had such a wonderful life together." He coyly retorted.

"I know you had another love. Perhaps, at one time, I thought the sun and moon set with you."

I am not one for deep reflection, and I don't dwell on past affairs. I hadn't been truthful with myself and did not contemplate what would arise once we delved into our prior romance. I realized the reality was that he had emotionally injured me.

My little outburst didn't dampen his feelings, and the calls and Internet chats continued until one thoughtless day he left town, leaving his computer on with all the evidence of our chatting. Ah, his wife spied the advantage and checked it out. Wow, that generated a call to my possessive mate. I don't think I have to diagram for you the results of that communication. What it did for me was to end the relationship immediately; we never spoke again.

In the meantime, he and his wife separated, as did we. Then, if you can believe this, my ex-husband began seeing his ex-wife.

The health gods were not good to my old infatuation. He had diabetes, and subsequently, he lost his legs (ugh). That undoubtedly hastened his demise. I received this information from no other than my ex-husband delivered maliciously with a snicker.

CHAPTER 39:

_____

MIRACLE

I managed the Marshall House Bed and Breakfast for twelve years, accommo-dating tourists and locals. In 1998, Tony showed up on my doorstep and rented Room 8 on the second floor. As we became acquainted with each other, a friendship blossomed, and eventually, a deeper bond. My twenty-six-year marriage to Jim ended on a sour note in September 2001, shortly before 9/11. The final decree came later, but once Jim was gone, Tony and I became a couple.

It was mid-May, one of those colder days before spring finally took hold. Tony and I were on a mission to locate a house for my son Jerry, who wanted a summer home in North Carolina. Tony found a place about a mile away. I parked the car and did not follow while Tony checked to see if the people were at home. A woman came to the door, they spoke a few moments, and Tony returned to the car.

Sitting in the car, I felt squeamish and waited impatiently for Tony to return. I cus-tomarily drove on weekends as he had a construction business and was on the move all week. When he returned to the car, I asked, "Will you please drive? I am not feeling too good. What happened at the house?"

"Is it a headache or a stomach ache; what does not feel well?"

"I just feel like I want to throw up."

"Well, don't do it in the car. I can pull over. I guess I was wrong about the house; she does not want to sell."

"I think I'll be ok until we get to Larry's house." Larry is Tony's long-time friend.

Tony had promised Chris, Larry's wife, to take her to the grocery store as their car was in the repair shop. While he was away, I spent my time in their bathroom. I did not throw up as expected but did not feel any better.

Upon Tony's return, he suggested, "Let me take you to the Sisters of Mercy just up the street." After a short wait, the receptionist ushered me inside. The nurse checked my vital signs, collected blood and body fluids, and then I threw up all over the table. The doctor came in, examined me briefly, at which point, I threw up again. He instructed the nurse to give me a cup of thick, chalky, white medicine to stop the vomiting. It didn't, and I heaved again. The clinic did not check the body fluids they had taken and released me. I had to throw up once more and choose the washroom near the lobby's exit while leaving. I found it more comfortable to sit on the floor and lean over the bowl. While in that position, I unexpectedly peed. I left the room physically uncomfortable, attempting to control the urge to throw up yet again. Rejoining Tony, he inquired, "How do you feel now?"

"Worse, worse than before; I want to go home."

I struggled up the stairs to my third-floor bedroom at home, changed clothes, and went to bed. Tony prepared a plate of canned fruit and a jug of ice water, which he brought to me, and then went to his room. At this point in the relationship, he felt it wise to keep his place with other people in the house. Although we saw each other, our rendezvous was sporadic.

Tony gave some thought to my condition. We had recently been away on a short vacation to meet up with Carol, Charlie, and son Charles, friends who live in Miami. Our destination was Washington, DC, and Baltimore, Maryland, to see the Orioles vs. Indian baseball game at Camden Yards. I had made the reservations at a Quality Inn in Alexandria, Virginia. It was not a top-notch accommodation. Charles felt it lacked the cleanliness that more expensive hotels possessed. Tony and I tend not to be so meticulous, and so we were satisfied. Now Tony wondered if something could have made me sick at that hotel.

A few hours later, Tony made another trip upstairs. On the third floor, the ceiling was low. At five-foot-two, I had no problem, but Tony, at six-foot-one, had to stoop to walk toward the bed. Over the bed, the roof sloped even lower toward the eves of the house.

As he bent over the bed with concern in his voice, he asked, "How are you doing now?"

"Ah, I have been throwing up. Even the water doesn't stay down."

"Do you want to try to eat some dry toast? That might work better to absorb the fluid." He offered to go downstairs, but I shook my head.

"No, instead, I will take some more fruit; my mouth is dry. Perhaps, it will stay down this time."

As the day continued, I did not get any better. By late afternoon, I wanted to fill the prescription the doctor had given me. It was Phenergan to stop the urge to vomit. A neighbor Sandy came to my house and offered to pick up the order. Before she left, I told her, "I have thrown up eleven times; maybe the medication will help."

The medicine had little or no effect. By morning, the pain in the middle of my chest had accelerated, so I could not endure it any longer. It was an agonizing pain, refusing to abate. I wanted to go to the hospital. Sandy offered to take me, and Tony said to Sandy, "If they admit her, then I will go. I can't make any health decisions on her behalf anyway."

On the drive to the hospital, Sandy said, "I wonder what could be causing you so much pain. The last time you were so sick was that rash you had from 1997 to 2001," Sandy said in her candid way. She has a way of bringing up past unpleasantries.

It was now May 20, 2002. To change the subject, I said, "Did I tell you Tony and I just came back from a trip to Washington and met Carol and family? We walked all around the National Mall, and I had a hard time keeping up. Something may have been brewing inside me already then. Tony enjoyed it so much he wants to go back and see the Smithsonian. Our friends' time was memorable, especially since Charlie, Carol's husband, was fighting cancer. Now, ten days later, I am sick. Maybe it isn't anything."

"Maybe it was something you ate recently?" Sandy inquired.

"If it is food, wouldn't that cause stomach upset, not the pain in my chest? But what could that be? We have been eating at home since we came back. I know my cooking isn't the greatest, but how could I be so sick? I've never had this type of pain before. Maybe it is gas pain, and they will not take me in the hospital." Dark thoughts clouded my mind. Sickness was not on my agenda.

"We will find out what it is when we get to the emergency room," Sandy commented.

At home, Tony was thinking these same thoughts. He remembered that he had German sausage at the last place we ate, and I had a fish dish. Maybe there was something wrong with the fish. He was worried; he thought, *she seldom gets sick, doesn't suffer from any ailments, and is very energetic.*

Keeping a house the size of Marshall House, with ten bedrooms, was a full-time job. Tourists and permanent residents kept me on the move. There was no time to get sick.

In the emergency room (ER), they put me in a cubicle, and a nurse took my vitals. After she left, Sandy asked, "Do you want me to stay until Tony gets here?"

"Yes, if they let you. Do you want to stay?"

"I would like to. I want to know what is wrong with you; I am worried about you. I need to call Tony and tell him we are at St. Joe's."

A friend for eight years, Sandy was a comfort to me in this unknown situation. She also knew about nursing, as she was a Certified Nursing Assistant 2 (CNA2), so I felt I had a nurse friend too.

The ER was buzzing. In and out of the room, they came, one test after another. Then, a doctor came in and began asking questions. I told the doctor about all the symptoms I was experiencing.

"I had a headache for one day and constant pain in my chest. Since the clinic bathroom incident, where I urinated all over myself, it seems I have not peed normally. Then, when I do pee, it comes out a dark color."

They poked and prodded, stuck me with needles, took blood, and inserted a catheter tube; the pain remained, but the medications given stopped the nausea and vomiting.

There were more questions upon questions. More doctors came into the room. "Did you ever experience anything like this in the past?" One of the doctors asked.

"No, I've never had anything like this before."

"Have you been in the woods lately?"

Then, I thought for a minute and said, "On our way back from Washington, we stopped at the Natural Bridge in Virginia, a geological formation made of limestone carved out by water. Woods surround it, but we only walked under the bridge, and I touched the sides, making me believe that is what possibly made me sick."

The doctors shook their heads and said, "Little Lady, I don't believe there is any possibility of that being the case. Lie back and let us do our work."

A nurse came in next and pulled the curtain closed.

"Please stand and remove your gown; I want to check for spider bites." She found none.

After replacing my gown, I requested a warm blanket.

Another doctor came into the room to look at me. He took my pulse, looked at my eyes, and instructed the nurse to take several blood samples. The nurse came back with a cart, took the samples, and left.

Next, a male nurse came to wheel me down the hall for a limited ultrasound. When I got back, Sandy had left, and Tony was waiting for me. He noted how pale I was: he was used to a healthy-looking girlfriend, one that laughed and kidded around. I was now a sickly-looking gal. He wanted to cheer me up. What could he do but watch me in pain?

I said to Tony, "I don't smoke, don't drink coffee, don't drink soda, don't take drugs or pills, do not care for beer, and alcohol and they do not know what is the matter with me after all these tests. Infectious disease and gastroenterology doctors have seen me. There was also discussion about bringing in a Nephrology doctor."

I then asked Tony, "Have they told you anything?"

Tony replied, "No, Sweetie, I have no idea and don't think they know what is going on with you either. The doctor told me to get in touch with a relative, said he couldn't tell me anything as I am not kin."

Tony sat down and put his head in his hands. He was distraught; what could he do. My fear was mounting; I was getting anxious and thought about crying. "No scenes," I told myself that will not fix anything.

Then, the nurse returned and said, "We will be admitting you to the hospital. We are getting a room ready for you upstairs."

Turning to Tony, she said, "Sir, it is going to take some time. We have more tests to perform; if you want to leave and come back when she is in a room, it will give her some time to rest."

He turned to me and said, "Honey, I wish I could just hold your hand and make it all go away." He leaned over and kissed me, "I think it would be best if I went home and gave your son Jerry a call."

"OK, Tony, I am tired. Love you."

Contrary to previous thinking, the doctors admitted me. A few hours later, a transport person pushed me to a room on the fourth floor with the speed of a hospital.

Dr. Aiello, who was a Nephrologist, he came into the room and informed me, "If there is no improvement in the next twenty-four to thirty-six hours, renal replacement therapy will be required. I think it best we move you across the street to Mission Hospital. They have a dialysis section that will be more capable of handling your needs."

A nurse brought the evening menu and ice water to the room and put them on the tray. Feeling it was not close enough, I took it to bed with me and shortly spilled it all over the bed. That happened on many occasions as I would fall asleep, and the ice water with cubes would wake me up. It was strange, though; everything, including the water, tasted salty.

Within a day, they transported me by ambulance across the street.

Tony frequently came, each time noticing there were more tubes on my body. I had an intravenous fluid drip, a bag full of sodium bicarbonate connected to my right arm, and the urine collection bag hanging off the bed. Leaning over, Tony told me, "I love you so much; nothing can happen to you. I can't live without you." He was so devastated; he wanted to spend more time with me. His work suffered: he did not feel he could handle the stress and go to work too.

"I want to get well to be with you, Tony. I do not intend to leave you. I love you too." He sat on the bed and held my hand. I turned my head to Tony for a kiss and, "Oh, that is so cold; ice cubes are under me. I'm so sorry; now they have to come and change me again." He tried to pull the ice away, change the bed but thought better of it and called the nurse. He was afraid to move me.

I wanted to tell him about my daily experience, saying, "I was wheeled through the hospital for CT scans and more ultrasound. Machines, those non-invasive body searches, are becoming a routine. I know there is a high demand for their use. I wait in line frequently, with three or four complaining patients. After one of those exams, someone mentioned I had a cyst on my right kidney."

Visiting time was over; Tony went home to feed the dogs and cats.

During the night, more doctors came into the room. Dr. Eubanks, my physician, told me I had pancreatitis that accounted for the constant pain in my chest. For the pain, I received morphine in a patch on my back. It gave relief and sleep, but it distorted my mind. The morphine did make me imagine situations, like the night I had the nurse call Tony at 2:00 a.m. to bring the Chamber of Commerce checkbook to the hospital. I thought I had some work to do. Poor fellow, he drove to the hospital with the book at 2:30 a.m.

Soon the hospital staff became aware of the seriousness of my condition. Social Services came to the room to discuss financial matters. I was sixty-four and not eligible for Medicare, although they submitted it, as I had end renal failure, which meant I might not survive.

The next question the worker asked me, "Do you have a will?"

"No."

My long-time friend Robbie was in the room and offered to call the local attorney in Marshall. When the document arrived, a hospital security officer brought it to my bedside and stood by while I signed it.

The doctors still did not know if I had a bacterial infection or a virus, although my temperature was one hundred three degrees. My condition was deteriorating. Some of the tests came back, and the results were surprising. Acute renal failure; my kidneys were failing to filter waste products. Dialysis was necessary and started on day four.

The symptoms of metabolic acidosis were present and commonly experienced at the end of life, reported, but not a certainty. I was also diagnosed with acute hepatic dysfunction, which is inflammation of the liver, shown in yellowing of the skin and eyes.

The following test results from my stay in the ER on May 20, 2002: My creatinine level was 7.3 (way above the normal range, which is 0.1 to 1.1.) This was considered acute hepatic dysfunction. There was too much acid that the kidneys did not remove; red blood cells destroyed before normal lifespan; anemia; pancreatitis with abdominal pain; and the potassium level in my blood was too high.

There was fear that I might not survive the night.

When Tony heard that, he was flabbergasted. It was time to follow the doctor's suggestion to call my son Jerry in Miami, Florida. Upon making the phone call, he was so relieved when Jerry said, "I'll be right up. I can make it in about eleven to twelve hours."

When Jerry walked through the door, Tony felt the weight fall off his shoulders. He told Jerry, "I just could not take it anymore all by myself seeing her lying in that bed and feeling so poorly. Every day, doctors came up with more and more diagnoses of what is wrong with her. I needed your support."

Jerry responded, "I know how you feel about Mom, but she is going to be alright. I know she will. She's my mom; nothing can happen to her." I listened to all this confidence from my only son, whom I trusted and loved. I knew that whatever it was that had taken me down, I would pull through.

There were more symptoms to disclose. Thrombocytopenia was a low red blood platelet count to treat with plasma transfusions during a dialysis treatment. Anemia and eosinophilia were pulmonary conditions treated with oxygen administered by attaching a hose to the nose. I received a feeding tube, but the doctors had it removed shortly after. I was wondering if anything else could go wrong. Every morning and evening, an orderly came to take blood.

It was now ten days in the hospital.

I could not eat breakfast before dialysis, and the wait for food after the procedure was causing excruciating pain in my lower abdomen. I suffered severe gas pains and hunger. One time after the treatment, I received a substantial plate of fruit. I expressed my pleasure to the cafeteria worker, telling her, "Oh, the fruit is so delicious. So juicy, thanks for bringing it for me." The nurse appeared in shock, "No, you are not to have that. It was a mistake." So, she took the remaining dish away. Everything I was fed was mild, soft, and not palatable. I watched cooking shows, so I could imagine I was eating that food. I wanted to concentrate on getting well and not watch silly sitcoms. The TV was of little interest. Dialysis treatments made me tired, sapping all the strength out of my body.

When Tony returned, he saw a yellow-skinned woman with snake-like yellow eyes. I was conscious, but I was not aware of my surroundings. I did not know where I was or if it was nighttime or daytime because the staff was restricting light.

Friends were arriving at the hospital to sit with me, giving me some companionship and support. Robbie and Sandy took turns coming on alternate days. On one sunny day, both girls were in the room. Sandy was following the nurses' orders not to give me any ice water due to the water surrounding my heart and lungs. I also wanted the shades opened, but Sandy refused. Sandy felt she should follow the nurse's orders; the light was to be blocked.

I got annoyed and told Sandy, "I'll throw you out the window." Was that the morphine talking?

Robbie could all but keep from laughing out loud. I had injured poor Sandy's feelings. That was mean; she meant well.

As time continued to drag, Esther, a friend I met in an arts and craft group, came to say,

"My church is praying for you. Besides, I have sent in a prayer request with a large TV audience." She felt prayers would help me get well.

I placed a call to my old nun teacher in New York. If I needed ecclesiastic help, she was the best one to contact. Surprised to hear from me, she told me, "All the nuns will pray for you. I love you, Ruthie; we wish you a speedy recovery."

The best visit I can remember was when the Baptist Minister Vince came from Marshall to see me. I was delirious that day and thought I was staying in Hot Springs. Since I always slept in the nude at home, the hospital was having trouble keeping me dressed, especially when drugged.

Upon seeing Vince, I uttered, "Vince, it is so nice to see you."

Then, I ceremoniously tossed the hospital gown aside, and poor Vince turned many shades of red. Robbie was there, and she attempted to apologize for my bad conduct. It was no use; I had already misbehaved, and he understood it was the morphine.

Word traveled to Miami, and my ex-husband Jim called. "What has happened? I'll come up."

"No, Jim, I am being taken care of by a staff of doctors and nurses. Don't worry." That was not enough assurance, and his calls continued to my annoyance. Robbie answered the phone to let him know I was cared for, and it was not necessary to keep calling.

Barbara Penland, and her daughter, Susan, owners of the Penland department store in Marshall, visited one evening after work. Barbara looked at me, and in an aston- ished tone, said,

"Ruth, your hair has turned gray."

"Not only that, it is falling out," I replied. The gray changed as I recovered, but the hair growth was slow in returning. Barbara had the Presbyterian Church in Marshall praying for me.

Kathy Wilkes from Florida was in the area and brought a purple orchid. Dick and Jane Morgan visited and, Jane told me, "Just think well. Concentrate on getting better." They were encouraging words.

Colleen Laroe, Wendy Danison, and Claudia Hiatt, and others I have forgotten came to cheer me.

Nexium, given for the ulcer that had suddenly appeared in my stomach; Reglan administered for high blood pressure; Paxil offered because I had said, "If it continues to feel so bad, I will kill myself." That was not my intention, and I never took the Paxil.

That frightened Dr. Aiello; he felt I was severely depressed. He became insistent I take Paxil. Robbie stepped in, "My friend does not want any tranquilizers. Listen to what she is telling you; she feels frustration at the situation and the beeping sounds during dialysis."

I said, "Every time the machines need medications added to the treatment or service or change of patients, they beep, and it was constant. The sounds of distress and need are disturbing." The doctor understood, and before he departed, he informed me I needed a transfusion of plasma.

The following day the transport personnel arrived and slid me from the bed onto a stretcher; transport placed me in a separate room within the dialysis section. That was the plasma transfer room closed off from the other patients. Dr. Eubanks arrived, plugged me into the plasma transfer, spent some time watching, and telling me I would be ok with time. I dozed on and off during the lengthy procedure.

Next, I had my dialysis treatment in the room where there were desperately ill people fighting for their lives. Loved ones sat with patients, and Sandy sat with me. On that occasion, when I was in more severe pain than usual and felt like I was losing my grip on life, Sandy begged, "Hold on; you are not going to die while I am here. Please do not die." She was desperate to keep me alive. Not that I wanted to die, but it was horrible, dreadful, and terrible with no words to describe the feelings in that room; I did not die, I did not suffer quietly, and I was determined to beat the thing that had ravaged my body.

After thirty days, the hospital discharged me, and Tony was there to take me home. I was weak, but joyful that it was over. Against all the odds, I had beaten the devil.

The creatinine level was 7.3 upon arriving at the hospital, a clear indication of kidney failure, and had come down to about 2.5. The hospital scheduled further dialysis as an outpatient to restore my kidneys to normal levels. On my first trip to the outpatient dialysis clinic in Weaverville, Doctor Manley greeted me with the words, "I didn't think you would make it. Most people don't live that have three or more major organs fail. Congratulations."

It was not entirely over. Each treatment left me weak and drained. There was food I could not eat. Nothing tasted quite the same. I had lost a lot of weight. My kidneys, although functioning, were only 55 percent. My immune system had attacked my joints, leaving me with a compromised immune system.

I received treatment three times a week. I was the only patient in the room who had to urinate during treatment. It was undetermined what had caused the problem. It must be an unknown, mysterious modern disease.

In March, before any inclination what was to come, Tony and I planned a trip to Maine in August. The clinic had arranged for me to continue dialysis in Bangor, Maine. I told them it was not necessary; I would be ok. Three days before the trip, my creatinine level came down to 1.5; that was a satisfactory level to discontinue treatment and have the plug removed from my chest.

On September 6, 2003, an appointment with Dr. E. Smith concluded I had rheumatoid arthritis, undoubtedly brought on by the kidney disease. Osteoporosis, scoliosis, and spinal stenos were not from the same cause. Perhaps, too many steroids shots to combat the rash of 1997 to 2001 could have been responsible for Osteo. Scoliosis may be from birth, and spinal stenos could have begun from overactivity or my life on the boat.

Hip replacement was due to falls and knee replacement from rheumatoid arthritis. Other joints affected are elbows and shoulders.

Many years later, in Miami, searching for pain treatment, I met a doctor. After discussion, he said, "People do not recover from end renal failure. You are a miracle."

Regardless of all the physical problems, my mind is intact. Although I feel I'm living on borrowed time, I am happy to do so.

CHAPTER 40:

_____

JIM BOYLAN

Jim was a changed man. His pallor was gray; he was a shadow of himself weighing a mere one hundred thirty pounds. His emphysema took the life out of him. Once a strong man, his body was showing the ravages of the disease. He was fading away.

What made him happy in the last years of his life was his granddaughter Josie. They often sat playing simple games like fish, with a stick, on a string in his room. They watched TV, read stories; conversations on many subjects were learning experiences, helping her imagination grow. Jim was an intelligent man, self-educated, and he expressed himself well, exhibiting a wealth of knowledge, even a young Josie understood.

Josie once said, "Grandpa knows everything."

Medical help was doing little to relieve the constant inability to catch his breath. The time was drawing near; he knew it and tried to convey this to a child.

The road he traveled was strenuous and steep each day, frustrating him with the simple tasks of dressing, eating, and requiring assistance walking. He felt he was a burden to the family. He desired to be a better grandfather, a better man. If only he were a man with no pain! Then, it came on Father's Day as he unexpectedly lost his balance and slipped from the bed to the floor. He never felt the fall, which sadly took his life.

Ah, the pain was gone. He was at peace.

God works in mysterious ways.

CHAPTER 41:

LIFE WITH TONY

In August 1998, I rented Room 8 at the end of the hall to Tony Dunkinson. He never left.

Tony was a good-looking mustached man until he smiled. A few teeth were missing in that grin. It was not long before a visit to the dentist put a smile back on his otherwise clean-shaven face.

Tony was quiet but friendly, and we soon became kitchen buddies. Every morning he prepared his daily lunch of hard-boiled eggs for sandwiches. He had a strange way of destroying the egg in the dish. He chopped it up with a knife until it became smashed eggs. The tink, tink sound was annoying to me. Taking a fork and mashing it would have been quieter, faster, and more efficient. He did not see it that way. Every day I heard the tick, tick, and then he was gone, out the door to work.

He was a construction worker who got his North Carolina General Contractor's License. He came home after a hard day, a few beers in hand, and went upstairs to his solitary room and watched sports on TV. Later, it was steak for dinner that he carried to his room, and then I never saw him again until I heard the tink, tink.

His room at the end of the hall allowed him to hear my movements, so when I went grocery shopping, he would listen for my car. When it drove in, he came downstairs to help me unload the food. On garbage day, he would show up to help me drag the cans down the driveway.

On a cool winter night, as we walked down the driveway, I attempted to snuggle with him. He would have none of that, saying, "You are a married woman."

It was December 4, 2000. Tony came home agitated over a job he worked that day. After consuming some beer, he left. The next call I received was from Mission Hospital. They called to say Mountain Area Medical Airlift (MAMA) airlifted him to the ER. He totaled his Toyota truck, tumbling down Jupiter Mountain. His injuries were severe with a damaged knee. Tony had bent forward and received bodily injuries. I went to see him, but he was too out-of-it to speak. They kept him for over a week and sent him home. On Christmas Eve, he was experiencing breathing problems and went back to the hospital by ambulance. After my holiday dinner with family in Asheville, I stopped in to see how he was doing. They had inserted a needle into his back to remove water and blood from his lungs. Jim expressed dissatisfaction that I stopped to visit Tony. I tried to explain he was a paying guest in our house, and I would do it for anyone sick in the hospital. That did not satisfy Jim, and he fussed all the way home.

After a few days, Tony came home.

Our relationship went from friendly to nurse, as I became his caregiver. He could not walk down the stairs because of his knee injury. I brought food to him and helped him with his shower. That was a trick to wash him and turn my head the other way. I was embarrassed. When I put his socks on, he complained I was too rough. It was difficult as I was tending to Tony and bringing food to the third floor for my husband Jim, who suffered from emphysema. I could not let Jim know about Tony, as he was a jealous husband. I was also working for H & R Block every day; I went to the Weaverville office until late afternoon.

As Tony slowly recovered, he worked on the rental house on Hill Street, which was previously a telephone switching station. Jim wanted to convert it into an apartment. After Jim interviewed four contractors, he gave the job to Tony. Jim complained about the plumber and electrician and was not satisfied with how Tony located the staircase. It turned out to be a comfortable living space, occupied for nineteen years by the same person.

Labor Day, Monday, September 3, 2001, Jim suffered a traumatic breathing situation that caused some mental disturbance. He walked into town to the sheriff's office, and they called an ambulance to take him to the hospital. A family upheaval followed with Jim being committed to St. Joe's Hospital Corner Stone psychiatric division. After discharge, he departed for Florida, where he lived with my son until his eventual death in 2010.

Within eight days, 9/11/2001 took place. Tony was repairing a splintered section in our reception room as the planes struck the World Trade Center towers. We shared that world-shattering day of horrifying disaster and sorrow.

Once Tony was well, he hired a crew to be part of his workforce.

On August 2002, we took a previously planned vacation to Maine. On our way, we stopped at the old Yankee Stadium for a game in the rain with Boston. The rain never stopped, and in the fifth inning, they called the game. We drove to Maine in heavy rain. A week later, we visited Margot, my stepmother in Phoenicia, New York, on the way home. The next time we came to see her, we saw the Yankees play again. Our seats were at the top of the bleachers, too high to decipher who was playing on the field. When I stood, I felt I would topple down onto the fans.

In 2004, Margot came to live with us. We took her out to dinners enjoying her company and watched TV. She loved Tony. Every night when he returned home, she insisted on spending time with him. She lived with us for approximately eight months, and in July 2005, she became ill, requiring amputation of her right leg. She suffered in silence because that was the type of lady she was. She passed peacefully on July 17 – ten days before her 97th birthday.

After her passing, I wrote to family in Germany, and due to this connection, Tony and I took a trip in 2007 to Germany to meet my father's side of the family. My cousin Manfred Langner managed a theater in Aachen, Germany. Nathalye, his French wife, had her own facial beauty business. They put us up on the third floor of an apartment building that housed their actors. There were no actors at the time of our visit. Much to my delight, there was a street flea market in progress, and we purchased a few items with Manfred's help, who spoke to the seller in German, reducing the price.

Marion, Werner, and Annarose are the children of Heintz and Hildegard. Their mixed marriage saved the family during the war. My grandfather Heinrich is the brother of Heintz, making us all cousins.

Marion, the eldest, married Albert Langler, who served in the German army and was captured by the Americans. He worked for his captors and learned English. Ingrid and Manfred, the children, are both involved in the film and theater business. Coincidentally, my son Jerry is in film and entertainment too.

Over the years, Ingrid and I have carried on an e-mail correspondence exchanging the political status of each Germany and the United States.

Werner, the middle son whom I resemble, married Sigrid. She and I became friends exchanging letters about the family ancestry. Their daughter, Sabine, studies in the states.

Annarose, the youngest of the three, married Werner Meyer, an architect, and has a son.

Sigrid Lichtenstein, Arthur, and Marion Langner took us on a day cruise on the Rhine River. Listening to the language of my childhood brought back memories of mom and grandma. Tony was amazed at how quickly the German words of my youth came back.

We saw the mystical, enticing Lorelei statue. She is a century-old legend. Lorelei was a siren attracting sailors with her beauty and causing ships to wreck and fall into the Rhine's deepest part. She sits on a high rock, jutting out into the river.

The family treated us to a hotel in the Black Forest. The bottom floor was a bowling alley. The first floor with the reception area and restaurant was where we ate a German breakfast. Soft boiled eggs, lox, bread, cheese, a deli platter were not an everyday fare. The soft-boiled egg Tony removed from the shell, making an American sandwich style. Eating it with a spoon in an eggcup was the European way.

Marion cooked dinner at their home in Simmern, and we met their daughter Ingrid, who lives in Frankfurt am Main. Marion's younger sister Annarose and her husband Werner Mayer met us at the gathering. Albert, Warner, and Siggy have passed since our visit.

Then, we traveled by rail to Brussels, where we had lunch while it rained on the cobblestone square. Across the street, Karl Marx wrote the Communist Manifesto. We visited the most magnificent church with an enormous wooden handcrafted organ.

We said good-bye to the family and railed to Munich, where we stayed in a Marriott. We bought Hummel figurines, jewelry and watched artists draw murals with colored charcoal pencils directly on the sidewalk only to last a day. In the early evening, we went to an outdoor Biergarten with a woman we met at the hotel. We taxied to a packed, wild, energetic, musical indoor Biergarten, where the entertainers dressed in lederhosen. Then, we went back to the Marriott, and the next day, we flew home. When traveling by rail, I could see the forests. There was no debris between the trees.

Over the next twelve years, we visited twelve baseball parks.

Tony's favorite is the Cincinnati Reds, where we have gone four times. We stayed at the Shenkle House Bed & Breakfast across the Ohio River in Covington, Kentucky, twice. We stayed at the Westin Hotel and shared an elevator ride with Joe Torre, the Yankees manager. Andy Pettitte was a pitcher for the Yankees, and although we did not share any space with him, we did see him leave the restaurant we were entering. On that trip, the Yankees were playing the Reds. The next time we came to Cincinnati, we stayed at the Westin hotel where Barry Larkin lived.

We went to Chicago and saw the Cubs game in the old Wrigley Field built in 1914. At the White Socks game, Tony spotted his old friend Tim Raines from his days at Sanford High School. They played in the schoolyard together. Tim was a future Baseball Hall of Fame candidate, and Tony chased him all around the ball field to get an autograph while I sat in the stands with my broken ankle. Tony pushed me around in a wheelchair at the Chicago Museum Art Institute, where we saw a Toulouse-Lautrec display of his Moulin Rouge poster art. We shopped in Marshall Field's department store. A treat for me as Nicky, my stepfather, spoke of that store. We ate at Lawry's Steak House, where many of the players frequented.

We went to Detroit to see the Tigers, who played well into the night with fifteen innings. We stayed in Winslow, Ontario, Canada, across the river from Detroit, and ate breakfast outside on the balcony.

We saw the Toronto Blue Jays, and on the way home, we stopped at Niagara Falls, where someone stole our camera.

We went to San Francisco to see Barry Bonds play in left field with the Giants. Then, we took the subway over to Oakland and saw the Athletics play the Seattle Mariners with Ichiro on the field. The hilly city's metropolitan area was a disgrace. On every corner stood a bum with his hand out looking for money or food; if there was one, there were three. The town supported several soup kitchens attempting to care for the masses. San Francisco is far from destitute, but the collection of indigents walking the streets was disheartening for an American city. I could compare it to Juarez, Mexico.

San Francisco's famous trolley ride took us down the hill to Fisherman's Wharf. We ate at Bubba Gump with a view of the Golden Gate Bridge and Alcatraz. The plentiful blubbery seals made their home at the wharf, calling each other and attempting to communicate with us.

We have been to Pittsburgh Park to see the Pirates. I thought it was one of the best laid-out parks.

We traveled to Miami to see the Marlins with Jerry and Carol. Carol's husband, Charlie, would have loved being along. Unfortunately, he passed from cancer.

We have been to see the Braves play in Atlanta's Turner field two times. We had a hell of a time getting into the new park as our tickets were incorrect. On this outing, we were a foursome with Travis and Andy, one of Tony's workers. The Hawthorn Hotel told us of the best Italian Restaurant in town, which gave us a bagged complimentary dinner to take back to our rooms.

In Indiana, we saw fields of corn and more corn. We went to South Bend and looked at Notre Dame's University cathedral. I went inside, but Tony did not, as he felt his flip-flops were inappropriate apparel to go into a cathedral. We also went to the Indianapolis Speedway and watched the cars on the first day of practice go round and round and make lots of noise.

We took a cruise to the Bahamas and stayed in St. Thomas for a week. We shopped in all the stores attracting tourists. Jewelry and porcelain items were at a low price. Tony swam in the blue waters, and I sat in a protected cove letting the waves lap over me.

Tony met my family, I met his, and on June 29, 2013, we married at the Marshall House in the conical tearoom on the porch. I wore a dark blue belted dress with a crinoline to make the skirt stand out and a small white straw hat. He wore a Panama Jack wide-brimmed hat along with a Panama Jack shirt and shorts. Sam Parker, the magistrate, performed the service. Travis stood to his right, and Jerry stood to my left. It was a small service with two observers.

Kathy Wilkes, from Lake Helen, Florida, in the center of the state, has been friends with both Tony and me. We met her in Marshall House some years ago when she was a guest more than once. She wanted to see us tie the knot. Kathy helped me dress, and unexpectedly, there came a knock on the bedroom door. She went to answer and found a strange man standing there with one-dozen red roses. She refused to let him in until he said, "I am Ruth's son." Jerry drove up from Miami for the day, and after the reception, he went back home.

We held the reception at Good Stuff. We supplied the food, plates, and cups, and they provided the drinks.

We had been together for twelve years before we got married, and now we are a married couple for seven-years. I got the bargain of a lifetime.

He calls me his Grand Cougar, and he is my Boy Toy.

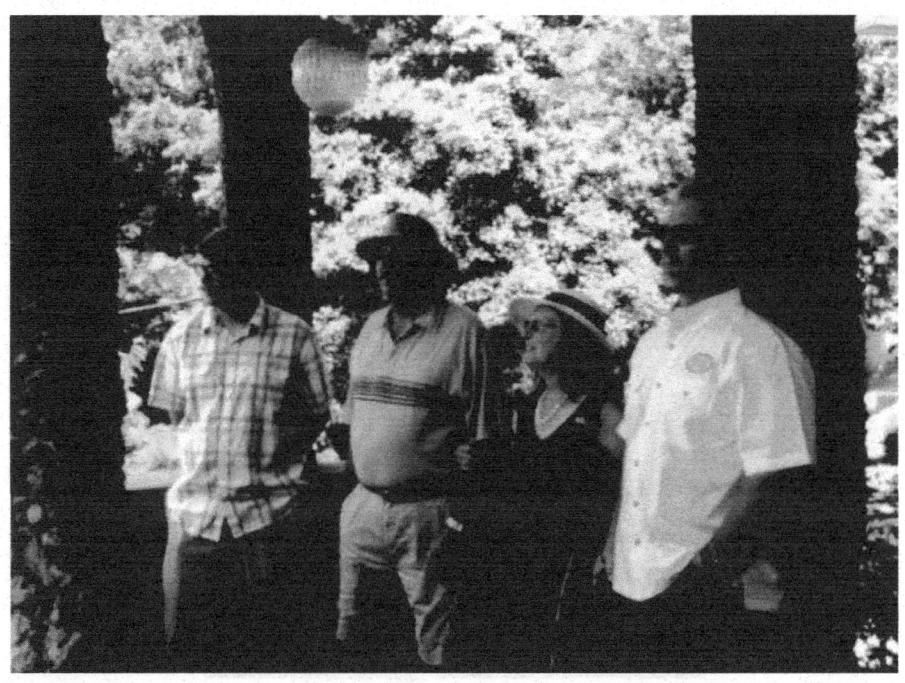

June 29, 2013 Travis, Tony and Ruth Dunkinson, and Jerry Blohm

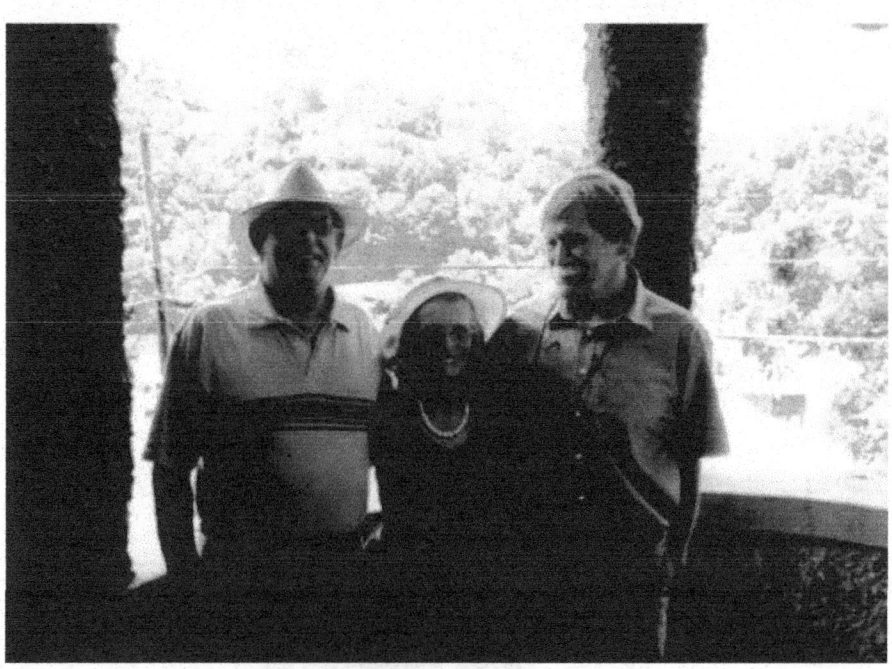

June 29, 2013 Ruth & Tony Dunkinson and Sam Parker

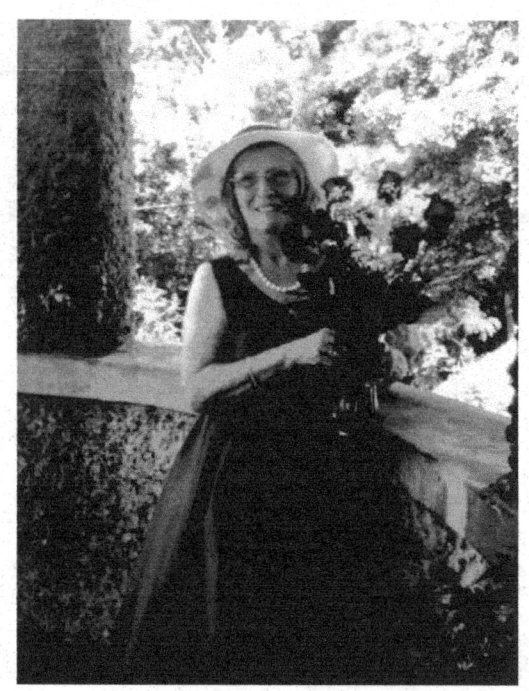

June 29, 2013 Ruth Dunkinson

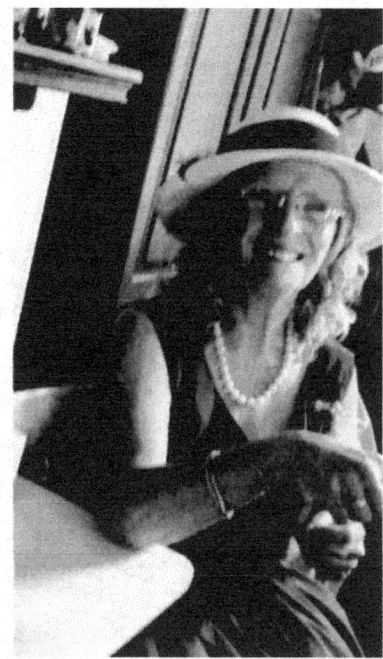

Ruth

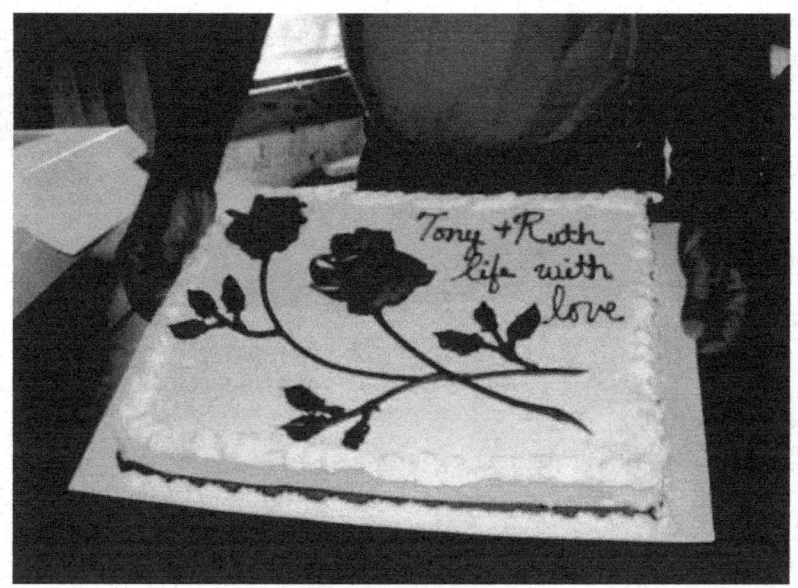

Tony holding the cake

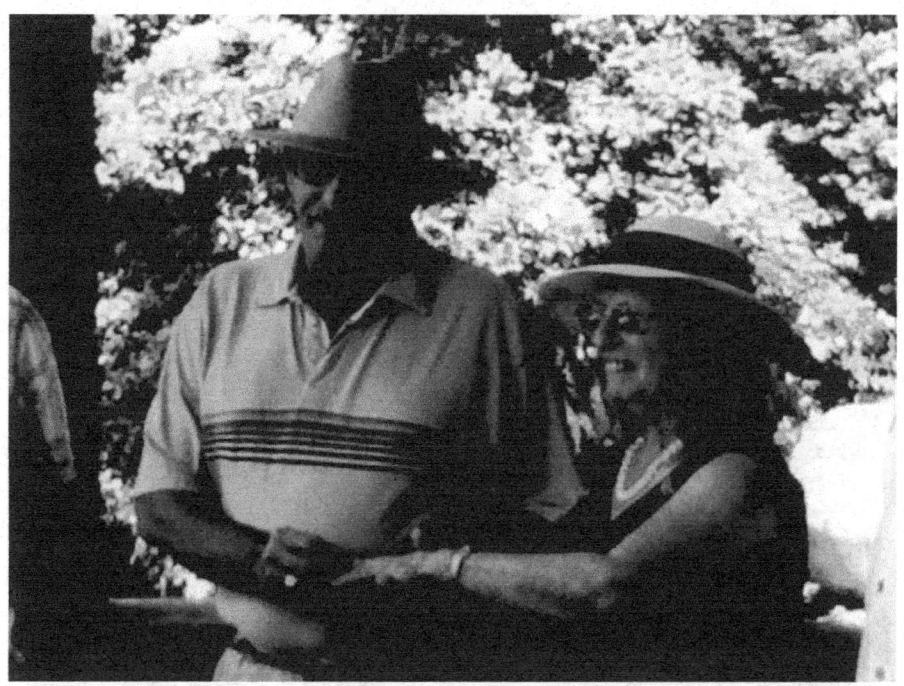

Ruth and Tony Dunkinson

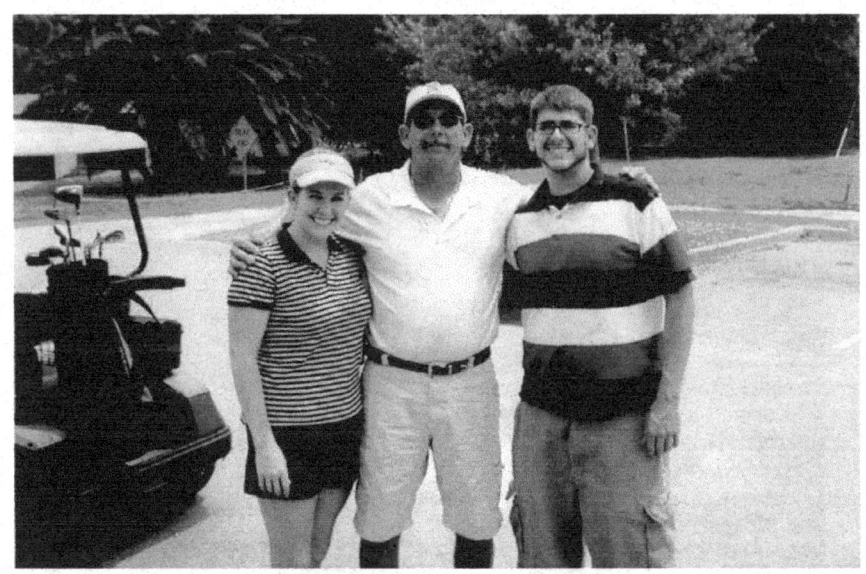

Samantha, Tony and Travis Dunkinson"

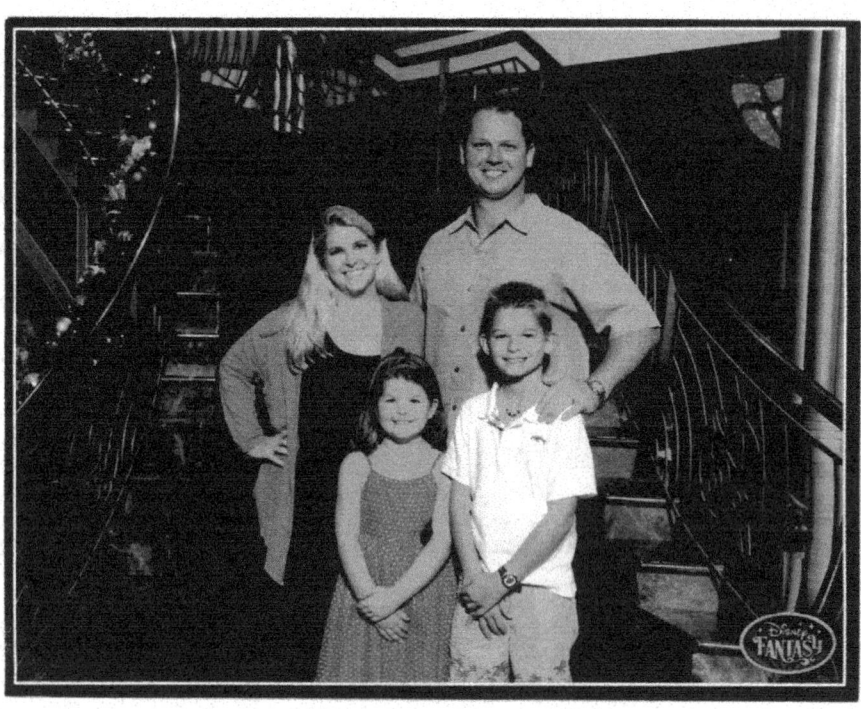

Samantha, Michael, Kaite and Sean

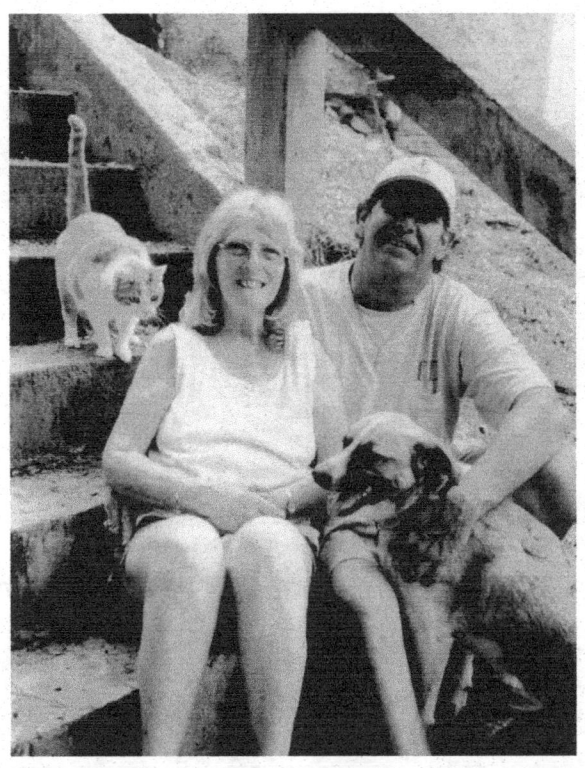

Ruth Eda Lichtenstein & Anthony "Tony" Ray Dunkinson and Ivy (cat) and Tar (dog)

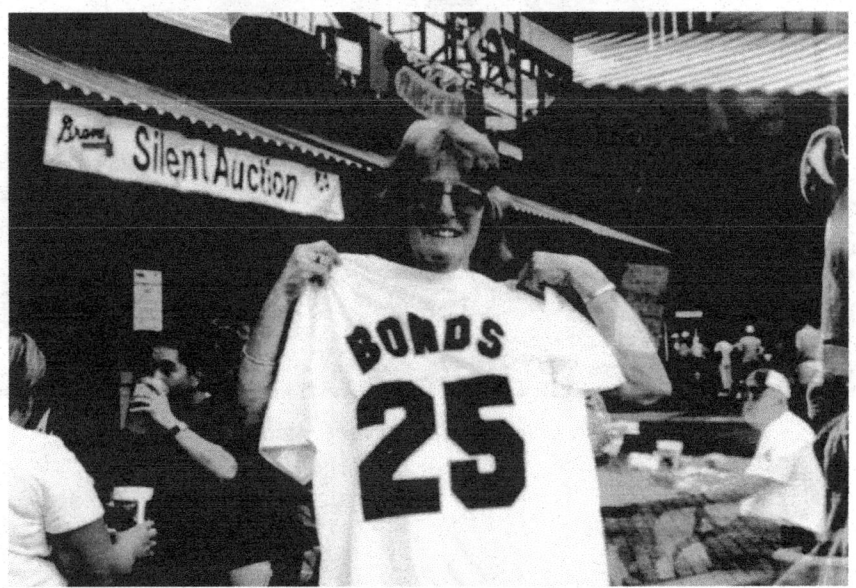

2004 Truner Field – Braves & San Fransisco Ruth Boylan 67 yrs old

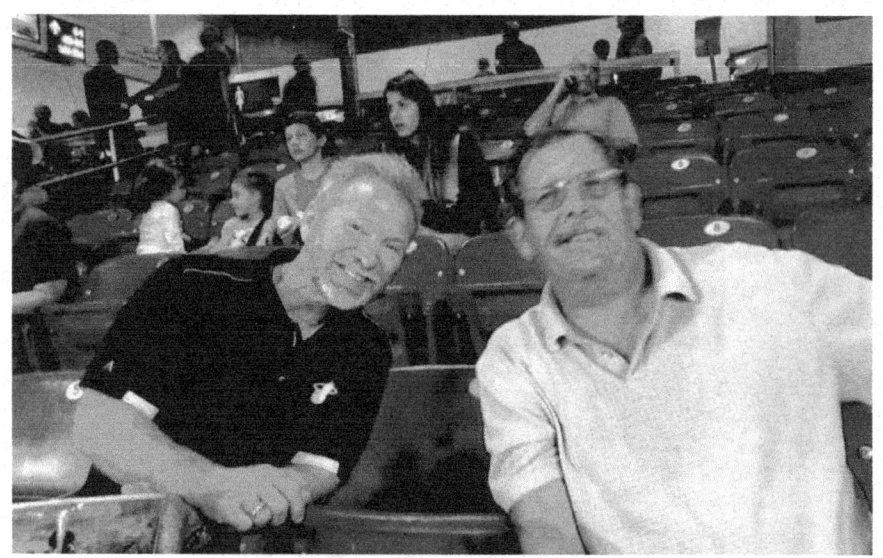

Jerry Blohm and Tony Dunkinson at a Miami Marlin Baseball Game

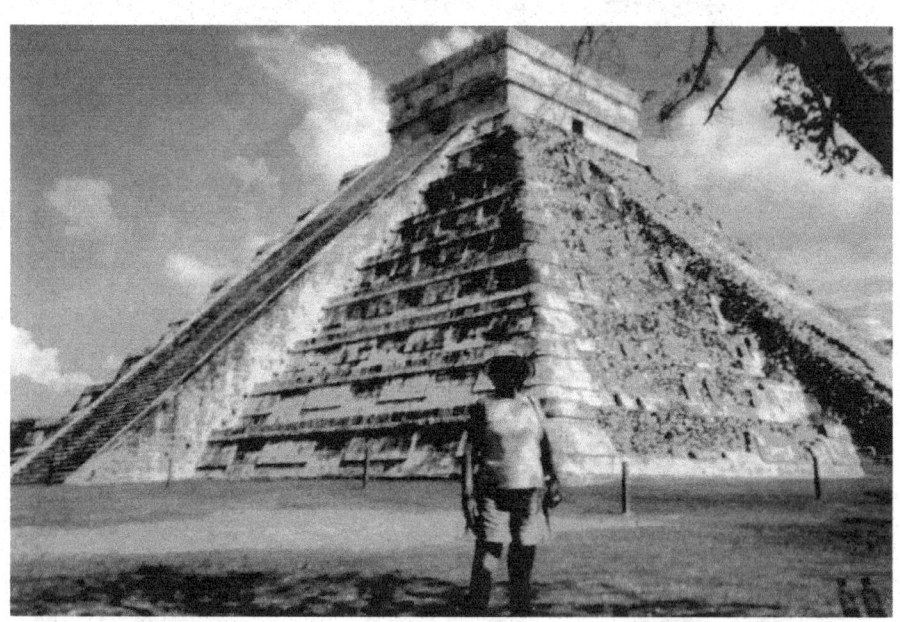

Chichen Itza Yacatan Peninsula, Mexico

CHAPTER 42:

GRANDKIDS

Josephine – October 31, 2003 --- Joslyn – May 21, 2010 --- Jacob – September 10, 2012

Due to miles and the length of time it took my son to start a family, I am not a devoted Grandparent. I want to play a game or sit comfortably on a pillowed couch. They are wild as the wind; only now, as the school has started, have they learned to calm down in the classroom, one can only hope.

Jerry says, "I put out a good product."

"Yes, I agree." They are healthy, strong, energetic children. They are intelligent little people.

All three are making good marks at school, and Josie is doing exceptionally well. She has grown up to be a respectful, attractive teenager. It is still too early in the lives of Joslyn and Jacob to know how they will develop. I hope to be around long enough to find out.

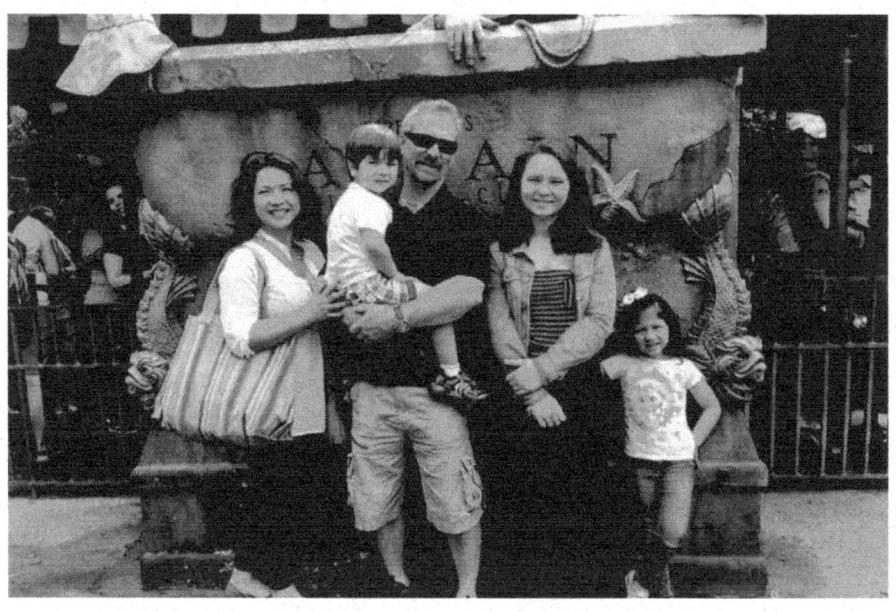

2016 Vacation in Winter Park, FL Mercedes, Jacob, Jerry, Josie and Joslyn

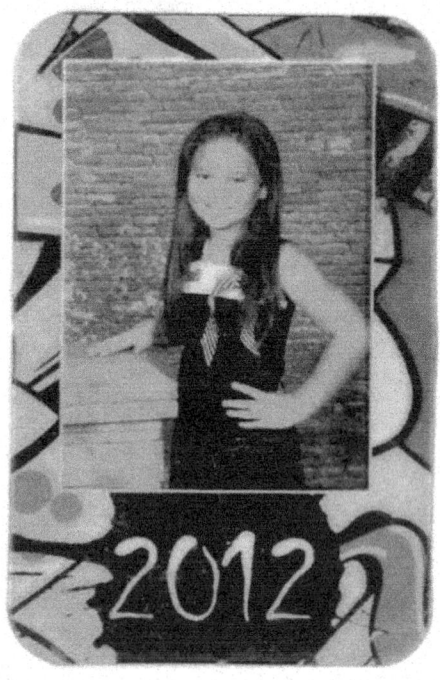

Josie Blohm

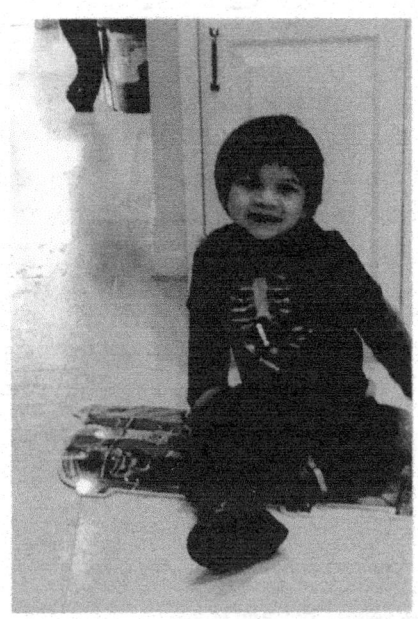

Jacob Blohm – 4 yrs old – 2016 Christmas, Marshall, NC

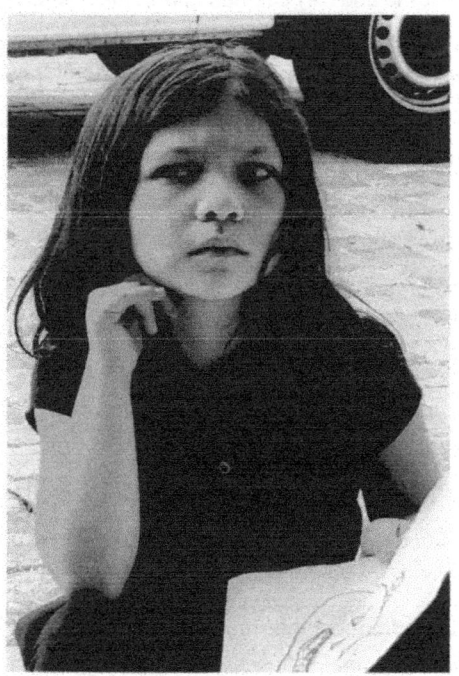

Joslyn Blohm 2016 Halloween Miami, FL

EPILOGUE

When I sat down to write this story, I took an online genealogy course to understand my family history better. I signed on to Ancestry.com and delved deeper into my origin to learn how to write a memoir; I took two courses at A-B Tech. The instructor did not read our submissions, but instead paired up two classmates and me to work together.

Steve Lewis and Sabine Carender, and I have been together for four years, meeting once a month to discuss our projects and give constructive criticism. They kept me on track, and without their dedication and guidance, I would never have completed the task.

At the UPS store on Merrimon Avenue, Susannah Haskell assisted in designing and printing the story.

Kathy Wilkes and Carol Berndt read the original drafts years ago. Robbie Gaulding helped with dates and storylines and supported my endeavor.

Over the past few years, Tony and I have made some wonderful friends. Meeting at Good Stuff every Monday evening became a habit, and after they closed, we moved on to Cinco de Mayo. Howie and Kay seemed to take the role of official greeters for new folks moving here from afar. We have made lasting friendships at Howie's home during parties celebrating national holidays. Frank Tedone is someone, who over a lifetime, you will only meet once. He is the first to say he loves women, and I have no problem saying it is easy to love Frank. He hugs me, and Kay, and Leslie, and any female that crosses his path. He is a charming Italian, a constant gentleman with the most patient wife Lynn, who has been putting up with him for forty-six years.

Now I could go on and mention Toby and Leslie, Dick and Dryna, Donna and Graeme, Frank and Debbie, Lorie and Bill, Jerry and Deb, Doug and Bonnie, Jim, Clark, Ricky and Lou, Nan and Terry, Holly and Jamie, Sue, Mo, and Joyce, but I'm afraid I may forget someone. They are all friendly, caring folks with whom it is a pleasure to share our time.

Susan Rector and Georgette Shelton – George & Barbara Penland's girls befriended me since I arrived in 1988. They have stood by me, making me feel like family in my new hometown.

Tony tolerated my frequent interruptions as I read a questioning phase of my literary talent. I needed his contribution, which he gave freely, and I thank him for taking time away from his sports.

To contact me: redruth676@gmail.com

A CLOSING THOUGHT

I've covered my life from the insignificant to the relevant. If I did not live to eighty-three, it would be shorter.

How I survived my end renal failure catastrophe remains a mystery. Not a devoted soul; many prayed for me in that time of sickness. I believe it assisted in my recovery. Blessed, I was blessed, I did nothing to be blessed, and it is a word I seldom use.

My transition from Marshall House, which was a labor of love, contributed to my physical decline. My boat life beat me up, and standing, for ten years, in the gun shop was a contributing factor.

Mentally sharp, physically weak, determined, and tenacious, I plan to stay here until my grandchildren are partially grown and have some knowledge about life.

Happy in my new surroundings with two cats, three dogs, and a husband that loves me, I revel in the birds, squirrels, rabbits, turkey, deer, an enormous visiting bear, and the lonely horse across the field.

The End